THE BEST OF
FOOD&WINE
1987 COLLECTION

THE BEST OF
FOOD&WINE
1987 COLLECTION

American Express
Publishing Corporation
New York

Cover: Peppered Chicken Breasts with Rosemary and Garlic (p. 82).

Sephardic-Style Haroset (p. 16) from *The Jewish Holiday Cookbook*, by Gloria Kaufer Greene. Copyright © 1985 by Gloria Kaufer Greene. Reprinted by permission of Times Books, a Division of Random House.

Minestrone with Artichokes, Sausage, Pistachios and Lemons (p. 45), Grilled Squab Marinated in Berry Puree (p. 91), Chopped Lamb Steak au Poivre with Garlic Cloves (p. 117), and Toasted Lobster Sandwich (p. 162) from *New American Classics* by Jeremiah Tower. © 1986 by Jeremiah Tower. Reprinted by permission of Harper & Row Publishers, Inc.

Siena Almond Cookies (p. 179) from *The Classic Cuisine of the Italian Jews*, by Edda Servi Machlin. Copyright © 1985 by Edda Servi Machlin. Reprinted by permission of Dodd, Mead & Company, Inc.

Country Gravy (p. 227) and Tomato Gravy (p. 227) from *Bill Neal's Southern Cooking*, by Bill Neal. Copyright © 1985 by William F. Neal. Reprinted by permission of The University of North Carolina Press.

THE BEST OF FOOD & WINE/1987 COLLECTION
Editor: Kate Slate
Art Director: Elizabeth G. Woodson
Designer: René-Julien Aussoleil

© 1987 American Express Publishing Corporation

Published by American Express Publishing Corporation
1120 Avenue of the Americas, New York, New York 10036

Manufactured in the United States of America

Library of Congress Cataloging in Publication Data

Main entry under title:

The Best of Food & Wine

Includes index.
1. Cookery, International. I. American Express Publishing Corporation.
II. Food & Wine (New York, N.Y.) III. Title: Best of Food and Wine.
TX725.A1B48233 1987   641.5   86-26506

ISBN 0-916103-06-4

TABLE OF CONTENTS

FOREWORD

Just a quick turn of this page will reveal a year's worth of the most mouth-watering and memorable recipes to appear in *Food & Wine* magazine. From the spicy surprise of Chinese-accented Caramel Pepper Nuts to the decidedly American Mint Jalapeño Jelly on the last page, you will find inspiration and guidance for preparing everything from a casual brunch to a gala dinner.

The recipes were chosen with a discerning eye by Kate Slate, who has been an important part of the staff of *Food & Wine* magazine and the editor of all the volumes in the *Best of Food & Wine* series. In this book, the dishes range from easy to ambitious, from up-to-the-minute contemporary to warmly nostalgic, but each recipe has something in common with all the others. It has been carefully tested—as well as tasted—in our *Food & Wine* kitchen, so that we can be sure it will work in yours.

You will find dishes as effortlessly elegant as Scallop and Shrimp Sauté with Pears and Tarragon, as deeply comforting as Thyme-Roasted Chicken with Onions and Potatoes, and as imaginative as Pumpkin and Ginger Soufflé.

But those are just a hint of what awaits. *Food & Wine*'s appetite is international, our mood relaxed. This book is meant to be part of your busy life, and with more than 450 recipes as reference, we hope it becomes an indispensable part of your kitchen, which is, after all, the heart of the house.

Ila Stanger
Editor-in-Chief

FOOD & WINE'S VINTAGE RATINGS
1975-1985

COMPILED BY ELIN McCOY & JOHN FREDERICK WALKER

	1975	1976	1977	1978	1979
Red Bordeaux	8½ Classic, concentrated. Start drinking. Will last.	7 Soft, full, attractive. Drink now.	4 Lightweight, lacks fruit. Best now.	9 Rich, full, good depth. Start tasting.	8 Fruity & delicious. Start drinking.
Sauternes	9 Deep, rich; some classics. Start drinking.	9 Elegant & luscious. Start drinking.	3 Very weak. Avoid.	5 Big, but lacks typical richness. Drink now.	6 Light but has character. Start drinking.
Red Burgundy	3 Thin, weak; most are poor. Avoid.	7 Deep, full, tannic. Drink now.	4 Light, thin, uneven. Drink now.	8 Outstanding; excellent balance. Drink now.	6 Soft, supple, appealing. Drink now.
White Burgundy	4 Very light wines. Drink up.	7 Big, soft, rich wines. Drink up.	5 Light, lean, acidic. Drink up.	9 Superb; well-balanced. Drink now.	7 Attractive, fruity wines. Drink now.
Napa/Sonoma Cabernet Sauvignon	7 Lacks power, but best have elegance. Drink now.	7 Variable. Many heavy and tannic. Drink now.	7½ Variable. Some well-balanced wines. Drink now.	8 Full, rich, balanced. Start drinking; best will keep.	7 Uneven quality; some very good. Start drinking.
Napa/Sonoma Chardonnay	8 Intense, well-balanced. Drink up.	6 Big, ripe; some too powerful. Drink up.	7 Uneven. Some attractive. Drink up.	8 Powerful, ripe wines. Drink up.	8 Rich, intense, impressive. Drink up.
Barolo & Barbaresco	5 Light & attractive. Drink now.	6 Light, well-balanced. Drink now.	4 Light, thin wines. Drink now.	9 Classic, concentrated & tannic. Wait 2-4 years; will last.	8 Elegant, well-balanced wines. Start drinking; will hold.
Chianti	9 Exceptional. Well-balanced wines. Drink now.	3 Lightweight, disappointing. Now or never.	7 Good to very good; firm, stylish. Drink now.	9 Exceptional; big, solid, tannic. Start drinking; will hold.	7 Attractive, ripe wines. Drink up.
Germany	8 Excellent balance, stylish. Drink up.	9½ Super-rich wines. Enjoy; best balanced will keep.	6 Lightweight, crisp. Drink up.	6 Lightweight, crisp. Drink up.	7 Good quality & balance. Drink now.
Vintage Porto	6½ Light & stylish. Try now. Some wines fast-maturing.	No vintage declared.	9½ Superlative; ripe & dense. Wait 8-10 years.	5 Not generally declared. Rich, soft. Try in 3-4 years.	No vintage declared.

The following ratings and comments reflect a variety of opinions, including our own, on the quality and character of various categories of wines from recent vintages. The ratings—0 for the worst, 10 for the best—are averages, and better or worse wine than indicated can be found in each vintage. Assessments of the most current vintages are more predictive and hence less exact than those of older vintages.

Scores are based on a wine's quality at maturity. A lower-rated but mature wine will often be superior to a higher-rated but immature wine. When-to-drink advice is based on how such wines seemed to be developing in mid-1986, and presumes good storage. The earliest date suggested for consumption applies to the lesser wines of the vintage, which will mature faster than the finest examples of the year.

1980	1981	1982	1983	1984	1985
5 Small-scale, lightweight, pleasant. Drink up.	7½ Well-balanced wines. Wait 1 year.	10 Fabulous. Try in 3-7 years.	8 Firm, powerful. Try in 4 years.	7 Small-scale, firm. Wait 3 years.	8½ Soft and elegant. Try in 6 years
7 Attractive, small-scale. Start drinking.	7½ Well-balanced wines. Start drinking.	7 Variable. Best are big, powerful wines. Sample now.	9 Very promising, rich, classic wines. Sample now.	7 Moderate quality. Some good. Sample now.	7 Good quality. Sample now.
6 Mostly light wines. Drink now.	6 Variable vintage. Most early maturing.	7 Big, soft wines. Drink now.	9 Some very good, powerful wines. Start sampling.	7 Variable quality.	9 Rich and round. Wait 2 years.
5 Variable; the best are attractive. Drink now.	8 Attractive wines. Drink now.	9 Excellent. Big, rich wines. Drink now.	8 Good, promising wines. Start drinking.	7 Some fine. Start sampling.	8½ Big but balanced. Start sampling.
8½ Powerful but well-balanced. Will keep.	7½ Variable. Early maturing; try now.	7½ Lighter style; some attractive. Try now.	7 Good, but not particularly promising.	8 Big, soft, promising.	9 Very promising. Wait 4 years.
9 Many have superb balance. Drink up.	7 Soft, ripe wines. Drink now.	8 Many light, some excellent. Drink now.	7 Good moderate year. Drink now.	7 Good year. Start sampling.	9 Fine balanced. Start sampling.
6 Uneven. Best are well-balanced, attractive. Start drinking.	7 Firm, solid wines. Start sampling.	8½ Big, powerful wines; very promising. Wait 1-4 years.	7½ Promising vintage.	5½ Light, variable. For early drinking.	9 Promising. Wait 4 years.
6 Uneven; best are small-scale.	7 Good, firm wines.	8 Attractive but early maturing.	8 Attractive, early maturing.	5 Spotty. For early drinking.	8½ Very good. Wait 2 years.
5 Light & lean. Drink now.	8 Well-balanced, attractive. Drink now.	7 Soft, fruity. Drink now.	9 Excellent year. Marvelous late-harvest wines. Start drinking.	7 Good. Drink now.	8½ Excellent. Start sampling.
7 Light but promising. Sample in 5-8 years.	No vintage declared.	7 Soft, well-balanced. Sample in 6-9 years.	8 Firm, solid wines. Sample in 7-10 years.	____	____

APPETIZERS

APPETIZERS

CARAMEL-PEPPER NUTS

These are Chinese "Cracker Jacks" that we serve at China Moon, [a Chinese bistro in San Francisco], one of those tidbits that the Chinese classify as "foods to make the wine go down." White wine, red wine or beer are equally appropriate. The recipe belongs to Barton Levenson, a wonderfully imaginative Bay Area cook.

MAKES ABOUT 2½ CUPS
1 cup hazelnuts (filberts)
1 cup raw skinned peanuts*
½ cup sugar
1 tablespoon coarse (kosher) salt
1 tablespoon freshly ground black pepper
¼ teaspoon freshly ground cinnamon
1½ whole star anise pods (equals 12 points)*
6 whole cloves
2 teaspoons Szechuan peppercorns*
1½ teaspoons whole Java peppercorns (optional)
*Available at Chinese markets and health food stores

1. Preheat the oven to 350°. Spread the hazelnuts and peanuts on separate baking sheets and toast, shaking the pans once or twice, until just beginning to brown, 10 to 15 minutes. Rub the hazelnuts in a kitchen towel to remove most of the skins.

2. In a small bowl, toss together the sugar, salt, ground black pepper and cinnamon to blend.

3. In a spice grinder, pulverize the star anise, cloves, Szechuan peppercorns and Java peppercorns. Strain through a fine-mesh sieve to eliminate husks. Add to the sugar mixture and toss to blend.

4. Heat a large heavy skillet, preferably cast iron, or a wok over high heat until hot enough to evaporate a bead of water on contact, about 1 minute. Add the nuts and toss for 1 minute, or until the nuts are hot and the nut oil

has come to the surface; reduce the heat if necessary to prevent scorching.

5. Sprinkle the nuts with half the sugar seasoning mixture, then toss by shaking the pan vigorously until the sugar melts and turns a dark caramelized brown, about 1 minute. Add the remaining seasoning mixture and continue shaking the pan until the sugar again melts and coats the nuts, about 3 minutes. Use the handle of a wooden spoon to stir the nuts and break apart any globs of sugar.

6. Immediately turn the nuts onto a foil-lined baking sheet. As soon as they are cool enough to handle, separate with your fingers. Let cool completely. Store in a tightly sealed glass jar for up to 2 weeks.

—Barbara Tropp

GORGONZOLA SPIRALS

MAKES ABOUT 5 DOZEN
1 pound frozen puff pastry, thawed
2 tablespoons Dijon-style mustard
1 egg yolk
1 cup (about 7 ounces) crumbled Gorgonzola cheese

1. Unfold the puff pastry on a lightly floured board. In a small bowl, whisk together the mustard and egg yolk until blended. Using a brush, paint the pastry with the mustard mixture. Distribute the Gorgonzola over half the pastry. Fold the pastry over to enclose the cheese and roll out to an 8-inch square. Cover with waxed paper and refrigerate until firm, at least 1 hour.

2. On a lightly floured board, roll out the pastry to a 10-by-15-inch rectangle about ¼ inch thick. Using a sharp knife, cut crosswise into thirds to form three 10-by-5-inch rectangles. Beginning with the long edge, tightly roll up each rectangle to form a cylinder. Wrap the rolls in waxed paper and place them in the freezer for 10 minutes to firm them up.

3. Preheat the oven to 400°. Unwrap the rolls and, using a sharp knife, slice ½ inch thick. Set the slices ½ inch apart on baking sheets and bake for 10 to 12 minutes, or until golden brown and crisp. Cool the spirals on a rack. (**Gorgonzola Spirals can be made several days ahead and stored in airtight containers.** Keep them in a cool place, but do not refrigerate. Reheat briefly before serving, if desired.)

—Molly O'Neill

MUSHROOM-LEEK TURNOVERS

A sophisticated savory just right for chilly evenings. The porcini, with their full, rich flavor, are a nice complement to the silky leeks. This is a filling you may want to try in a tartlet or work into a cream cheese pastry quiche.

MAKES ABOUT 4 DOZEN
1 ounce dried mushrooms, such as porcini
4 tablespoons unsalted butter
3 medium leeks (white part only), finely chopped
½ pound fresh mushrooms, finely chopped
1 tablespoon all-purpose flour
2 tablespoons Cognac or brandy
¼ cup heavy cream
½ teaspoon salt
¼ teaspoon freshly ground black pepper
Pinch of crushed hot pepper
Pinch of thyme

¼ *cup freshly grated Parmesan cheese*
Cream Cheese Dough (p. 169)
1 egg

1. Put the dried mushrooms in a small bowl. Pour 1 cup of boiling water over the mushrooms and let them soak until softened, about 20 minutes. Lift out the mushrooms and squeeze as much liquid as possible back into the bowl; reserve the liquid. Chop the reconstituted mushrooms.

2. Strain the soaking liquid through a sieve lined with a double thickness of dampened cheesecloth into a heavy skillet. Add the chopped reconstituted mushrooms and 1 tablespoon of the butter. Bring the liquid to a boil over moderately high heat and cook, stirring occasionally, until the liquid evaporates, about 3 minutes. Scrape the mushrooms into a bowl.

3. Melt the remaining 3 tablespoons butter in the skillet over moderately high heat. Add the leeks and sauté until softened but not browned, about 5 minutes. Add the fresh mushrooms and sauté, tossing, until their juices evaporate, about 5 minutes.

4. Return the cooked dried mushrooms to the pan. Sprinkle on the flour and cook, stirring, for about 1 minute. Stir in the Cognac and cook until it evaporates, about 1 minute. Stir in the cream and remove from the heat.

5. Add the salt, black pepper, hot pepper, thyme and Parmesan cheese. Scrape the filling into a bowl and let cool to room temperature. (**The filling can be prepared to this point up to 3 days ahead.** Refrigerate, covered.)

6. Remove half the dough from the refrigerator and let rest for about 10 minutes, until malleable. Divide the dough in half. On a lightly floured surface, roll out one piece of the dough into a 12-by-8-inch rectangle. Cut the dough lengthwise in half and then crosswise at 2-inch intervals to form 12 rectangles 2 by 4 inches each.

7. Place 1 heaping teaspoon of filling in the center of one half of each rectangle. Moisten the edges of the pastry lightly with water. Fold the dough over the filling to form squares and, gently squeezing out the air, pinch to close. Trim any edges that are ragged. Crimp the edges of the pastries with the tines of a fork to seal. Repeat with the remaining piece of dough and more filling. Then remove the second half of the dough from the refrigerator and repeat to form all the turnovers. Refrigerate the turnovers for at least 30 minutes, or for up to 24 hours. (**The turnovers can be made ahead to this point and frozen, well wrapped, for up to 1 month.** Bake without defrosting.)

8. Preheat the oven to 400°. In a small bowl, beat the egg with 1 teaspoon of cold water to make a glaze. Brush the glaze over the squares. With a small knife, cut a slit in the top of each turnover.

9. Bake for about 15 minutes, or until golden brown. (Frozen turnovers will take about 5 minutes longer.)

—*Dorie Greenspan*

CHICKEN LIVER AND APPLE CRESCENTS

This liver filling, flecked with apples and hazelnuts, is a favorite recipe of mine, for it works well both hot and cold: baked in a pastry wrapper, as suggested here, or chilled and served as an excellent spreadable pâté.

MAKES ABOUT 3 DOZEN
2 tablespoons hazelnuts (filberts)
1 large garlic clove, quartered
1 medium onion, quartered
2 tablespoons unsalted butter
½ *medium, tart apple—peeled,*
 quartered and cored

½ *pound chicken livers, trimmed*
1 tablespoon Calvados
½ *teaspoon salt*
¼ *teaspoon freshly ground pepper*
Pinch of allspice
Pinch of ground cloves
Pinch of freshly grated nutmeg
¼ *teaspoon cinnamon*
2 tablespoons heavy cream
Cream Cheese Dough (p. 169)
1 egg

1. Finely chop the nuts in a food processor, turning the machine on and off several times. Transfer to a small bowl.

2. Place the garlic and onion in the food processor and chop.

3. In a large heavy skillet, melt 1 tablespoon of the butter over moderately high heat. Add the garlic and onion and sauté until softened but not browned, about 5 minutes.

4. Meanwhile, chop the apple in the food processor. Scrape the apple into the skillet and cook until softened, 3 to 4 minutes longer. Scrape the mixture back into the processor.

5. Melt the remaining 1 tablespoon butter in the same skillet. Add the chicken livers and sauté, tossing frequently, until browned outside but still pink in the center, about 5 minutes. Add the Calvados and cook for 30 seconds.

6. Add the livers and the pan juices to the processor. Add the salt, pepper, allspice, cloves, nutmeg, cinnamon and cream. Puree until smooth. Add the chopped nuts and turn the

machine quickly on and off several times until just incorporated. Let cool to room temperature before using. (**The chicken liver filling can be made up to 3 days ahead.** Refrigerate, covered.)

7. Remove half the dough from the refrigerator and let stand for about 10 minutes, until malleable. Divide this piece of dough in half. On a lightly floured work surface, roll out one piece of the dough about ⅛ inch thick. Using a 3- or 3¼-inch round cutter, cut the dough into circles. Collect the scraps, chill them briefly and reroll them; cut out to make about 10 circles in all.

8. Put about 1 heaping teaspoon of filling in the center of each round. Moisten the edges of the dough with water. Fold one side of the circle over the filling to form a crescent and pinch the pastry together. Crimp the edges with the tines of a fork to seal. Refrigerate for at least 30 minutes, or up to 24 hours. Repeat with all the remaining dough and filling. (**The crescents can be made ahead to this point and frozen, tightly wrapped, for up to 1 month.** Bake the crescents without defrosting.)

9. Preheat the oven to 400°. Place the crescents on a buttered baking sheet, preferably nonstick. In a small bowl, beat the egg with 1 teaspoon of water to make a glaze. Brush the glaze over the crescents. Slash with a small knife or prick with a fork to make steam vents.

10. Bake for about 15 minutes, or until golden brown. (Frozen crescents will take about 5 minutes longer.)
—*Dorie Greenspan*

RICOTTA PESTO CRESCENTS

MAKES ABOUT 3 DOZEN

1 cup (loosely packed) fresh basil leaves
¼ cup olive oil, preferably extra-virgin
2 tablespoons walnuts
2 tablespoons freshly grated Parmesan cheese
2 medium garlic cloves
½ teaspoon salt
¼ teaspoon freshly ground pepper
1 cup whole-milk ricotta cheese, drained of excess liquid
Cream Cheese Dough (p. 169)
1 egg

1. Put the basil, olive oil, walnuts, Parmesan cheese, garlic, salt and the pepper into a food processor. Puree until the pesto is well blended.

2. Scrape the pesto into a bowl and stir in the ricotta cheese. (**The filling can be made up to 3 days ahead.** Cover and refrigerate.)

3. Form and bake the crescents as in Steps 6 through 9 of the Chicken Liver and Apple Crescents (p. 13).
—*Dorie Greenspan*

MINIATURE WELSH RAREBITS

Though these hors d'oeuvre are small, they are easy to make in quantity and are particularly appropriate for a large cocktail party.

MAKES 80 PIECES

3 cups (¾ pound) grated Cheddar cheese
5 tablespoons unsalted butter, cut into small pieces
¼ cup lager beer
1 tablespoon Dijon-style mustard

Salt and freshly ground pepper
20 slices buttered white toast, crusts removed
1 large Granny Smith apple—peeled, cored and cut into matchsticks
10 flat anchovy fillets—rinsed, patted dry and quartered (optional)

1. In a heavy medium saucepan, combine the Cheddar cheese, butter and beer. Cook over low heat, stirring constantly, until the cheese melts and the mixture is smooth, about 5 minutes. Stir in the mustard and season with salt and pepper to taste.

2. Preheat the broiler. Place the toast on a baking sheet lined with aluminum foil. Spoon the cheese mixture evenly over the toast and broil 2 inches from the heat until the cheese bubbles and browns, 3 to 4 minutes.

3. Cut each slice into 4 triangles. Garnish with the apple sticks and anchovy fillets, if using, and serve hot.
—*W. Peter Prestcott*

PIERINO'S OLIVE-STUFFED PEPPER WEDGES WITH TOMATOES AND ANCHOVIES

This is my all-time favorite hors d'oeuvre, based on a recipe my chef friend Sandra Gluck brought back from Pierino Govene, chef-owner of Ristorante Gambero Rosso in Cesenatico, on Italy's Adriatic coast. Prepared in advance and served at room temperature, it couldn't be easier.

F&W BEVERAGE SUGGESTION
Robust Italian white wine, such as Greco di Tufo

6 TO 8 SERVINGS
10 to 12 Calamata or other brine-cured black olives, pitted and chopped

2 garlic cloves, minced
3 tablespoons chopped Italian
    flat-leaf parsley
2½ tablespoons rinsed and chopped
    capers
2 to 3 anchovy fillets, to taste,
    chopped
5 canned plum tomatoes, drained and
    chopped
½ teaspoon freshly ground black
    pepper
3½ tablespoons extra-virgin olive oil
2 large red bell peppers
2 large yellow bell peppers

1. Preheat the oven to 375°. In a medium bowl, combine the olives, garlic, parsley, capers, anchovies, tomatoes, black pepper and 1½ tablespoons of the olive oil. Set the stuffing aside.

2. Cut the peppers in half lengthwise and remove the stems, seeds and ribs. Make 2 diagonal crisscross cuts in each half to form 4 triangular wedges.

3. Lightly oil a large shallow baking dish and arrange the pepper pieces in a single layer, hollow-sides up. Spoon 1 heaping teaspoon of the olive stuffing into each piece of pepper. Cover the dish with foil.

4. Bake until the peppers begin to soften, about 15 minutes. Uncover and bake until they are tender but not limp, about 10 minutes. Let cool to room temperature. Transfer the stuffed pepper wedges to a serving platter and drizzle with the remaining 2 tablespoons extra-virgin olive oil.
—Richard Sax

PROSCIUTTO AND CHEESE APPETIZER TOASTS

A generous squeeze of lemon juice cuts nicely through the seasoned oil in which these little appetizer sandwiches are fried.

F&W BEVERAGE SUGGESTION
Italian white, such as Gavi

8 SERVINGS

4 not-too-thin slices of prosciutto
    (about 3 ounces)
8 slices of Italian or French bread,
    about 3 inches in diameter, cut ½
    inch thick
¼ pound Italian Fontina or
    mozzarella cheese, shredded
4 fresh sage or basil leaves
About ¼ cup extra-virgin olive oil
1 large garlic clove, smashed and
    peeled
1 small fresh or dried hot pepper
1 lemon, quartered
Sprig of fresh sage or basil, for
    garnish

1. Fold a slice of prosciutto on each of 4 slices of the bread. Top each with 1 heaping tablespoon of the grated cheese and a sage or basil leaf. Sandwich each with a second slice of bread.

2. In a large heavy skillet, heat ¼ cup olive oil with the garlic and hot pepper over moderate heat. When the garlic sizzles, carefully lay the sandwiches in the oil. Fry until the bottom slice of the bread is golden, about 4 minutes. With a wide spatula, turn the sandwiches over, add a little more oil if needed and reduce the heat slightly. Fry until the second side is golden and the cheese is melted but not runny, about 3 minutes.

3. Place the sandwiches on a serving plate and cut them in half. If desired, warm the remaining oil in the pan and drizzle a little of the seasoned oil over the sandwiches. Garnish with the lemon quarters and a small sprig of fresh sage or basil. Serve hot.
—Richard Sax

ARTICHOKE FRITTERS WITH REMOULADE SAUCE

MAKES 40

¼ cup fresh lemon juice
5 large artichokes
1 cup all-purpose flour
1 teaspoon baking powder
1 quart vegetable oil, for deep-frying
Remoulade Sauce (p. 229)

1. Pour the lemon juice into a large noncorrodible saucepan with about 2 quarts of water.

2. Trim each artichoke by snapping off the stem; bend back and pull off the tough outer dark green leaves. Using a serrated stainless steel knife, cut off the top ⅔ of the artichoke, leaving about 1½ inches of the heart. Pare away the bases of the dark green outer leaves. As you trim each artichoke, drop immediately into the acidulated water to prevent discoloration.

3. When all the artichokes are in the saucepan, bring to a boil over high heat. Reduce the heat to moderate and boil until the artichokes hearts are tender, 20 to 25 minutes. Let the hearts cool in the cooking liquid to retain their color. (**The artichokes can be cooked a day ahead and refrigerated in their cooking liquid overnight.**)

4. When cool, remove the artichokes from the liquid and cut each heart into eighths. Remove the hairy

choke and drain well.

5. In a medium bowl, combine the flour and baking powder with 1 cup of water. Blend thoroughly.

6. In a deep-fryer or large deep saucepan, heat the oil to 400°. One by one, dip each piece of artichoke into the batter and add to the hot oil. Fry in batches without crowding until crisp and brown, about 3 minutes. Drain on paper towels. Serve the fritters hot with the remoulade sauce for dipping.

—*John Robert Massie*

ORIENTAL FRIED
FETA DUMPLINGS

These dumplings can be assembled and fried early in the day. Keep them at room temperature. About 10 minutes before serving, place the dumplings on baking sheets in a single layer and crisp them in a preheated 300° oven.

MAKES 96

1 ounce dried shiitake mushrooms*
½ pound feta cheese
1 package (8 ounces) cream cheese
3 medium scallions, minced
3 tablespoons minced fresh ginger
1 can (5 ounces) water chestnuts,
*   drained and finely chopped*
1 medium garlic clove, minced
¼ cup sesame seeds
½ cup pine nuts (pignoli)
2 packages (¾ pound each) fresh
*   wonton skins**
3 cups peanut or corn oil, for
*   deep-frying*
*Available at Oriental markets

1. In a medium bowl, cover the mushrooms with hot water and soak until soft, about 30 minutes. Drain well. Cut off and discard the stems; mince the caps.

2. In a food processor, combine the feta cheese, cream cheese and scallions. Process until smooth. Scrape the mixture into a medium bowl. Add the ginger, water chestnuts, garlic, sesame seeds, pine nuts and minced mushrooms and blend well.

3. Using a 3-inch round cookie cutter, stamp out circles from the wonton skins. Cover the circles with a damp cloth to keep them moist.

4. Moisten the rim of a wonton circle with water. Place 1 teaspoon of the cheese filling in the center of the circle and fold the edges over the filling to form a semicircle. Press the edges together to seal. Repeat with the remaining wonton circles and cheese filling.

5. In a large heavy saucepan or a deep-fryer, heat the oil to 375°. Fry the dumplings in small batches until golden and crisp, about 1 minute. Using a slotted spoon, transfer the dumplings to paper towels to drain. Serve hot.

—*W. Peter Prestcott*

MADRONA MANOR'S
FRIED CHEESE

4 SERVINGS

¼ cup extra-virgin olive oil
¼ pound caciocavallo or imported
*   provolone cheese, cut into ½- to*
*   ¾-inch dice*
1 teaspoon oregano
1 garlic clove, minced
1 tablespoon red wine vinegar
2 teaspoons minced parsley
1 loaf of French bread, sliced

1. In a small skillet, heat the oil. Add the cheese and cook over moderately high heat until the cheese begins to melt, about 2 minutes.

2. Add the oregano and garlic, shake the pan and remove from the heat. Add the vinegar and sprinkle on the parsley. Serve immediately, directly from the skillet, with the bread for dunking.

—*Todd Muir, Madrona Manor,*
Healdsburg, California

SEPHARDIC-STYLE HAROSET

This tempting fruit-and-nut spread, one of the traditional Passover dishes, can be made up to a day ahead and refrigerated. Let return to room temperature before serving. For best results, the dried fruit used in this recipe should be soft.

MAKES ABOUT 4 CUPS

1 cup walnut pieces
½ cup blanched almonds
5 large dried Calimyrna figs
8 large pitted prunes
½ cup dark raisins
½ cup pitted dates
1 medium, tart apple—peeled, cored
*   and cut into chunks*
1 tablespoon freshly grated orange
*   zest*
1 medium navel orange, peeled and
*   cut into chunks*
¼ teaspoon cinnamon
1 regular or whole wheat matzoh,
*   broken into large pieces*
2 to 4 tablespoons dry red wine, or to
*   taste*

1. Place the walnuts, almonds, figs, prunes, raisins, dates, apple, orange zest, orange chunks, cinnamon and matzoh in a food processor. With quick on/off motions, process until the ingredients are coarsely chopped.

2. Continue to process, adding just

enough wine to form a soft, coarse paste (the mixture should not be smooth). Transfer the *haroset* to a bowl, cover and refrigerate for up to 2 days before serving. If the *haroset* is too stiff to spread, stir in some additional wine. Serve with matzoh.

—*Gloria Kaufer Greene*

GINGERED EGGPLANT MOUSSE

As this delicately flavored mousse drains overnight in the refrigerator, it takes on the pattern of the basket in which it was molded.

F&W BEVERAGE SUGGESTION
Côtes du Rhône

8 TO 10 SERVINGS
2 medium eggplants (about 1¼ pounds total)
½ pound farmer cheese
½ cup sour cream
2 tablespoons tomato paste
1 medium garlic clove, minced
1 cup minced scallions (about 1 bunch)
1 teaspoon ground ginger
1 teaspoon salt
2½ teaspoons freshly ground pepper
1 cup heavy cream
1 tablespoon olive oil

1. Preheat the oven to 400°. Place the eggplants on a baking sheet, prick them with a fork and roast for 40 minutes, or until very tender when pierced. Let cool completely. Peel the eggplants and puree the pulp in a food processor. Scrape the puree into a large bowl.

2. Combine the farmer cheese, sour cream, tomato paste and garlic in the food processor and puree until smooth. Scrape this mixture into the bowl of eggplant puree and add the

scallions, ginger, salt and 2 teaspoons of the pepper; mix well.

3. In a medium bowl, whip the heavy cream until it forms stiff peaks. Fold the cream into the eggplant mixture. Season to taste with additional salt, pepper and ginger.

4. Line a 6- to 8-cup wicker basket with dampened cheesecloth. Gently pour in the mousse mixture and cover with any overhanging cheesecloth. Cover with plastic wrap, place on a large plate and refrigerate overnight.

5. About 30 minutes before serving, remove the mousse from the refrigerator and set aside. Just before serving, unwrap the mousse and unmold onto a decorative platter. Drizzle with the olive oil and sprinkle with the remaining ½ teaspoon pepper.

—*W. Peter Prestcott*

CHEVRE MOUSSE

This fragrant herbed cheese mousse is made on the same principle as *coeur à la crème*. Make it the night before so that the whey has a chance to drain.

12 SERVINGS
½ pound Bucheron or other mild goat cheese, at room temperature
¼ cup sour cream
¼ cup walnuts, coarsely chopped
½ teaspoon rosemary, crumbled
1½ teaspoons salt
¼ teaspoon freshly ground white pepper
3 teaspoons Calvados or applejack
1 cup heavy cream
Bay leaves and walnut halves, for garnish

1. In a medium bowl, using an electric mixer, beat the goat cheese with the sour cream until smooth. Stir in the walnuts, rosemary, salt, white pepper and 2 teaspoons of the Calvados (or apple jack).

2. In another bowl, beat the heavy cream until almost stiff. Blend in the remaining 1 teaspoon Calvados. Gently stir half the whipped cream into the cheese mixture to lighten it; then fold in the remaining cream.

3. Line a 4- to 5-cup wicker basket with three layers of dampened cheesecloth, cutting the cloth large enough to overlap the mousse. For garnish, arrange bay leaves and walnut halves upside down on the cheesecloth in a decorative pattern.

4. Carefully turn the cheese mixture into the mold and smooth the surface. Fold the cheesecloth over the mousse. Place the basket on a rack set over a bowl to drain. Refrigerate the mixture overnight.

5. To unmold, fold back the cheesecloth. Place a serving plate over the top of the basket and invert carefully. Peel off the cheesecloth. Serve chilled.

—*W. Peter Prestcott*

PUMPKIN SEED PUREE

This pumpkin seed puree is delicious as a dip. Serve it chilled with raw vegetables or lightly toasted pita triangles for dunking.

MAKES ABOUT 1½ CUPS
1½ cups (8 ounces) hulled, unsalted pumpkin seeds (pepitas)*
3 tablespoons olive oil
2 garlic cloves, crushed
¾ to 1 cup chicken stock or canned broth

¼ cup fresh lime juice
1 to 2 jalapeños—seeded, deveined
   and chopped—or hot pepper sauce
   to taste
1 teaspoon salt
¼ teaspoon freshly ground pepper
*Available at health food stores and
   Mexican markets

1. In a medium ungreased skillet, cook the pumpkin seeds over high heat, stirring occasionally, until they begin to pop and turn golden brown, 2 to 3 minutes. Place the seeds in a food processor or blender and puree until finely ground.

2. In the same skillet, heat the oil. Add the garlic and cook over moderate heat until fragrant, about 30 seconds. Pour the oil and garlic into the processor. Add ¾ cup of the chicken stock, the lime juice, jalapeños, salt and pepper. Puree until smooth. (If the mixture is too thick, add a bit more stock, 1 tablespoon at a time.)

—Jim Fobel

SHAD ROE SPREAD

MAKES ABOUT 1¾ CUPS
2 slices of bacon
3 tablespoons unsalted butter, at
   room temperature
1 large pair of shad roe (about ¾
   pound)
2 tablespoons minced scallion
1 tablespoon fresh lemon juice
Salt and freshly ground pepper
6 drops hot pepper sauce, or to taste

1. Cook the bacon in a medium skillet over moderate heat, turning oc-

casionally, until crisp. Reserve the drippings in the pan. Drain the bacon on paper towels; crumble and set aside.

2. Add 2 tablespoons of the butter to the bacon drippings and place over moderate heat. When the butter has melted, add the shad roe. Cook, covered, turning once, for about 10 minutes, or until the roe is firm and lightly browned. Transfer the roe to a bowl.

3. Add the scallion to the skillet and cook over low heat for 1 minute until softened. Remove from the heat, stir in the lemon juice, scraping up any browned bits on the bottom of the pan, and pour the mixture over the roe.

4. Using a fork, break up the roe and mix the ingredients together. Stir in the reserved bacon, the remaining butter, salt and pepper to taste and the hot pepper sauce. Transfer to a crock or serving dish, cover and refrigerate. Serve at room temperature with toast rounds.

—Jim Fobel

SHRIMP LEGS WITH CRISPY NORI

This is a funny name for a delicious appetizer. Actually logs of shrimp puree wrapped in bands of crisp, smoky seaweed (nori, in Japanese), these deep-fried nuggets are easy to prepare and perfect finger food for a party. I serve them with a dry, cool white wine or Champagne.

🍷 F&W BEVERAGE SUGGESTION
Mosel, such as Deinhard Green Label

MAKES ABOUT 20
¾ pound fresh shrimp, shelled and
   deveined
1½ tablespoons finely minced fresh
   pork fat

1 scallion, minced
1½ tablespoons finely minced fresh
   ginger
1 teaspoon coarse (kosher) salt
1 tablespoon Chinese rice wine or dry
   sherry
1½ teaspoons cornstarch
6 fresh water chestnuts,* cut into
   ⅛-inch dice or ⅓ cup finely diced
   jicama
1 egg white
20 strips of nori,* cut 3½ inches long
   and 1¼ inches wide
1 to 1½ quarts corn or peanut oil, for
   deep-frying
Fresh coriander sprigs or scallion
   brushes, for garnish
Roasted Szechuan Pepper-Salt
   (p. 236)
*Available at Oriental markets

1. In a food processor, combine the shrimp, fat, scallion, ginger, salt, rice wine and cornstarch; process to a paste, about 20 seconds. Scrape into a bowl and stir in the water chestnuts.

2. Beat the egg white until stiff but not dry. Fold into the shrimp paste.

3. Lay a piece of nori flat on your work surface with a short edge closest to you. Spoon about 1 tablespoon of the shrimp mixture in the middle. Mold the paste into a log running perpendicular to the nori; the length of the shrimp log should be equal to the width of the nori. Roll the shrimp log up in the nori. Seal the log with a dab of shrimp paste. Smooth the filling at the ends of the log with your finger, then set aside on a lightly oiled baking sheet or flat plate. Repeat with the remaining nori and shrimp filling. **(The recipe can be prepared ahead to this point. Cover with plastic wrap**

and refrigerate for several hours. Let return to room temperature before frying.)

4. Preheat the oven to 325°. In a large wok or deep-fat fryer, heat at least 1½ inches of oil to 350°, hot enough to foam up around a dab of shrimp paste on contact. One by one, add as many logs to the oil as will float comfortably in a single layer, adjusting the heat so they remain rimmed by a crown of white bubbles. Fry until the shrimp paste is light golden, about 1 minute, using chopsticks or tongs to turn the logs as they fry. With a Chinese mesh spoon or flat strainer, remove the logs to a paper towel-lined baking sheet and place in the oven to keep warm. Repeat with the remaining logs.

5. Increase the oil temperature to 375°. Return all the shrimp logs to the oil and fry until they turn a deeper gold and swell, 15 to 30 seconds. Drain on fresh paper towels. Serve garnished with fresh coriander or scallion brushes and accompanied with a dish of Szechuan pepper-salt.

—Barbara Tropp

SESAME CHICKEN

The marinade here has the same flavor as the traditional sauce for cold spicy noodles with sesame sauce. Running the chicken breasts under the broiler gives them an almost black, crusty exterior and a wonderful flavor. Cut into chunks, Sesame Chicken makes an excellent room-temperature appetizer. The chicken needs to be marinated overnight, so plan accordingly.

6 SERVINGS
¾ cup sesame paste (tahini)
⅓ cup brewed Chinese black tea
¼ cup dark soy sauce*
1½ tablespoons Chinese hot oil

3 medium garlic cloves, crushed
  through a press
2 tablespoons Oriental sesame oil
2 tablespoons sugar
2 tablespoons red wine vinegar
½ cup thinly sliced scallions
2 pounds skinless, boneless chicken
  breasts trimmed of excess fat
1 bunch of watercress, for garnish
*Available at Oriental markets

1. In a small bowl, combine the sesame paste, tea, soy sauce, hot oil, garlic, sesame oil, sugar and vinegar. Whisk until well blended. Stir in the scallions.

2. Place the chicken in a large glass baking dish. Pour the marinade over the chicken. Turn to coat well. Cover and refrigerate for 24 hours. Let the chicken return to room temperature before proceeding.

3. Preheat the broiler. Place the chicken on a rack over a broiler pan. Broil the chicken about 3 inches from the heat, turning carefully so as not to break the crust, for about 5 minutes on each side, until the outside is slightly charred and the chicken is still juicy but no longer pink.

4. Let rest for 10 minutes. Cut into 1-inch cubes. Serve warm or at room temperature, garnished with the sprigs of watercress.

—Karen Lee & Alaxandra Branyon

BROILED CLAMS WITH FLAVORED BUTTER AND BACON

🍷 F&W BEVERAGE SUGGESTION
Brouilly Nouveau, such as Georges Duboeuf

MAKES 2 DOZEN
24 cherrystone or littleneck clams, on
  the half shell
4 tablespoons Red Pepper and Herb
  Butter (p. 231) or Tarragon-Pernod
  Butter (p. 231)
3 slices of bacon, cut into 8 pieces
  each

Preheat the broiler. Place the clams on a large ovenproof platter covered with rock salt. Top each clam with ½ teaspoon of the flavored butter and a piece of bacon. Broil as close to the heat as possible for 4 to 6 minutes, or until the clams are cooked, and the bacon is crisp. Serve immediately.

—Anne Disrude

THE MILANESE RESTAURANT'S BAKED STUFFED CLAMS

The crabmeat and mushrooms in these stuffed clams make them especially good.

6 SERVINGS
1 stick (4 ounces) unsalted butter
1 small onion, minced
½ pound fresh mushrooms, minced
¼ cup dry white wine
1 pound lump crabmeat, flaked
12 medium clams—shucked and
  minced, shells rinsed and reserved
½ cup fresh bread crumbs
¼ cup minced Italian flat-leaf parsley
1 teaspoon salt
¼ teaspoon freshly ground pepper
Paprika

1. Preheat the oven to 375°. In a

medium skillet, melt the butter. Add the onion and cook over moderate heat until softened but not browned, about 3 minutes. Add the mushrooms and cook until they've softened, about 4 minutes.

2. Stir in the wine, crabmeat, minced clams, bread crumbs, parsley, salt and pepper. Remove from the heat and stir well to combine.

3. Fill all 24 reserved shells with the clam mixture and sprinkle lightly with paprika. Place on a baking sheet and bake for 12 minutes, or until heated through.

—Rita Milanese, The Milanese Restaurant, Poughkeepsie, New York

COLD SHRIMP WITH FOUR-HERB MAYONNAISE

This sauce is also delicious spooned over raw oysters and clams, and it makes a great sauce for spooning over roasted clams, oysters and shrimp. Feel free to substitute other fresh herbs if those called for below are un-available.

MAKES ABOUT 5 DOZEN
2¼ teaspoons salt
3½ pounds large shrimp—shelled and deveined, with tails and last section of shell left on
1 egg yolk
¼ teaspoon Dijon-style mustard
1½ tablespoons lemon juice

1 tablespoon dry white wine
5 to 6 drops of hot pepper sauce
Pinch of sugar
1 teaspoon anchovy paste
¾ cup safflower or other light vegetable oil
¼ cup extra-virgin olive oil
1 tablespoon warm water
3 tablespoons minced fresh chives
2 tablespoons minced parsley
3 tablespoons minced fresh tarragon or 2 teaspoons dried
2 tablespoons minced fresh basil

1. Bring a large pot of water to a boil with 2 teaspoons of the salt. Add the shrimp, let the water return to a boil and cook until shrimp are loosely curled and just opaque throughout, 1 to 2 minutes for medium shrimp, 2 to 3 minutes for large and 3 to 4 minutes for jumbo. Drain under cold running water and pat dry with paper towels. Cover with a damp towel and refrigerate until serving time. (The shrimp can be prepared up to 5 hours ahead.)

2. In a medium bowl, combine the egg yolk, mustard, lemon juice, wine, hot sauce, sugar, anchovy paste and the remaining ¼ teaspoon salt. Whisk until thoroughly blended.

3. Gradually whisk in the safflower and olive oils, drop by drop at first, then in a thin stream. When all the oil has been incorporated, whisk in 1 tablespoon of warm water. Stir in the mixed fresh herbs. Serve immediately, with the shrimp, or cover and refrigerate for up to 6 hours.

—Anne Disrude

MUSSELS DIJONNAISE

These mussels are as tasty as they are simple to prepare.

6 SERVINGS
¼ cup vegetable oil
24 mussels
1 cup white wine
2 medium shallots, minced
1 garlic clove, minced
1 tablespoon Dijon-style mustard
1½ tablespoons soy sauce
1 tablespoon fresh lemon juice
⅛ teaspoon salt
⅛ teaspoon freshly ground pepper
¼ cup olive oil

1. In a large stockpot, heat the vegetable oil until it begins to smoke. Add the mussels and wine, cover and cook over moderate heat, shaking the pot occasionally, until the mussels open, 5 to 7 minutes. Remove the mussels with a slotted spoon, let cool and set aside; discard the cooking liquid and any mussels that have not opened.

2. In a small bowl, combine the shallots, garlic, mustard, soy sauce, lemon juice, salt and pepper. Gradually whisk in the olive oil in a slow steady stream.

3. Arrange the mussels on the half shell and spoon some of the sauce over each.

—Fio Antognini, Fio's La Fourchette, St. Louis, Missouri

FIRST COURSES

BEGGAR'S POUCHES

Beggar's Pouches, caviar tied up in a crêpe pouch, make an elegant first course. The batter must be refrigerated overnight, so plan accordingly.

MAKES 8
½ cup milk
¼ cup all-purpose flour
Pinch of salt
2 tablespoons unsalted butter, melted
1 ounce caviar, preferably beluga
8 whole chives or long thin strips of
  scallion green

1. In a blender or food processor, combine the milk, flour, salt and 1 tablespoon of the melted butter. Blend until smooth, stopping to scrape down the sides of the bowl. Pour the batter into a small bowl, cover and refrigerate overnight.

2. Grease a small, well-seasoned crêpe or omelet pan with a little of the remaining butter and heat over moderately high heat. Pour in about 1½ tablespoons of batter, to make a crêpe 2½ to 3 inches in diameter. Cook until the bottom is barely browned, about 45 seconds. Turn and cook until the second side is dry, 10 to 15 seconds. (**The crêpes can be made several hours before serving.** Cover them with plastic wrap and store at room temperature.)

3. Shortly before serving, dab about ¾ teaspoon caviar into the center of each crêpe. Carefully gather the edges to shape each crêpe into a little pouch and tie securely with a chive.
—John Robert Massie

SHAD WRAPPED IN
PHYLLO PASTRY

These phyllo-wrapped shad packages can be assembled ahead of time and refrigerated. Bake just before serving.
🔖 F&W BEVERAGE SUGGESTION
California Dry Chenin Blanc, such as Dry Creek

6 FIRST-COURSE SERVINGS
2 shad fillets (about ¾ pound each)
½ cup fresh lemon juice
3 bay leaves, broken in half
½ teaspoon freshly ground pepper
2 carrots, cut into 1-by-⅛-inch
  julienne strips
2 celery ribs, cut into 1-by-⅛-inch
  julienne strips
12 sheets of phyllo pastry*
1½ sticks (6 ounces) unsalted butter,
  melted and cooled slightly
½ cup minced chives or thinly sliced
  scallion greens
1 small onion, sliced into thin rounds
  and separated into rings
Salt
*Available at specialty food stores

1. Cut each shad fillet diagonally into three equal pieces. Place in a shallow glass dish; add the lemon juice, bay leaves and pepper. Let the fillets marinate at room temperature, turning several times, for 1 hour.

2. Bring about 1 quart of water to a boil in a medium saucepan over high heat. Add the carrots and celery; when the water returns to a boil, cook for 1 minute and then drain; set aside.

3. Preheat the oven to 450°. Lightly butter a baking sheet.

4. Place 1 sheet of phyllo on a flat work surface. (Keep the remaining sheets covered with a damp cloth to prevent them from drying out.) Brush the sheet of phyllo lightly with butter

and top it with a second sheet. Lightly brush again with butter and evenly scatter ½ teaspoon of the chives over the phyllo. Add a third sheet of phyllo, brush it lightly with butter and scatter ½ teaspoon of the chives over it. Top with a fourth sheet and brush it lightly with butter. Cut the layered phyllo in half crosswise to make two rectangles, about 12 by 8 inches each.

5. Remove the fillets from the marinade and pat dry with paper towels; reserve the marinade. Place one piece of fish, boned-side down, in the center of one rectangle of phyllo. Scatter one-sixth of the carrots, celery and onion over the shad. Sprinkle with 1 tablespoon of the chives, 2 teaspoons of the butter, 1 teaspoon of the reserved marinade and salt and pepper to taste.

6. Fold one corner of the phyllo over the fish, making the fold close to the fillet. Brush the dough lightly with butter. Working clockwise, fold up each remaining corner, brushing with butter, until the fish is snugly wrapped. Fold any extra dough under the fish to make a neat package. Repeat with the remaining ingredients to make 6 wrapped packages in all.

7. Place the phyllo-wrapped shad on the baking sheet, leaving at least 1 inch between the packages. Bake for about 15 minutes, or until the phyllo is crisp and golden brown. Serve hot.
—Jim Fobel

SALMON CABBAGE SASHIMI

Sashimi, which literally means, "fresh slice," here refers to medallions of pale cabbage and avocado, dark green watercress and coral smoked salmon.

4 FIRST-COURSE SERVINGS
8 large cabbage leaves
2 large bunches of watercress, leaves and small stems only
6 scallions, trimmed to 6 inches and minced
2 tablespoons olive oil
1 teaspoon prepared white horseradish
1 teaspoon salt
Freshly ground pepper
3½ teaspoons fresh lime juice
1 avocado
6 ounces thinly sliced Scotch smoked salmon
1 egg yolk
1 tablespoon dry white wine
Pinch of sugar
1 cup safflower oil
1½ tablespoons capers, or chopped fresh dill or coriander

1. Cook the cabbage leaves in a large saucepan of boiling salted water until tender and translucent, 15 to 20 minutes. Drain, cool under cold running water and pat dry. Cut out the tough end of the central rib on each leaf.

2. Blanch the watercress leaves in boiling salted water for 10 seconds, just until limp. Drain, cool under cold running water. Squeeze in cheesecloth to remove excess moisture; chop.

3. In a medium bowl, thoroughly mix the watercress, scallions, olive oil, horseradish, ½ teaspoon of the salt, a

pinch of pepper and ½ teaspoon of the lime juice. Set aside.

4. Peel and pit the avocado. Slice into thin strips. Toss with 2 teaspoons of the lime juice, ¼ teaspoon of the salt and a pinch of pepper.

5. On a sheet of plastic wrap, overlap 4 cabbage leaves evenly in a rectangular shape. Distribute half of the watercress mixture (about ⅓ cup) over the leaves. Cover with half of the salmon to form a complete layer. (Don't worry about covering the edges since they will be trimmed off.) Lay half of the avocado strips, end on end, crosswise in the center. Lift the edges of the plastic wrap to begin the roll as you would for a jelly roll. Finish rolling with your hands, using your palms to keep the roll tight and even as it gets larger. Then fold the plastic wrap over the completed roll, tuck under and squeeze gently to tighten. Finish wrapping the roll in plastic and twist the ends to tighten and seal. Refrigerate and repeat with the remaining cabbage, watercress, salmon and avocado.

6. In a medium bowl, whisk to blend the egg yolk, wine, 1 teaspoon of water, the remaining 1 teaspoon lime juice, the sugar and the remaining ¼ teaspoon salt and ⅛ teaspoon pepper. Drizzle in the oil, whisking constantly to make the mayonnaise. Add the capers.

7. To serve, unwrap the rolls. Use a thin sharp knife to trim off the ends on the diagonal. Slice each roll into 6 diagonal slices. Arrange 3 slices on each of 4 chilled plates. Add a pool of the sauce and serve.

—Anne Disrude

GOLD COIN CRAB CAKES

I'm wild about these wonderfully flavorful, *green* crab cakes! I serve them as a sit-down appetizer accompanied with sprigs of lightly dressed watercress and flutes of cold, dry Champagne. The mixture can be made a full night ahead. Leftover crab cakes are quite delicious.

F&W BEVERAGE SUGGESTION
Hanns Kornell Brut

MAKES ABOUT 16 LARGE OR 24 SMALL CRAB CAKES
1 cup coarsely chopped fresh coriander
2 tablespoons finely minced or pureed fresh ginger
2 scallions, thinly sliced
1½ to 2 tablespoons Chinese chili sauce*
½ teaspoon coarse (kosher) salt
½ cup Thick Coconut Milk (p. 232) or canned unsweetened
1 pound fresh crabmeat—carefully picked over and well drained
½ cup fresh bread crumbs
2 eggs, lightly beaten
1½ to 2 cups corn or peanut oil, for frying
1 to 2 tablespoons unseasoned Japanese rice vinegar, to taste
Sprigs of watercress or fresh coriander, for garnish
*Available at Oriental markets

1. In a food processor or blender, combine the coriander, ginger, scallions, chili sauce, salt and coconut milk. Process until green and well blended, about 15 seconds. Transfer to a medium bowl. Add the crabmeat and toss lightly to combine.

2. Sprinkle the bread crumbs into the bowl, add the eggs and toss light-

ly, until thoroughly blended. Seal airtight with plastic wrap pressed directly on the surface and refrigerate for at least 1 hour, or overnight. (The crab cakes are easier to shape and absorb less oil when the mixture is chilled.)

3. About 15 minutes before serving, preheat the oven to 300°. In a large heavy skillet, heat ⅛ inch of oil until it is hot enough to foam up around a dab of crab mixture. Using 1 heaping tablespoon for each, shape the crab mixture into oval cakes about 3 inches long and ½ inch thick (see Note) and add to the skillet. Add as many crab cakes to the skillet as fit comfortably in a single layer. Adjust the heat so that the crab cakes will sizzle without scorching.

4. Brown the cakes lightly on both sides, then reduce the heat and cook through, turning once, 6 to 7 minutes. Transfer to a baking sheet lined with a triple layer of paper towels to drain. Keep the crab cakes warm in the oven. Wipe out the pan with dry paper towels, add more oil and repeat with the remaining crab mixture.

5. Serve the crab cakes hot, sprinkled with a dash of vinegar and garnished with a sprig of watercress or fresh coriander.

NOTE: These large crab cakes are plate and fork food. If you prefer to make them into small pick-up hors d'oeuvre, form scant tablespoonfuls of the crab mixture into 1½-inch rounds and fry only 5 to 6 minutes.

—Barbara Tropp

TEA-AND-SPICE-SMOKED QUAIL

This is a simple yet exceedingly elegant and impressive appetizer to make. The wee birds may be marinated and smoked a day in advance, then served alone as a first course or on an appetizer plate alongside Peking Cold Noodles with Chili-Orange Oil (p. 29) or a lightly dressed salad of interesting lettuces, depending on whether you're inclined East or West. Fingers are the stylish and only way to eat the quail. Put out a bone bowl or two for the celebrants.

🍷 F&W BEVERAGE SUGGESTION
Beaujolais

MAKES 6 QUAIL
6 fresh quail
¼ cup (packed) plus 1 tablespoon dark brown sugar
1 tablespoon plus ¾ teaspoon Roasted Szechuan Pepper-Salt (p. 236)
1 tablespoon slivered fresh ginger
1 tablespoon slivered scallion
2 tablespoons coarsely chopped orange zest plus 2 teaspoons finely minced
¼ cup fragrant black tea leaves
¼ cup rice
1 tablespoon Szechuan peppercorns*
1 cinnamon stick, crushed
About 1 tablespoon Oriental sesame oil
*Available at Oriental markets

1. For smoking, the quail must be absolutely clean. Remove the kidneys from either side of the tail bone, then flush the cavity of the quail clean with cold water. Reach again inside with your fingers to remove any loose innards, then rinse again. Dry the quail inside and out with paper towels.

2. In a small bowl, combine 1 tablespoon of the brown sugar with the Szechuan pepper-salt, mashing with a fork to blend the seasoning mixture.

In another bowl, combine the ginger and scallion. Dust the inside of each quail with ⅜ teaspoon of the seasoning mixture. Stuff each with several slivers of the ginger and scallion. Fold the wings back, with the tips tucked under the bird, and tie the legs together with string. Sprinkle the outside of each quail with ¾ teaspoon of the seasoning mixture and arrange, breast-side up, on a flat plate or tray. Sprinkle with the 2 teaspoons minced orange zest. Cover tightly with plastic wrap and set the birds aside to cure for 8 hours at cool room temperature or overnight in the refrigerator. (The longer time yields a richer flavor.)

3. Line a 14-inch wok or a broad heavy pot with enough heavy-duty aluminum foil to allow an extra 6 inches all around. Similarly line a matching lid. Combine the tea leaves, remaining ¼ cup brown sugar, rice, Szechuan peppercorns, cinnamon and chopped orange zest and scatter over the bottom of the lined wok. Choose a round rack that will fit at least 1½ inches above the bottom of the pan. (I use a 12-inch rack in my 14-inch wok for 6 quail. If you are using a flat Western pot, stand the rack on several cut-out cans to keep it distanced from the smoking mixture.) Brush the rack with sesame oil and set in the wok.

4. Arrange the quail, breast-side up, on the rack. Turn on the heat to its highest setting. (If smoking in a wok over a gas flame, invert the burner grid to nestle the wok close to the flame.) When several broad plumes of smoke appear from several spots in the wok, after 4 to 7 minutes, cover with the lined lid and using mitts or tongs, roll together the edges of foil

on the wok and lid to seal the contents. Smoke over high heat for 10 minutes. Turn off the heat and let the pot stand unopened for 5 minutes longer.

5. Promptly unseal the foil and remove the lid, avoiding the smoke that will suddenly vent. Remove the quail and immediately discard the foil and burnt smoking mixture. Brush the hot quail with a thin film of sesame oil. Cut in half through the breast bone and back bone, discard the ginger and scallion stuffing and serve hot, warm or at room temperature.

—*Barbara Tropp*

BEEF DUMPLINGS WITH ORANGE-SPICE DRESSING

Making dumplings from scratch is a labor of love in my servantless kitchen, but I find it well worth it. To offset the labor, I often double the recipe and freeze half. To cut labor even further, these dumplings can be made with storebought *shao mai* wrappers or wonton skins (see Note). The results will be slightly different but equally delicious.

Follow the dumplings with something simple—grilled fish and stir-fried greens or a single platter of stir-fried eggplant nuggets—to assuage the dumpling chef.

MAKES ABOUT 2 DOZEN LARGE DUMPLINGS
2½ cups all-purpose flour
¼ pound bok choy,* chopped (about 1½ cups)
1½ teaspoons coarse (kosher) salt
3 tablespoons tree ears*—soaked in cool water until pliable, about 30 minutes, rinsed and drained
6 ounces ground beef round
1½ teaspoons finely minced fresh ginger

1 scallion, minced
1½ tablespoons thinly sliced Chinese chives* or garlic shoots (optional)
½ cup plus ½ tablespoon soy sauce
2½ tablespoons Chili-Orange Oil (p. 236), plus ½ to 1 tablespoon minced seasonings from the oil, to taste
½ tablespoon Chinese rice wine or dry sherry
⅛ teaspoon freshly ground pepper
⅓ cup unseasoned Japanese rice vinegar
Chopped fresh coriander or sliced scallion, for garnish
*Available at Oriental markets

1. To make the dough for the dumpling wrappers, put the flour in a food processor. With the machine on, add about ¾ cup of cold water in a thin stream until the dough comes together in a ball; then process for 15 seconds to knead. Remove with floured hands and knead for about 15 seconds longer, until smooth and elastic enough to spring back when pressed with a finger. Cover the dough and let rest for at least 30 minutes. The dough is ready to be rolled when it does not spring back when pressed with a fingertip. (**The dough can be prepared ahead and refrigerated overnight.** Let return to room temperature before rolling out.)

2. To make the filling, sprinkle the bok choy with 1 teaspoon of the salt and let stand for 20 minutes. Drain and squeeze out excess liquid. Put the bok choy in a large bowl.

3. Put the tree ears in a food processor and pulse about 8 times, until coarsely chopped. Add the beef,

ginger, scallion, chives, ½ tablespoon each of the soy sauce and chili-orange oil, the minced seasonings from the oil, the rice wine, the remaining ½ teaspoon salt and the pepper. Pulse about 10 times to combine. Add the beef mixture to the bowl with the bok choy and stir lightly with a fork to blend. (**The filling can be made a day ahead.** Seal airtight with plastic wrap pressed directly on the surface and refrigerate. The flavors will develop overnight.)

4. To form the dumplings, divide the dough in half and roll out each piece as thin as possible on a floured surface, dusting the dough lightly with flour as needed to prevent sticking. Cut the dough into rounds with a floured 3½-inch cutter. Knead the scraps lightly into a ball, roll out and cut more rounds.

5. Put 1 level tablespoon of filling off-center on each wrapper. Fold the dough over the filling and press the edges together to seal in a plain half-moon, or pleat the edges decoratively if desired.

6. As the dumplings are shaped, set on a baking sheet covered with no-stick parchment or floured waxed paper. (**At this point, they can be frozen or covered and refrigerated.**)

7. In a small bowl, combine the remaining ½ cup soy sauce, 2 tablespoons chili-orange oil and the vinegar for the dressing.

8. To cook the dumplings, bring 3 quarts of water to boil in a stockpot over high heat. Add the dumplings, stir gently to separate them, cover and bring just to a boil. Immediately add 1 cup of cold water, replace the cover and wait for the water to return to a boil, 1½ to 2 minutes. Repeat twice more, for a total of 3 cups cold water.

9. As soon as the dumplings come to a final boil (after about 7 minutes), turn off the heat and remove the dumplings with a large mesh or slotted skimmer, dividing them among heated bowls. Ladle the sauce on and garnish liberally with coriander or scallions. Serve hot.

NOTE: To make the dumplings with storebought *shao mai* wrappers or wonton skins cut into 3½-inch rounds, skip Steps 1 and 4, and in Step 5, rub the edges of the dough rounds with water to seal. In Step 8, return to a boil only twice.

—*Barbara Tropp*

POTATO CASES WITH SHIITAKE AND MOREL FILLING

4 FIRST-COURSE SERVINGS
8 baking potatoes (10 ounces each), about 5 inches long and 2 inches wide
½ ounce dried morels
2 tablespoons unsalted butter, melted (preferably clarified)
3 tablespoons extra-virgin olive oil
3 garlic cloves, sliced
¾ pound fresh shiitake mushrooms— stemmed, caps cut crosswise into slices and then halved
¼ cup dry white wine
¼ cup chicken stock or canned broth
⅓ cup heavy cream
1 teaspoon fresh lemon juice
½ teaspoon salt
⅛ teaspoon freshly ground pepper
1 tablespoon minced parsley

1. With a paring knife, trim the potatoes to make straight-sided rectangular boxes (3 by 1½ by 1½ inches). Holding a paring knife vertically, cut completely around the inside of the potato box, leaving a shell ⅛ to ¼ inch thick. Insert the paring knife horizontally ⅛ to ¼ inch from the bottom of the box. Without enlarging the cut, work the knife back and forth in a swiveling motion to loosen the inside piece. If necessary, insert the paring knife in several different spots. Keep the potato cases submerged in cool water while you prepare the filling.

2. Preheat the oven to 450°. Soak the morels in 2 cups of hot water until softened, about 10 minutes. Remove the morels, squeezing gently. Strain the soaking liquid through a double layer of dampened cheesecloth into a small saucepan. Rinse the morels and trim. Chop coarsely and add to the saucepan. Boil gently until the liquid is completely absorbed, about 20 minutes. Set aside.

3. Meanwhile, pat the potato cases dry and brush completely with the butter. Place on a baking sheet and bake for 20 minutes, or until golden brown, turning the cases on a different side every 5 minutes.

4. In a large heavy skillet, heat the oil. Add the garlic and cook over moderately high heat until light golden, about 1 minute. Add the morels and the shiitake. Cook, stirring frequently, until the shiitake are softened, about 2 minutes.

5. Add the wine and stock and cook over moderately high heat until the liquid is slightly reduced, about 1 minute. Stir in the cream and boil until thickened, about 2 minutes. Add the lemon juice, salt and pepper. Keep warm.

6. To serve, season the potato cases lightly with salt. Stir the parsley into the filling. (If the filling is too thick, stir in 1 to 2 tablespoons additional cream, stock or water.) Place 2 potato cases on each serving plate. Spoon filling into each potato and serve.

—*Anne Disrude*

ANGELI'S POTATO CROQUETTES

Chef Evan Kleiman serves these as a first course.

MAKES 12
4 baking potatoes (about 2½ pounds)
1¼ teaspoons salt
5 eggs
4 tablespoons unsalted butter
⅔ cup freshly grated Parmesan cheese
¼ cup chopped parsley
¼ pound Italian salami, minced (about 1 cup)
½ teaspoon freshly ground pepper
2 ounces smoked mozzarella, cut into 12 strips, 2½ by ¼ by ¼ inch each
2 cups dry fresh bread crumbs
Vegetable oil or solid shortening, for deep-frying

1. In a large saucepan, cover the potatoes with cold water and bring to a boil over high heat. Add 1 teaspoon of the salt and cook until the potatoes are tender, about 40 minutes. Discard the water. Cook the potatoes over low heat until dry, about 5 minutes.

2. Peel the potatoes. Cut into chunks and place in a large mixing bowl. Using an electric mixer, beat the potatoes until smooth. In a small bowl, beat 2 of the eggs. Add the beaten eggs and butter to the potatoes and blend. Add the Parmesan, parsley, salami, pepper and remaining ¼ teaspoon salt. Beat well.

3. Shape the potato mixture into 2 logs. Cut each log into 6 pieces. Flatten each piece and press a strip of the mozzarella into the center. Fold the potato mixture around the cheese to enclose it completely. Roll the croquettes into 3½-inch cylinders, closing the ends neatly.

4. Place the bread crumbs in a wide shallow dish. In a similar dish, beat the remaining 3 eggs. Roll the croquettes first in the eggs, then in bread crumbs. Be sure to coat the ends as well. **(The recipe can be prepared a day ahead up to this point.** Place the croquettes on a cookie sheet, cover and refrigerate. Remove them from the refrigerator at least 1 hour before frying.)

5. In a deep fryer or a heavy, deep saucepan, heat 4 inches of oil or shortening to 360°. Add the croquettes, in batches of 3 or 4, and fry until deep golden brown, 7 to 8 minutes. Using a slotted spoon, transfer to paper towels to drain. Serve immediately.

—*Evan Kleiman, Angeli,*
Los Angeles, California

ZUCCHINI RIBBONS WITH ARUGULA AND CREAMY GOAT CHEESE SAUCE

4 FIRST-COURSE SERVINGS
1¼ cups heavy cream
½ cup finely chopped onion
3 sprigs of fresh thyme plus ½
teaspoon minced fresh thyme (or a
total of 1½ teaspoons dried thyme)
3 parsley stems
3 black peppercorns
2 medium garlic cloves, unpeeled and
lightly crushed
3 ounces mild goat cheese
4 teaspoons balsamic vinegar
Salt and coarsely cracked pepper
16 lengthwise slices of zucchini, cut
⅛ inch thick (from about 3
medium)

3 tablespoons extra-virgin olive oil
1 bunch of arugula, large stems
removed

1. In a heavy medium saucepan, combine the cream, onion, thyme sprigs (or 1 teaspoon dried), parsley stems, peppercorns and garlic. Bring just to a simmer, cover and cook over low heat until the garlic is very soft, about 20 minutes. Strain into a small saucepan; discard the solids.

2. Place the saucepan over low heat and whisk in the goat cheese, 1 teaspoon of the vinegar and the minced thyme (or ½ teaspoon dried). Stir until the sauce is smooth. Season with salt and pepper to taste.

3. Meanwhile, heat a large heavy skillet over high heat. Brush the zucchini slices with the olive oil and place in the skillet. Cook until lightly browned, about 1 minute on each side. Remove and keep warm.

4. To assemble, toss the remaining 3 teaspoons vinegar with the arugula. Gather together 3 arugula leaves and place crosswise on one of the zucchini slices; fold the zucchini slice over the arugula. Repeat with the remaining zucchini and arugula. Arrange four zucchini bundles decoratively on each serving plate. Spoon one-fourth of the sauce over each serving and top with more cracked pepper.

—*Anne Disrude*

WARM MOZZARELLA AND TOMATO SALAD WITH PROSCIUTTO

Serve this summery salad with a loaf of crusty French bread and a crock of sweet butter.

4 FIRST-COURSE SERVINGS
½ pound whole-milk mozzarella,
preferably fresh, cut into 12 slices,
about ¼ inch thick
4 medium tomatoes, sliced ¼ inch
thick
8 teaspoons extra-virgin olive oil
Coarse (kosher) salt and freshly
ground pepper
2 teaspoons fresh thyme leaves or 1
teaspoon dried
8 thin slices of imported prosciutto
12 fresh basil leaves

1. Cut the slices of mozzarella in half crosswise. On 4 individual flame-proof plates, alternate the tomato and mozzarella slices in an overlapping pattern to form a circle.

2. Drizzle each serving with 1 teaspoon of the oil and sprinkle with coarse salt, a grinding of pepper and ½ teaspoon of the fresh thyme or ¼ teaspoon dried. **(The recipe can be prepared to this point up to 2 hours ahead.** Cover loosely and set aside at room temperature.)

3. Preheat the broiler. Broil the salads, as close to the heat as possible, until the mozzarella is just warmed through but not melting, 20 to 30 seconds. Remove from the broiler and drizzle 1 teaspoon oil over each salad.

4. Drape 2 slices of the prosciutto over each serving and garnish with 3 basil leaves. Serve warm.

—*Perla Meyers*

CARAMELIZED ONION WITH SALSA

6 FIRST-COURSE SERVINGS
1 pound plum tomatoes—peeled,
seeded and coarsely chopped
4 medium scallions, trimmed to 6
inches and thinly sliced
1 jalapeño pepper, seeded and minced
2 tablespoons minced flat-leaf parsley
1½ teaspoons minced fresh coriander
3 tablespoons extra-virgin olive oil
4 teaspoons sherry wine vinegar
½ teaspoon salt
⅛ teaspoon cayenne pepper
6 large slices of Spanish onion, about
¾ inch thick and 3½ inches in
diameter
Freshly ground black pepper
Fresh coriander leaves, for garnish

1. In a large bowl, combine the tomatoes, scallions, jalapeño pepper, parsley, minced coriander, 2 tablespoons of the olive oil, 2 teaspoons of the vinegar, the salt and cayenne. Let marinate at room temperature for 1 hour.

2. Meanwhile, in a large heavy skillet, heat the remaining 1 tablespoon oil over moderately high heat. Reduce the heat to moderate, add the whole onion slices in a single layer and cook, turning once and pressing down on them occasionally with a spatula, until they are deep golden brown and shiny and tender throughout, about 45 minutes.

3. Add the remaining 2 teaspoons vinegar and 1 tablespoon of water. Flip the onion slices twice, being careful to keep them whole, to coat well. Season with salt and pepper to taste.

4. To serve, place one onion slice on each plate and top with ¼ cup salsa. Garnish with fresh coriander leaves.

—*Anne Disrude*

10-INGREDIENT VEGETABLE FRITTERS

6 FIRST-COURSE SERVINGS
¼ pound bean sprouts (about 2 cups)
1 red bell pepper, cut into thin slivers
8 scallions, thinly sliced into rounds
3 mushrooms, slivered
2 teaspoons capers, rinsed and patted
dry
1 tablespoon slivered black olives
1 teaspoon minced garlic
1 teaspoon minced fresh tarragon or
½ teaspoon dried
½ teaspoon minced fresh rosemary or
¼ teaspoon dried
2 tablespoons chopped sun-dried
tomatoes
Vegetable oil, for deep-frying
1 cup all-purpose flour
1 teaspoon baking powder
1 cup ice water
Coarse salt and lemon wedges

1. In a bowl, toss together the bean sprouts, bell pepper, scallions, mushrooms, capers, olives, garlic, tarragon, rosemary and sun-dried tomatoes.

2. Preheat the oven to 250°. Place a baking sheet with a rack on it in the oven. Fill a deep-fryer with 4 inches of oil and heat to 390°.

3. Meanwhile, sift the flour and baking powder into a medium bowl. Make a well in the center, pour in the ice water and whisk until smooth.

4. Add the batter to the vegetables and stir to coat well. Using a large flat spoon, slide about ¼ cup of the fritter mixture into the hot oil, trying not to make the fritters too thick in the center. Add as many as will fit without crowding and fry, turning once, until browned and crisp, 3 to 4 minutes. Drain on paper towels; then transfer to the rack in the oven to keep warm until all the batter is used up.

5. Serve the fritters in a napkin-lined basket and pass coarse salt and wedges of lemon on the side.

—*Anne Disrude*

BRAISED PEAR, CELERY AND ENDIVE WITH PARMESAN AND BASIL

4 FIRST-COURSE SERVINGS
1 Bosc pear
Juice of ½ lemon
1 head of celery
4 small Belgian endive
1 tablespoon unsalted butter
1 cup rich chicken or veal stock,
preferably homemade
½ teaspoon salt
¼ teaspoon freshly ground pepper
4 teaspoons freshly grated Parmesan
cheese
2 teaspoons minced fresh basil

1. Preheat the oven to 350°. Peel, quarter and core the pear. Sprinkle with the lemon juice. Remove and discard the tough outer ribs of celery until you reach the light-green inner ribs, or heart. Trim the celery heart to 5 inches, core and cut lengthwise into quarters.

2. Place the celery heart and endive in a single layer in a large flameproof baking dish. Dot with the butter and pour in the stock. Bring to a boil over high heat. Loosely cover with parchment or waxed paper and bake in the oven for 15 minutes. Turn the vegetables over and bake for another 10 to 15 minutes, until almost tender. Add the pear quarters and braise until tender, about 15 minutes longer.

3. Preheat the broiler. There should be only 3 to 4 tablespoons of liquid in the bottom of the baking dish. If there's more, boil over high heat to reduce.

4. Tip the baking dish and baste the vegetables with the reduced stock. Sprinkle with the salt, pepper and Parmesan cheese and broil 3 to 4 inches from the heat until the cheese begins to brown, 1 to 2 minutes.

5. Place a piece of celery heart, pear and endive on each of 4 warmed plates. Drizzle over any remaining juices. Sprinkle with the basil and serve.

—*Anne Disrude*

PEKING COLD NOODLES WITH CHILI-ORANGE OIL

Like Italians, northern Chinese love serving pasta as an appetizer. In Peking, it is traditionally cold and spicy, though the orange-accented oil is of my own eclectic making. For a large crowd, I know of no easier way to begin a meal with zest. For a smaller group, simply cut the recipe in half.

8 TO 10 FIRST-COURSE SERVINGS
1 pound very thin fresh Chinese or Italian egg noodles
1 pound bean sprouts
⅓ cup plus 1 tablespoon Chili-Orange Oil (p. 236) plus 1 to 2 tablespoons minced seasonings from the oil, to taste
¼ cup dark soy sauce*
¼ cup distilled white vinegar
2 tablespoons sugar
2 teaspoons coarse (kosher) salt
2 large carrots, shredded into long thin strips
5 scallions, thinly sliced
1 cup coarsely chopped fresh coriander
1 cup raw skinned peanuts,* freshly roasted (see Note) and coarsely crushed
*Available at Oriental markets and health food stores

1. Bring a large pot of salted water to a boil. Fluff the noodles to separate the strands, add to the water and swish with chopsticks. Cook until just tender but still slightly firm to the bite, 2 to 3 minutes. Immediately drain and rinse under cold water to chill. Drain well and turn into a large bowl.

2. Bring a large pot of unsalted water to a boil. Blanch the bean sprouts for 5 seconds. Immediately drain and plunge into a bowl of ice water to chill. Drain well, then toss with the noodles.

3. Combine the chili-orange oil, the minced seasonings from the oil, the soy sauce, vinegar, sugar and salt; stir to dissolve the sugar. Pour the sauce over the noodles and toss well to coat. Scatter the carrots, scallions and half the coriander on top and toss again.

4. To serve, heap the noodles in individual bowls and scatter the remaining coriander and about 1 tablespoon peanuts on top of each. Serve with a bowl of the remaining nuts on the side.

NOTE: To roast peanuts, spread them out in a small baking pan and bake in a 350° oven, shaking the pan occasionally, until lightly browned, about 10 minutes.

—*Barbara Tropp*

SOUPS

 SOUPS

SOUTHWESTERN BLACK BEAN SOUP

Inspired by several soups I tasted throughout New Mexico and Arizona, this main-course soup is rich in spices typical of southwestern fare and full of the zesty heat of their local green chiles. (Reduce the amount of jalapeños if you wish, but the soup is meant to be quite hot.) Serve with buttery hot corn bread and a green salad with avocados and oranges. To drink, nothing is more appropriate than good Mexican beer such as Bohemia or Dos Equis, but a lightly chilled fruity red wine, such as Zinfandel, works too.

6 SERVINGS
¼ cup rendered bacon fat or olive oil
4 medium onions, chopped
8 garlic cloves, minced
2 cans (13¾ ounces each) beef broth
2 cans (13¾ ounces each) chicken
    broth
1 pound dried black beans
1 meaty ham hock or ham bone
1 pig's foot, split (optional)
3 tablespoons ground cumin
2 tablespoons oregano, preferably
    Mexican
1 tablespoon thyme
¼ teaspoon ground cloves
5 pickled jalapeños, minced
    (about ¼ cup)
Sour cream, diced tomatoes and
    chopped scallions, for garnish

1. In a large saucepan or flameproof casserole, heat the bacon fat. Add the onions and garlic, cover and cook over moderately low heat, stirring occasionally, until tender, about 20 minutes.

2. Add the beef and chicken broths, the black beans, ham hock, pig's foot, cumin, oregano, thyme, cloves, jalapeños and 2 cups of water. Bring to a boil, reduce the heat to moderately low and simmer, partially covered, stirring and skimming occasionally, for about 2½ hours, or until the beans are tender.

3. Remove and discard the pig's foot. Remove and reserve the ham hock. In a food processor, puree half of the soup; return the puree to the pan with the remaining soup.

4. Remove the meat from the ham hock, shred and add to the soup. Simmer for 10 minutes.

5. To serve, ladle the soup into bowls. Top each with a dollop of sour cream and a generous sprinkling of diced tomato and scallion.
—*Michael McLaughlin*

SILKY LENTIL SOUP WITH HAM HOCKS AND ORANGE

A final blending (in Step 2) gives this soup a lovely velvet texture. The ham hocks lend a deep, smoky flavor, while the orange zest imparts a refreshing citrus finish.

8 SERVINGS
2 medium red bell peppers
1 tablespoon olive oil
5 garlic cloves, coarsely chopped
1 pound onions, coarsely chopped
    (about 1 large Spanish onion)
2 smoked ham hocks (about 1½
    pounds total), trimmed of fat
6 sprigs of fresh thyme or 1 teaspoon
    dried
5 sprigs of fresh rosemary or
    1 teaspoon dried
3 bay leaves
½ cup chopped parsley
5 pieces of orange zest (3 by ½ inch)
6 cups beef stock or canned broth
1 pound lentils, rinsed and drained
1 teaspoon freshly ground black
    pepper
About ⅔ cup plain low-fat yogurt

1. Coarsely chop 1 of the red peppers. In a large heavy saucepan or flameproof casserole, heat the olive oil over moderately high heat. Add the garlic, chopped red pepper and onions. Reduce the heat to low and cook until the vegetables are softened but not browned, 15 to 20 minutes.

2. Add the ham hocks, thyme, rosemary, bay leaves, parsley and 3 pieces of the orange zest. Pour in the beef stock and 8 cups of water; then add the lentils. Bring the soup to a boil over high heat. Reduce the heat to low and simmer the soup for 2 hours. The lentils will be extremely soft.

3. Remove the ham hocks and set aside to cool. Remove and discard the bay leaves. In batches, coarsely puree the soup in a blender or food processor, then press through a mesh sieve, discarding the solids.

4. Again working in batches, pour the strained soup into a blender and blend for 1 minute. (This step is not mandatory but produces a wonderfully silky soup. You can use a food processor here, but a blender will produce a better texture.)

5. Pour the soup back into the saucepan and season with the black pepper. Let cool to room temperature.

6. Meanwhile, cut the remaining 2 strips of orange zest into very thin strands. Blanch the zest in 1 cup of boiling water for 30 seconds. Remove with a slotted spoon and set aside. Cut the remaining red pepper into ⅛-inch-thick strips. Remove the meat from the ham hocks and cut it into ¼-inch-thick strips.

7. When ready to serve, ladle the soup into individual bowls and place a dollop of yogurt in the center. Scatter the strips of red pepper, orange zest and ham on top. Serve at room temperature.
—*Marcia Kiesel*

A first-course serving of Gulf Crab Cakes with Lemon Butter (p. 62).

Above, Prosciutto and Cheese Appetizer Toasts (p. 15). At right, left to right: Mushroom-Leek Turnovers (p. 12) and Ricotta Pesto Crescents (p. 14).

WHITE BEAN AND BACON SOUP

With a crusty loaf of French bread, this soup becomes a meal in itself.

6 TO 8 SERVINGS
1 pound dried white beans, such as Great Northern
½ pound thickly sliced bacon, diced
1 small onion, minced
1 garlic clove, minced
8 cups chicken stock or canned broth
1 teaspoon thyme
1 bay leaf
1 teaspoon salt
2 teaspoons freshly ground pepper
½ cup freshly grated Parmesan cheese

1. Place the beans in a large bowl, add water to cover and soak overnight. Alternatively, place the beans in a large saucepan, add water to cover and bring to a boil over high heat. Boil for 2 minutes, then remove from the heat and let the beans soak, covered, for 1 hour. Drain the beans.

2. In a large heavy saucepan, cook the bacon over low heat until crisp, about 7 minutes. Transfer the bacon to paper towels.

3. Add the onion and garlic to the bacon fat and cook over moderate heat until softened but not browned, about 5 minutes. Add the chicken stock, thyme, bay leaf, salt, pepper and beans. Reduce the heat to low, cover and simmer, stirring occasionally, until the beans are soft and the soup is thick, about 3 hours.

4. Thin the soup with stock or water if necessary. Taste for seasoning. Ladle the soup into bowls and garnish each serving with grated Parmesan cheese and the bacon. Serve hot.
—*Molly O'Neill*

Steamed Shrimp and Vegetables with Ta-penade Sauce (p. 77) and for dessert (upper left), Lavender-Pepper Pears (p. 216).

MILLECOSEDDE
(PASTA AND BEAN SOUP)

8 TO 10 SERVINGS
¼ pound dried cranberry beans
½ pound dried cannellini or Great Northern white beans
¼ cup olive oil
2 medium carrots, cut into ¼-inch dice
1 medium onion, cut into ¼-inch dice
1 medium celery rib, cut into ¼-inch dice
½ pound mushrooms, cut into ¼-inch dice
½ small head of Savoy cabbage, shredded
1 can (28 ounces) Italian peeled tomatoes, drained and chopped
8 cups boiling water
¼ pound lentils, rinsed and drained
1 can (19 ounces) chick-peas, drained and rinsed
½ pound tubetti or other short tubular pasta
1½ teaspoons salt
¼ teaspoon freshly ground pepper
1 cup (4 ounces) freshly grated Pecorino Romano cheese

1. Place the cranberry and cannellini beans in a large bowl and soak overnight in enough cold water to cover by 2 inches; drain. Or place the beans in a large saucepan, add water to cover and bring to a boil over high heat. Boil for 2 minutes, then remove from the heat and let the beans soak, covered, for 1 hour; drain.

2. In a stockpot or large flameproof casserole, heat the olive oil over moderate heat. Add the carrots, onion and celery and cook until the vegetables are softened but not browned, 10 to 12 minutes. Add the mushrooms and cook until they lose their juices and begin to brown, about 10 minutes. Add the cabbage and cook until wilt-ed, about 5 minutes. Add the tomatoes and cook for 5 minutes. Add the drained cranberry and cannellini beans and the boiling water. Simmer over moderately low heat, partially covered, for 45 minutes.

3. Add the lentils to the soup and cook, partially covered, until the beans are tender, 1 to 1½ hours. (If the soup becomes too thick, add 1 to 3 cups of additional hot water.)

4. Add the chick-peas, pasta, salt and pepper. Cook until the pasta is al dente, tender but still firm to the bite. Serve hot with a generous sprinkling of grated cheese. Pass the remaining cheese separately.
—*Nancy Verde Barr*

SUMMER PISTOU

The vegetables in this Mediterranean soup are cooked in a clean, clear herbal broth that is infused with a dollop of pesto before serving.

F&W BEVERAGE SUGGESTION
Spanish white, such as
Torres Viña Sol

6 SERVINGS
⅓ pound Great Northern white beans (about ¾ cup)
2 medium Spanish onions
3 tablespoons fresh thyme leaves or 2 teaspoons dried
3 garlic cloves
2 teaspoons olive oil
1½ cups diced (½-inch) rutabaga (about 5 ounces)
2 medium carrots, cut into ½-inch dice
2 medium celery ribs, cut into ½-inch dice
5 cups chicken stock or canned broth

SOUPS

1 large tomato, peeled and chopped,
  or 1 cup drained, chopped canned
  Italian tomatoes (14-ounce can)
1 medium zucchini, halved lengthwise
  and then cut into ¼-inch slices
2 cups chopped spinach (from about
  ½ pound untrimmed)
1 teaspoon salt
1 teaspoon freshly ground pepper
Pesto (p. 229; see Note)

1. Soak the beans overnight in cold water to cover by about 4 inches. Alternatively, cover the beans with 4 inches of cold water and bring to a boil over high heat. Boil for 2 minutes, remove from the heat and let the beans soak, covered, for 1 hour.

2. Drain the beans, place in a medium saucepan and cover with 4 inches of fresh, cold water. Halve one of the onions and add one half to the beans. Add 1½ teaspoons of the thyme leaves (or ¼ teaspoon dried) and 1 of the garlic cloves. Bring to a boil over high heat. Reduce the heat to low and simmer until the beans are cooked through and tender, about 2 hours. Drain the beans. Discard the onion half and garlic clove. (**The recipe can be prepared to this point 1 day ahead. Refrigerate the beans, covered.**)

3. Dice the remaining 1½ onions and mince the remaining 2 garlic cloves. In a large heavy saucepan or flameproof casserole, warm the olive oil over moderately high heat. Add the diced onion, garlic, rutabaga, carrots and celery. Reduce the heat to low and cook the vegetables, stirring occasionally, until the onions are soft and translucent, about 7 minutes.

4. Add the chicken stock and remaining 2½ tablespoons fresh (or 1¾ teaspoons dried) thyme and simmer the soup over moderately low heat until the vegetables are just tender, about 25 minutes. Add the tomato, zucchini and spinach and cook for 1 minute.

5. Transfer the soup to a serving bowl to cool off. When the soup has cooled to room temperature, season with the salt and pepper. To serve, top each portion with 1 tablespoon of pesto. Pass the remaining pesto on the side.

NOTE: The recipe for pesto makes more than will probably be used for the soup, but pesto keeps well for about 1 week in the refrigerator, and even a small amount is useful to have on hand for a quick pasta dish or a salad dressing.

—Marcia Kiesel

PANCOTTO COME A FOGGIA (COOKED BREAD SOUP)

Pancotto (which means cooked bread) is a splendid way to use up stale bread. This particular recipe is a specialty of the province of Foggia in the region of Apulia, but similar versions exist all over southern Italy.

8 SERVINGS
¼ pound pancetta or prosciutto,
  minced
2 medium onions, coarsely chopped
3 garlic cloves, chopped
5 tablespoons olive oil
3 medium potatoes, peeled and cut
  into 1-inch cubes
⅓ pound spinach or arugula—
  washed, trimmed and torn into
  bite-size pieces
1 medium head of chicory—washed,
  trimmed and torn into bite-size
  pieces
½ cup leafy fennel tops, chopped
  (optional)
¼ teaspoon crushed hot pepper
½ teaspoon salt

5 cups hot Meat Broth (p. 46)
2 cups stale Italian bread, cut into
  1-inch cubes (from 1 Italian loaf)

1. In a stockpot or large flameproof casserole, combine the pancetta, onions, garlic and 3 tablespoons of the olive oil. Cook over low heat, stirring occasionally, until the vegetables are softened but not browned, about 15 minutes.

2. Add the potatoes and toss to coat with oil. Add the spinach, chicory, fennel tops, hot pepper and salt. Cook, covered, until the greens begin to wilt, about 3 minutes.

3. Add the broth, increase the heat to high and bring to a boil. Reduce the heat to moderately low and simmer, partially covered, for 45 minutes.

4. Meanwhile, preheat the oven to 450°. Place the bread cubes on an ungreased baking sheet and toast until dry, about 5 minutes. Stir the toasted bread cubes into the soup and simmer for 15 minutes. Ladle the soup into bowls and drizzle about 1 teaspoon olive oil over each serving. Serve hot.

—Nancy Verde Barr

CHARRED CARROT SOUP

Charring shredded carrots in a cast-iron skillet caramelizes the vegetable's natural sugars and adds a deep, rich, nutty flavor to the soup. This slight sweetness is brought back into balance by a small amount of red wine vinegar added at the end.

4 SERVINGS
½ tablespoon vegetable oil
5 to 6 medium carrots, peeled and
  shredded (about 3 cups)
2 shallots, coarsely chopped
2 garlic cloves, coarsely chopped
½ teaspoon thyme
1 small Idaho potato, peeled and
  coarsely chopped
3½ cups rich chicken stock

½ cup heavy cream
1 tablespoon red wine vinegar
¼ teaspoon salt
¼ teaspoon coarsely cracked pepper
1 tablespoon unsalted butter, softened
1 tablespoon chopped parsley or
   chives

1. Preheat a 12-inch cast-iron skillet over high heat for 5 minutes. Add the oil, then the carrots. Stir to coat the carrots with oil and cook, stirring frequently, until the carrots are partially charred, about 15 minutes.

2. Reduce the heat to moderate and add the shallots, garlic and thyme. Cook until the shallots are softened, 2 to 3 minutes.

3. Add the potato and stock. Simmer over low heat until the carrots and potato are very soft, about 15 minutes.

4. In a food processor or blender, puree the soup until smooth. (For an extra-silky texture, press the puree through a fine sieve after pureeing.)

5. Transfer the soup to a saucepan and add the cream (use extra chicken stock or water for a thinner consistency if desired). Add the red wine vinegar, salt and pepper. Stir in the butter and serve hot, sprinkled with the chopped parsley.

—Anne Disrude

CORN SOUP WITH SPICY PUMPKIN SEEDS

Based on traditional corn chowder, this soup is thickened with pureed corn and potatoes instead of the usual flour or egg yolks. The spicy pumpkin seeds are more than a garnish; they are an intense final flavoring. The light cool cream added just before serving helps to mellow the fiery pumpkin seeds.

F&W BEVERAGE SUGGESTION
California white Zinfandel, such as Beringer

4 TO 6 SERVINGS
1 tablespoon olive oil
1 medium onion, chopped
1 garlic clove, minced
1 small jalapeño pepper, seeded and
   minced or 1 small dried hot red
   pepper, seeded and crushed
¼ teaspoon ground cumin
1 medium baking potato, peeled and
   cut into ¼-inch dice
3 cups corn kernels, fresh or frozen
   (see Note)
1 cup light cream or half-and-half
½ teaspoon salt
½ teaspoon freshly ground black
   pepper
Spicy Pumpkin Seeds (recipe follows)

1. In a large saucepan or flameproof casserole, heat the olive oil over moderate heat. Add the onion, garlic, jalapeño pepper and cumin. Reduce the heat to low and cook until the onion is softened but not browned, about 5 minutes.

2. Add the potato and 4 cups of water. Bring to a boil over high heat. Add the corn, reduce the heat and simmer until the potato is tender, about 20 minutes.

3. Measure out 3 cups of the soup and puree in a food processor. Combine the pureed soup with the rest of the soup in a large serving bowl and let cool to room temperature.

4. Just before serving, stir in the light cream and season with the salt and pepper. Ladle the cooled soup into bowls and sprinkle each serving with some of the spicy pumpkin seeds. Pass the remaining pumpkin seeds on the side.

NOTE: If you use fresh corn for this, reserve the corn cobs and throw them into the soup in Step 2 for added flavor. Remove and discard them at the end of Step 2.

—Marcia Kiesel

SPICY PUMPKIN SEEDS

These seeds are deliciously addictive! Make a double or triple batch to have on hand for nibbling.

MAKES ABOUT ½ CUP
1 garlic clove, minced
1 tablespoon olive oil
2 teaspoons ground cumin
1 teaspoon sweet paprika
½ teaspoon cayenne pepper
½ cup shelled pumpkin seeds
   (pepitas)*
1 teaspoon coarse (kosher) salt
*Available at Latin American
   markets and health food stores

1. Preheat the oven to 400°. In a small skillet, cook the garlic in the oil over low heat for about 5 minutes without browning. Strain the oil through a fine sieve and discard the garlic. Return the garlic-flavored oil to the skillet and add the cumin, paprika and cayenne. Cook over low heat, stirring occasionally, until fragrant, about 1 minute.

2. Place the pumpkin seeds on a baking sheet. Scrape the spice mixture over the seeds, sprinkle with the salt and toss to coat evenly. Spread the seeds in a single layer and bake in the oven for about 5 minutes, or until they turn light brown. The seeds will pop and dance while cooking.

—Marcia Kiesel

ZUPPA DI FINOCCHIO (FENNEL SOUP)

6 SERVINGS
3 medium-to-large bulbs of fennel
   (about 2½ pounds with stalks)—
   trimmed to the bulb, stalks
   discarded and leafy tops reserved
3 garlic cloves, minced
¼ cup olive oil

SOUPS

1 teaspoon salt
½ teaspoon freshly ground pepper
4 cups Meat Broth (p. 46)
6 slices of day-old Italian bread, cut
    ½ inch thick and lightly toasted
¾ cup freshly grated Pecorino
    Romano cheese

1. Remove the tough cores of the fennel and coarsely chop the bulbs. Chop the feathery green fennel tops until you have ½ cup and set aside.

2. In a large saucepan, cook the garlic in the olive oil over moderate heat until it is light golden, about 10 minutes.

3. Add the chopped fennel bulbs and cook, stirring occasionally, until they begin to soften, about 10 minutes. Stir in the reserved fennel tops and the salt and pepper. Add the meat broth. Increase the heat to high and bring to a boil. Reduce the heat to moderate and simmer the soup for 30 minutes.

4. To serve, place a slice of toasted bread in the bottom of each bowl and sprinkle each with 2 tablespoons of cheese. Ladle the soup over the bread.

—Nancy Verde Barr

ZUPPA DI FUNGHI
(MUSHROOM SOUP)

8 SERVINGS
1 ounce dried porcini mushrooms
3 tablespoons unsalted butter
3 tablespoons olive oil
1 small onion, minced
3 garlic cloves, minced
1½ pounds mushrooms, sliced
2 medium tomatoes—peeled, seeded
    and chopped—or 1 can (14 ounces)
    Italian peeled tomatoes, drained
    and chopped
1 teaspoon salt
¼ teaspoon freshly ground pepper

1 tablespoon minced fresh marjoram
    or 1 teaspoon dried
1 tablespoon minced fresh thyme or
    1 teaspoon dried
6 cups Meat Broth (p. 46)
8 slices Italian bread, cut ½ inch
    thick
3 egg yolks
⅓ cup freshly grated Parmesan
    cheese, plus about 1 cup for passing
2 tablespoons freshly grated Pecorino
    Romano cheese
3 tablespoons chopped parsley, plus
    about ¼ cup chopped for garnish

1. Soak the porcini mushrooms in ½ cup of warm water for 30 minutes. Drain, reserving the soaking liquid. Rinse, dry and chop the mushrooms. Strain the soaking liquid through paper towels or a double layer of dampened cheesecloth. Set aside.

2. In a large saucepan or flame-proof casserole, melt the butter and 1 tablespoon of the olive oil over low heat. Add the onion and garlic. Cook, stirring frequently, until the onion is softened but not browned, about 5 minutes.

3. Add the porcini mushrooms and cook over low heat for 8 minutes. Increase the heat to moderate and add the fresh mushrooms. Cook until the juices run, about 10 minutes. Add the reserved porcini soaking liquid and continue to cook until reduced by half, about 5 minutes. Add the tomatoes, salt, pepper, marjoram and thyme. Cook for 5 minutes longer.

4. Preheat the broiler. Add the broth to the soup and simmer over moderate heat for 15 minutes to blend the flavors.

5. Toast the bread slices on both sides under the broiler. Remove and brush with the remaining 2 tablespoons olive oil.

6. In a small bowl, beat the egg yolks with ⅓ cup of the Parmesan cheese, the Romano cheese and 3 tablespoons of the parsley. Gradually whisk ¼ cup of the hot broth into the beaten eggs to warm them. Slowly whisk the mixture into the soup. Cook, stirring constantly, over low heat until the soup thickens slightly, about 2 minutes. (Do not boil, or the soup will curdle.)

7. Place a slice of toast in each of 8 bowls. Ladle in the soup and garnish with chopped parsley. Pass a bowl of grated Parmesan cheese on the side.

—Nancy Verde Barr

ROASTED PEPPER SOUP
WITH ZUCCHINI

This is one of my favorite room-temperature soups, adapted from a recipe that appeared in *Cucina Fresca* by Viana La Place and Evan Kleiman. Extra-virgin olive oil not only emulsifies and smooths out this soup but adds, along with the balsamic vinegar, a distinct fruity flavor.

4 TO 6 SERVINGS
4 large red bell peppers
2 cups peeled, chopped and seeded
    fresh tomatoes or 1 can (35 ounces)
    Italian peeled tomatoes, drained
¼ cup extra-virgin olive oil
2 garlic cloves, minced
3 cups chicken stock or canned broth
½ teaspoon salt
¼ teaspoon freshly ground black
    pepper
1 medium zucchini, cut into 2-by-¼-
    inch julienne strips
1½ tablespoons chopped fresh basil
2 tablespoons balsamic vinegar

1. Roast the peppers under a broiler or directly over a gas flame, turning, until the skin is charred all over, about 10 minutes. Enclose in a plastic bag and let stand for 10 to 15 minutes.

Peel off the skin; remove the stems and seeds. In a food processor, coarsely puree the roasted peppers and the tomatoes.

2. In a medium saucepan, heat 3 tablespoons of the olive oil. Add the garlic and sauté over moderately high heat until fragrant but not browned, about 30 seconds. Add the pepper-tomato puree and the stock. Simmer the soup over low heat, stirring occasionally, until slightly thickened, 10 to 12 minutes.

3. Pour the soup into a serving bowl, season with the salt and black pepper and allow it to cool to room temperature.

4. Just before serving, warm the remaining 1 tablespoon olive oil in a medium skillet over high heat. Add the zucchini and sauté, stirring occasionally, until barely softened, about 2 minutes. Stir the zucchini into the soup and add the basil and balsamic vinegar. Season with additional salt, black pepper and vinegar to taste.

—*Marcia Kiesel*

KALE, BEAN AND SQUASH SOUP

This hefty main-course soup is lightly seasoned with herbs and spices. You can use any one of a number of dried beans for the soup, but they should be pale enough to present a prettily contrasting plateful of vegetables to each diner: chick-peas, small limas, black-eyed peas, Great Northern, navy and pink are all possibilities. As with all compound soups, this one improves if allowed to mellow for about a day before it is served.

8 SERVINGS
¾ pound dried beans (see above)
2 bay leaves
1 teaspoon marjoram
2 tablespoons lard, bacon fat or olive oil
3 medium leeks (white and tender green), thinly sliced
1 teaspoon curry powder
2½ pounds butternut squash, peeled and cut into ¾-inch dice
6 cups meat stock or canned broth
1¼ pounds small, tender kale—cleaned, stemmed and cut into fine slivers
Salt and freshly ground pepper
Freshly grated Parmesan or aged Gruyère cheese

1. Place the beans in a large saucepan with water to cover and boil for 2 minutes. Turn off the heat, cover and let stand for 1 hour. Drain.

2. In a large saucepan, combine the beans with the bay leaves and marjoram. Add fresh water to cover by several inches and bring to a simmer over high heat. Simmer the beans, covered, until barely tender. (Timing can vary from 15 minutes to over an hour, depending on the variety of bean used and the state of dehydration—keep close watch, testing often.) Drain the beans and reserve the cooking liquid.

3. Meanwhile, in a large pot, melt the lard over moderate heat. Add the leeks and cook until softened, 4 to 5 minutes. Stir in the curry powder. Add the squash and stock and bring to a boil over high heat. Add the beans, reduce the heat and simmer gently, partly covered, until the squash is tender, about 15 minutes.

4. Add the kale and enough of the reserved bean liquid to almost cover (you'll probably use all the liquid). Simmer until the kale is tender, pressing it gently into the soup as it wilts, 5 to 10 minutes.

5. Cool the soup, then cover and refrigerate. To serve, reheat the soup and season with salt and pepper to taste. Pass grated cheese separately.

—*Elizabeth Schneider*

BUTTERNUT SQUASH SOUP

For a meatless supper, serve with a savory nut bread and a sharp Cheddar cheese.

6 SERVINGS
2 tablespoons unsalted butter
1 small onion, chopped
¼ to ½ teaspoon rosemary, to taste, crumbled
1 small butternut squash, peeled and cut into chunks
6 cups chicken stock or canned broth
1 cup heavy cream
1 teaspoon salt
½ teaspoon freshly ground white pepper
Dash of hot pepper sauce
½ cup chopped toasted walnuts

1. In a large heavy saucepan, melt the butter over moderate heat. Add the onion and rosemary and cook until the onion is soft, about 5 minutes. Add the squash, chicken stock, heavy cream, salt, white pepper and hot pepper sauce. Reduce the heat to low, cover and simmer, stirring occasionally, until the squash is very soft, about 2 hours.

2. Puree the hot soup in a blender or food processor, adding additional stock if necessary. To serve, ladle the soup into bowls and garnish with the walnuts.

—*Molly O'Neill*

ARTICHOKE AND OYSTER SOUP

4 TO 6 SERVINGS
4 tablespoons unsalted butter
8 scallions, minced
1 small onion, minced
1 celery rib, minced
1 small garlic clove, minced
6 tablespoons all-purpose flour
3½ cups bottled clam juice

24 oysters, shucked, with liquor
    reserved
½ cup heavy cream
1 package (10 ounces) frozen
    artichoke hearts, thawed and
    coarsely chopped
¼ cup chopped parsley
½ teaspoon salt
⅛ teaspoon freshly ground white
    pepper
Pinch of cayenne pepper

1. In a large saucepan, melt the butter over moderate heat. Add the scallions, onion, celery and garlic and
cook until the onion is translucent,
about 5 minutes.

2. Add the flour, reduce the heat
and cook over low heat, stirring constantly, for 5 minutes.

3. Add enough clam juice to the
oyster liquor to equal 4 cups. Gradually add this liquid and the heavy cream
to the saucepan. Bring to a simmer
and cook, stirring constantly, until
slightly thickened, about 5 minutes.

4. Add the artichoke hearts and the
oysters and cook just until the edges
of the oysters begin to curl, about 2
minutes. Stir in the parsley, salt,
white pepper and cayenne. Serve hot.

—LeRuth's, Gretna, Louisiana

FISH CONSOMME
WITH POACHED OYSTERS AND
BEGGAR'S POUCHES

8 SERVINGS

3 medium leeks
2 tablespoons unsalted butter
3 medium onions, coarsely chopped
8 pounds non-oily fish bones, heads
    and trimmings—gills removed, well
    rinsed and cut up
2 large tomatoes, chopped
½ pound medium mushrooms
Bouquet garni: 12 parsley stems, 10
    peppercorns, ¼ teaspoon thyme and
    1 bay leaf tied in cheesecloth

3 cups dry white wine
24 small oysters, shucked, with liquor
    reserved
3 egg whites, lightly beaten
2 carrots, chopped
1 pound sole or flounder fillets,
    coarsely chopped
¼ teaspoon salt
Pinch of freshly ground pepper
Beggar's Pouches (p. 22)
1½ tablespoons very finely diced
    carrot, for garnish

1. Trim off the dark green tops of
the leeks and set aside for use in Step
7. Coarsely chop the white and tender
green portion of the leeks.

2. In a large stockpot, melt the butter over moderate heat. Add the onions and white and tender green of
the leeks and cook until softened but
not browned, about 5 minutes. Add
the fish bones, 1 of the tomatoes, the
mushrooms, bouquet garni, white
wine and enough water to cover the
bones (about 3 quarts).

3. Slowly bring to a simmer, skimming frequently. Reduce the heat to
maintain a slow simmer and cook for
20 minutes.

4. Strain the stock through a double
layer of dampened cheesecloth. Skim
off any fat from the surface and pour
the stock into a large saucepan, leaving any sediment behind. Bring the
stock to a full boil over high heat,
reduce the heat slightly to maintain a
slow boil and cook, skimming frequently, until the stock is reduced to 6
cups, about 50 minutes. (**The stock
can be made ahead.** Let cool to room
temperature; then seal in airtight containers and refrigerate for up to 3 days
or freeze for up to 1 month. Defrost
the stock before proceeding.)

5. Strain the liquor from the oysters
through several thicknesses of dampened cheesecloth and add to the reduced fish stock.

6. Bring the stock to a boil over
high heat. Drop in the oysters and

cook until the edges just begin to curl,
about 1 minute. Immediately remove
the oysters; cover and refrigerate. Let
the stock cool to tepid. (**The recipe
can be prepared to this point several
hours ahead.**)

7. In a large bowl, lightly beat the
egg whites until foamy. In a food processor, puree the leek greens, carrots,
fish fillet and remaining tomato.
Whisk this mixture into the egg
whites.

8. Stir the mixture into the fish
stock and cook over moderate heat,
stirring constantly, until the eggs begin to coagulate, about 10 minutes.
Stop stirring. Move the pot off the
center of the burner; simmer gently
for about 30 minutes (a crust of egg
white and pureed vegetables and fish
will form on top).

9. With a serving spoon, scoop out
a small hole on the edge of the crust.
Place the opening directly over the
heat with the rest of the pot off the
center of the burner. Simmer for 30
minutes. (The stock will bubble up
through the opening in the crust, fil-
tering out impurities.) Do not boil, or
the crust will break, and the soup will
be cloudy.

10. Remove the pot from the heat.
Scoop up enough of the crust to allow
you to ladle up the consommé. Strain
it through a double layer of dampened cheesecloth into a clean saucepan. Season with the salt and pepper.
Set the consommé aside over low
heat. Dip the oysters in the hot consommé just long enough to reheat
them, about 30 seconds.

11. To serve, ladle about ¾ cup hot
consommé into each soup plate. Place
3 oysters and a Beggar's Pouch in
each bowl. Sprinkle each serving with
about ½ teaspoon of diced carrot.
Serve hot.

—John Robert Massie

OYSTER AND SPINACH RAGOUT

6 TO 8 SERVINGS
3 tablespoons unsalted butter
1 shallot, minced
4 ounces spinach, stemmed and finely
 chopped (about 2 cups)
2 teaspoons Pernod
2 pints shucked oysters with their
 liquor or 36 oysters, shucked,
 liquor reserved
4 cups heavy cream
4 cups milk
Dash of Worcestershire sauce
Dash of cayenne pepper
Salt

1. In a large heavy saucepan, melt the butter over moderately low heat. Add the shallot and cook until soft, about 5 minutes. Add the spinach and toss until wilted, about 3 minutes. Stir in the Pernod and cook for 2 minutes. Add the oyster liquor, cream, milk, Worcestershire sauce and cayenne. Cook until heated through.

2. Stir in the oysters and cook just until their edges begin to curl, about 30 seconds. Season with salt to taste. Serve piping hot.

—Molly O'Neill

ZUPPA DI VONGOLE (CLAM SOUP) WITH GARLIC TOASTS

4 SERVINGS
2 dozen littleneck or cherrystone
 clams, well scrubbed
⅓ cup plus 1 tablespoon olive oil
6 garlic cloves, minced
1 medium onion, chopped
2 cups chopped plum tomatoes, with
 their juice (about 5 medium)
1 cup dry white wine
¾ cup chopped parsley
1½ teaspoons oregano
¼ teaspoon crushed hot pepper
¼ cup minced pancetta or prosciutto
Salt
Garlic Toasts (recipe follows)

1. Place the clams in a large bowl of lightly salted cold water and set aside for 1 hour.

2. In a large saucepan or flame-proof casserole, combine ⅓ cup of the olive oil, 2 tablespoons of the minced garlic and the onion. Cook over low heat until the onion is softened but not browned, about 6 minutes.

3. Add the tomatoes with their juice, the wine, ½ cup of the chopped parsley, the oregano and hot pepper. Increase the heat to moderately high and bring to a boil. Reduce the heat to moderately low and simmer for 15 minutes.

4. In a small skillet, combine the pancetta with the remaining garlic and olive oil. Cook over moderately low heat until the pancetta is slightly crisped, about 8 minutes. Add the remaining ¼ cup parsley and cook for 3 minutes longer. Remove from the heat.

5. Drain the clams and add to the soup. Increase the heat to high, cover and cook until the clams open, about 3 minutes. Season with salt to taste.

6. To serve, divide the clams and broth among 4 soup bowls. Sprinkle the pancetta topping over each and serve with the garlic toasts.

—Nancy Verde Barr

GARLIC TOASTS

4 SERVINGS
8 slices day-old Italian bread, cut
 ½ inch thick
1 garlic clove, cut in half
¼ cup extra-virgin olive oil

Preheat the oven to 450°. Toast the bread slices in the oven, turning once, until lightly browned on both sides, about 5 minutes. Rub one side of the hot bread with the garlic, drizzle with the olive oil and serve warm.

—Nancy Verde Barr

LIGHT MANHATTAN CLAM CHOWDER

The steamer clam produces a brinier broth than the hard-shell clam. In either case, use the smallest clams you can find, as they will be sweeter and tenderer.

F&W BEVERAGE SUGGESTION
California Sauvignon Blanc,
such as Cakebread

4 SERVINGS
1 cup dry white wine
3 pounds soft-shell steamer clams or
 hard-shell littlenecks or
 cherrystones, as small as possible,
 scrubbed
¼ pound slab bacon
1 medium onion, cut into ¼-inch dice
1 carrot, cut into ½-inch dice
1 celery rib, cut into ¼-inch dice
1 small red bell pepper, cut into
 ½-inch dice
1 garlic clove, minced
1 small baking potato, unpeeled and
 cut into ½-inch dice
1 teaspoon chopped fresh rosemary
 (about 1 sprig) or ½ teaspoon dried
1 bay leaf
½ cup chopped tomato or ½ cup
 drained and chopped canned Italian
 tomato
1 sprig of fresh thyme, chopped, or
 ½ teaspoon dried
1 tablespoon chopped parsley
½ teaspoon freshly ground black
 pepper

1. In a large, wide saucepan or flameproof casserole, bring the wine plus 3 cups of water to a boil over

high heat. Add the clams, cover and steam for about 3 minutes, or until the clams just barely open. Turn off the heat and leave the lid on for 1 minute.

2. Place a colander over a large bowl and pour the clams and liquid into the colander. Discard any clams that have not opened. Set the clam broth aside.

3. Remove the clams from their shells and pull off the outer neck skins and discard them and the shells. Set the clams aside.

4. Carefully strain the clam broth through a sieve lined with a double thickness of dampened cheesecloth, discarding the gritty liquid and grit at the bottom of the pan.

5. With a sharp knife, trim off all the fat from the slab bacon and cut the meat into ¼-inch dice. You should have about ½ cup.

6. In a large saucepan or flame-proof casserole, cook the bacon over moderate heat until it browns, about 3 minutes. Add the onion, carrot, celery, red pepper and garlic. Reduce the heat to low and cook the vegetables slowly, stirring occasionally, until the onion is translucent, about 4 minutes.

7. Increase the heat to high and add the strained clam broth, potato, rosemary and bay leaf. Bring to a boil, immediately reduce the heat to low and simmer until the vegetables are just tender, about 15 minutes. Add the tomato, thyme and parsley. Cook for 1 minute longer. Discard the bay leaf.

8. Add the clams, pour the soup into a serving bowl and let cool to room temperature. Season with the black pepper before serving.

—Marcia Kiesel

SALMON AND MUSSEL CHOWDER

This attractive salmon-flecked chowder is wonderfully rich.

6 SERVINGS
2 tablespoons unsalted butter
1 leek (white and tender green), cut into thin julienne strips
1 teaspoon salt
2 pounds mussels, scrubbed and debearded
1 cup dry white wine
1 medium potato, peeled and cut into ¼-inch dice
2 cups heavy cream
2 cups milk
2 tablespoons minced fresh basil
¼ teaspoon saffron threads
½ pound salmon fillet, cut into ¼-inch dice
Freshly ground pepper

1. In a large heavy saucepan, melt the butter over low heat. Add the leek and salt and cook until very soft, about 15 minutes.

2. Meanwhile, in a large pot, combine the mussels and wine. Cover and steam the mussels over high heat until barely open, about 4 minutes. Using a slotted spoon, transfer the mussels to a large bowl to cool. Strain the broth through several layers of dampened cheesecloth.

3. Add the potato and broth to the leeks and simmer over low heat for 15 minutes. Add the cream, milk, basil and saffron and simmer for 10 minutes longer. Meanwhile, remove the mussels from their shells.

4. Add the salmon and mussels to the chowder and simmer for 5 minutes. Season with salt and pepper to taste and serve hot.

—Molly O'Neill

TURKEY SOUP WITH DUMPLINGS

6 SERVINGS
2 tablespoons unsalted butter
1 small onion, minced
9 cups Turkey Stock (p. 226)
Salt and freshly ground white pepper
½ teaspoon thyme
Pinch of freshly grated nutmeg
1 cup all-purpose flour
2 eggs

1. In a large saucepan, melt the butter. Add the onion and cook over moderate heat until softened, about 3 minutes. Stir in 8 cups of the turkey stock and bring to a simmer. Season with salt and white pepper to taste.

2. Meanwhile, in a medium saucepan, combine the remaining 1 cup stock with the thyme, nutmeg, ½ teaspoon salt and a pinch of white pepper. Bring to a boil over high heat. Remove from the heat and beat in the flour until thoroughly blended. Let the mixture cool slightly, then beat in the eggs, one at a time.

3. Drop tablespoons of the dumpling mixture into the simmering soup and cook until the dumplings begin to firm, about 5 minutes. Remove from the heat, cover the saucepan and set aside to steam the dumplings for 3 minutes before serving.

—Molly O'Neill

COOL HOT-AND-SOUR SOUP

It is surprising how well the complex flavors of this Chinese classic work at room temperature. To lighten the soup, the amount of cornstarch is reduced so that the soup will not thicken when cooled. To enhance its silky texture and add visual interest, a beaten egg is swirled into the soup while it's still hot.

6 TO 8 SERVINGS
1 ounce dried shiitake mushrooms (about 6 large)*
1 ounce dried tiger lily buds (about 20)*
½ ounce dried tree ears (about 5 large)*
7 cups chicken stock or canned broth
2 to 3 small dried hot red peppers, crumbled
6 ounces pork shoulder, trimmed of fat and cut into 2-by-¼-inch julienne strips
1 garlic clove, minced
1 quarter-size piece of fresh ginger, peeled and minced
3 tablespoons cider vinegar
3 tablespoons dark soy sauce*
1½ tablespoons cornstarch
1 small cake of bean curd, halved and cut crosswise into ¼-inch slices
1 egg
2 teaspoons Oriental sesame oil
¼ teaspoon salt
¼ teaspoon freshly ground black pepper
1½ tablespoons chopped fresh coriander
3 scallions, chopped
*Available at Oriental markets

1. In a small bowl, soak the mushrooms in 1 cup of hot water for 1 hour. In another small bowl, soak the tiger lily buds and tree ears in hot water to cover for 1 hour.

2. Remove the mushrooms from the soaking liquid. Strain the liquid through a double thickness of dampened cheesecloth and set aside. Rinse any grit from the mushrooms, trim off the woody stems and slice the mushrooms ¼ inch thick.

3. Remove the tree ears and tiger lily buds from their water and discard the water. Trim any tough knobs from the tree ears and slice ¼ inch thick. Halve the tiger lily buds lengthwise.

4. In a large 4-quart saucepan or flameproof casserole, combine the chicken stock and hot peppers; bring to a boil over moderate heat. Add the mushrooms and their soaking liquid, the tree ears, tiger lily buds, pork, garlic and ginger and return to a boil. Reduce the heat to low and simmer the soup for about 10 minutes. Add the vinegar and soy sauce.

5. Mix the cornstarch with 2 tablespoons of water. Increase the heat to high and bring the soup to a boil. Whisk in the cornstarch mixture and keep stirring until the soup boils and thickens. Reduce the heat to low. Add the slices of bean curd.

6. In a small bowl, lightly beat the egg with the sesame oil. Remove the soup from the heat and pour the egg mixture into the soup in a thin stream. Do not stir the soup for 15 seconds, then swirl the egg with a spoon or fork into lacy strands. Season with the salt and black pepper.

7. Pour the soup into a large serving bowl and let cool to room temperature. Just before serving, taste the soup and add more vinegar, salt and pepper to taste. Sprinkle the coriander and scallions on top.

—*Marcia Kiesel*

HARVESTER'S SOUP

Spicy zucchini or pumpkin bread makes a good counterpoint to this soup.

6 SERVINGS
2 tablespoons olive oil
1 cup diced spicy sausage, such as chorizo
2 cups shredded cabbage (½ small)
6 cups chicken stock or canned broth
2 teaspoons salt
1 teaspoon freshly ground pepper
1 medium apple, peeled and grated

In a large saucepan, warm the oil over moderate heat. Add the sausage and cook until browned, about 10 minutes. Add the cabbage and toss well. Stir in the chicken stock, salt and pepper. Reduce the heat to low, cover and simmer for 1 hour, stirring occasionally. Stir in the grated apple and serve.

—*Molly O'Neill*

MINESTRONE WITH ARTICHOKES, SAUSAGE, PISTACHIOS AND LEMONS

"This soup," says Jeremiah Tower, "was inspired by a 17th-century recipe that called for black truffles and artichokes—an idea so appealing that I decided to put in other things as well. The sausage and lemons replace the roast partridge and orange called for in the original, which also had different vegetables. Basically one should feel free to make up one's own minestrone. Here's mine."

■ BEVERAGE SUGGESTION
Dry sherry or Sercial Madeira

4 SERVINGS
2 small lemons, preferably thin-skinned
6 small or 3 medium artichokes
3 thin Oriental eggplants, cut lengthwise into ¼-inch-thick slices, or 3 small eggplants, halved lengthwise and then cut lengthwise into ¼-inch slices
8 baby pattypan squash
2 small zucchini, quartered lengthwise
2 small golden zucchini or yellow squash, quartered lengthwise
3 cups chicken stock, preferably homemade

12 small green beans, trimmed
1 roasted red bell pepper—peeled,
  seeded and cut into thin strips
½ pound garlic sausage, poached and
  thinly sliced
24 shelled pistachio nuts, peeled
  (see Note)
16 flat Italian parsley leaves
12 fresh marjoram leaves (optional)
12 thyme flowers (optional)
4 drops of truffle oil* (optional)
½ teaspoon salt
¼ teaspoon freshly ground black
  pepper
*Available at specialty food shops

1. In a large noncorrodible saucepan, combine 2 quarts of cold water with the juice of one of the lemons. Trim the artichokes by first snapping off the tough outer leaves. Using a stainless steel knife, cut off the stems and the crowns to within about 1½ inches of the bases. Drop the trimmed artichokes into the saucepan and bring to a boil over moderately high heat. Simmer until tender, 15 to 20 minutes. Let them cool in their cooking liquid.

2. Preheat the grill or broiler. Thinly slice the remaining lemon. Grill or broil the slices 5 to 6 inches from the heat, turning once, until they are lightly browned on both sides, about 5 minutes.

3. Grill or broil the eggplant, pattypan squash and the green and golden zucchini, turning once, until lightly charred on all sides, about 10 minutes. Set aside.

4. In a large saucepan, bring the chicken stock to a boil. Add the pattypan squash, green and golden zucchini and beans; cook until the beans are just tender, about 5 minutes.

5. Meanwhile, using a teaspoon, scoop out the hairy chokes from the artichokes. Quarter the small hearts or cut the larger ones into eighths; add to the soup. Add the red pepper strips, eggplant, sausage, lemon

slices, pistachios, Italian parsley, marjoram, thyme flowers, truffle oil, salt and black pepper and cook until heated through.

NOTE: To peel pistachio nuts, blanch in boiling water for 30 seconds. Drain and rinse under cold water. Rub off the skins with your fingers.

—Jeremiah Tower

MINESTRA MARITATA (MARRIED SOUP)

6 TO 8 SERVINGS
¾ pound smoked ham hock
¾ pound boneless pork shoulder,
  trimmed of excess fat and cut into
  ½-inch dice
6 ounces Genoa salami, cut into
  ¼-inch dice
3-inch-square piece of cheese rind,
  from a wedge of Parmesan or
  Romano (optional)
Pinch of crushed hot pepper
1 medium onion, coarsely chopped
1 medium carrot, coarsely chopped
1 celery rib, coarsely chopped
7 cups boiling water
¾ pound broccoli rabe, chopped
¾ pound escarole, chopped
¾ pound Savoy cabbage, chopped
1 cup (4 ounces) freshly grated
  Pecorino Romano cheese

1. Blanch the ham hock in a large saucepan of boiling water for 10 minutes. Drain and rinse. When cool enough to handle, remove and reserve the rind and scrape off any excess fat. Remove the meat and cut it into ¼-inch dice; reserve the bones.

2. In a stockpot or large flameproof casserole, place the ham rind, bone and diced ham and pork. Add the salami, cheese rind, hot pepper, onion, carrot and celery. Add the boiling water and bring to a boil. Reduce the heat to moderately low and simmer, partially covered, for 1½ hours.

3. Meanwhile, fill a large pot with water and a pinch of salt. Bring to a boil; add the broccoli rabe, escarole and cabbage and blanch until limp, about 5 minutes. Drain and rinse under cold water; drain well.

4. Add the greens to the soup. Cook, partially covered, over moderately low heat for 45 minutes. Remove and discard the bones and ham and cheese rinds. Ladle the soup into bowls and add a sprinkling of grated cheese. Pass the remaining cheese separately.

—Nancy Verde Barr

MEAT BROTH

This simple meat broth (*brodo*) can be used immediately or cooled and stored for three days in the refrigerator or frozen. Make sure you bring the broth to a boil before using.

MAKES ABOUT 6 QUARTS
5 pounds meaty chicken, beef and/or
  veal bones and meaty trimmings
2 medium onions, quartered
2 medium carrots, halved
2 celery ribs with tops, halved
5 sprigs of parsley
2 canned Italian plum tomatoes or
  1 large fresh tomato, chopped

1. Place the bones and trimmings in a stockpot. Add warm water to cover and bring to a boil over high heat. Drain and rinse the bones and meat under warm running water. Rinse the pot and return the bones and meat to it. Fill with enough cold water to cover by 2 inches and bring to a boil.

2. Add the onions, carrots, celery, parsley and tomatoes. Reduce the heat to low and simmer, uncovered, for 3 to 4 hours. (Do not boil.)

3. Strain the broth through a double layer of dampened cheesecloth. Skim off the fat.

—Nancy Verde Barr

EGGS & CHEESE

EGGS & CHEESE

LIGHTENING DEVILED EGGS

I've used six different ingredients in "lightening" these deviled eggs, more as an example of what *might* work than as a requirement. One or two of those listed here are certainly enough to lighten the dish, but be sure to choose contrasting flavors and use a total of ¾ cup. I'm partial to an apple/radish combination.

6 TO 8 SERVINGS
6 jumbo eggs, hard cooked and peeled
2 tablespoons mayonnaise, preferably
   homemade
¼ teaspoon salt
Pinch of cayenne pepper
3 tablespoons finely diced, peeled
   green apple
2 tablespoons finely diced green bell
   pepper
2 tablespoons finely diced radish
   (daikon, red, white or black)
2 tablespoons finely diced fresh water
   chestnuts
2 tablespoons finely diced jicama
1 tablespoon minced scallion
Coarsely ground black pepper
   (optional)

1. Quarter the eggs lengthwise, place the egg yolks in a medium bowl and mash well. Add the mayonnaise, salt and cayenne. Continue mashing until the mixture is completely smooth.

2. Stir in the diced vegetables. Season with additional salt to taste.

3. Spoon 1 heaping teaspoon of the egg yolk mixture into each egg quarter; press slightly to help adhere. Sprinkle with black pepper if desired.
   —*Anne Disrude*

HUEVOS RANCHEROS NEW YORK STYLE

In this variation on the Mexican classic, thin egg crêpes, spiked with scallions and cayenne, replace the traditional fried eggs and tortillas.

F&W BEVERAGE SUGGESTION
Amber beer, such as New
Amsterdam

4 SERVINGS
6 tablespoons olive oil
1 large onion, chopped
2 large garlic cloves, minced
½ teaspoon oregano
½ teaspoon chili powder
¾ teaspoon ground cumin
1¼ teaspoons salt
1 teaspoon Dijon-style mustard
2 cans (15 ounces each) pinto beans,
   rinsed and drained
1 can (14 ounces) Italian peeled
   tomatoes, drained and chopped
½ cup sour cream
2 large fresh plum tomatoes—peeled,
   seeded and chopped
½ cup coarse fresh bread crumbs
   (made from 1½ slices of firm-
   textured white bread)
8 eggs
Pinch of cayenne pepper
¼ cup minced scallion greens
Fresh Tomato Salsa (p. 230)

1. In a large skillet, heat 3 tablespoons of the olive oil over moderate heat. Add the onion and sauté until golden, about 10 minutes. Add the garlic, oregano, chili powder, ½ teaspoon of the cumin and ½ teaspoon of the salt. Sauté for 1 minute longer.

2. Add the mustard, beans and canned tomatoes to the skillet and cook over low heat, stirring occasionally, until the beans form a puree, about 20 minutes. Stir in ¼ cup of the sour cream and the chopped fresh plum tomatoes. Remove from the heat and set aside. **(The recipe can be made to this point several days ahead.)**

3. In a medium skillet, heat 2 tablespoons of the olive oil over moderate heat. Add the bread crumbs and cook, tossing frequently, until golden and very crunchy, about 15 minutes. Toss with ¼ teaspoon of the salt and the remaining ¼ teaspoon cumin.

4. Beat the eggs with 2 tablespoons of water, the remaining ½ teaspoon salt, the cayenne and the minced scallion greens.

5. Preheat the oven to 250°. Heat a 7-inch crêpe pan or nonstick skillet over moderate heat. Brush with some of the remaining olive oil to grease lightly. Add about 2 tablespoons of the beaten egg mixture and immediately tilt and swirl the skillet to form a thin, even crêpe. Cook until the egg is set and only slightly wet on top. Turn and cook for 5 seconds on the second side. Transfer the egg crêpe to a cookie sheet and place in the oven to keep warm. Continue cooking the remaining eggs in the same manner, lightly oiling the skillet each time, to make 8 egg crêpes.

6. To assemble the dish, reheat the bean mixture over moderate heat until warm. Spread about 1 heaping tablespoon of beans onto each crêpe. Fold into a triangle and place 2 on each of 4 warmed plates. Spoon about 3 tablespoons of fresh tomato salsa, a sprinkling of bread crumbs and a small dollop of sour cream over each serving.
   —*Anne Disrude*

SCRAMBLED EGGS WITH BLACK TRUFFLES (BROUILLADE AUX TRUFFES)

These buttery eggs are incredibly rich and so soft you may want to eat them with a spoon. Toast or French bread is a must for sopping up every last bit. Although the cooking time is less than half an hour, the eggs must sit overnight with the truffles (see Step 1), so plan accordingly.

3 TO 4 SERVINGS

8 eggs
2 ounces fresh black truffles
1 garlic clove, peeled
1 stick (4 ounces) unsalted butter
¼ teaspoon salt
⅛ teaspoon freshly ground pepper

1. Place the uncracked eggs in a bowl with the whole truffles, cover tightly and refrigerate overnight.
2. Break the eggs into a medium bowl. Spear the garlic clove on a fork and use it to beat the eggs. Set the eggs aside, leaving the fork-speared garlic in the bowl.
3. Thinly slice the truffles. Add them to the beaten eggs and let stand for 15 minutes.
4. In a small saucepan, melt 5 tablespoons of the butter over low heat and set aside. Thinly slice the remaining 3 tablespoons butter into the eggs.
5. Pour 3 tablespoons of the melted butter into a heavy nonaluminum double boiler or medium saucepan set in a larger pan of hot water. Remove the fork with the garlic and pour the beaten eggs into the double boiler. Add the salt and pepper. Cook, over steaming water, stirring constantly with a small whisk, until the eggs have a thick, custardlike consistency, 15 to 20 minutes. Do not let the eggs curdle at all. Whisk in the remaining melted butter and serve at once.

—Judith Olney

SCRAMBLED EGGS WITH DUCK CRACKLINGS

This recipe provides a perfect excuse to not waste any bit of the duck, especially if you are making something that does not use the whole bird, such as our Sautéed Breast of Duck with Wild Mushrooms (p. 90) or Duck Confit (p. 90), which uses only the legs and thighs. If you have only one duck, divide the recipe by three for two servings. Serve the eggs with a light Salad of Bitter Greens with Grapefruit Vinaigrette (p. 132).

6 SERVINGS

Skin and fat from 3 ducks (see Note), cut into 1-inch pieces
9 eggs
¼ cup light cream or half-and-half
1½ teaspoons salt
¼ teaspoon freshly ground pepper
6 tablespoons unsalted butter
2 tablespoons chopped parsley
1 garlic clove, minced

1. In a large skillet, combine the duck skin with enough water to barely cover. Bring to a simmer and cook over low heat until all the fat is rendered, about 2 hours.
2. Increase the heat to moderately high and cook until the cracklings are brown and crisp, about 30 minutes. Using a slotted spoon, transfer the cracklings to paper towels to drain. Strain the fat and reserve for another use, such as making confit or frying potatoes.
3. In a medium bowl, beat the eggs with the cream, salt and pepper.
4. In a large skillet, melt the butter. Add the parsley, garlic and duck cracklings; toss lightly. Add the eggs and cook over moderate heat, stirring occasionally, until soft and set but not dry, about 7 minutes. Serve hot.

NOTE: Assuming that you are saving the larger parts—such as breasts, legs and thighs—for another recipe, use all the skin and fat that remain once those parts have been removed.

—Deirdre Davis & Linda Marino

GARLIC FLAN

This flavorful flan makes a lovely accompaniment to simple roast meats. Note that the custard must sit for about 15 minutes before serving.

4 SERVINGS

1 large head of garlic (no more than 15 cloves)
2 cups heavy cream
Pinch of ground cloves
Freshly grated nutmeg
Salt and freshly ground white pepper
4 egg yolks, at room temperature

1. Separate the garlic cloves and blanch in a pot of boiling water for 3 to 4 minutes. Cool the garlic under cold running water and slip off the skins. Roughly chop the garlic.
2. In a small heavy saucepan, cook the garlic and heavy cream over moderate heat until the cream is almost scalded, 3 to 4 minutes. Reduce the heat to low and simmer for 10 minutes. Pass the mixture through a

strainer, pressing down on the garlic to puree as much as possible. Season the strained mixture with the cloves and nutmeg and salt and white pepper to taste.

3. Preheat the oven to 325°. Lightly coat four ½-cup ramekins with butter.

4. In a large bowl, beat the egg yolks lightly. Stir in the garlic cream. Divide the custard among the prepared ramekins and place in a baking pan. Add enough hot water to reach halfway up the sides of the custard cups. Cover the pan loosely with foil.

5. Bake the custards until a knife inserted in the center comes out clean, 30 to 40 minutes.

6. Remove the custards from the hot water bath and let them stand for about 15 minutes to set. Run a sharp knife around the edges of each custard and unmold. Serve warm.

—*Christopher Idone*

BACON, LETTUCE AND TOMATO CUSTARD

This savory bread pudding recalls a familiar sandwich combination. With it I suggest a pile of home fries. A spicy white wine, such as Gallo Gewürztraminer, would be good to drink, but then so would freshly squeezed orange juice.

This dish is almost as good at room temperature as it is warm, and it is easier to cut neatly after it has had a chance to set. Leftovers are delicious, too, served cold the next day.

8 SERVINGS

1 pound slab bacon, sliced ¼ inch thick
1 medium head of romaine lettuce, coarsely chopped
10 eggs
⅓ cup mild deli-style mustard
¼ to ½ teaspoon cayenne pepper, to taste
2 teaspoons salt
1 quart heavy cream
4 cups whole wheat bread cubes (½- to 1-inch)
3 firm, ripe plum tomatoes, thickly sliced

1. Remove any tough rind from the bacon and cut the bacon into ¼-inch dice. In a large skillet, cook the bacon over moderate heat, stirring frequently, until crisp and brown, about 20 minutes. Using a slotted spoon, transfer the bacon to paper towels and drain.

2. In a large saucepan of boiling salted water, cook the lettuce for 1 minute. Drain immediately and refresh in a bowl of ice water. Drain well and squeeze dry.

3. Preheat the oven to 375°. In a large bowl, whisk the eggs thoroughly. Beat in the mustard, cayenne and salt. Slowly beat in the cream.

4. Butter a 9-by-13-inch baking dish. Sprinkle the bacon, lettuce and bread cubes evenly over the bottom of the dish. Pour in the egg mixture. Arrange the tomato slices on top.

5. Bake in the center of the oven for 45 to 50 minutes, until puffed, golden brown and firm in the center. Let cool on a rack for at least 20 minutes before cutting into squares and serving.

—*Michael McLaughlin*

GREEN CHILE AND SHRIMP TIMBALE

4 SERVINGS

¼ cup finely diced cooked shrimp
1 teaspoon finely diced fresh jalapeño chile
2 eggs
½ cup heavy cream
¼ teaspoon salt
Pinch of freshly ground white pepper
⅛ teaspoon freshly grated nutmeg

1. Preheat the oven to 325°. Butter four ½-cup molds. Line the bottoms of the molds with waxed paper and butter the paper.

2. Toss together the shrimp and chile and divide among the molds. In a small bowl, whisk together the eggs, cream, salt, white pepper and nutmeg. Divide this mixture among the molds.

3. Set the molds in a shallow baking pan and pour in enough hot water to reach two-thirds of the way up the sides of the molds. Bake the timbales in the middle of the oven for 20 minutes, or until a knife inserted halfway between the center and edge of the molds comes out clean.

4. Leave the timbales in the water bath for up to 45 minutes until serving time. To serve, run a knife around the sides of the molds, invert onto plates and peel off the waxed paper.

—*Ken Dunn*

MOLDED SWISS CHARD, LEEK AND HAM CUSTARD

In this recipe, large, beautiful, deep green chard leaves enclose a smoky filling to make a broad, flat cake for a lunch or light supper entrée, or to serve as a first course for dinner.

8 FIRST-COURSE OR 4 MAIN-COURSE SERVINGS

1½ pounds Swiss chard
2 tablespoons unsalted butter
2 medium leeks (white and tender green), thinly sliced
1 tablespoon all-purpose flour
¾ cup milk
2 eggs
¼ teaspoon marjoram
½ teaspoon coarse (kosher) salt
Freshly ground pepper
1 medium potato (about 6 ounces), peeled
¼ pound ham, in one piece, cut into ¼-inch dice

1. Cut the chard stems from the leaves. Stack 12 of the most perfect large leaves together and set in a colander; pour boiling water over them to soften; then spread them flat on a towel. Slice the remaining leaves and set them aside. Cut the stems into ¼- to ½-inch-long pieces.

2. In a large skillet, melt the butter over moderately high heat. Add the leeks and the chard stems and sauté for 1 minute. Reduce the heat to low. Cover and cook, stirring occasionally, until the vegetables are tender, about 8 minutes. Add the sliced leaves and cook over high heat, stirring, until most of the liquid has evaporated.

3. In a medium bowl, blend the flour with 1 tablespoon of the milk. Gradually stir in the remaining milk to make a smooth liquid. Add the eggs, marjoram, salt and pepper to taste and beat well to blend.

4. Butter a 9-inch round cake pan. Line the pan with whole chard leaves, overlapping them with their tips meeting in the center and the wider ends draped over the rim of the pan. Place a few extra leaves in the center and cover any holes.

5. Preheat the oven to 375°. Spread one-third of the cooked vegetable mixture in the lined pan. Finely grate half the potato over the mixture; top with half the diced ham. Ladle one-third of the custard mixture over this. Repeat once, then spread the remaining vegetable mixture on top and pour on the last of the custard. Cover with any remaining leaves and fold the overhanging ends into the center to cover the mixture.

6. Cover the pan with foil and set on a rack in a pan of hot water. Bake in the preheated oven for about 1 hour, or until the custard is set.

7. Let cool for about 15 minutes. Then run a knife around the edge of the pan and invert the cake onto a serving plate. Serve warm, lukewarm or at room temperature.

—Elizabeth Schneider

FOUR-CHEESE TART

Though best served at room temperature, this elegant tart makes a wonderful cold picnic dish accompanied with a tossed green salad and a chilled white wine.

■ F&W BEVERAGE SUGGESTION
California Chardonnay, such as Burgess Cellars Vintage Reserve

6 TO 8 SERVINGS

1½ cups all-purpose flour
2 teaspoons dried dill
⅜ teaspoon salt
1 stick (4 ounces) cold unsalted butter, cut into small pieces
1 tablespoon brandy
3 to 4 tablespoons ice water
1 cup (4 ounces) freshly grated Parmesan cheese
1 cup (4 ounces) freshly grated Emmentaler cheese
4 ounces mild goat cheese, such as Bucheron, mashed
¼ cup freshly grated Cheddar cheese
1 small onion, minced
1 large garlic clove, minced
3 eggs
½ cup heavy cream
¼ teaspoon freshly ground pepper
¼ cup minced parsley

1. In a food processor, combine the flour, dill and ⅛ teaspoon of the salt. Process until well blended, about 3 seconds. Add the butter and turn the machine quickly on and off until the mixture resembles coarse meal, 10 to 20 seconds. Add the brandy and the ice water, 1 tablespoon at a time; process until the dough just begins to form a ball. Gather the dough together and flatten into a 6-inch disk, wrap in waxed paper and refrigerate for at least 1 hour.

2. On a lightly floured surface, roll out the dough to an 11-inch circle. Line a 9½-inch tart pan with a removable bottom with the dough. Trim the edge to the rim. Place the pastry shell in the freezer until very firm, at least 30 minutes.

3. Preheat the oven to 400°. Line the frozen tart shell with a large sheet of aluminum foil and fill with pie weights or dried beans. Bake the shell in the lower third of the oven for 20 minutes. Remove the pie weights or beans and the foil. Return the shell to the oven for 5 to 7 minutes, or until dry all over. Set aside to cool for 5 minutes.

4. Reduce the oven temperature to 350°. In a medium bowl, combine the Parmesan, Emmentaler, goat and Cheddar cheeses with the onion and garlic. Distribute evenly in the cooled tart shell.

5. In a small bowl, beat the eggs with the heavy cream. Season with the pepper and the remaining ¼ teaspoon salt; pour the mixture over the cheese. Tap the pan a few times to settle the liquid.

6. Set the tart on a baking sheet and bake for 20 minutes, until the cheese filling is puffed and browned and a knife tip inserted near the center comes out clean.

7. Let the tart stand at room temperature for at least 20 minutes before serving. Remove the tart from the pan, sprinkle the parsley on top and serve warm or at room temperature.

—*W. Peter Prestcott*

ALMOND GOUGERE RING

This splendid cheese dish can be served as a light lunch along with a tossed green salad and a glass of good Burgundy.

8 TO 10 SERVINGS
1 stick (4 ounces) unsalted butter, cut into small pieces
¼ teaspoon salt
¼ teaspoon freshly ground pepper
1 cup all-purpose flour
4 whole eggs
1½ cups (6 ounces) freshly grated Gruyère cheese
Pinch of freshly grated nutmeg
1 egg yolk
1 tablespoon milk
½ cup slivered almonds

1. Preheat the oven to 375°. In a heavy medium saucepan, combine the butter, salt and pepper with 1 cup of water. Bring to a boil over high heat. Remove from the heat and add the flour all at once. Using a wooden spoon, beat until the mixture is smooth and pulls away from the sides of the pan to form a ball. Continue to beat over low heat for 1 minute.

2. Remove from the heat and let cool for 1 minute. Beat in the whole eggs, 1 at a time, making sure each egg is completely incorporated before adding the next. Stir in 1¼ cups of the cheese and the nutmeg. Mound large heaping spoonfuls of the mixture on a buttered baking sheet to form a wreath; the inside edges should measure about 7 inches across.

3. In a small bowl, lightly beat the egg yolk with the milk. Using a pastry brush, paint the top of the wreath with this glaze. Sprinkle the remaining ¼ cup Gruyère and the almonds over the wreath.

4. Bake the gougère for 15 minutes, until puffed and set. Reduce the heat to 350° and cook for 45 minutes longer, until golden brown and firm to the touch. Let cool for 10 minutes and serve warm.

—*W. Peter Prestcott*

FISH & SHELLFISH

FISH & SHELLFISH

SKILLET-GRILLED AND SMOKED FISH

With this treatment of fish, a variety of seasonings can be used. Fennel seeds impart a subtle licorice flavor. Coriander seeds have a perfumed, citrus effect, and a mix of spices and herbs with hot pepper add some zing. Feel free to experiment with your own blends. Just be sure to soak the seasonings well so that they will smolder and give off smoke rather than burn.

F&W BEVERAGE SUGGESTION
Sancerre or California Fumé Blanc

2 SERVINGS
3 tablespoons fennel or coriander seeds, or a mixture of 1 tablespoon cumin seeds, 1 tablespoon oregano, 1 tablespoon thyme and 1 tablespoon red pepper flakes
2 fish steaks, such as swordfish or salmon, cut about 1½ inches thick
1 tablespoon vegetable oil
¼ teaspoon salt
1 tablespoon unsalted butter, melted (optional)

1. Place the spices in a small bowl and soak them in 2 to 3 tablespoons of water until well saturated, about 20 minutes.
2. Select a cast-iron skillet that can accommodate a small-footed rack (such as a cake rack) and that can be covered with a fairly close-fitting lid. Place the empty skillet over high heat until smoking, about 10 minutes.
3. Brush the fish with the oil to coat. Add the fish to the skillet and

cook for 1 minute on each side to brown.
4. Transfer the fish to the rack and place the soaked spices in the skillet. Place the rack over the spices and cover the skillet. Reduce the heat to moderately high and smoke for 4 to 5 minutes, until the fish is still slightly translucent when checked in the center with a small sharp knife.
5. Sprinkle the fish with the salt and serve as is or drizzled with a little melted butter.

—*Anne Disrude*

BAKED FISH WITH LEMON AND VEGETABLES

This dish is adapted from a recipe for baked fish with preserved lemons from Ginette Spier, a Maryland-based caterer who is from Morocco. If you have preserved lemons (see Note), add four wedges, slivered, in place of the lemon juice in Step 3.

3 TO 4 SERVINGS
Pinch of saffron threads
3 tablespoons boiling water
4-pound whole red snapper, sea trout or sea bass—cleaned and scaled, head and tail intact
2 teaspoons coarse (kosher) salt
½ teaspoon freshly ground pepper
⅓ cup fresh lemon juice
⅓ cup chopped parsley
3 garlic cloves, crushed
1 lemon, very thinly sliced
3 small baking potatoes, peeled and thinly sliced
1 green bell pepper, cut into ¼-inch strips
1 red bell pepper, cut into ¼-inch strips
2 medium tomatoes, cut into ½-inch wedges
½ teaspoon crushed hot pepper

1 teaspoon paprika
¼ cup vegetable oil

1. In a small bowl, crumble the saffron threads into the boiling water and set aside. Preheat the oven to 400°.
2. Season the inside of the fish with ½ teaspoon of the salt, ⅛ teaspoon of the pepper and 1 tablespoon of the lemon juice. Sprinkle the parsley and garlic in the bottom of a 17-by-10-by-2-inch noncorrodible baking dish and place the fish on top.
3. Place a few of the lemon slices under the head and tail of the fish and the remainder in a row on top of the fish. Arrange the potato slices, green and red pepper strips and tomato wedges in rows on both sides of the fish. Sprinkle on the hot pepper, paprika and remaining 1½ teaspoons salt and ⅜ teaspoon pepper. Pour the saffron water, oil and remaining lemon juice over the fish and vegetables.
4. Cover the baking dish tightly with aluminum foil, tenting it to avoid touching the fish. Bake for 30 minutes. Remove the foil. Tilt the dish and with a bulb baster, baste the vegetables with the pan juices. Return to the oven and bake, uncovered, until the fish is cooked through and opaque at its thickest point, about 10 minutes.

NOTE: A shortcut recipe for homemade preserved lemons appears on page 238.

—*Ginette Spier*

54

MARINATED SEAFOOD AND VEGETABLE KEBABS

One of my favorite grilling ideas is skewered foods. Meat and vegetables, usually marinated in advance, are placed on long metal or bamboo skewers and cooked over a hot fire. Traditionally this is done with lamb or beef, which is very good, but in the summer I find seafood a pleasant change. Shrimp, scallops, swordfish and monkfish are my usual choices. Vegetables might include onions, cherry tomatoes, peppers (green, yellow and red), mushrooms, zucchini and eggplant. Because these ingredients cook at different rates, if you try cooking an assortment on the same skewer, you end up with some nearly raw and others overcooked. To avoid this, I skewer each food separately, placing the one that takes the longest cooking time on the grill first.

Rice pilaf is traditional with this type of meal, though I find that a good French bread and perhaps a mixed green salad is all that is needed. A light dry Muscadet or Rosé de Provence will be pleasurable drinking, and a refreshing lime or lemon mousse is an ideal ending to this summer meal.

8 SERVINGS
24 jumbo shrimp
32 large sea scallops
3 pounds swordfish or monkfish
    steaks, cut about 1 inch thick
4 medium onions, quartered
6 bell peppers—preferably 2 red,
    2 green and 2 yellow
1 medium eggplant
3 medium zucchini
¾ pound medium mushrooms
1 pint cherry tomatoes (24 to 32)
¼ cup tarragon vinegar
¼ cup fresh lemon juice
¾ cup light olive oil

1 cup light vegetable oil
Salt and freshly ground pepper
Possible additions: Honey, grated
    fresh ginger, mustard, garlic, curry
    powder, soy sauce, fresh or dried
    herbs (thyme, tarragon, basil,
    oregano or marjoram)

1. I recommend leaving the shells on the shrimp. Although removing the shells makes for easier dining, grilling the shrimp in the shell enhances their flavor. Choose large sea scallops, and cut the swordfish or monkfish into 1-inch cubes. The monkfish has a membrane covering the flesh that should be removed because it becomes tough when cooked and has an off taste.

2. If you prefer your onions tender rather than crunchy, boil them until tender before browning them on the grill. You can cut the peppers and eggplant into large cubes, the zucchini into thick slices; the mushrooms and cherry tomatoes can be left whole.

3. Whisk together the vinegar, lemon juice, olive oil, vegetable oil and salt and pepper to taste. Then adjust the flavor to complement each item being grilled. For example, divide the marinade into 5 bowls and add a touch of honey and ginger for the shrimp, mustard and garlic for the fish, curry for the scallops, garlic and soy sauce for the eggplant, and herbs for the vegetables.

4. After marinating for several hours, the seafood and vegetables are ready for grilling. The vegetables have the longest cooking time and should be put on the grill first, the fish and shrimp next and the scallops last. If you are cooking for a large group or if your grill is small, keep the vegetables

warm in the oven while you finish cooking the fish and seafood. The grill should be very hot and the skewers turned several times. When everything is cooked, remove individual portions from the skewers onto serving plates or platters for your guests to help themselves.

—Richard Grausman

GRILLED SNAPPER WITH FRAGRANT PEPPER (TAI NO SANSHOYAKI)

F&W BEVERAGE SUGGESTION
Light white wine, such as Tormes Vinho Verde

4 SERVINGS
2 red snapper fillets (about 12 ounces
    each) or 4 fillets (about 6 ounces
    each), skin intact
1½ tablespoons sake
1 teaspoon vegetable oil
½ teaspoon coarse (kosher) salt
½ teaspoon sansho (fragrant Japanese
    pepper)*
1 small lemon, cut into 4 wedges
*Available at Oriental markets

1. Rinse the fish fillets under cold water and remove any scales. Pat dry and place in a flat-bottomed dish. Add the sake and marinate for 10 minutes, turning the fish after 5 minutes. Remove the fish and pat dry.

2. Preheat the broiler. Lay the fish, skin-side up, on a rack fitted over a broiling pan or on a ridged disposable broiling pan, and brush lightly with ½ teaspoon of the vegetable oil. Sprinkle with ¼ teaspoon of the salt and ¼ teaspoon of the sansho.

3. Broil the fish 1½ to 2 inches from the heat for 1 minute. Flip the fillets with a wide spatula and brush the fish with the remaining ½ teaspoon oil. Sprinkle with the remaining ¼ tea-

spoon salt and ¼ teaspoon *sansho*. Broil the snapper until the fish is opaque around the edges but translucent in the center, 1½ to 2 minutes. Turn the fish again and broil until the skin is blistered and the fish is just opaque throughout, 30 seconds to 1 minute. Serve hot with lemon wedges.

—*Elizabeth Andoh*

PAPILLOTE OF RED SNAPPER WITH SAGE

This recipe is equally delicious with any of your favorite fresh herbs.

F&W BEVERAGE SUGGESTION
California Sauvignon Blanc

1 SERVING
1 tablespoon clarified or melted butter
1 red snapper fillet (8 ounces), skinned
½ teaspoon fresh lemon juice
Salt and freshly ground pepper
Sprig of fresh sage (5 to 6 medium leaves), basil, tarragon or thyme

1. Preheat the oven to 400°. Fold a 15-by-20-inch sheet of butcher's paper, parchment or aluminum foil in half crosswise to make a 15-by-10-inch rectangle. Using scissors, cut the rectangle into a heart shape with the fold running vertically down the center. Open up the heart and brush with ½ tablespoon of the butter.

2. Put the snapper fillet in the center of half of the papillote. Brush with the remaining ½ tablespoon butter.

3. Sprinkle the fillet with the lemon juice and season lightly with salt and pepper. Place the sage on top.

4. Fold the paper over the fish and beginning at the top of the heart,

make a series of tight overlapping folds to seal the papillote.

5. Place the papillote on a cookie sheet and bake for 8 minutes; the papillote will be puffed and lightly browned. Serve at once.

—*John Robert Massie*

BARBECUED SALMON STEAKS

Salmon, popular in America but not available in China, is flavored with Chinese seasonings and then broiled under a very hot flame. Though only the marinade is Chinese, the resulting dish is a seductive blend of the two cultures. If salmon is not available, any thick fish steak, such as swordfish or halibut, can be substituted.

F&W BEVERAGE SUGGESTION
Chilled rosé, such as Domaines Ott

2 SERVINGS
1 tablespoon unhulled sesame seeds*
3 tablespoons medium-dry sherry
1 tablespoon dark soy sauce*
1 tablespoon Oriental sesame oil
2 teaspoons minced fresh ginger
2 scallions, thinly sliced
1 medium garlic clove, minced
2 salmon steaks, cut about 1 inch thick (½ pound each)
*Available at Oriental markets

1. In a bowl, combine the sesame seeds, sherry, soy sauce, sesame oil, ginger, scallions and garlic.

2. Preheat the broiler for 20 minutes. Meanwhile, place the salmon steaks in a flameproof dish with a lip. Pour the marinade over the salmon and let stand while the broiler is preheating.

3. Place the dish with the salmon steaks under the broiler as close to the heat as possible. Broil for 10 minutes without turning. Serve immediately or at room temperature.

NOTE: For catering, I sometimes use this dish as part of a buffet of room-temperature Chinese dishes, in which case I use a whole piece of boneless salmon fillet weighing about 3 or 4 pounds, increasing the marinade accordingly. Cooking time remains the same.

—*Karen Lee & Alaxandra Branyon*

GRILLED SALMON FILLETS WITH BEURRE BLANC SAUCE

For company, I serve a beurre blanc sauce over the salmon; for an everyday meal, I simply use melted butter with fresh herbs. I generally accompany the fish with steamed new potatoes, followed by a mixed green salad. The potatoes can be fully cooked in advance and reheated while the fish is on the grill. I find that a rich Chardonnay complements the delicate smoky flavor of salmon.

6 SERVINGS
6 salmon fillets, about 6 ounces each (see Note)
2 to 3 tablespoons soy sauce and/or fresh lemon or lime juice (optional)
Olive oil (optional)
Beurre Blanc Sauce (p. 228) or 1 stick of unsalted butter, melted and mixed with 2 tablespoons chopped fresh chives, tarragon or basil

1. To prepare the salmon for grilling, rinse under cold water and dry with paper towels. If the fillets are very fresh, I generally do nothing else to them. If they are not, sprinkle them with a little soy sauce and/or lemon or lime juice several hours ahead. The fish should be kept refrigerated until shortly before grilling. Salmon is con-

sidered to be a fatty fish and generally remains moist after cooking. Salmon that has a deep orange color as compared to a lighter pink will be less fatty and drier. For this reason, when I have dark salmon, I coat the fish with a little oil as well.

2. Preheat your grill so that it is very hot. Before putting the fish on the grill, make sure the rest of the dinner is ready because the salmon fillets cook very quickly. Arrange the salmon on the grill, skin-side down. Cover the grill. If you do not have a lid, make one by loosely tenting the grill with heavy-duty aluminum foil, or use a large pot lid to cover the fish. The fish will take only 5 to 10 minutes. There are many people today who like their fish rare. I prefer to cook the fish thoroughly without overcooking it. It will be fairly firm to the touch, yet still have a little spring. Moisture or juices from the fish will pool on the surface and become opaque in appearance. The skin should be stuck to the grill by now.

3. The technique I have developed for removing the fillets solves this sticking problem with a simple procedure. I slide a metal spatula between the skin and fish and lift the fish onto a plate, leaving the skin on the grill to be scraped off and discarded later.

4. Serve the fish immediately, either topped with a generous spoonful of beurre blanc sauce or some of the melted butter with fresh herbs.

NOTE: The fillets will most likely be cut from a side of boned salmon. The belly section is thinner than the back, so try to have the fillets of even thickness and cut from the sections in attractive serving pieces of about 6 ounces.

—*Richard Grausman*

SALMON EN PAPILLOTE WITH PERNOD AND MINT

Paper around the salmon keeps the fish moist. Since the wrapping is only for cooking and not for presentation at table (the salmon is presented separated from the skin and bones), no fancy folding is required.

Menu suggestion: To start, Summer Tossed Salad with Mushrooms and Fresh and Pickled Peppers (p. 134); with the salmon, steamed broccoli or baby carrots; for dessert, Strawberry-Cream Cheese Galette (p. 170).

🍷 F&W BEVERAGE SUGGESTION Full-bodied white, such as Meursault or white Hermitage, or California Chardonnay, such as Glen Ellen

6 SERVINGS

3 salmon steaks, cut about 1 inch thick (10 to 12 ounces each)
3 tablespoons Pernod
3 tablespoons shredded fresh mint
¼ teaspoon salt
Freshly ground white pepper
1 tablespoon plus 1 teaspoon olive oil
4 tablespoons unsalted butter, cut into pieces
¼ cup heavy cream
6 sprigs of mint, for garnish

1. Rub the salmon steaks with 2 tablespoons of the Pernod and place them on a platter. Season the salmon with 2 tablespoons of the mint, the salt and white pepper to taste. If you have time, cover with plastic wrap and refrigerate for 2 or 3 hours.

2. Preheat the oven to 400°. Rub a large baking dish with 1 teaspoon of the olive oil. Line the dish with enough parchment paper, overlapping where necessary, to completely line the dish and allow a 4-inch overhang all around. Drizzle the remaining 1 tablespoon oil over the bottom

of the lined dish and arrange the salmon steaks in a single layer. Sprinkle on the remaining 1 tablespoon Pernod. Dot each steak with 1 teaspoon butter. Enclose the salmon in the paper by bringing the two long sides of parchment together and folding and crimping to seal, allowing room for expansion. Tuck the remaining edges of paper underneath the fish to form a loose bundle.

3. Bake the salmon in the center of the oven for 20 minutes, or until the fish is just opaque throughout.

4. Unwrap the fish and transfer to a warm plate. Pour the pan juices into a small saucepan. Add the cream and bring to a boil over high heat. Boil until the liquid thickens slightly, 1 to 2 minutes; there will be about ⅓ cup.

5. Remove from the heat and whisk in the remaining 3 tablespoons butter, a few pieces at a time. Season with additional salt and pepper to taste and stir in the remaining 1 tablespoon shredded mint.

6. To serve, skin and bone the salmon and present ½ steak per person, garnished with a sprig of mint. Pass the sauce separately.

—*Lydie Marshall*

PAPILLOTE OF SALMON WITH OYSTERS AND MUSHROOMS

🍷 F&W BEVERAGE SUGGESTION Chardonnay, such as Sanford, or Sauvignon Blanc, such as Cakebread Cellars

1 SERVING

1 tablespoon clarified or melted butter
2 medium mushrooms, thinly sliced
2 tablespoons crème fraîche

FISH & SHELLFISH

Salt and freshly ground pepper
8 ounces salmon fillet, cut 1 inch
*   thick or less, skinned*
3 medium oysters, shucked
5 or 6 whole chives

1. Preheat the oven to 400°. Fold a 15-by-20-inch sheet of butcher's paper, parchment or aluminum foil in half crosswise to make a 15-by-10-inch rectangle. Using scissors, cut the rectangle into a heart shape with the fold running vertically down the center. Open up the heart and brush with ½ tablespoon of the butter.

2. In a medium bowl, combine the mushrooms, crème fraîche and a pinch of salt and pepper. Scrape the seasoned mushrooms onto half of the heart in an even layer about the size of the fish.

3. Place the salmon fillet on top of the mushrooms. Brush the fish with the remaining ½ tablespoon butter; season lightly with salt and pepper.

4. Arrange the oysters in a line down the length of the salmon and garnish with the chives.

5. Fold the paper over the fish and beginning at the top of the heart, make a series of tight overlapping folds to seal the papillote.

6. Put the papillote on a cookie sheet and bake for 10 minutes for a salmon fillet 1 inch thick (slightly less time for a thinner fillet); the papillote will be puffed and lightly browned. Serve at once.

—*John Robert Massie*

SALMON AND CHIVE CAKES WITH CORIANDER BUTTER

Buttered boiled potatoes make a terrific companion to these salmon cakes.

F&W BEVERAGE SUGGESTION
Vouvray, such as Martin Soret

4 SERVINGS

3 tablespoons mayonnaise
1 tablespoon fresh lemon juice
1 teaspoon dry mustard
Dash of hot pepper sauce
2 teaspoons salt
1 teaspoon freshly ground pepper
½ cup minced fresh chives
1 pound salmon fillet, minced
1 cup plus 2 tablespoons fresh bread
*   crumbs*
1 stick (4 ounces) unsalted butter
1 cup dry white wine
1 tablespoon fresh lime juice
½ cup minced fresh coriander

1. In a large bowl, combine the mayonnaise, lemon juice, mustard, hot sauce, salt, pepper and chives. Add the salmon and 1 cup of the bread crumbs; toss lightly to blend.

2. Shape the salmon mixture into 4 cakes, about 3½ inches in diameter and almost 1 inch thick. Dust the cakes with the remaining 2 tablespoons bread crumbs and place on a rack; cover and refrigerate for 1 hour.

3. In a large skillet, melt 4 tablespoons of the butter over moderate heat. Add the salmon cakes and fry until nicely browned and resistant when lightly pressed, about 5 minutes per side. Transfer to a plate and keep warm.

4. Discard the butter and wipe the skillet clean. Add the wine and lime juice and bring to a boil over moderate heat. Boil until the mixture is reduced by half, about 4 minutes. Reduce the heat to low and whisk in the remaining 4 tablespoons butter, 1 ta-

blespoon at a time. Remove from the heat and add the coriander. Season with salt and pepper to taste. Serve one salmon cake per person, with some of the sauce spooned over the top.

—*Molly O'Neill*

SALMON SCALLOPS WITH SCALLION CREAM

F&W BEVERAGE SUGGESTION
A fresh, clean Chardonnay, such as Chateau Ste. Michelle

4 SERVINGS

½ cup all-purpose flour
½ teaspoon salt
Dash of freshly ground pepper
12 salmon scallops (2 ounces each),
*   about ¼ inch thick*
2 tablespoons clarified butter or light
*   vegetable oil*
½ cup dry white wine
1 tablespoon fresh lemon juice
1 cup heavy cream
2 scallions, minced

1. On a flat plate, combine the flour, salt and pepper. Lightly dust the salmon scallops in the seasoned flour; shake off the excess.

2. In a large noncorrodible skillet, heat the clarified butter until smoking. Add the salmon scallops in batches and sauté over high heat for 5 seconds on each side. Transfer to a warm platter and cover loosely with foil.

3. Discard the butter from the pan. Add the wine and lemon juice and bring to a boil over high heat. Cook until the wine reduces by half, 2 to 3 minutes. Add the cream and boil until reduced by half, about 4 minutes. Stir in the scallions and season with additional salt and pepper to taste.

4. Arrange the salmon on heated plates. Spoon the sauce over the scallops and serve immediately.

—*Molly O'Neill*

SALMON "AUBERGE DE L'ILL"

🍷 F&W BEVERAGE SUGGESTION
Hugel Gewürztraminer

4 SERVINGS
*4 salmon steaks (about 8 ounces
    each), cut about 1 inch thick*
¼ pound sole fillet
*¼ pound medium shrimp, shelled and
    deveined*
½ cup heavy cream, chilled
1 whole egg, separated
Pinch of freshly grated nutmeg
½ teaspoon salt
¼ teaspoon freshly ground pepper
2 egg whites
1 stick (4 ounces) unsalted butter
4 shallots, minced
2 tablespoons fresh lemon juice
1 cup Alsatian Riesling
1 cup fish stock or bottled clam juice
1 cup crème fraîche

1. Cut the salmon steaks in half lengthwise along the central bone. Remove and discard the bones. Using a sharp knife, cut off the skins and discard. Re-form the steaks and pin together with 2 wooden toothpicks.

2. In a food processor, combine the sole and shrimp. Puree until smooth. With the machine on, add the heavy cream and the egg yolk and process until blended. Pass the mixture through the medium disk of a food mill. Scrape the fish puree into a stainless steel bowl set in a larger bowl half-filled with ice and water. Add the nutmeg and half the salt and pepper. Using a wooden spoon, stir the mixture until chilled completely.

3. Preheat the oven to 400°. In a medium bowl, beat the 3 egg whites until soft peaks form. Gently fold the beaten whites into the chilled puree.

4. In a large noncorrodible oven-proof skillet, melt 2 tablespoons of the butter over moderately high heat. Add the shallots and cook, stirring occasionally, until softened, about 5 minutes.

5. Season the salmon with the lemon juice and the remaining ¼ teaspoon salt and ⅛ teaspoon pepper. Mound ½ cup of the fish mixture on top of each steak, smoothing with a wet spatula. Place the steaks in the skillet. Pour the Riesling and the stock around the fish.

6. Bake the salmon until the topping is firm, about 10 minutes. Transfer to the broiler and lightly brown the tops. Transfer the steaks to a warmed platter and place in a warm oven.

7. Add the crème fraîche to the skillet and bring to a boil over high heat. Cook until the liquid reduces to 1 cup, about 12 minutes. Reduce the heat to low and whisk in the remaining 6 tablespoons butter, 1 tablespoon at a time. Adjust the seasoning if necessary and strain the sauce through a fine-mesh sieve. To serve, place the salmon steaks on warmed plates and surround each with about ⅓ cup of sauce.

—*l'Auberge de l'Ill, Illhaeusern, France*

BROILED SHAD

2 SERVINGS
2 teaspoons coarse (kosher) salt
1 shad fillet (about ¾ pound)
1 tablespoon vegetable oil
Lemon wedges
2 pats of butter (optional)

Preheat the broiler. Sprinkle the salt over a rectangular metal baking pan. Place the shad fillet, skin-side down, in the pan and rub the oil over the fillet. Broil, about 4 inches from the heat, without turning, for about 4 minutes, or until the fish is firm, lightly browned and easily flakes when pierced with a fork. Serve hot, with lemon wedges. Add butter if desired.

—*Jim Fobel*

BLACKENED SHAD

Chef Paul Prudhomme inspired this method of preparing shad. Blackened redfish is a popular entrée at his New Orleans restaurant, K-Paul's. A word of caution—because of the intense heat and smoke in this method of preparation, do not attempt this indoors unless you have a good ventilating system.

🍷 F&W BEVERAGE SUGGESTION
White Rhône, such as Hermitage Blanc

2 SERVINGS
1½ teaspoons coarse (kosher) salt
1 shad fillet (about ¾ pound)

1. Sprinkle a large well-seasoned cast-iron skillet with the salt and place it over high heat for 10 minutes.

2. Cut the shad fillet in half crosswise and place the pieces, skin-side down, in the pan. Cook over high heat, without turning or moving, for 6 minutes. Turn and cook the other side for 10 seconds. Serve the shad, blackened-side up, as a main course with potatoes or potato salad.

—*Jim Fobel*

FISH & SHELLFISH

BAKED SHAD

4 SERVINGS
3 tablespoons unsalted butter, at
  room temperature
2 shad fillets (about ¾ pound each)
Salt and freshly ground pepper
1 lemon, thinly sliced

Preheat the oven to 400°. Lightly butter a baking sheet with 1 tablespoon of the butter. Season the shad with salt and pepper. Place the fillets, skin-side down, on the baking sheet and smear 1 tablespoon of butter over each. Arrange the lemon slices in a row down the center of each fillet. Bake for about 10 minutes, or until the fish easily flakes when pierced with a fork. Serve hot with additional lemon if desired.

—Jim Fobel

PAN-FRIED SHAD WITH BAY BUTTER

The bay butter needs to sit for 3 hours, so plan accordingly.

❚ F&W BEVERAGE SUGGESTION
California Chardonnay, such as Bacigalupi, or Spanish white, such as Torres Viña Sol

4 SERVINGS
1 stick (4 ounces) unsalted butter
5 bay leaves
⅓ cup all-purpose flour
1 teaspoon salt
¼ teaspoon freshly ground pepper
3 tablespoons olive oil
2 shad fillets (about ¾ pound each)
Lemon wedges

1. Place the butter and bay leaves in a small skillet over low heat. After the butter melts, remove the pan from the heat and let the mixture remain at room temperature for 3 hours. Warm over low heat shortly before serving.

2. Combine the flour, salt and pepper in a large bag. Place one fillet in the bag and shake to coat; repeat with the second fillet.

3. Place the oil in a large, heavy skillet over moderate heat until almost smoking. Add the shad fillets, skin-side down, to the hot oil. Fry for about 2 minutes; turn the fillets and fry for 15 seconds. Serve hot with warm bay butter and lemon wedges.

—Jim Fobel

CREAMY BAKED SHAD ROE

4 SERVINGS
2 tablespoons unsalted butter, at
  room temperature
1 large pair of shad roe (about ¾
  pound)
½ cup heavy cream
1 egg yolk
½ teaspoon basil
½ teaspoon salt
¼ teaspoon freshly ground pepper
½ small onion, sliced into thin
  rounds
2 tablespoons chopped parsley

1. Preheat the oven to 350°. Spread the butter over a medium baking pan or gratin dish. Without piercing or separating the roe, place them in the pan.

2. In a small bowl, beat the cream, egg yolk, basil, salt and pepper with a fork until well blended. Pour the mixture over the roe. Separate the onion into rings and arrange over the roe. Sprinkle with the parsley and bake, uncovered, for 30 to 35 minutes, or until golden and bubbly.

—Jim Fobel

SAUTEED SOLE WITH GINGER SAUCE

Fresh ginger has traditionally been a Chinese seasoning. Sole, popular and widely available in America, is not indigenous to Chinese waters. Sautéing, a French technique (appropriate for keeping the fish fillets intact, where Chinese stir-frying would break the fish up), fuses this mix of East/West cuisines.

2 SERVINGS
1 teaspoon water chestnut powder* or
  cornstarch
2 tablespoons medium-dry sherry
2 tablespoons dark soy sauce*
1 pound fresh fillet of sole (4 fillets, 4
  ounces each, or halved larger
  fillets)
½ cup all-purpose flour
3 tablespoons peanut oil
1 tablespoon finely shredded fresh
  ginger
3 tablespoons minced shallots
½ cup unsalted chicken stock or ¼
  cup canned broth diluted with ¼
  cup water
*Available at Oriental markets

1. Preheat the oven to 250°. Place a heatproof platter in the oven to warm.

2. In a small bowl, dissolve the water chestnut powder in the sherry. Add the soy sauce and set aside.

3. Rinse, drain and dry the fillets. Dredge in the flour and shake off any excess.

4. In a large skillet, heat 2 tablespoons of the peanut oil over moderately high heat until hot but not smoking. Place the fillets in the pan in a single layer. Sauté, turning once, until opaque throughout, 1 to 2 min-

utes per side, depending on the thickness of the fish.

5. Transfer the fish to the heated serving platter and place uncovered in the oven to keep warm.

6. Add the remaining 1 tablespoon oil to the skillet and return to moderate heat. Add the ginger and shallots. Sauté, stirring, until the shallots soften, 1 to 2 minutes.

7. Add the stock, increase the heat to high and bring to a boil. Reduce the heat and simmer for 1 minute.

8. Stir the soy sauce mixture and add all at once. Cook, stirring, until the sauce thickens slightly, about 30 seconds. Add any fish juices that have accumulated on the platter to the sauce. Pour the sauce over the fish fillets and serve immediately.

—*Karen Lee & Alaxandra Branyon*

PAPILLOTE OF TROUT STUFFED WITH TOMATO AND BASIL

1 SERVING

1 tablespoon olive oil
1 whole trout (about 10 ounces)—
  cleaned, with head and tail intact
¼ teaspoon salt
⅛ teaspoon freshly ground pepper
2 plum tomatoes—peeled, seeded and
  coarsely chopped
2 tablespoons chopped fresh basil
1 medium garlic clove, minced

1. Preheat the oven to 400°. Fold a 15-by-20-inch sheet of butcher's paper, parchment or aluminum foil in half crosswise to make a 15-by-10-inch rectangle. Using scissors, cut the rectangle into a heart shape with the fold running vertically down the center. Unfold the heart and brush with ½ tablespoon of the oil.

2. Season the inside of the trout

with half the salt and pepper. In a small bowl, combine the tomatoes, basil, garlic and the remaining oil, salt and pepper. Spoon the mixture into the trout. Place the trout on the oiled paper.

3. Fold the paper over the fish and beginning at the top of the heart, make a series of tight overlapping folds to seal the papillote.

4. Place the papillote on a cookie sheet and bake for 8 to 10 minutes; the papillote will be puffed and lightly browned. Serve at once.

—*John Robert Massie*

GLAZE-GRILLED SWORDFISH (KAJIKI NO TERIYAKI)

If you like, the glaze in Step 1 can be doubled or even tripled and stored, covered, in the refrigerator for two to three weeks. Use it when broiling any oily fish, such as salmon or kingfish.

F&W BEVERAGE SUGGESTION
California Sauvignon Blanc, such as Silverado

4 SERVINGS

¼ cup soy sauce
3 tablespoons mirin (sweet rice wine)
1 tablespoon sugar
4 pieces of swordfish steak, cut at
  least ¾ inch thick (about 4 ounces
  each)
¼ cup sake
1 tablespoon fresh ginger juice (see
  Note)
¼ teaspoon salt

1. In a small saucepan, combine the soy sauce, *mirin* and sugar. Cook over low heat, stirring constantly, until the sugar dissolves. Continue to simmer

until the liquid is reduced to ⅓ cup, 5 to 10 minutes. Pour the glaze into a bowl and set aside to cool.

2. Place the swordfish in a flat-bottomed dish and sprinkle with the sake and ginger juice. Turn the fish to moisten all over and let marinate for 5 minutes before broiling.

3. Preheat the broiler. Remove the swordfish from the marinade and pat dry. Lightly salt both sides of each fish steak just before broiling.

4. Arrange the pieces of fish about ½ inch apart on a rack fitted over a broiling pan or a ridged disposable broiling pan. Broil 1½ to 2 inches from the heat until the surface becomes opaque, 1 to 1½ minutes. Paint with glaze and continue to broil the fish on the same side, brushing twice more with glaze, for 1½ to 2 minutes. Using a spatula, flip the fish and broil, brushing twice with glaze, for about 2½ minutes longer, until just opaque throughout.

5. Drizzle each swordfish steak with any remaining glaze and serve hot.

NOTE: To make ginger juice, grate a 3-inch piece of fresh ginger, collect the gratings on a plate and squeeze with your fingers to extract the juice.

—*Elizabeth Andoh*

FISH & SHELLFISH

GULF CRAB CAKES WITH LEMON BUTTER

🍷 F&W BEVERAGE SUGGESTION
California Chardonnay, such as
Iron Horse

*6 FIRST-COURSE OR
3 MAIN-COURSE SERVINGS*

9 tablespoons unsalted butter
3 eggs
*1 pound fresh lump crabmeat, picked
over to remove any cartilage*
*3¼ cups (lightly packed) fresh bread
crumbs, made from day-old French
bread, crusts removed*
1 small shallot, minced
*¼ cup plus 1 tablespoon chopped
parsley*
*2 tablespoons plus 1 teaspoon fresh
lemon juice*
Pinch of freshly grated nutmeg
Pinch of cayenne pepper
¾ teaspoon salt
*¼ teaspoon freshly ground black
pepper*
1 tablespoon peanut oil
¼ cup dry white wine
*Lemon wedges and parsley sprigs, for
garnish*

1. Melt 4 tablespoons of the butter.
Set aside and let cool to tepid.

2. In a large bowl, lightly beat 1 of
the eggs with 1 tablespoon of water.
Add the crabmeat, 1¾ cups of the
bread crumbs, the melted butter, the
shallot, ¼ cup of the parsley, 2 tablespoons of the lemon juice, the nutmeg, cayenne, ½ teaspoon of the salt
and the black pepper. Stir well to
combine. Shape the mixture into 6

patties, about ½ inch thick.

3. Place the remaining 1½ cups
bread crumbs in a shallow bowl. In
another shallow bowl, lightly beat the
remaining 2 eggs with 2 tablespoons
of water. Dip each crab cake first in
the eggs, then in the bread crumbs,
pressing lightly so the crumbs adhere.
Shake off the excess. Set the cakes on
a rack. **(The crab cakes can be prepared to this point 2 hours ahead and
refrigerated.)**

4. In a large noncorrodible skillet,
preferably nonstick, melt 1 tablespoon
of the remaining butter in the oil over
moderately high heat until foaming.
Add the crab cakes, reduce the heat to
moderate and cook until a golden
crust forms on the bottom, about 3
minutes. Turn and cook the other side
until lightly browned, about 3 minutes. Remove and set aside.

5. Pour off any fat from the skillet.
Add the white wine and the remaining 1 teaspoon lemon juice and bring
to a boil over moderately high heat.
Boil until reduced by half, about 2
minutes. Off the heat, whisk in the
remaining 4 tablespoons butter, 1 tablespoon at a time. Stir in the remaining 1 tablespoon parsley and season
with the remaining ¼ teaspoon salt
and a pinch of black pepper. Garnish
each crab cake with a lemon wedge
and a sprig of parsley. Serve the sauce
on the side.

—*Frank Stitt, Highlands:
A Bar & Grill, Birmingham, Alabama*

CRAB AND OYSTER GUMBO

Colorful and highly seasoned, this
festive gumbo will spark any large
dinner party. Serve in shallow soup
bowls over steamed white rice.

Menu suggestion: To start, Cajun
martinis and Artichoke Fritters with
Remoulade Sauce (p. 15); with the
gumbo, steamed white rice; for dessert, Flambéed Maple-Rum Bananas
(p. 215) and Café Brûlot.

🍷 F&W BEVERAGE SUGGESTION
California dry Chenin Blanc, such
as Chappellet, or cold lager beer.

10 TO 12 SERVINGS

¼ cup vegetable oil
*½ pound chorizo, cut into ¼-inch
rounds*
*½ pound smoked ham, cut into
½-inch dice*
1 large onion, chopped
3 garlic cloves, minced
1 large green bell pepper, chopped
1 large red bell pepper, chopped
2 celery ribs, chopped
*1 can (14 ounces) Italian peeled
tomatoes with their juice*
6 cups fish stock or chicken broth
3 imported bay leaves
1 teaspoon paprika, preferably hot
½ teaspoon thyme
½ teaspoon oregano
¼ teaspoon cayenne pepper
1 teaspoon salt
*¼ teaspoon freshly ground black
pepper*
*¼ pound okra, cut into ½-inch
rounds*
*½ cup thinly sliced scallions
(about 4)*
*4 dozen oysters, shucked, with 1 cup
of the liquor strained and reserved*

FISH & SHELLFISH

2 tablespoons filé powder* (optional)
1 pound lump crabmeat, picked over
* to remove any cartilage*
*Available at specialty food shops

1. In a large flameproof casserole, heat the oil over moderately high heat. Add the chorizo and smoked ham and sauté until lightly browned, about 8 minutes. Using a slotted spoon, lift out the meat and set aside.

2. Add the onion and garlic to the fat in the pan and cook, stirring frequently, until the vegetables are softened, about 5 minutes. Add the green and red bell peppers and the celery and cook until they begin to soften, about 5 minutes.

3. Add the tomatoes, with their juice, breaking them up with a wooden spoon. Stir in the fish stock, bay leaves, paprika, thyme, oregano, cayenne, salt and black pepper. Add the reserved chorizo and ham. Bring the mixture to a simmer and cook, stirring occasionally, for about 45 minutes, skimming excess fat from the top. **(The gumbo can be made ahead to this point and held at room temperature for several hours or refrigerated overnight.** Return to a simmer before proceeding.)

4. Add the okra and scallions and cook for 10 minutes. Stir in the reserved oyster liquor and the filé powder. Add the crab and oysters and simmer until the edges of the oysters curl, about 5 minutes. Serve at once.

—*John Robert Massie*

CRABMEAT RAVIOLI WITH CREAM SAUCE (AGNOLOTTI ALLA FRACCARO)

Using precut, fresh wonton skins simplifies the ravioli-making process.

9 FIRST-COURSE OR 4 MAIN-COURSE SERVINGS
RAVIOLI:
1½ tablespoons unsalted butter
½ tablespoon all-purpose flour
¼ cup milk
1 egg, separated
2 scallions, chopped
½ pound lump crabmeat, picked over
* to remove any cartilage*
1 tablespoon chopped parsley
2 tablespoons unsalted cracker
* crumbs*
½ teaspoon salt
⅛ teaspoon freshly ground white
* pepper*
Pinch of cayenne pepper
1½ packages (¾ pound each) fresh or
* defrosted frozen wonton skins**

CREAM SAUCE:
2 cups heavy cream
1 stick (4 ounces) unsalted butter
½ teaspoon salt
⅛ teaspoon freshly ground white
* pepper*
Pinch of cayenne pepper
4 scallions, thinly sliced
Freshly grated Parmesan cheese
*Available at Oriental markets

1. *Make the ravioli:* In a small saucepan, melt ½ tablespoon of the butter over low heat. Add the flour and cook, whisking constantly, for 1 minute without letting the flour brown. Gradually add the milk, and bring to a boil, whisking constantly. Cook the sauce for 3 minutes, whisking from time to time. Remove from the heat

and stir in the egg yolk. Set aside.

2. In a small skillet, melt the remaining 1 tablespoon butter. Add the scallions and cook over low heat until wilted, about 5 minutes. Scrape the scallions into a medium bowl and add the crabmeat, egg white, parsley, cracker crumbs, reserved sauce, salt, white pepper and cayenne.

3. Mound 2 teaspoons of the filling in the center of a wonton skin. Paint the edges with water, top with another wonton skin and press the edges together to seal. Repeat with the remaining wonton skins and filling. Cut the edges of each ravioli with a jagged-edged pastry wheel. Set the filled ravioli on a wire rack or lightly floured surface and let stand for 30 minutes, turning once.

4. *Meanwhile, make the sauce:* In a medium saucepan, bring the cream to a boil. Cook over moderate heat until reduced by one-third, 7 to 10 minutes. Remove from the heat and whisk in the butter, 1 tablespoon at a time. Season with the salt, pepper and cayenne and stir in the scallions.

5. Bring 2 large pots of salted water to a boil. Add half the ravioli to each and cook until tender, but still firm to the bite, about 8 minutes. Transfer the ravioli to a colander to drain.

6. Reheat the sauce and pour it into a large serving bowl. Add the ravioli and toss to coat. Pass the Parmesan cheese separately.

—*Goffredo Fraccaro, La Riviera, Metairie, Louisiana*

LOBSTER CHOWDER AMERICAINE WITH FLOUNDER MOUSSE

F&W BEVERAGE SUGGESTION
Acacia "Winery Lake" Chardonnay

8 SERVINGS
8 lobsters, 1½ pounds each
1 stick (4 ounces) unsalted butter
½ cup olive oil
8 medium shallots, minced
4 medium garlic cloves, minced
1 teaspoon tarragon
1 teaspoon thyme
2 cups dry white wine
2 cups Cognac or brandy
1 cup chicken stock or canned broth
*1 can (35 ounces) Italian plum
   tomatoes, drained and minced*
Salt and freshly ground pepper
Flounder Mousse (recipe follows)

1. In each of 2 large pots, bring 1 quart of water to a boil over high heat. Add 4 lobsters to each pot, cover and steam for 20 minutes. Remove the lobsters and let cool. Combine the broths in 1 pot and set aside.

2. As soon as the lobsters are cool enough to handle, remove the meat from the tails and claws. Cut into bite-size pieces and place in a bowl. Cover tightly and refrigerate. Reserve the shells for the broth in Step 4.

3. Remove any coral from the tails and place in a food processor or blender. Scoop out the tomalley and add to the coral. Add the butter and puree until smooth. Scrape into a small bowl, cover and refrigerate.

4. Return the lobster shells to the broth in the pot. Add 4 cups of cold water, bring to a boil and simmer for 2 hours. Strain the broth and let cool slightly.

5. In a large heavy saucepan, heat the oil. Add the shallots and garlic and cook over low heat until softened but not browned, about 5 minutes. Add the tarragon, thyme, wine, Cognac, chicken stock, tomatoes and 10 cups of the reserved lobster broth and simmer for 2 hours. Season with salt and pepper to taste. (**The chowder can be prepared to this point up to 1 day ahead.** Let cool, then cover and refrigerate.)

6. About 10 minutes before serving, bring the soup to a simmer. Whisk in the reserved coral-tomalley butter and add the reserved lobster meat. Cut the flounder mousse into 16 thin slices. Carefully ladle the chowder into warmed soup plates and garnish each serving with 2 slices of flounder mousse.

—*Molly O'Neill*

FLOUNDER MOUSSE

*½ pound flounder fillets, cut into
   1-inch cubes*
½ egg white (see Note)
1 teaspoon salt
Dash of hot pepper sauce
¼ cup heavy cream, chilled

1. In a food processor or blender, combine the flounder with the egg white; puree until smooth. Add the salt and hot pepper sauce and puree until blended. Scrape the fish mixture into a large bowl.

2. Beat the heavy cream until soft peaks form. Fold the cream into the flounder puree.

3. Cut out a 10-inch square of aluminum foil and butter lightly. Spoon the flounder mixture into the center, fold the foil over and roll into a sausage shape, leaving a 1-inch foil border at each end. Tightly seal the ends.

4. In a large shallow saucepan or flameproof casserole, bring 4 inches of water to a boil over high heat. Reduce to a simmer and gently slide the foil-wrapped mousse roll into the water. Cover with a heatproof plate to keep submerged and simmer for 5 minutes.

5. Remove the pan from the heat and set aside for 10 minutes. Then remove the roll and carefully unwrap the mousse. (**The mousse can be prepared up to 1 day ahead.** Let cool completely, then cover tightly with plastic wrap and refrigerate. Let the mousse return to room temperature before serving.)

NOTE: For ½ egg white, lightly beat 1 egg white and measure out half (about 1 tablespoon).

—*Molly O'Neill*

THE PERFECT LOBSTER— GRILLED AND STEAMED

There are two schools of thought on the best way to cook lobster. Steaming and boiling, the most commonly used methods, yield moist, sweet results. Grilling—often confused with broiling—is praised by many for its unequaled flavor, but is sometimes criticized for dryness. When this happens, it is the result of overcooking, and it is usually the claws and legs that are most noticeably dry. I have devised a technique that delivers the best of both cooking styles: a body of unequaled flavor and limbs that are sweet and moist.

I serve a half a lobster per person, and therefore choose 3- to 4-pound lobsters. The large halves are the easiest size to fit on the grill and can take the length of time needed to absorb a delicate smoky taste without drying out. Call and reserve lobsters this size a day in advance because they are less common than smaller ones. Ask the fish market to split them in half shortly before you pick them up. Have the stomach and intestine removed and the legs and claws twisted from the body and placed in a separate bag. The claws should also be cracked. This is easily done with a sharp blow of a knife before cooking; *after* cooking, the shells harden and you need lobster crackers or nutcrackers to open them. It is best to have your lobsters prepared as close as possible to cooking time, not more than 2 to 3 hours in advance. At home, keep them well iced in the refrigerator until cooking time.

With grilled lobster, I always enjoy corn on the cob. We often start with a chilled fresh pea or watercress soup. Either a crisp Muscadet or fuller-bodied Meursault would go nicely, and a summer fruit tart provides a perfect ending.

6 SERVINGS

3 lobsters (3 to 4 pounds each), split in half, legs and claws removed and reserved
1 stick (4 ounces) unsalted butter
2 tablespoons chopped fresh herbs— tarragon, chives or basil
2 lemons, cut into wedges
2 sticks (8 ounces) unsalted butter, melted, for dipping (optional)

1. To prepare the lobsters for grilling, place them flesh-side up on a large tray or baking sheet. Cut off the antennae if they are unwieldy. A fe-

male will contain roe, or eggs, that are dark green when raw; aficionados consider them a treat. Melt 1 stick of the butter and add the fresh herbs. Using a pastry or basting brush, brush the herb butter over the lobster meat.

2. Have ready a large pot containing 1 to 2 inches of boiling water. Be sure the coals are very hot. If you do not have a cover for the grill, make one with aluminum foil. Place the lobsters on the grill, shell-side down, cover and grill for 10 to 15 minutes. During the same time, put the legs and claws into the boiling water, cover and steam. When the bodies are done, the juices in the shell will be sizzling, the meat will be opaque and firm to the touch and the roe (if the lobster is female) will be bright red.

3. Lift or slide the grilled lobsters onto individual serving plates. Bring the legs and claws to the table in a large bowl; let your guests know that they each get one claw and several legs. Put out lemon wedges and melted—not clarified—butter for those who like to dip. A large bowl in which to discard the empty shells is always appreciated.

—*Richard Grausman*

MUSSELS AND RICE WITH TWO CHILES, TOMATOES AND GARLIC

Subtly complex, with a hot chile nip, the tender grains in this dish will be separate and light from their initial sauté in oil.

When you buy mussels, ask for the cultivated ones. They are slightly more expensive than the wild variety, but there's less waste, they require little cleaning and are more consistent in quality.

4 TO 6 SERVINGS

4 pounds mussels, scrubbed and debearded
¼ cup olive oil
2 medium-large dried New Mexico or ancho chiles—stemmed, seeded and torn into large pieces
¾ cup boiling water
1½ tablespoons coarsely sliced garlic
2 medium tomatoes—peeled, cored and seeded
2 cups medium-grain white rice
1 teaspoon salt
¼ cup coarsely chopped parsley
½ cup coarsely chopped fresh coriander
¼ cup minced medium-hot fresh green chile (1 large), such as Anaheim or New Mexico

1. In a large saucepan, combine three-quarters of the mussels with 1 cup of water. Cover and cook over high heat, shaking the pot now and then, until the mussels just open, 3 to 4 minutes; do not overcook. Discard any mussels that do not open. Strain the cooking liquid and reserve. Set the mussels aside.

2. In a large, heavy casserole, heat the oil. Add the dried chiles and sauté over moderately high heat until fragrant, about 1 minute; do not allow to burn. With a slotted spoon transfer the chile pieces to a food processor or blender. Pour the boiling water over the chiles and cover.

3. In the same casserole, over moderate heat, gently sauté the garlic in the oil until golden. With a slotted spoon, add the garlic to the chiles. Add the tomatoes and puree.

4. Add the rice to the oil that remains in the casserole. Sauté the rice over moderately high heat until almost opaque.

5. Combine the tomato and chile puree with the reserved mussel broth and the salt to make 3¼ cups of liquid, adding water if necessary. Pour the liquid over the rice and bring to a full boil over high heat, stirring. Reduce the heat to very low, cover and cook for 15 minutes. Remove the rice from the heat and let rest, covered, for 5 minutes.

6. Meanwhile, shell the cooked mussels and place the meat in a small saucepan. When the rice has finished cooking but has not yet "rested," place the uncooked mussels in a wide saucepan. Add 2 tablespoons of water, cover and cook over moderate heat until the mussels open, 3 to 4 minutes. Leave the mussels in their shells.

7. Strain the broth into the small saucepan of shelled mussels. Bring to a bare simmer over moderate heat. Fluff the cooked rice. Fold in the mussel meats and three quarters of the parsley, coriander and minced green chile. Mound the rice on a serving platter or in a large bowl and set the mussels in their shells on top. Sprinkle with the remaining parsley, coriander and chile. Serve at once.

—Elizabeth Schneider

BAKED OYSTERS OR CLAMS WITH FLAVORED BUTTERS

▮ F&W BEVERAGE SUGGESTION
Muscadet, such as Jean Savion

MAKES 2 DOZEN
24 oysters or cherrystone or littleneck clams, on the half shell
4 tablespoons Red Pepper and Herb Butter (p. 231) or Tarragon-Pernod Butter (p. 231)

1. Cover a large ovenproof platter or baking sheet with rock salt and place it in the oven. Preheat the oven to 500°, about 30 minutes.

2. Set the shellfish on top of the hot rock salt. Top each clam or oyster with ½ teaspoon of flavored butter and bake for 3 to 5 minutes, or until the shellfish is warm or hot, to your taste. Serve immediately.

—Anne Disrude

MANDICH BORDELAISE OYSTERS

Having grown up in Louisiana, I'm very partial to seafood—especially fried oysters. This is a fairly simple recipe, but I consider it an indulgence, because after frying the oysters, you usually have to repaint the kitchen. . . . I solve the whole problem by going down to New Orleans a couple of times a year and having Oysters Bordelaise at Restaurant Mandich.

▮ F&W BEVERAGE SUGGESTION
California Fumé Blanc, such as Robert Mondavi

4 MAIN-COURSE OR 8 FIRST-COURSE SERVINGS
¼ cup extra-virgin olive oil
¾ cup safflower oil
3 tablespoons minced garlic
1 tablespoon minced scallion
¾ teaspoon salt
⅛ teaspoon freshly ground pepper
1 tablespoon dry sherry
1 quart vegetable oil, for deep-frying
2 eggs
1 cup all-purpose flour
1 tablespoon paprika
4 dozen medium oysters, shucked, with the deeper half of the shell reserved
2 tablespoons chopped parsley
Lemon wedges, for garnish

1. In a small heavy saucepan, combine the olive oil, safflower oil, garlic, scallion, salt and pepper. Over moderate heat, simmer gently for about 30 minutes, or until the garlic is tender. Remove from the heat and stir in the sherry. Set aside.

2. Meanwhile, in a deep-fryer or large deep saucepan, preheat 1 quart of vegetable oil to 400°.

3. In a small bowl, lightly beat the 2 eggs. In a shallow dish, combine the flour and paprika. Dip the oysters into the beaten eggs; then dredge them in the flour mixture, shaking off any excess. Working in batches, deep-fry the oysters until crisp, 15 to 20 seconds.

4. Place a fried oyster in each half shell. Spoon about 1 teaspoon of the reserved oil with the garlic and scallions over each. Sprinkle the parsley on top. Garnish with lemon wedges.

—Lee Bailey

SCALLOP AND SHRIMP SAUTE WITH PEARS AND TARRAGON

🍷 **F&W BEVERAGE SUGGESTION**
California Chenin Blanc, such as
Robert Mondavi

2 TO 3 SERVINGS
½ pound medium shrimp, shelled and deveined
Flour, for dredging
1 tablespoon unsalted butter
1 tablespoon vegetable oil
½ pound sea scallops, quartered
¼ cup dry vermouth
2 tablespoons fresh lemon juice
2 small Bosc or Bartlett pears—peeled, cored and cut into ½-inch dice
½ cup heavy cream
1 tablespoon chopped fresh tarragon or 1 teaspoon dried
¼ teaspoon salt
Pinch of freshly ground white pepper
2 to 3 tarragon or parsley sprigs

1. Dust the shrimp lightly with flour. Shake off any excess. In a large skillet, melt ½ tablespoon of the butter in ½ tablespoon of the oil over high heat until shimmering. Add the shrimp and sauté, tossing, for 3 minutes. Transfer the shrimp to a bowl.

2. Dust the scallops lightly with flour and shake off the excess. Add the remaining ½ tablespoon butter and ½ tablespoon oil to the skillet and heat until shimmering. Add the scallops and sauté until lightly browned, about 1 minute. Add the scallops to the shrimp.

3. Pour any excess fat out of the skillet and set over high heat. Stir in the vermouth and lemon juice and bring to a boil, scraping up any browned bits from the bottom of the pan. Add the diced pears and cream and return to a boil. Reduce the heat

and simmer until thickened slightly, about 4 minutes.

4. Return the shrimp and scallops to the skillet. Add the chopped tarragon, salt and pepper. Cook over moderate heat until warmed through, about 1 minute. Garnish with sprigs of tarragon or parsley.

—*The Gazelle Restaurant, North Quincy, Massachusetts*

PAPILLOTE OF SCALLOPS WITH SPINACH, CARROTS AND LEEKS

4 SERVINGS
4 tablespoons clarified butter
4 large spinach leaves, tough stems removed
16 sea scallops, tough membranes removed
1 small leek (white and tender green), cut into very thin 2-inch julienne strips
1 small carrot, cut into very thin 2-inch julienne strips
1 plum tomato—peeled, seeded and cut into ¼-inch dice
4 tablespoons dry white wine
½ teaspoon salt
¼ teaspoon freshly ground pepper

1. Preheat the oven to 400°. Fold four 15-by-20-inch sheets of butcher's paper, parchment or aluminum foil in half crosswise to make 15-by-10-inch rectangles. Using scissors, cut each rectangle into a heart shape with the fold running vertically down the center. Open the hearts and brush each with ½ tablespoon of the butter.

2. Put a spinach leaf in the center of half of each sheet. Arrange 4 scallops in a single layer on top of the spinach. Scatter the julienned leek and carrot over and around the scallops. Sprinkle the diced tomato on top.

3. Drizzle ½ tablespoon of the butter over each. Sprinkle each with 1 tablespoon of the wine and season with the salt and pepper.

4. Fold the paper over the scallops and beginning at the top of the hearts, make a series of tight overlapping folds to seal the papillotes.

5. Place side by side on 2 cookie sheets and bake for 8 minutes; the papillotes will be puffed and lightly browned. Serve at once.

—*John Robert Massie*

GRILLED MARINATED SHRIMP (EBI NO KUSHIYAKI)

4 FIRST-COURSE OR 2 MAIN-COURSE SERVINGS
12 large shrimp in their shells
1 tablespoon sake
1 tablespoon soy sauce
1 tablespoon mirin (sweet rice wine)* or ½ tablespoon corn syrup
1 teaspoon grated fresh ginger
1 teaspoon minced scallion
2 to 3 drops Oriental sesame oil, preferably dark, or hot chili oil (rayu)*
*Available at Oriental markets

1. Rinse the shrimp in cold water and pat dry. If you want to remove the thicker part of the vein, carefully grasp it at the open end of the shrimp and straighten the curve in the shrimp's back as you gently pull.

2. In a medium bowl, combine the

sake, soy sauce, *mirin*, ginger, scallion and sesame oil. Add the shrimp and marinate at room temperature for at least 1 hour or in the refrigerator for up to 12 hours.

3. Lightly oil 8 to 10 metal skewers. Thread the shrimp onto pairs of skewers, securing them well by bending into a C shape. Alternating the direction of the shrimp, head to tail, will help them to brown more evenly.

4. Preheat the broiler. Rest the tips of the skewers on the edges of a foil broiling pan so that the shrimp will be suspended about 1½ inches from the heat. Broil, basting once with marinade, for 3 minutes. Turn the shrimp and broil, basting once more, for 2½ minutes or until they are just opaque throughout.

5. Remove the shrimp from the skewers and serve hot in their shells or let the shrimp cool slightly and remove the shells before serving.

—*Elizabeth Andoh*

UPPERLINE'S BARBECUED SHRIMP

Serve these spicy shrimp with plenty of warm French bread to sop up the fiery sauce. At the restaurant these shrimp are served with their heads on. If using shrimp with heads, simply remove the feelers before cooking.

2 SERVINGS
4 tablespoons clarified butter
1 pound large shrimp in their shells
2 tablespoons coarsely ground pepper
1 teaspoon salt

1 tablespoon Worcestershire sauce
½ cup lager beer

1. In a large skillet, warm the butter over moderately high heat until shimmering. Add the shrimp and sauté for 1 minute on each side. Add the pepper, salt and Worcestershire sauce and cook, tossing, for 1 minute.

2. Stir in the beer. Bring to a boil and cook for 2 minutes longer. Pour the shrimp and their sauce into two shallow soup plates and serve hot.

—*Jason Clevinger, Upperline,
New Orleans, Louisiana*

SHRIMP BAKED IN BLACK BEAN SAUCE

The sauce used in this dish is extremely versatile. Served hot, it makes a flavorful accompaniment for roasted clams, oysters and shrimp. Or spoon it on raw clams or oysters just before baking. Try it cold, as a dip for boiled shrimp or a topping for clams or oysters served on the half shell.

MAKES ABOUT 38
2 tablespoons Chinese salted black beans*—rinsed, drained and coarsely chopped
2 tablespoons dry sherry
1 tablespoon Chinese black tea leaves*
8 garlic cloves, minced
6 scallions, minced (about ½ cup)
2-inch piece of fresh ginger, peeled and minced
¼ teaspoon crushed hot pepper
2 tablespoons soy sauce
1 teaspoon Oriental sesame oil
1 teaspoon red wine vinegar or sherry wine vinegar
1 teaspoon sugar
1 tablespoon cornstarch
2 tablespoons vegetable oil

3 pounds large shrimp—shelled and deveined, with tails and last section of shell left on
¼ cup very thinly julienned or finely diced cucumber
*Available at Oriental markets

1. Soak the black beans in the sherry for at least 15 minutes.

2. Meanwhile, cover the tea with 1½ cups boiling water and let steep for 5 minutes. Strain the tea and measure out 1 cup for the sauce.

3. In a small bowl, combine the garlic, scallions, ginger and hot pepper.

4. In another small bowl, combine the soy sauce, sesame oil and vinegar. Add the sugar and cornstarch and whisk until dissolved.

5. Preheat the oven to 500°, about 30 minutes. In a heavy medium saucepan, heat the vegetable oil until shimmering. Add the garlic and ginger mixture and cook over moderately high heat, stirring, until softened, about 2 minutes. Add the black beans and sherry and cook for 30 seconds longer. Stir in the brewed tea, reduce the heat and simmer for 5 minutes.

6. Increase the heat to high. Stir the cornstarch mixture and add it to the sauce. Bring to a boil, stirring, and cook until the sauce is shiny and slightly thickened, about 1 minute.

7. Spread about ½ cup of the black bean sauce over the bottom of a large ovenproof serving dish. Place the shrimp in the dish, vein-sides down and with the tails in the air. Top the flat surface of each one with 1 teaspoon of the sauce. Bake in the preheated oven for 5 to 7 minutes, or until the shrimp are just opaque throughout. You may top with additional sauce. Garnish the shrimp with the cucumber and serve immediately.

—*Anne Disrude*

A fennel-flavored Stuffed Breast of Veal with Mushroom Gravy (p. 94).

Left to right: Spicy Greek Lamb Stew (p. 115) and Swedish Limpa Bread (p. 159).

Orange-Spiced Duck (p. 89).

Thyme-Roasted Chicken with Onions and Potatoes (p. 80).

Left, The Perfect Lobster—Grilled and Steamed (p. 65).
Above, top to bottom: Stir-Fried Scallop and Sweet Pepper
Salad (p. 143) and Barbecued Salmon Steaks (p. 56).

RED PRAWN CURRY

I first tasted this curry in one of the little open-air seafood restaurants that line the beach at Bangsaen on the northern coast of the Gulf of Thailand. Maybe it was the sea air, or the ambience, but I have seldom tasted a more deliciously sauced shrimp dish.

Buy the freshest, largest shrimp you can obtain, between 12 and 15 count per pound if you can find them. The citrus leaves must, unfortunately, be an optional ingredient, as few of us have access to orange, lemon or lime trees. For a different but interesting result, scatter a few fresh mint or basil leaves in the curry instead.

6 TO 8 SERVINGS
3 cups Thick Coconut Milk (p. 232)
3½ tablespoons Red Curry Paste (p. 237)
2 tablespoons fish sauce (nam pla, nuoc mam or patis)*
3 dried hot red peppers, seeded and cut into fine slivers
2 pounds large shrimp—shelled and deveined, with tails left on
4 citrus leaves, torn in half, or 6 fresh mint or basil leaves
¼ cup fresh coriander leaves
2 limes, quartered
*Available at Southeast Asian and some Chinese markets

1. Set a wok over moderately high heat and add the coconut milk. As the milk begins to get hot, blend in the curry paste. Add the fish sauce and chiles. Stirring constantly, bring the mixture to a slow boil. Reduce the heat to low and gently simmer the sauce for 5 minutes.

2. Add the shrimp and citrus leaves and cook, stirring, until the shrimp are just cooked through (they will be loosely curled and opaque throughout), 2 to 3 minutes.

3. Transfer the curry to a large serving bowl and sprinkle with the fresh coriander leaves. Serve with the lime quarters.

—Jennifer Brennan

STEAMED SHRIMP AND VEGETABLES WITH TAPENADE SAUCE

This recipe is easily adapted to serve a crowd. Be sure to allow for more cooking time and a greater quantity of Tapenade Sauce.

F&W BEVERAGE SUGGESTION
Chilled light white wine, such as Corvo

2 SERVINGS
12 large shrimp in their shells, legs removed
1 small bunch of broccoli, broken into 1-inch florets
4 medium red potatoes, peeled and sliced into ⅛-inch rounds
Tapenade Sauce (p. 229)

Arrange the shrimp, broccoli and potato slices in a single layer in a large steamer, (a bamboo steamer makes an attractive presentation at table). Steam for 10 minutes, or until the shrimp are opaque and the vegetables tender. Serve hot, warm or cold with tapenade sauce on the side.

—Anne Disrude

BAKED SHRIMP WITH SEASONED BREAD CRUMBS

As these shrimp bake, the bread crumbs are infused with melted butter and crisped by the heat of the oven.

MAKES ABOUT 2½ DOZEN
2 pounds large shrimp—shelled and deveined, with tails and last section of shell left on
¾ cup fresh bread crumbs
About 5½ tablespoons Red Pepper and Herb Butter (p. 231) or Tarragon-Pernod Butter (p. 231)

Preheat the oven to 500°. In a large, buttered ovenproof serving dish, arrange the shrimp vein-sides down with their tails in the air. Top the flat surface of each shrimp with about 1 teaspoon of the bread crumbs and ½ teaspoon of a flavored butter. Bake for about 5 minutes, or until the shrimp are just opaque throughout.

—Anne Disrude

SAGE CRUMB TOPPING FOR SHELLFISH

Sprinkle these crisp, tasty crumbs over roasted oysters or clams just before you pop them in your mouth. This makes enough for about 3 dozen.

MAKES ABOUT ¾ CUP
3 tablespoons extra-virgin olive oil
¾ cup fresh bread crumbs

Marinated Sirloin with Sherry Vinaigrette (p. 100) and Hearts of Palm, Beet and Endive Salad (p. 135).

FISH & SHELLFISH

¼ teaspoon salt
1 tablespoon minced fresh sage leaves
or 1½ teaspoons dried, crumbled

In a small saucepan, heat the oil until it begins to shimmer. Add the bread crumbs and toss to coat well with oil. Sprinkle with the salt and cook over moderate heat, stirring frequently, until the crumbs are lightly browned and crisp, about 5 minutes. Stir in the sage and transfer the crumbs to a small serving bowl.

—Anne Disrude

SHRIMP AND WATER CHESTNUTS IN LIGHT CREAM SAUCE

Succulent pink shrimp and crisp, sweet water chestnuts are briefly simmered in a light cream-enriched stock. The dusting of spices acts to highlight the natural flavors.

3 SERVINGS
1 pound small shrimp in their shells
¼ teaspoon salt
¼ teaspoon freshly ground white pepper
⅛ teaspoon ground cardamom
⅛ teaspoon freshly grated nutmeg
¾ cup chicken stock or canned broth
½ pound fresh water chestnuts—scrubbed, peeled and cut into ¼-inch slices
¼ cup heavy cream
2 scallions
1 tablespoon unsalted butter
1 teaspoon sherry, preferably medium-dry
1 teaspoon cornstarch

1. Peel the shrimp; place the shells in a medium saucepan. Toss the shrimp in a bowl with the salt and white pepper, cardamom and nutmeg; set aside.

2. Add the stock to the shells and boil for 5 minutes. Strain, reserving the stock; discard the shells. Add the water chestnuts to the stock and simmer for 5 minutes. Remove the water chestnuts with a slotted spoon and set aside.

3. Add the cream to the stock and boil until reduced to ½ cup, about 1 minute. Mince enough of the white part of the scallions to measure 2 tablespoons. Mince enough of the scallion greens to measure 1 tablespoon.

4. In a medium skillet, heat the butter over moderate heat. Add the minced scallion whites and cook, stirring, until softened, about 1 minute. Add the shrimp and water chestnuts and toss to combine. Add the cream-stock mixture, reduce the heat and simmer, stirring, until the shrimp turn opaque, about 5 minutes.

5. In a small bowl, stir the sherry into the cornstarch. Add to the shrimp and stir over moderate heat until the sauce boils and thickens. Season with salt and pepper to taste. Spoon into a warmed serving dish and sprinkle with the minced scallion greens and serve hot.

—Elizabeth Schneider

FROG'S LEGS IN RIESLING WITH FRESH HERBS

4 SERVINGS
1 stick (4 ounces) unsalted butter
2 shallots, minced
1 garlic clove, minced
40 pairs of frog's legs
1 cup Alsatian Riesling
1 cup chicken stock, preferably homemade
½ teaspoon salt
¼ teaspoon freshly ground pepper
½ cup crème fraîche or heavy cream
1 tablespoon fresh lemon juice
1 tablespoon chopped parsley
1 tablespoon minced fresh chives

1. In a large flameproof casserole, melt 3 tablespoons of the butter over moderate heat. Add the shallots and garlic and cook, stirring frequently, until tender, about 5 minutes.

2. Add the frog's legs, Riesling, stock, salt and pepper. Increase the heat to moderately high and cook, stirring occasionally, until the frog's legs are tender, about 10 minutes. Transfer the frog's legs to a platter.

3. Bring the liquid in the casserole to a boil over high heat. Stir in the crème fraîche and cook until the liquid reduces to 1½ cups, about 10 minutes. Reduce the heat to moderate. Cut the remaining 5 tablespoons butter into small pieces and whisk into the sauce, a few pieces at a time. Stir in the lemon juice and more salt and pepper to taste.

4. Return the frog's legs to the casserole; toss gently until heated through. Add the parsley and chives and toss.

—l'Auberge de l'Ill, Illhaeusern, France

POULTRY

THYME-ROASTED CHICKEN WITH ONIONS AND POTATOES

Menu suggestion: To start, Charred Carrot Soup (p. 38); with the chicken, buttered green beans; for dessert, Strawberry-Peach Cobbler (p. 170).
🍴 F&W BEVERAGE SUGGESTION
California Chardonnay, such as Simi, or Beaujolais Nouveau

4 TO 6 SERVINGS
1 stick (4 ounces) unsalted butter, softened
1 large onion, coarsely chopped
1 teaspoon salt
½ teaspoon freshly ground pepper
1 tablespoon fresh thyme leaves or 1 teaspoon dried
1 whole chicken (3½ pounds)
6 medium all-purpose potatoes, scrubbed and quartered

1. In a large ovenproof skillet, preferably cast iron, melt 1 tablespoon of the butter over moderately high heat. Add the onion, ¼ teaspoon of the salt and a pinch each of the pepper and thyme. Cook, tossing frequently, until the onion is lightly browned, about 10 minutes. Remove from the skillet and let cool to room temperature.
2. In a small bowl, combine the remaining 7 tablespoons butter, ¼ teaspoon of the salt, a pinch of pepper and the remaining thyme; blend well.
3. Preheat the oven to 400°. Using your fingers, gently loosen the breast, thigh and leg skin of the chicken. Rub 4 tablespoons of the thyme butter under the skin.
4. Stuff the cavity with the browned onion and truss the chicken. Rub the skin with 1 tablespoon of the thyme butter. Place the chicken in the skillet.
5. Toss the potatoes with the re-maining 3 tablespoons thyme butter and arrange around the chicken. Set the skillet, uncovered, in the oven and bake for 1 hour and 15 minutes, or until the juices run clear when the thigh of the chicken is pierced.
—*John Robert Massie*

APRICOT- AND SHIITAKE-STUFFED CHICKEN WITH TURNIPS

This dish can also be made with two large chicken breasts instead of a whole chicken. Preheat the oven to 375° and cook the chicken and vegetables together for 50 minutes.
🍴 F&W BEVERAGE SUGGESTION
Alsace Riesling, such as Trimbach

4 SERVINGS
4 tablespoons unsalted butter
1 small onion, minced, plus 2 medium onions, quartered
¼ pound prosciutto, coarsely chopped
½ cup dried apricots
¼ pound fresh shiitake (Golden Oak) mushrooms (or 1 ounce dried, reconstituted), stemmed and minced
⅔ cup fresh bread crumbs
¼ teaspoon salt
1 whole chicken (3 to 3½ pounds)
1 tablespoon vegetable oil
½ teaspoon freshly ground pepper
1¾ pounds turnips, peeled and cut into 1-inch cubes
4 small carrots, halved on the diagonal

1. In a small skillet, melt the butter over moderately low heat. Add the minced onion and cook until softened, 3 to 4 minutes.
2. Preheat the oven to 425°. In a food processor, combine the prosciutto and apricots. Process until finely chopped; scrape into a bowl. Add the mushrooms, the cooked onion, the bread crumbs and salt and toss to combine.
3. With your fingers, loosen the chicken breast skin and lightly pack the stuffing under the skin in an even layer. Place the chicken in a large oval gratin dish or roasting pan. Brush with the oil. Sprinkle the pepper over the chicken and bake for 20 minutes.
4. Remove the chicken from the oven and reduce the temperature to 375°. Place the turnips, quartered onions and carrots around the chicken and toss the vegetables with the fat in the pan. Return to the oven and bake until the vegetables are tender, about 50 minutes.
—*Mary Lynn Mondich*

GLAZE-GRILLED CHICKEN AND BELL PEPPER (YAKITORI)

This glaze keeps two to three weeks in the refrigerator and can be used for basting broiled chicken, veal or pork.
🍴 F&W BEVERAGE SUGGESTION
California Sauvignon Blanc, such as Silverado

6 TO 8 FIRST-COURSE OR 2 MAIN-COURSE SERVINGS
¼ cup soy sauce
3 tablespoons mirin (sweet rice wine)*
1 tablespoon sugar
1 large whole chicken breast (about 12 ounces), boned with skin intact
1 large green bell pepper, cut into 1½-by-½-inch pieces
½ teaspoon salt
⅛ teaspoon shichimi togarashi (7-blend spice powder; optional)*
*Available at Oriental markets

1. In a small saucepan, combine the soy sauce, *mirin* and sugar. Cook over low heat, stirring constantly, until the sugar dissolves. Continue to cook until the glaze is reduced to ⅓ cup, 5 to

10 minutes. Pour the glaze into a bowl and set aside to cool.

2. Cut the chicken breast into 1½-by-½-inch pieces (ideally each piece should have some skin attached).

3. Preheat the broiler. Lightly oil 6 to 8 metal skewers. Starting and ending with green pepper, thread the chicken and peppers onto parallel pairs of skewers set about 1½ inches apart. This will hold the ingredients in place and make flipping easier.

4. Rest the tips of the skewers on the edges of a disposable foil, or lined, broiling pan so that the chicken and peppers will be suspended. Sprinkle lightly with half the salt and broil as close to the heat as possible, basting twice with glaze, for 1½ to 2½ minutes. Flip the skewers and sprinkle lightly with the remaining salt. Broil, basting twice more with glaze, until the chicken is cooked through and the skin is blistered and slightly charred, about 1½ to 2½ minutes.

5. Drizzle any remaining glaze over the chicken and peppers and sprinkle with *shichimi togarashi*, if desired. Serve hot or at room temperature.

—*Elizabeth Andoh*

SAUTE OF CHICKEN BREASTS WITH GORGONZOLA AND FRESH HERBS

Menu suggestion: To start, Scallop and Sweet Pepper Salad with Avocado (p. 149); with the chicken, steamed rice; for dessert, Summer Fruit in Lime Caramel (p. 214).

❚ F&W BEVERAGE SUGGESTION
Dry Chenin Blanc, such as Chappellet

4 SERVINGS
*6 skinless, boneless chicken breast
　halves
Salt and freshly ground white pepper
Flour, for dredging
2 tablespoons unsalted butter*
*2 teaspoons peanut oil
⅓ cup plus 3 tablespoons chicken
　stock or canned broth
3 ounces Gorgonzola cheese
1 cup heavy cream
1 tablespoon softened unsalted butter
　blended to a paste with 1
　tablespoon flour (optional)
2 tablespoons minced fresh tarragon
2 tablespoons minced fresh chives*

1. Season the chicken breasts with salt and white pepper. Dredge lightly in flour; shake off the excess.

2. In a large heavy skillet, melt the butter in the oil over high heat. Add the chicken breasts and sauté, turning once, until browned on the outside (they will still be quite pink inside), 2 to 3 minutes per side.

3. Reduce the heat to moderately low. Add 3 tablespoons of the chicken stock, cover and cook for 5 minutes. With a slotted spoon, transfer the chicken to a plate.

4. Meanwhile, in a food processor, puree the Gorgonzola with ¼ cup of the cream.

5. Add the remaining ⅓ cup stock to the skillet. Cook over high heat, scraping the bottom of the pan, until the sauce reduces to a glaze, about 2 minutes. Add the remaining ¾ cup cream and cook, stirring, until reduced to ½ cup, about 5 minutes. Whisk in the Gorgonzola cream. If the sauce seems thin, bring to a boil and whisk in bits of the butter paste until the sauce lightly coats a spoon. Add the tarragon and season with salt and pepper. **(The recipe can be prepared to this point up to 2 hours ahead.)**

6. Add the chicken breasts to the sauce, cover and cook over low heat until just heated through, about 2 minutes. Transfer to a serving platter and spoon the sauce over the chicken. Sprinkle with the chives.

—*Perla Meyers*

ORANGE-CURRY GRILLED CHICKEN WITH TARRAGON

A recipe I use often, originally developed on the spur of the moment when friends dropped by at dinner time, is this Orange-Curry Grilled Chicken with Tarragon. Not needing a sauce, it benefits from the sweet pungency of a mango chutney. It goes well with wild rice and mushrooms as do most grilled birds, and I enjoy serving sweet, fresh snap peas or a salad at the same time. A summer melon and chilled Sauternes add a touch of elegance to end the simple summer meal.

❚ F&W BEVERAGE SUGGESTION
Dry Chenin Blanc, such as
Chateau Ste. Michelle

8 SERVINGS
*8 skinless, boneless chicken breast
　halves
4 teaspoons Dijon-style mustard
1 cup orange juice
4 teaspoons curry powder
4 teaspoons tarragon*

1. Trim off any fat or cartilage from the chicken and rinse under cold water. Pat dry with paper towels.

2. In a large bowl, thin the mustard with ¼ cup of the orange juice. Blend in the curry powder, tarragon and remaining orange juice. Marinate the chicken for at least 15 minutes at room temperature or refrigerate for up to 24 hours.

3. Since the chicken cooks quickly, have the rest of the meal well underway before putting the meat on the fire. Grill the chicken breasts for 5 minutes on each side over a very hot grill. If not done, baste with marinade, turn and cook 1 to 2 minutes longer on each side. The chicken should be slightly springy to the touch and juicy and moist but not pink on the inside.

—*Richard Grausman*

MIXED SKILLET GRILL

This grill can be served on a platter, but it's more appealing (and convenient) to serve it from the skillet.

🍷 **F&W BEVERAGE SUGGESTION**
Rioja, such as 1978 C.U.N.E.

2 SERVINGS

3 tablespoons olive oil
1 tablespoon Dijon-style mustard
¼ teaspoon thyme
1 large skinless, boneless chicken breast, halved and pounded to ¼ inch
2 baby eggplants, halved lengthwise, or 1 small eggplant, quartered lengthwise
Salt
4 sticks of mozzarella cheese (1½ by ½ inch)
4 large radicchio leaves
2 basil leaves, minced, or ¼ teaspoon oregano
Freshly ground pepper
2 small zucchini, halved lengthwise
1 large plum tomato, halved crosswise

1. In a small bowl, combine 2 teaspoons of the olive oil with the mustard and thyme; blend well. Brush the chicken breast halves on both sides with the mustard mixture. Cover and refrigerate for 1 to 4 hours.

2. With a sharp knife, score the eggplant halves in a diamond pattern and sprinkle with a little salt. Set aside cut-side down.

3. Place a piece of mozzarella on each radicchio leaf. Top each piece of cheese with one-fourth of the minced basil and a sprinkle of salt and pepper. Roll the cheese up in the radicchio and set aside.

4. Remove the chicken from the refrigerator. Heat a 12-inch cast-iron skillet over high heat for 5 minutes.

5. Pat the eggplant dry and paint the cut sides with 1 tablespoon of the olive oil. Place them in the skillet and cook over high heat, turning, until they are softened and well browned all over, about 10 minutes. Remove the eggplant to a platter.

6. Brush the cut sides of the zucchini with 1 teaspoon of the olive oil. Place in the skillet and cook, turning, until browned on both sides, 3 to 4 minutes. Season with salt and pepper to taste and set aside on the platter.

7. Brush the cut sides of the tomato halves with 1 teaspoon of the olive oil, place in the skillet and cook until browned on the bottom, about 1 minute. Set aside on the platter.

8. Add the chicken to the skillet and cook for 2 minutes on the first side; turn and cook 1 minute on the second side, or until browned and cooked through. Season with salt and pepper to taste. Add to the platter.

9. Brush the radicchio rolls with the 2 remaining teaspoons olive oil and place seam-side down in the skillet. Cook for 30 seconds on the first side; turn the rolls over and remove from the heat.

10. Arrange the chicken and vegetables in the skillet to keep them warm. Serve directly from the skillet.

—Anne Disrude

PEPPERED CHICKEN BREASTS WITH ROSEMARY AND GARLIC

🍷 **F&W BEVERAGE SUGGESTION**
1979 Barbaresco, such Gaja, or California Sauvignon Blanc, such as Groth

4 SERVINGS

2 tablespoons fresh lemon juice
2 tablespoons olive oil
½ teaspoon rosemary, crumbled
⅛ to ¼ teaspoon crushed hot pepper, to taste
½ to 1 teaspoon coarsely cracked black pepper, to taste
4 garlic cloves, crushed
4 skinless, boneless chicken breast halves
1 teaspoon unsalted butter
1 teaspoon vegetable oil
¼ teaspoon salt

1. In a glass dish just large enough to hold the chicken breasts, combine the lemon juice, olive oil, rosemary, hot pepper, black pepper and garlic. Add the chicken breasts and let marinate at room temperature, turning once or twice, for 1 hour.

2. Remove the chicken from the marinade and pat dry. In a large skillet, melt the butter in the oil. Add the chicken, smooth-side down, and sauté over moderate heat, turning once, for 4 to 5 minutes on each side, until lightly browned and cooked through. Season with the salt. Serve hot or warm.

—Anne Disrude

PAPILLOTE OF CHICKEN WITH KALE AND PROSCIUTTO

🍷 **F&W BEVERAGE SUGGESTION**
California dry Chenin Blanc, such as Chappellet

2 SERVINGS

3 tablespoons extra-virgin olive oil
2 cups chopped kale, turnip greens or mustard greens
Salt and freshly ground pepper
2 skinless, boneless chicken breast halves (about 5 ounces each)
1 thin slice of prosciutto, cut in half

1. Preheat the oven to 400°. Fold two 15-by-20-inch sheets of butcher's paper, parchment or aluminum foil in half crosswise to make 15-by-10-inch

rectangles. Using scissors, cut each rectangle into a heart shape with the fold running vertically down the center. Open up the hearts and brush each with ½ tablespoon of the oil.

2. Toss the kale with 1 tablespoon of olive oil. Season lightly with salt and pepper. Dividing evenly, place in the middle of one side of each heart.

3. Fold out the small fillet from each breast to even the thickness of the chicken. With a sharp knife, make 4 deep, evenly spaced cuts crosswise on the diagonal.

4. Roll up each piece of prosciutto and cut each into 4 pieces. Tuck 1 spiraled piece of prosciutto into each cut in the chicken. Place on top of the greens. Season the chicken lightly with salt and pepper. Drizzle the remaining 1 tablespoon oil on top.

5. Fold the paper over the chicken and beginning at the top of each heart, make a series of tight overlapping folds to seal the papillotes.

6. Place the papillotes on a cookie sheet and bake for 10 minutes (if the breast is larger than 5 ounces increase the time to 12 minutes). Serve hot.
—*Anne Disrude*

CHICKEN DRUMSTICK RAGOUT WITH BELL PEPPERS AND ARTICHOKES

The skillet supper below, particularly the use of chicken legs, stirs a fond memory of growing up. In a house with three hungry boys, there could never be enough drumsticks on a normal chicken to satisfy us all. If you can find red, green and yellow peppers, they make this creamy fricassee a gorgeous presentation. (If not, use whatever you have on hand; the flavor will be fine.)

As accompaniments, serve white rice, hot garlic bread and a crisp Italian white wine, such as Pinot Grigio.

4 TO 6 SERVINGS
16 chicken drumsticks, about 4 pounds
1 cup all-purpose flour
1 stick (4 ounces) unsalted butter
1 teaspoon salt
½ teaspoon freshly ground black pepper
2 medium onions, chopped
4 garlic cloves, minced
1 teaspoon thyme
1 teaspoon basil
1 imported bay leaf
2 cups chicken stock or canned broth
1 cup dry white wine
1 large red bell pepper, quartered
1 large green bell pepper, quartered
1 large yellow bell pepper, quartered
1 package (10 ounces) frozen artichoke hearts, thawed and drained
1 cup heavy cream

1. Dredge the chicken in the flour; shake off any excess. In a large skillet or flameproof casserole, melt 4 tablespoons of the butter over moderate heat. Working in batches, add the legs, season with the salt and black pepper and cook, turning, until lightly browned, about 10 minutes for each batch. As they brown, transfer the legs to a dish and set aside.

2. Add 2 tablespoons of butter to the pan. Stir in the onions, garlic, thyme, basil and bay leaf. Reduce the heat to moderately low, cover and cook, stirring occasionally, until the onions are tender, 10 to 15 minutes.

3. Return the chicken to the skillet. Add the stock and wine and bring to a boil. Reduce the heat to moderately low, cover, and simmer, turning the legs occasionally, until very tender, about 40 minutes. Remove to a bowl.

4. Meanwhile, in a medium skillet, melt the remaining 2 tablespoons butter over moderately high heat. Add the bell peppers, season with a pinch of salt and pepper and cook, tossing frequently, until lightly browned, about 5 minutes. Add the artichoke hearts and cook for 2 minutes. Transfer the chicken, peppers and artichokes to a bowl.

5. Strain the cooking liquid and return it to the skillet. Place over high heat, stir in the cream and bring to a boil. Boil until the liquid is reduced by one-third, about 15 minutes. Season with salt and pepper to taste. Return the chicken, peppers and artichokes to the skillet. Simmer gently until heated through, about 5 minutes.
—*Michael McLaughlin*

SWEET AND SOUR CHICKEN WITH CARROTS

This unusual "dry curry,' which is moist but has very little sauce, originated in the Jewish community of Calcutta. It is traditional to remove the skin from the chicken, which produces an almost fat-free dish. If you prefer to leave the skin on, degrease the sauce just before serving.

8 TO 10 SERVINGS
3 tablespoons corn or peanut oil
4 medium carrots, finely shredded
2 medium onions, thinly sliced
3 garlic cloves, minced
1½ tablespoons minced fresh ginger
¾ teaspoon turmeric
1½ teaspoons salt
2 chickens (3 pounds each)—skinned, trimmed of excess fat and cut into 8 serving pieces each (include the giblets)
3 imported bay leaves
6 cardamom pods, lightly cracked
⅓ cup fresh lemon juice
2 tablespoons light brown sugar

1. In a large skillet, heat 1½ table-

spoons of the oil over moderately low heat. Add the carrots and sauté until wilted, about 3 minutes. Set aside.

2. In a large flameproof casserole, heat the remaining 1½ tablespoons oil. Add the onions, garlic, ginger, turmeric and salt and cook until the onions are soft and translucent, 2 to 3 minutes. Add the chicken and cook, turning, until white all over, 8 to 10 minutes.

3. Add 1½ cups of water, the bay leaves and cardamom. Cover and cook, turning the chicken occasionally, for 15 minutes. Add the sautéed carrots and continue to cook for 10 minutes. Add the lemon juice and sugar; stir well and cook, partially covered, over moderately low heat, until the chicken is so tender it is almost falling off the bone, about 10 minutes.

4. Uncover and boil over moderately high heat until the liquid is almost evaporated, 5 to 10 minutes. Season with additional lemon juice and sugar to taste if desired.

—Copeland Marks

CHICKEN WITH RICE AND OLIVES

4 SERVINGS
3 tablespoons olive oil
3 garlic cloves, lightly crushed
1 chicken (3 pounds), cut into 8 pieces
½ pound smoked ham, cut into ¼-inch dice
2 medium onions, chopped
½ green bell pepper, chopped
1½ cups converted rice
1 can (14 ounces) Italian peeled tomatoes, drained and coarsely chopped
1½ cups chicken stock or unsalted canned broth
1½ cups lager beer
½ cup pitted green olives, chopped
¼ cup chopped pimientos

1 teaspoon salt
½ teaspoon freshly ground black pepper

1. Preheat the oven to 375°. In a large skillet, heat the oil with the garlic cloves. Add the chicken pieces and cook over moderate heat until browned, about 10 minutes. Transfer the chicken and garlic to a flameproof casserole.

2. Add the ham, onions and bell pepper to the skillet. Cook over moderate heat until softened, 5 to 7 minutes. Add to the casserole.

3. Add the rice to the skillet and cook, stirring constantly, until translucent, 2 to 3 minutes. Add the rice, tomatoes, chicken stock, beer, olives, pimientos, salt and black pepper to the casserole, stirring to combine. Bring to a boil over moderate heat. Stir once, cover the casserole and bake until the rice and chicken are tender, about 25 minutes.

—Mary Lynn Mondich

CHICKEN FRICASSEE WITH ARTICHOKES AND PEARL ONIONS

🍷 F&W BEVERAGE SUGGESTION
Chianti, such as 1979 Badia a Coltibuono

4 TO 6 SERVINGS
1 lemon plus ¼ cup fresh lemon juice
6 medium artichokes
1 chicken (3½ to 4 pounds), cut into 8 pieces
½ teaspoon salt
¼ teaspoon freshly ground pepper
2 tablespoons unsalted butter
2 tablespoons vegetable oil
¾ pound pearl onions, blanched and peeled
¾ pound small mushrooms or quartered large mushrooms

½ cup dry white wine
½ cup chicken stock or unsalted canned broth
1 cup heavy cream
1 bay leaf
2 tablespoons chopped parsley

1. In a large noncorrodible saucepan, squeeze the lemon into 2 quarts of water. Add the lemon halves to the water. Trim the artichokes by first snapping off the tough outer leaves. Then, using a stainless steel knife, cut off the stems; cut the crown to within about 1½ inches of the base. Drop the trimmed artichokes into the saucepan.

2. Bring to a boil over moderately high heat and cook the artichokes until just tender when pierced with a knife, about 25 minutes. Remove from the heat and let them cool in the cooking liquid. When cool enough to handle, scoop out the hairy chokes with a spoon. Cut the hearts into quarters and set aside. (**The hearts can be prepared up to one day ahead.** Return the artichoke hearts to their cooking liquid, cover with plastic wrap and refrigerate overnight.)

3. Season the chicken pieces with the salt and pepper. In a large noncorrodible skillet or flameproof casserole, melt the butter in the oil over moderately high heat. Add the chicken and cook, turning, until browned on all sides, about 10 minutes. Remove from the skillet and set aside.

4. Add the pearl onions to the skillet and cook, tossing frequently, until evenly browned, about 10 minutes. Using a slotted spoon, remove from the skillet and set aside.

5. Add the mushrooms to the skillet and cook, tossing frequently, until lightly browned, about 8 minutes. Using a slotted spoon, remove from the skillet and set aside.

6. Drain any fat from the skillet. Pour in the white wine and bring to a boil, scraping up any browned bits

from the bottom of the pan. Add the chicken stock and cook until the liquid is reduced to 3 tablespoons, about 5 minutes.

7. Pour in the cream and add the artichoke hearts, chicken, onions, mushrooms and bay leaf. Reduce the heat to moderately low and simmer for 35 minutes. Stir in the ¼ cup lemon juice and season with salt and pepper to taste. Sprinkle with the parsley just before serving.

—*John Robert Massie*

YELLOW CHICKEN CURRY

Chicken curries are traditionally prepared in Thailand with the chicken either cut into parts or hacked through the bone, Chinese style, into bite-size pieces. If the chicken is to serve a large number of people, then the latter style is preferable. You will need a heavy cleaver to penetrate the bones, or ask the butcher to do it for you.

▯ F&W BEVERAGE SUGGESTION
Alsace Gewürztraminer

8 SERVINGS
3 pounds chicken parts, skinned and cut through the bone into large bite-size pieces
3 cups Thin Coconut Milk (p. 232)
2 tablespoons fish sauce (nam pla, nuoc mam or patis)*
½ cup Yellow Curry Paste (p. 236)
4 thin slices of peeled fresh ginger
4 dried hot red chiles (optional)
2 cups Thick Coconut Milk (p. 232)
2 tablespoons chopped fresh coriander
*Available at Southeast Asian and some Chinese markets

1. In a wok set over moderately high heat, combine the chicken

pieces, thin coconut milk and fish sauce. Bring the mixture to a gentle boil. Reduce the heat to low and simmer uncovered, stirring occasionally, until the chicken is no longer pink but still juicy, about 20 minutes.

2. Using a slotted spoon, remove the chicken pieces from the wok and set aside covered loosely with foil to keep warm. Blend the curry paste into the liquid. Add the ginger and chiles. Increase the heat to moderate and boil the sauce, stirring occasionally, until it is reduced by one-third, about 10 minutes.

3. Return the chicken to the wok and simmer for 5 minutes longer. Add the thick coconut milk, increase the heat to moderately high and cook, stirring, for 3 minutes. Pour into a serving bowl and sprinkle with the coriander.

—*Jennifer Brennan*

ANA'S CIORBA

This recipe for *ciorbă*, a cross between a soup and a stew, is from Ana Cotaescu, a wonderful Rumanian cook who now lives in New York City.

8 SERVINGS
1 chicken (3½ to 4 pounds), cut into 8 pieces
2 medium carrots, coarsely grated
1 green bell pepper, cut into thin strips 1½ inches long
1 red bell pepper, cut into ¼-inch squares
8 scallions, chopped
2 medium tomatoes, chopped
¼ pound green beans, as thin as possible, cut into 2-inch lengths
1 cup small cauliflorets (about 4 ounces)
2 cups chicken stock or unsalted canned broth
1 teaspoon salt
½ teaspoon freshly ground white pepper

½ cup chopped fresh dill
½ cup chopped parsley
4 ounces dry egg vermicelli
2 egg yolks
⅔ cup sour cream
¼ cup fresh lemon juice

1. In a large noncorrodible saucepan, combine the chicken, carrots, green and red bell peppers, scallions, tomatoes, green beans and cauliflower. Add the stock, salt, white pepper and 3 cups of water. Bring to a boil over moderate heat. Reduce the heat to low and simmer, partially covered, skimming occasionally, until the chicken is tender, about 1 hour.

2. Add the dill, parsley and vermicelli. Cook until the noodles are tender, about 5 minutes. Remove from the heat and set aside for 5 minutes. Skim off any fat that rises to the surface.

3. In a small bowl, beat the egg yolks and sour cream until blended. Gradually whisk in ¼ cup of the hot cooking liquid. Stir the mixture into the hot *ciorbă*. Stir in the lemon juice and season with additional salt and white pepper to taste and serve hot. (**The recipe can be made a day ahead.** Let cool completely, then cover and refrigerate. Reheat gently before serving. Do not boil.)

—*Ana Cotaescu*

BRAISED CAPON WITH TRUFFLES

Menu suggestion: To start, Fish Consommé with Poached Oysters and Beggar's Pouches (p. 42); with the capon, Buttered Spaetzle with Spinach (p. 152), Creamed Parsley and Shallots (p. 128); for the salad course, Green Salad with Lemon and Fennel

(p. 133); for dessert, Hazelnut Succès (p. 196).

🍷 F&W BEVERAGE SUGGESTION
Margaux, such as Giscours, or full-bodied California Chardonnay, such as Matanzas Creek

8 SERVINGS
2 sticks (8 ounces) plus 4 tablespoons unsalted butter, softened
4 medium onions, finely diced
4 medium carrots, finely diced
4 large celery ribs, finely diced
2 large leeks (white and tender green), finely diced
4 ounces Black Forest Ham, finely diced (about 1 cup)
1 teaspoon salt
½ teaspoon freshly ground pepper
⅛ teaspoon freshly grated nutmeg
1 fresh capon (7 to 8 pounds)—neck, gizzard and large pieces of fat reserved
½ lemon
2 medium black truffles, preferably fresh, thinly sliced
2½ cups rich chicken stock
7 ounces truffle essence*
2 tablespoons all-purpose flour
*Available at specialty food shops

1. In a large oval flameproof casserole, melt 6 tablespoons of the butter over moderate heat. Add the onions, carrots, celery, leeks and ham. Cook until the vegetables are softened but not browned, about 15 minutes. Add ½ teaspoon of the salt, ¼ teaspoon of the pepper and the nutmeg.

2. In a small saucepan, melt 1 stick of the butter. Remove from the heat and let cool to lukewarm.

3. Meanwhile, rinse and dry the capon. Rub all over with the cut lemon. With your fingers, carefully loosen the skin from the breast, thighs and legs without tearing it. Stuff 4 tablespoons of the softened butter under

the skin and massage it into the bird. Sprinkle the inside and outside of the bird with the remaining ½ teaspoon salt and ¼ teaspoon pepper.

4. Reserve 6 slices of truffle for decoration. Slip the remainder under the skin of the bird, working them carefully onto the legs, thighs and breast. Truss the bird and place it on top of the vegetables in the casserole. Tuck a sheet of cheesecloth over and around the bird. Pour the lukewarm butter over the top of the bird, completely moistening the cheesecloth. (**The recipe can be prepared ahead to this point.** Cover and refrigerate overnight. Let return to room temperature before proceeding.)

5. Preheat the oven to 325°. Lay a piece of parchment paper or buttered brown paper over the bird and cover with a tight-fitting lid. Cook in the middle of the oven, basting thoroughly with the pan juices every 30 minutes, for about 1½ hours, or until an instant-reading thermometer measures 150° when inserted in the thigh of the bird.

6. Meanwhile, put the capon neck, gizzard and pieces of fat in a medium saucepan. Add the stock and simmer slowly for 1 hour. Do not let boil, or the sauce will become greasy.

7. Transfer the capon to a heatproof platter. Cover loosely with aluminum foil and let rest in a warm oven while you finish the sauce.

8. Strain the stock into the vegetables and butter in the casserole. Add the truffle essence and simmer over low heat for 20 minutes. (Do not let boil.) Strain, reserving the vegetables. Skim off the fat from the surface (see Note). Return the vegetables to the broth.

9. Knead the remaining 2 tablespoons butter with the flour to make a beurre manié. Bring the broth and vegetables to a simmer over moderate heat. Gradually whisk in the beurre manié. Bring to a boil and cook, stir-

ring, until thickened, 1 to 2 minutes. Season the sauce with salt and pepper to taste. Set aside over low heat.

10. Remove the trussings from the bird. Add any juices that have accumulated on the platter to the sauce. Decoratively arrange the reserved truffle slices on top of the breast. Serve the capon with the sauce on the side.

NOTE: This flavorful fat can be saved for cooking potatoes or other poultry.

—Anne Disrude

ROAST CAPON WITH SHIITAKE MUSHROOMS

Capon is a particularly meaty and juicy bird, but this recipe can also be made with two chickens, 3½ to 4 pounds each. They will require two pans, and the roasting time will be shorter.

Menu suggestion: To start, Ratatouille with Goat Cheese (p. 128) and warm French bread; with the capon, buttered asparagus; for dessert, Délice Maison (p. 214).

🍷 F&W BEVERAGE SUGGESTION
Gigondas or a California Zinfandel or Chardonnay

6 TO 8 SERVINGS
1 capon (6 to 7 pounds)
1½ teaspoons salt
½ teaspoon freshly ground pepper
5 tablespoons unsalted butter
1 tablespoon olive oil
1 cup dry white wine
1 pound fresh shiitake (Golden Oak) mushrooms, stems removed and caps sliced
2 tablespoons Cognac

1. Season the inside of the capon

with ½ teaspoon of the salt and ⅛ teaspoon of the pepper; truss the bird.

2. Preheat the oven to 375°. In a large ovenproof skillet or flameproof oval gratin dish, melt 2 tablespoons of the butter in the oil over moderate heat. Brown the capon on all sides, turning carefully to avoid tearing the skin, about 20 minutes. Remove the capon to a plate. Discard the fat in the skillet and add the wine. Bring to a boil, scraping up the browned bits that cling to the bottom of the pan. Boil for 1 minute. Return the capon to the skillet.

3. Sprinkle ½ teaspoon salt and ⅛ teaspoon pepper over the capon. Roast uncovered in the oven, basting with the pan juices every 15 minutes and adding ½ cup water at a time as necessary when the juices become syrupy, for 1½ to 2¼ hours, or until the juices from the capon run golden when the thigh is pierced and the internal temperature in the thickest part of the meat registers 155° to 160°.

4. Meanwhile, melt the remaining 3 tablespoons butter in a large skillet over moderate heat. Add the mushrooms and sauté for 2 to 3 minutes. Season with the remaining ½ teaspoon salt and ¼ teaspoon pepper. Cover the pan, reduce the heat to low and braise the mushrooms, stirring frequently, until they are tender, 15 to 20 minutes.

5. In a very small saucepan or large ladle, heat the Cognac. Ignite and pour over the capon. Transfer the bird to a carving board and cut into serving pieces. Pour the juices from the skillet and the cutting board back into a large measuring cup. Skim off the fat and add water if necessary to equal 1½ cups. Pour back into the oven-proof skillet and bring to a boil. Add the mushrooms and season with additional salt and pepper to taste. Pour over the capon and serve.

—*Lydie Marshall*

CHESTNUT AND SAUSAGE STUFFING FOR POULTRY

This makes enough stuffing for four Cornish hens or one large chicken. With ¼ cup of heavy cream stirred in, the stuffing becomes a delicious filling for savory crêpes.

MAKES ABOUT 3½ CUPS
1 tablespoon unsalted butter
7 medium shallots, chopped
1 medium celery rib, chopped
½ pound country sausage meat
½ pound mushrooms, chopped
½ pound Peeled Chestnuts (p. 123), chopped
½ cup chicken stock or canned broth
Salt and freshly ground pepper

1. In a large skillet, melt the butter over moderately high heat. Add the shallots and celery; sauté until softened and lightly browned, about 15 minutes.

2. Add the sausage meat and stir to break up the meat. Cook until lightly browned, about 10 minutes.

3. Add the mushrooms and chestnuts and cook for 10 minutes, stirring occasionally.

4. Add the chicken stock and season to taste with salt and pepper. Continue cooking until most of the liquid has evaporated, about 10 minutes. Let cool completely before using as a stuffing.

—*John Robert Massie*

ROAST TURKEY WITH PAN GRAVY AND SWEET PEPPER AND RICE STUFFING

You will need a large roasting pan with a rack and a cover.

Menu suggestion: To start, Braised Fennel with Prosciutto and Parmesan Cheese (p. 125); with the turkey, Baked Yams with Amaretti Crumble Topping (p. 129), Sweet and Sour Onions (p. 238); for the salad course, Tricolor Salad (p. 134); for dessert, Cappuccino Ice Cream Cake with Hot Chocolate Sauce (p. 198).

F&W BEVERAGE SUGGESTION
Italian white, such as Cortese di Gavi or Corvo; or Italian red, such as Barolo or Chianti Classico

8 SERVINGS
8- to 10-pound fresh turkey, liver and
giblets reserved (see Note)
½ teaspoon salt
½ teaspoon freshly ground pepper
1 stick (4 ounces) unsalted butter,
softened
3 cups Sweet Pepper and Rice
Stuffing (recipe follows)
Quick Turkey Stock (p. 226)
1 tablespoon all-purpose flour
½ cup dry white wine

1. Up to 3 hours before you plan to roast the turkey, trim the bird of excess fat. Season inside and out with the salt and pepper. Rub 6 tablespoons of the butter over the bird, inside and out.

2. Fold the wings of the turkey under. Spoon the stuffing into the body cavity; do not pack too tightly. Truss securely, sewing up the cavity.

3. Preheat the oven to 450°. In a medium saucepan, bring the stock to a simmer over moderately high heat. Reduce the heat and keep the stock hot.

4. Place the turkey, breast-side up,

on a rack in a large roasting pan. Pour 1 cup of the hot stock into the bottom of the pan. Put the turkey in the oven and roast uncovered for 30 minutes, basting frequently, adding up to 1½ cups more stock, plus water if necessary, to the roasting pan as needed. (Reserve 1 cup of stock to make the gravy in Step 7.)

5. Cover the bird and continue roasting for about 1½ hours, basting frequently. Remove the cover for the last 15 minutes to brown and crisp the skin. The turkey is done when the legs move freely and the juices from the pierced thigh run clear.

6. Transfer to a warmed platter and let rest, loosely covered with foil, for 20 minutes before carving.

7. Meanwhile, make a pan gravy. Blend the flour with the remaining 2 tablespoons butter to make a beurre manié. Skim off most of the fat from the juices in the roasting pan. Place the pan over high heat, add the wine and remaining 1 cup stock and bring to a boil, scraping up any browned bits from the bottom of the pan. Gradually stir in the beurre manié and boil the gravy until slightly thickened, 2 to 3 minutes. Season with additional salt and pepper to taste.

NOTE: Reserve the liver for the Sweet Pepper and Rice Stuffing and the giblets for the Quick Turkey Stock.

—*Arthur Gold & Robert Fizdale*

SWEET PEPPER AND RICE STUFFING

MAKES ABOUT 8 CUPS

3 teaspoons salt
1 stick (4 ounces) unsalted butter
2 cups converted rice
6 tablespoons olive oil
2 medium red bell peppers, cut into ½-inch squares
2 medium green bell peppers, cut into ½-inch squares
2 medium yellow bell peppers (see Note), cut into ½-inch squares
½ teaspoon crushed hot pepper
¼ teaspoon freshly ground black pepper
1 medium onion, chopped
1 large garlic clove, minced
1 turkey liver, reserved from the Roast Turkey (above), trimmed and cut into ½-inch pieces
½ pound chicken livers, trimmed and cut into ½-inch pieces

1. In a medium saucepan, bring 1 quart of water to a boil over high heat. Add 2 teaspoons of the salt and 2 tablespoons of the butter. Stir in the rice, cover and reduce the heat to moderately low. Cook for about 15 minutes, or until the rice is just tender but still firm to the bite; the water will not all be absorbed. Drain and put the rice in a large bowl.

2. In a large skillet, heat 3 tablespoons of the oil. Add the red, green and yellow bell peppers and the hot pepper flakes and sauté over high heat for 2 minutes. Reduce the heat to moderate, add 2 tablespoons of the butter and cook until the peppers are slightly tender but still quite crisp, about 5 minutes. Season with ¾ teaspoon of the salt and ⅛ teaspoon of the black pepper. Add to the rice and toss to mix.

3. In the same large skillet, melt 1 tablespoon of the butter in 1 table-spoon of the oil over high heat. Add the onion and sauté for 30 seconds. Reduce the heat to moderate and cook until wilted, about 5 minutes. Add the garlic and cook for 1 minute longer. Combine the onion and garlic with the rice.

4. In the skillet, heat the remaining 3 tablespoons butter and 2 tablespoons oil. Add the turkey and chicken livers and sauté over high heat until they are browned outside but still rosy inside, 2 to 3 minutes. Season with the remaining ¼ teaspoon salt and ⅛ teaspoon pepper and add them to the rice mixture. Adjust the seasoning if necessary. Let the stuffing cool to room temperature. (**The recipe can be made to this point up to a day ahead.** Cover and refrigerate.)

5. Use about 3 cups of the stuffing in the turkey (see Step 2 of the Roast Turkey recipe, above). Turn the remainder into a 6- to 8-cup baking dish. Cover with foil and bake in the 450° oven for 20 minutes during the end of the turkey's cooking time.

NOTE: If yellow peppers are not available, increase the quantity of red and green peppers.

—*Arthur Gold & Robert Fizdale*

TURKEY MOLE BURRITOS

F&W BEVERAGE SUGGESTION
California Zinfandel, such as 1983 Kendall-Jackson

MAKES 12

4 tablespoons unsalted butter
1 small onion, minced
2 garlic cloves, minced
¼ cup tomato paste
½ cup slivered almonds, minced
¼ cup chili powder
1 tablespoon oregano

1 tablespoon unsweetened cocoa
  powder
½ teaspoon cinnamon
½ teaspoon ground cloves
½ teaspoon freshly grated nutmeg
½ teaspoon allspice
½ teaspoon ground ginger
½ teaspoon ground cumin
1 cup Turkey Stock (p. 226) or
  unsalted chicken broth
4 cups coarsely shredded cooked
  turkey
Hot pepper sauce
12 flour tortillas
Sour cream, chopped red onion and
  shredded iceberg lettuce, for garnish

1. In a large saucepan, melt the butter over moderate heat. Add the onion and garlic and cook until softened, about 3 minutes. Add the tomato paste, almonds, chili powder, oregano, cocoa, cinnamon, cloves, nutmeg, allspice, ginger and cumin; stir well to combine. Add the turkey stock and bring to a boil. Reduce the heat and simmer for 5 minutes. Stir in the turkey and cook until warmed through, about 3 minutes. Add hot sauce to taste. (**The recipe can be prepared to this point up to 3 days ahead.** Cover and refrigerate. Reheat the turkey mixture before proceeding.)

2. Preheat the oven to 250°. To assemble the burritos, heat the tortillas in the oven until warmed through but still soft, 2 to 3 minutes. Spoon ⅓ cup of the turkey mole along the center of each tortilla and roll up neatly. Place 2 burritos on each plate and garnish each serving with sour cream, chopped onion and shredded lettuce.

—Molly O'Neill

CREAMED TURKEY AND APPLE HASH

Serve this creamy hash with oven roasted new potatoes or buttered wild rice.

6 SERVINGS

4 tablespoons unsalted butter
1 small onion, minced
1 cup Turkey Stock (p. 226) or
  unsalted chicken broth
1 teaspoon fresh lemon juice
2 cups heavy cream
2 teaspoons soy sauce
4 cups shredded cooked turkey
2 medium Granny Smith apples—
  peeled, cored, quartered and thinly
  sliced
Salt and freshly ground pepper
Minced scallions, for garnish

1. In a medium saucepan, melt the butter over moderate heat. Add the onion and cook until softened, about 3 minutes.

2. Stir in the turkey stock and lemon juice and bring to a boil. Boil over high heat until the mixture reduces by half, about 5 minutes. Add the heavy cream and soy sauce and simmer until reduced again by half, about 12 minutes. Stir in the turkey and cook for 10 minutes. Add the apples and cook until just tender, about 5 minutes. Season with salt and pepper to taste. Serve the hash garnished with minced scallions.

—Molly O'Neill

ORANGE-SPICED DUCK

This recipe uses the three French cooking techniques that have most influenced my Chinese cooking: deglazing, degreasing and reducing. When I first tasted Chinese Orange-Spiced Duck, it was presented swimming in a greasy, watery sauce. Removing the fat and reducing the sauce to a thick, syrupy glaze produces a much more elegant dish with greater intensity of flavor.

Although Orange-Spiced Duck must simmer a long time, it can be made a day in advance and rewarmed in the oven or on top of the stove. The skin is usually not eaten, as it remains soft, but it makes for a beautiful presentation, so I like to leave it on for serving.

❖ F&W BEVERAGE SUGGESTION
Alsace Gewürztraminer, such as Hugel

3 TO 4 SERVINGS

1 fresh duck (about 5 pounds),
  preferably Long Island
2 medium leeks (white and tender
  green), cut into 2-inch lengths and
  well rinsed
2 cups unsalted duck or chicken stock
  or water
¼ cup dark soy sauce* (see Note)
½ cup medium-dry sherry
2 tablespoons honey
1 teaspoon five-spice powder*
1 piece of dried tangerine peel,*
  2-by-1-inch strip
2 navel oranges
*Available at Oriental markets

1. Preheat the oven to 400°. Remove the giblets and fat from the cavity of the duck. Trim the skin extending from the neck, leaving about 3 inches. Lift the skin on the neck side and remove excess fat, glands and membranes. Rinse the duck under cold running water. Drain and wipe dry.

2. Place the duck on a rack in a roasting pan. To help drain the fat, prick the duck all over with a trussing

POULTRY

needle or sharp fork. Roast the duck for 1 hour, pricking it after 20 minutes and again after 45 minutes.

3. Place a cake rack on the bottom of a wok or oval Dutch oven. Spread the leeks on top of the rack.

4. Insert a wooden spoon into the cavity of the duck. Carefully remove it from the roasting pan, keeping the duck level so as not to lose any juices. Place the duck, breast-side up, on top of the leeks. Pour out the fat from the roasting pan.

5. Pour the duck stock into the roasting pan. Place over high heat and boil, scraping up the browned bits that cling to the bottom of the pan. Add the soy sauce and sherry. Pour over the duck.

6. Bring the stock in the wok to a boil over high heat, then reduce to a simmer. Cover the duck and cook for 30 minutes.

7. Spoon the honey over the duck. Dissolve the five-spice powder in 2 tablespoons of water and add to the duck stock in the wok. Add the tangerine peel. With a swivel-bladed vegetable peeler, remove a 2-by-1-inch strip of orange zest from one of the oranges. Add to the wok. Baste the duck. Cook, covered, for another 1½ hours, basting every 20 minutes. (If the liquid evaporates, add water ¼ cup at a time.)

8. Preheat the oven to 200°. Peel the oranges, removing all the white pith. Halve lengthwise, then cut them into ¼-inch slices.

9. Remove the duck to a warm platter and hold uncovered in the oven. Set the leeks aside. Strain the sauce into a small saucepan. Let the fat rise to the top of the sauce, then skim off. Boil the sauce until reduced to ¾ cup. Add the leeks to the sauce. Pour the sauce over the duck. Garnish with the orange slices and serve hot.

NOTE: If your duck is smaller than 5 pounds, reduce the amount of soy sauce accordingly.

—*Karen Lee & Alaxandra Branyon*

SAUTEED BREAST OF DUCK WITH WILD MUSHROOMS

If you are using whole ducks for this recipe, save the legs and thighs for Duck Confit (recipe follows) and the remaining skin and fat for Scrambled Eggs with Duck Cracklings (p. 49).

We like to serve this dish with breaded pan-fried tomatoes and a fennel, red onion and green bean stir-fry.

F&W BEVERAGE SUGGESTION California Merlot, such as Stephen Zellerbach, or Tuscan red, such as Carmignano

6 SERVINGS
6 tablespoons olive oil
Necks from 3 ducks, cut into 1-inch pieces
4 cups White Veal Stock (p. 225)
1 stick (4 ounces) unsalted butter
½ pound fresh chanterelles, cèpes or oyster mushrooms, stemmed and sliced into ¼-inch strips
¾ teaspoon salt
¼ teaspoon freshly ground pepper
2 teaspoons Cognac
Breasts from 3 ducks

1. In a large skillet, heat 2 tablespoons of the oil. Add the necks and cook over moderately high heat until browned all over, about 8 minutes.

2. Drain the fat from the skillet, add the veal stock and cook until reduced to 1½ cups, about 25 minutes.

3. Meanwhile, melt 2 tablespoons of the butter in a medium skillet. Add the mushrooms, salt and pepper and sauté over moderately high heat until tender, about 10 minutes. Keep warm.

4. Strain the reduced stock into a medium saucepan and bring to a boil over high heat. Remove from the heat and whisk in the remaining 6 tablespoons butter, 1 tablespoon at a time. Stir in the Cognac and keep the sauce warm over very low heat.

5. In a large skillet, heat the remaining 4 tablespoons oil until almost smoking. Add the duck breasts and sauté over moderately high heat until lightly browned, about 3 minutes on each side for medium-rare. Transfer to a large serving platter. Pour the sauce over the duck and spoon the mushrooms on top. Alternatively, cut each duck breast crosswise into ¾-inch slices or lengthwise into ¼-inch strips and fan out on individual plates.

—*Deirdre Davis & Linda Marino*

DUCK CONFIT

The duck must marinate overnight, so plan accordingly. Accompany this confit with the Turnip-Shallot Compote (p. 129) and Sicilian Citrus Salad (p. 132).

F&W BEVERAGE SUGGESTION Full-bodied red, such as Cahors or California Zinfandel

6 SERVINGS
1 teaspoon cinnamon
1 teaspoon allspice
1 teaspoon cardamom
1 teaspoon ground cloves
Legs and thighs from 3 ducks
1 tablespoon coarse (kosher) salt
1 bay leaf, crumbled
1 teaspoon thyme
10 garlic cloves, peeled
4 whole cloves
4½ cups duck or goose fat

90

1. In a small bowl, combine the cinnamon, allspice, cardamom and ground cloves. Rub the duck with the spice mixture and sprinkle each piece lightly with the kosher salt. Place the duck in a glass dish, cover with plastic wrap and refrigerate overnight.

2. Preheat the oven to 350°. Wipe the salt from each piece of duck and place in a medium casserole. Add the bay leaf, thyme, garlic, whole cloves and duck fat. Bake for about 1½ hours, or until the duck is tender and the skin is brown and crisp. Drain on paper towels before serving. (**The confit can be prepared up to 1 week ahead.** Store the duck in the refrigerator in a glass crock or bowl, covered by the strained fat in which it was cooked. Reheat the duck in the fat in a casserole on the stove. The fat can be strained and reused.)

—*Deirdre Davis & Linda Marino*

DUCK AND BAMBOO CURRY

A rather hearty curry, this dish relies on the green curry paste for zip and balance.

6 TO 8 SERVINGS
4 cups Thin Coconut Milk (p. 232)
1 small (3-pound) duck—skinned, surplus fat removed and cut through the bone into bite-size pieces (see Note)
3 tablespoons Green Curry Paste (p. 237)
2 cups sliced canned bamboo shoots
3 fresh green serrano peppers, seeded and finely slivered
2 citrus leaves, slivered, or 6 fresh mint leaves
1 cup Thick Coconut Milk (p. 232)
3 tablespoons fish sauce (nam pla, nuoc mam or patis)*
2 scallions, thinly sliced
*Available at Southeast Asian and some Chinese markets

1. In a wok set over moderately high heat, bring the thin coconut milk to a boil. Add the duck pieces. When the mixture returns to a boil, blend in the green curry paste. Continue to cook, stirring occasionally, until the duck is tender and the sauce is thick, about 30 minutes.

2. With a bulb baster, draw off as much of the fat as you can. Stir in the bamboo shoots, serrano peppers and citrus leaves. Reduce the heat to moderate and continue cooking for 5 minutes. Again remove any accumulated fat from the surface.

3. Stir in the thick coconut milk and fish sauce. Reduce the heat to low and simmer, stirring occasionally, for 5 minutes longer. Pour the curry into a serving bowl and garnish with the scallions.

NOTE: If you can't find a small duck, you can make this curry with a 4- to 5-pound duck. Increase the green curry paste to 4 tablespoons and the amount of thick coconut milk to 1½ cups. In Step 1, increase the cooking time to 45 minutes.

—*Jennifer Brennan*

GRILLED SQUAB MARINATED IN BERRY PUREE

"The purpose of the berry puree is to glaze the skin for crispness and color," says Jeremiah Tower. "The acid in the berries counteracts and balances the richness of the squab. The recipe was inspired by a 17th-century cookbook called *Le Cuisinier François,* which includes a recipe for raspberry vinegar."

BEVERAGE SUGGESTION
Full-bodied red Burgundy

4 SERVINGS
4 squabs, including hearts and livers

2½ cups fresh or unsweetened frozen red raspberries, blackberries or blueberries
1 stick (4 ounces) unsalted butter, cut into chunks and softened
1¼ teaspoons salt
½ teaspoon freshly ground pepper
¼ cup olive oil
½ pound salt pork, cut into 1-by-¼-inch strips
1 tablespoon chopped fresh thyme
16 small mushrooms (about ½ pound)
2 tablespoons fresh lemon juice
½ cup walnut oil
2 bunches of watercress, tough stems removed

1. Using kitchen shears, cut out the backbones of the squabs. Set the hearts and livers aside. Place the squabs on their backs and use the heel of your hand to flatten them. Fold the wings under the bodies.

2. In a food processor, puree 2 cups of the berries. Strain the puree through a stainless steel sieve into a bowl. Return one-fourth of the puree to the processor. Add the butter, ½ teaspoon of the salt and ¼ teaspoon of the pepper and process until well blended. Scrape the berry butter into a small bowl, cover and refrigerate until needed.

3. Season the squabs with ½ teaspoon salt and the remaining ¼ teaspoon pepper; place in a shallow dish.

4. Stir 2 tablespoons of the olive oil into the remaining berry puree and pour over the squabs; toss to coat well. Let marinate at room temperature for 1 hour, turning them after 30 minutes.

5. Meanwhile, blanch the salt pork strips in boiling water for 1 minute;

drain into a colander, rinse and drain well. Pat dry with paper towels. Trim the reserved livers.

6. In a medium bowl, mix the remaining 2 tablespoons olive oil with the thyme. And the blanched salt pork, livers, hearts and mushrooms and toss well. Let marinate at room temperature for 45 minutes.

7. Preheat the grill or broiler. Thread the salt pork, livers, hearts and mushrooms onto four 6-inch skewers. Remove the squabs from the marinade; discard the marinade.

8. Grill or broil the squabs about 5 inches from the heat, breast-side away from the heat, for 8 minutes. Turn the squabs and cook the second side until the skin is very brown and crisp but the meat is still rare, 5 to 8 minutes (see Note). Remove the squabs from the heat and let rest for 5 minutes.

9. Meanwhile, grill or broil the skewered meats and mushrooms for 5 minutes, turning often to brown evenly.

10. In a small bowl, combine the lemon juice with the remaining ¼ teaspoon salt and a pinch of pepper. Gradually whisk in the walnut oil. Toss the watercress with the walnut vinaigrette and arrange on 4 dinner plates. Place a squab in the center of each plate and a skewer beside it. Arrange the remaining ½ cup berries around the squabs and top each bird with a dollop of the reserved berry butter.

NOTE: Squabs are traditionally served rare, but you may cook them longer if desired.

—Jeremiah Tower

CABBAGE STUFFED WITH FOIE GRAS AND CABBAGE

🍷 F&W BEVERAGE SUGGESTION
Red Burgundy, such as Mercurey

8 FIRST-COURSE OR
4 MAIN-COURSE SERVINGS
1 large head of cabbage, about 3 pounds
3 tablespoons goose or duck fat
2 medium onions, chopped
2 medium celery ribs, chopped
3 garlic cloves, chopped
1 medium carrot, finely diced
½ teaspoon salt
⅛ teaspoon freshly ground pepper
4 to 6 ounces cooked terrine of foie gras (goose or duck) or canned pâté de foie gras, cut into ¼-inch dice
1 cup unsalted chicken stock or canned broth
¼ teaspoon arrowroot or cornstarch
¾ teaspoon sherry wine vinegar
Thin ribbons of carrot, for garnish

1. Remove the 3 or 4 toughest outer leaves of the cabbage and discard. Cut out a broad deep core. Put the cabbage in a large pot of boiling water and cook, removing 8 leaves as they loosen. Reserve in a bowl. Remove the cabbage head. Return the 8 leaves to the pot and boil until tender and translucent, 15 to 20 minutes. Drain, pat dry, and let cool. Trim off the thickest part of the central rib on each leaf.

2. Coarsely chop the cabbage head. In a large skillet, melt the goose fat over moderate heat. Add the chopped cabbage, onions, celery, garlic and the diced carrot. Cook, stirring frequently, until the vegetables are golden brown, about 1 hour. Season with the salt and pepper. Remove from the heat and let cool slightly.

3. Gently toss the foie gras with the cooked vegetable mixture. Divide this filling among the leaves. To form each cabbage roll, fold up the bottom, fold in the sides and roll up into small neat cylinders.

4. In a large skillet, heat the chicken stock, add the cabbage rolls, seam-side down, and simmer over low heat for 10 minutes to heat through. Transfer the rolls to a warm platter.

5. Dissolve the arrowroot in the vinegar. Bring the chicken stock to a boil. Stir in the vinegar mixture. Cook, stirring, until the sauce is clear and slightly thickened, about 15 seconds. Drizzle the sauce over the cabbage rolls and garnish with the ribbons of carrot.

—Anne Disrude

MEAT

MEAT

ROLLED BREAST OF VEAL STUFFED WITH TUNA

This rolled veal breast must be refrigerated overnight in its cooking liquid to firm it up and allow the flavors to fully develop. But because this is served at room temperature, there is no last-minute fussing, making this an ideal buffet dish.

F&W BEVERAGE SUGGESTION
California Chardonnay, such as Jekel

10 TO 12 SERVINGS
2 tablespoons olive oil
1 medium onion, minced
2 large garlic cloves, minced
½ pound ground veal
1 can (6½ ounces) tuna in oil,
  preferably Italian, drained
3 tablespoons drained capers
3 tablespoons fresh lemon juice
1 egg
2 teaspoons salt
1½ teaspoons freshly ground pepper
4½ pounds boneless breast of veal
3 quarts chicken stock or canned
  broth
Lemon Mayonnaise (p. 228)

1. In a medium skillet, heat the olive oil. Add the onion and garlic and cook over moderate heat until softened but not browned, about 5 minutes. Remove from the heat and let cool.

2. In a medium bowl, combine the ground veal, tuna, capers, lemon juice, egg, salt and pepper. Add the onion and garlic and mix well.

3. Place the veal breast on a cutting board, fat-side down, and trim off any excess fat and untidy edges. Spread the stuffing evenly over the meat, leaving a 1½-inch border all around.

4. Carefully roll up the breast, following the grain of the meat. Tightly wrap the meat in a double thickness

of cheesecloth or muslin and tie with string at 2-inch intervals to make a neat roll.

5. Preheat the oven to 375°. Place the veal roll in a large flameproof casserole and add the chicken stock. Add enough water to cover the meat completely and bring to a simmer over high heat. Cover the casserole and cook the veal in the oven for 2 hours.

6. Remove the casserole from the oven, uncover and let the veal cool completely in the liquid; refrigerate, covered, overnight.

7. One to two hours before serving, remove the veal from the casserole. Cut the strings and carefully unwrap the meat. With a very sharp knife, cut the veal into ¼-inch slices and place on a decorative serving platter. Serve at room temperature with the lemon mayonnaise.

—W. Peter Prestcott

STUFFED BREAST OF VEAL WITH MUSHROOM GRAVY

Buttered orzo, glazed carrots and/or steamed green beans would make a fine accompaniment to this fennel-flavored roast.

F&W BEVERAGE SUGGESTION
1979 Bordeaux, such as Château Gloria

6 TO 8 SERVINGS
6 ounces fresh mushrooms
1 cup fresh bread crumbs
1 egg, lightly beaten
½ cup freshly grated Parmesan cheese
2 tablespoons fennel seeds
½ teaspoon salt
¼ teaspoon freshly ground pepper
½ pound ground veal (see Note)
½ cup diced ham (about ¼ pound)
4 scallions, chopped
¼ cup finely chopped parsley
2½-pound boned and trimmed breast
  of veal, ribs and trimmings
  reserved (see Note)

5 pounds veal rib bones (see Note)
3 medium onions, coarsely chopped
3 medium carrots, coarsely chopped
3 celery ribs, coarsely chopped
3 tablespoons all-purpose flour

1. Preheat the oven to 500°. Finely chop half the mushrooms. Slice the remaining mushrooms.

2. In a medium bowl, combine the bread crumbs with the egg, 1 tablespoon of water, the Parmesan cheese, fennel, salt and pepper. Stir in the ground veal, chopped mushrooms, ham, scallions and parsley; blend lightly.

3. Lay the breast of veal flat and spread the stuffing over the inside of the meat to cover. (Extra stuffing can be lightly packed into a small greased casserole and baked 30 minutes alongside the roast.) Roll up lengthwise and tie securely with string; set aside.

4. Place the veal bones in a heavy roasting pan. Roast, turning the bones occasionally, for 20 minutes, or until browned. Reduce the oven to 350°. Transfer the bones to a large saucepan and add 4 cups of water; set the roasting pan aside. Simmer the bones over low heat until the liquid has been reduced to 2 cups, about 45 minutes. Strain the stock.

5. Meanwhile, add the onions, carrots, celery and sliced mushrooms to the roasting pan and cook on top of the stove over moderately high heat until slightly softened, about 3 minutes. Add the veal breast and cook, turning without piercing the meat, until lightly browned all over, about 8 minutes.

6. Cover the roasting pan with aluminum foil, transfer to the oven and roast for 45 minutes, basting the veal twice. Remove the foil and roast for 15 minutes to brown the top. The inter-

nal temperature of the meat should be 120° to 125° (the meat will continue to cook as it rests). Transfer the veal to a carving board, cover loosely with foil and let rest for 20 to 30 minutes.

7. Pour off all but 3 tablespoons fat from the roasting pan. Sprinkle in the flour and cook over moderate heat, stirring constantly, about 3 minutes or until lightly browned. Slowly whisk in the veal stock. Bring to a boil, reduce the heat and simmer, stirring occasionally, until the sauce thickens, about 3 minutes. Season with salt and pepper to taste.

8. To serve, carve the veal into thin slices. Strain the gravy into a warmed sauceboat and pass separately.

NOTE: A 7½-pound (8-rib) veal breast when trimmed of fat will yield a 2½-pound boned veal roast plus 4 to 5 pounds rib bones and about ½ pound trimmings that can be ground.
—*Alyssa Alia*

RACK OF VEAL BRAISED WITH TARRAGON

For this extravagant roast, ask your butcher for the best cut of the rack, which includes the first five ribs. On less important occasions, you can enjoy the same flavors at less cost by making the recipe with a breast of veal (see Note).

Menu suggestion: To start, Arugula and Watercress Salad with Swiss Cheese Beignets (p. 133); with the veal, sautéed green beans or haricots verts; for dessert, Chocolate Fondant with Fresh Blueberries (p. 205).

F&W BEVERAGE SUGGESTION
Red Bordeaux, such as Château d'Angludet, or Bandol Domaine Tempier

6 TO 8 SERVINGS
5 tablespoons unsalted butter
2 tablespoons olive oil

Rack of veal with 5 ribs, about 5¼ pounds untrimmed; ask the butcher to crack and french the bones
16 small red potatoes (1 to 1½ inches in diameter), peeled
8 small white onions (about 1 inch in diameter), peeled
1 bunch of fresh tarragon
1 teaspoon salt
¼ teaspoon freshly ground pepper
½ cup dry white wine

1. In a large flameproof casserole, melt 1 tablespoon of the butter in the oil over moderately high heat until the foam subsides. Add the veal and brown all over, about 15 minutes.

2. Add the potatoes, onions and 3 or 4 sprigs of tarragon. Season with the salt and pepper. Add the wine, cover, reduce the heat to moderately low and cook for 1 hour, or until the internal temperature of the meat registers 140°.

3. Transfer the veal to a carving board. Discard the tarragon and with a slotted spoon, place the potatoes and onions in a covered serving bowl. Reserve the liquid in the casserole.

4. Working as quickly as you can, carve the rack to separate the ribs. Cut the meat away from the bones and slice the meat on a diagonal as thinly as possible. Arrange the veal on a heated serving platter. Cover with foil to keep warm.

5. Add any meat juices that have collected on the carving board to the liquid in the casserole. Boil over moderately high heat until slightly syrupy and reduced to ⅓ cup, about 3 minutes. Remove from the heat and gradually whisk in the remaining 4 tablespoons butter, 1 tablespoon at a time. Season with salt and pepper to taste.

6. To serve, overlap several pieces of meat in the center of individual plates and ladle 1 to 2 tablespoons of the sauce over each serving. Garnish with the remaining sprigs of tarragon.

Serve the potatoes and onions on the side.

NOTE: A 3½-pound boned breast of veal, trimmed of excess fat, rolled and tied, can be substituted for the rack; ask your butcher to compact the roast so that it is no longer than 8½ inches. The instructions and cooking time remain the same.
—*Lydie Marshall*

HERB-PRESSED VEAL CHOPS

Menu suggestion: To start, Risotto with Spring Vegetables (p. 153) and grissini; with the veal chops, Garlic Flan (p. 49) and sautéed wild mushrooms; as the salad *and* cheese course, Pear and Blue Cheese Salad with Parmesan (p. 132); and with after-dinner coffee, Miniature Berry and Cherry Tartlets (p. 168).

F&W BEVERAGE SUGGESTION
Beaujolais Cru, such as Morgon or Moulin-à-Vent

4 SERVINGS
4 veal rib chops, cut 1 inch thick (9 to 10 ounces each), frenched
Salt and coarsely cracked pepper
¼ cup all-purpose flour
1 teaspoon of chopped fresh thyme
2 teaspoons of chopped fresh rosemary
3 to 4 tablespoons safflower oil

1. Preheat the oven to 400°. Season the veal chops with salt and pepper to taste. Dredge the chops in the flour and shake off any excess. Press the thyme and rosemary into both sides of each chop.

2. Pour enough oil into a large ovenproof skillet to coat the bottom; heat over high heat until the oil is hot but not smoking. Add the chops and

MEAT

cook until well browned on the bottom, 3 to 4 minutes. Reduce the heat to moderate, turn and cook 3 to 4 minutes longer, to brown the second side. Transfer the skillet to the oven. Bake the chops for an additional 7 minutes for medium rare or 10 minutes for medium.

—*Christopher Idone*

VEAL CHOPS WITH SWEETBREADS IN BOURBON AND MOREL SAUCE

🍷 F&W BEVERAGE SUGGESTION
Red Bordeaux, such as Château d'Angludet

4 SERVINGS
¾ pound sweetbreads
2½ cups chicken stock or canned broth
1 small onion, sliced
1 teaspoon white wine vinegar
1 bay leaf
5 peppercorns
1 ounce dried morels
1 small shallot, minced
⅓ cup bourbon
¾ cup heavy cream
½ teaspoon fresh lemon juice
1 cup all-purpose flour seasoned with salt and pepper, for dredging
4 tablespoons unsalted butter, softened
2 tablespoons vegetable oil
4 veal loin chops, cut 1 inch thick
¼ teaspoon salt
Pinch of freshly ground pepper

1. Soak the sweetbreads in cold water for at least 1 hour or overnight; drain. Remove as much membrane as possible and any fat.

2. In a saucepan just large enough to hold the sweetbreads, combine the stock, onion, vinegar, bay leaf and peppercorns. Bring to a boil over high heat. Reduce the heat to low and simmer the stock for 15 minutes. Add the sweetbreads and cook until firm, about 10 minutes. Drain and rinse under cold running water until cooled.

3. Using a small sharp knife, peel off any remaining membrane and cut out the tough connective tissues. Loosely wrap the sweetbreads in a clean kitchen towel and place on a tray. Cover with a second tray or platter weighted with about 5 pounds (two #2½ cans work well); refrigerate for 2 hours. **(The sweetbreads can be returned to the stock at this point and refrigerated, covered, for up to 2 days.)**

4. In a small bowl, soak the morels in 1 cup of warm water until softened, about 30 minutes. Remove the morels, squeezing any liquid back into the bowl. Strain the soaking liquid through several layers of dampened cheesecloth or a coffee filter. (You should have about ½ cup.) Set aside. Rinse the morels to get rid of any sand. Trim off any hard pieces and sandy ends. Halve any large morels.

5. In a medium skillet, warm the shallot in the bourbon over moderate heat; ignite. When the flames subside, boil the bourbon until only a glaze remains. Add the strained morel liquid and boil until reduced by half, about 5 minutes. Add the cream and morels, reduce the heat to low and simmer until the sauce thickens, about 5 minutes. Stir in the lemon juice and remove from the heat. **(The sauce can be prepared ahead to this point.** Let cool completely, then cover and refrigerate for up to 2 days.)

6. Preheat the oven to 200°. Place a large heatproof platter in the oven to warm. Cut the sweetbreads on the diagonal into 4 slices. Pat dry. Dust the slices in the seasoned flour and shake off the excess.

7. In a large skillet, melt 1 tablespoon of the butter in 1 tablespoon of the oil over moderately high heat. Add the sweetbreads and sauté until lightly browned, about 1 minute on each side. Transfer to the platter in the oven.

8. Pat the veal chops dry, dust with flour and shake off the excess. Melt 1 tablespoon of butter in the remaining 1 tablespoon oil in the skillet. Add the chops and sauté on one side for 4 minutes. Turn and cook the second side for 3 minutes. Transfer to the platter.

9. Reheat the sauce. Whisk in the remaining 2 tablespoons butter. Add the salt and pepper. To serve, place a chop and a slice of sweetbread on each plate. Stir any accumulated meat juices into the sauce. Spoon the sauce over the veal and serve hot.

—*Near Elan, Mama Maria, Boston, Massachusetts*

VEAL SCALLOPS WITH BRAISED LEEKS AND GLAZED CARROTS

Menu suggestion: To start, Warm Mozzarella and Tomato Salad with Prosciutto (p. 27); with the veal, buttered green fettuccine; for dessert, Melon Melba (p. 216).

4 SERVINGS
8 to 9 tablespoons unsalted butter
4 medium leeks (white and 2 inches of green), sliced ¼ inch thick
1 cup plus 3 tablespoons chicken stock or canned broth
Salt and freshly ground white pepper
⅓ cup heavy cream
3 medium carrots, cut into ⅛-inch rounds
Pinch of sugar
8 thin veal scallops
Flour, for dredging
1 to 2 teaspoons peanut oil
¼ cup fresh lemon juice
2 tablespoons minced parsley

1. Butter a rectangular flameproof baking dish large enough to hold the veal in a single layer.

2. In a large skillet, melt 3 tablespoons of the butter over moderate heat. Add the leeks and 2 tablespoons of the stock. Reduce the heat to low and season with salt and white pepper to taste. Cover and braise the leeks until tender, 8 to 10 minutes. Uncover, increase the heat to high and cook, stirring constantly, until all the liquid evaporates, about 1 minute. Add the cream, bring to a boil and cook, stirring, until most of the cream has been absorbed by the leeks, about 3 minutes. Remove from the heat and set aside.

3. In a small skillet, melt 2 tablespoons of the butter over moderate heat. Add the carrots and 1 tablespoon of stock. Season with the sugar and salt and white pepper to taste. Reduce the heat to low, cover and simmer until just tender, about 5 minutes. Uncover, increase the heat to moderately high and cook, stirring constantly, until the liquid evaporates and the carrots are lightly browned and glazed, about 5 minutes. Remove from the heat.

4. Season the veal scallops with salt and white pepper. Dredge lightly in flour; shake off the excess.

5. In a large heavy skillet, melt 2 tablespoons of the butter in 1 teaspoon of the oil over high heat. Add the veal scallops in batches and sauté, turning once, until lightly browned, about 30 seconds per side; transfer to the buttered baking dish. Repeat with the remaining scallops, adding more butter and oil as necessary.

6. Add the lemon juice and the remaining 1 cup stock to the skillet. Bring to a boil over high heat, scraping up any browned bits from the bottom of the pan. Pour this sauce over the veal. (**The recipe can be prepared to this point up to 2 hours in advance.** Set the veal aside at room temperature.)

7. About 45 minutes before you plan to serve the main course, preheat the oven to 350°. Cover the veal tightly with buttered foil and bake in the center of the oven for 25 minutes.

8. To serve, reheat the vegetables. Spoon the leeks onto the center of 4 heated plates. Arrange 2 veal scallops on top. Surround with the glazed carrots. Place the baking dish over high heat and boil the pan juices to thicken slightly, about 1 minute. Pour some of the juices over each serving and sprinkle with the parsley.

—*Perla Meyers*

CABBAGE-WRAPPED VEAL TONNATO WITH SEASONED MAYONNAISE

8 SERVINGS
16 large cabbage leaves
¼ cup plus 2 tablespoons olive oil
1 small onion, minced
2 celery ribs, minced
2 garlic cloves, minced
1 can (6½ ounces) tuna fish, drained
1 pound ground veal
3 eggs
1 tablespoon anchovy paste
1 teaspoon salt
¼ teaspoon freshly ground pepper
½ cup heavy cream
1 cup cooked white rice
⅓ cup chopped parsley
2 tablespoons capers
1 tablespoon dry white wine
½ teaspoon Dijon-style mustard
1 teaspoon fresh lemon juice
¾ cup safflower oil
Tomato wedges, hard-cooked eggs
    and black olives, for garnish

1. Boil the cabbage leaves in a large saucepan of boiling water until tender and translucent, 15 to 20 minutes. Drain, let cool and pat dry. Trim away the tough ends of the central ribs.

2. In a medium skillet, heat 2 tablespoons of the olive oil. Add the onion, celery and garlic and sauté over moderate heat until softened, about 5 minutes. Remove from the heat and let cool.

3. In a food processor, puree the tuna and veal until finely ground. Add 2 of the eggs, 2 teaspoons of the anchovy paste and the salt and pepper. Blend well.

4. With the machine on, add the cream slowly through the feed tube. Transfer the mixture to a bowl. Add the rice, ¼ cup of the parsley, the capers and the sautéed vegetables. Mix well.

5. Scoop about ¼ cup of filling onto the center of one of the prepared cabbage leaves; set on a larger square of cheesecloth. Gather the ends of the cloth together and twist to form a compact ball. Remove the cheesecloth and trim off any extra cabbage to form a smooth ball. Repeat with the remaining cabbage leaves and filling.

6. Steam the stuffed cabbage on a steamer rack over boiling water for 20 minutes. Let cool to room temperature, then refrigerate for several hours, or overnight, until chilled.

7. Make a seasoned mayonnaise by whisking together the remaining egg, remaining 1 teaspoon anchovy paste, the wine, mustard, lemon juice and an additional pinch of pepper. Gradually whisk in the remaining ¼ cup olive oil and the safflower oil in a slow stream. Add 1 tablespoon of warm water when the mayonnaise starts to thicken.

8. Serve the cabbage rolls whole or sliced, accompanying each serving with tomato and egg wedges, olives and a spoonful or two of the seasoned mayonnaise. Garnish the mayonnaise with the remaining chopped parsley.

—*Anne Disrude*

MEAT

ROASTED CALF'S LIVER WITH PROSCIUTTO AND SAGE CREAM GRAVY

This is an especially attractive presentation of rosy liver slices in a cream sauce. Serve with a simple rice pilaf.

▯ F&W BEVERAGE SUGGESTION
California Merlot, such as Zellerbach

6 SERVINGS
2½ pounds calf's liver, in one piece
1 tablespoon olive oil
¼ pound prosciutto, coarsely chopped
1 large onion, chopped
2 garlic cloves, chopped
½ teaspoon thyme
10 dried sage leaves
1½ tablespoons sherry wine vinegar
¼ cup dry Marsala
1½ cups heavy cream
2 tablespoons minced parsley
¼ teaspoon salt
Pinch of freshly ground pepper

1. Preheat the oven to 450°. Pull the membrane off the surface of the liver. Cut away large blood vessels. Brush ½ tablespoon of the olive oil over the liver. Place in a roasting pan.

2. Set aside 1 tablespoon of the prosciutto. Toss the remaining prosciutto, the onion, garlic, thyme and sage leaves with the remaining ½ tablespoon oil. Scatter around the liver.

3. Roast until the internal temperature reaches 150°, about 20 to 25 minutes for medium-rare. Transfer to a platter. Loosely cover with foil to keep warm while making the sauce.

4. Place the roasting pan over moderately high heat and pour in the vinegar, Marsala and ½ cup of water. Bring to a boil and cook until almost no liquid remains, 3 to 4 minutes. Add the cream and boil over moderate heat, stirring, until thickened, 4 to

5 minutes. Strain through a sieve, pressing on the solids to extract as much liquid as possible. Return to a small saucepan over low heat to keep warm. Stir in the parsley, salt, pepper and any accumulated juices from the liver.

5. To serve, slice the liver crosswise into ¼-inch slices. Drizzle the gravy over the meat or spoon on the side. Sprinkle with the reserved prosciutto.
—*Anne Disrude*

EMINCE DE FILET DE BOEUF

▯ F&W BEVERAGE SUGGESTION
Châteauneuf-du-Pape, such as Château Beaucastel

2 SERVINGS
¾ pound beef tenderloin or sirloin, cut into 2-by-½-by-½-inch strips
½ teaspoon salt
¼ teaspoon freshly ground pepper
1 teaspoon paprika
1 tablespoon unsalted butter
1 medium shallot, chopped
1 tablespoon finely diced ham
1 tablespoon finely diced sour pickle
1 medium mushroom, finely diced
1 tablespoon finely diced pimiento
2 tablespoons Cognac or brandy
1 tablespoon dry white wine
¼ cup beef stock or canned chicken broth
1 tablespoon Dijon-style mustard
1 teaspoon Worcestershire sauce
3 drops of hot pepper sauce
2 tablespoons sour cream
1 tablespoon minced parsley

1. In a medium bowl, toss the beef with the salt, pepper and paprika.

2. In a large skillet, melt the butter

over moderately high heat. Add the beef and sauté, turning, until browned outside, about 2 minutes.

3. Add the shallot, ham, pickle, mushroom and pimiento and cook for 30 seconds. Add the Cognac and ignite. When the flames subside, transfer the beef mixture to a bowl.

4. Place the skillet over high heat. Add the wine and stock and bring to a boil, scraping up any browned bits from the bottom of pan. Stir in the mustard, Worcestershire and hot sauce. Reduce the heat to low. Blend in the sour cream and parsley. Return the beef to the skillet and cook until heated through, about 2 minutes. (Do not let the sauce boil.)
—*Walter Ruttimann, Le Midi, Newport Beach, California*

BEEF WITH CUCUMBERS AND GREEN PEPPERCORNS

▯ F&W BEVERAGE SUGGESTION
1976 Bordeaux, such as Château Branaire-Ducru

4 SERVINGS
1 boneless beef rib roast, cut about 3 inches thick (about 2½ pounds boned weight)
¼ teaspoon salt
⅛ teaspoon freshly ground black pepper
2 tablespoons grapeseed or safflower oil
3 medium cucumbers—peeled, seeded and cut into 2-by-¼-inch julienne strips
3 shallots, minced
½ cup dry white wine
1 cup veal or beef stock, preferably homemade
¼ cup heavy cream
1 stick (4 ounces) unsalted butter
1 tablespoon drained green peppercorns

1 small red bell pepper—roasted,
   peeled, seeded and cut into ¼-inch
   dice
1 tablespoon minced fresh chives

   1. Preheat the oven to 400°. Season
the meat with the salt and pepper. In
a noncorrodible ovenproof skillet,
heat the oil. Add the meat and sauté
over high heat until browned on all
sides, about 8 minutes. Place in the
oven and roast the beef until the internal temperature reaches 140°, about
15 minutes.

   2. Meanwhile, bring a pot of lightly
salted water to a boil. Add the cucumbers and cook until barely tender,
about 2 minutes. Rinse and drain
well.

   3. Transfer the beef to a platter and
cover with foil. Drain the fat from the
skillet. Add the shallots and cook over
moderate heat until softened, about 2
minutes. Add the wine and bring to a
boil over high heat. Cook until reduced to a syrupy glaze, about 3 minutes. Stir in the stock and heavy
cream and boil until reduced to 1 cup,
8 to 10 minutes.

   4. Remove from the heat and whisk
in 6 tablespoons of the butter, 1 tablespoon at a time. Add the green peppercorns; season with salt and pepper
to taste. Set aside, covered, to keep
warm.

   5. In a large skillet, melt the remaining 2 tablespoons butter over
moderately high heat. Add the cucumbers and red bell pepper, season
with a pinch of salt and pepper and
sauté until hot, 2 to 3 minutes.

   6. To serve, cut the beef into 8
slices and overlap them on a heated
platter. Arrange the vegetables
around the beef. Spoon a little of the
sauce over the meat and sprinkle with
the chives. Pass the remaining sauce
separately.

   —l'Auberge de l'Ill, Illhaeusern, France

STANDING RIB ROAST AU JUS

For a grand Sunday dinner, accompa-
ny the roast with fresh-from-the-oven
popovers and buttered broccoli.
▌F&W BEVERAGE SUGGESTION
   Burgundy, such as 1980
   Chambolle-Musigny (Grofier), or
   California Pinot Noir, such as 1983
   Sanford

6 TO 8 SERVINGS
6½-pound rib roast (3 ribs)
¼ teaspoon salt
¼ teaspoon freshly ground pepper
3 tablespoons Dijon-style mustard
   (optional)
1 tablespoon vegetable oil

   1. Preheat the oven to 500°. Place
the meat, fat-side up, in a roasting
pan; the bones, which form a slight
arc, will act as a natural rack.

   2. Sprinkle the top and sides with
the salt and pepper. Blend together
the mustard and oil and smear it over
the roast. If you are using a meat thermometer, push it deep into the center
of one of the meaty ends.

   3. Roast the meat for 15 minutes.
Reduce the heat to 350° and roast until
the thermometer registers 120° for
rare roast beef, another 1¼ hours;
130° for medium and 150° for well
done. The meat will continue to cook
as it rests after roasting. (If you wish
to calculate the cooking time for a different weight roast, allow 15 minutes
per pound for rare, 20 minutes per
pound for medium and 25 minutes
per pound for well done.)

   4. Remove the meat from the roasting pan without piercing it. Let rest
for at least 15 minutes before carving.
Take care to capture the juices as the
meat is carved and spoon some over
each serving. Rare meat will, of
course, provide more juices than well-
done meat.

   —Diana Sturgis

BRISKET STUFFED WITH SPINACH AND CARROTS

As a reminder that Passover is a
spring holiday, this brisket is stuffed
with spinach and scallions, with carrots added for a contrast in color. The
recipe can be made a day ahead and
reheated before serving.
▌F&W BEVERAGE SUGGESTION
   Sequoia Grove Cabernet
   Sauvignon

8 TO 10 SERVNGS
4-pound brisket of beef, from the first
   cut (wide end)
2 tablespoons vegetable oil
2 garlic cloves, minced
6 scallions, sliced
1¾ pounds fresh spinach, stemmed
1 egg
1 cup matzoh farfel
1 teaspoon salt
¾ teaspoon freshly ground pepper
6 medium carrots, peeled
2 large onions, sliced
¾ cup dry red wine
¾ cup beef stock or canned broth

   1. Cut a pocket horizontally along
one long side of the brisket, leaving a
½-inch border around three sides.

   2. In a large saucepan, heat the oil.
Add the garlic and cook over moderate heat until fragrant, about 30 seconds. Add the scallions and cook 2
minutes longer. With a slotted spoon,
transfer the garlic and scallions to a
large bowl.

   3. Add the spinach to the same
saucepan and cook, stirring, until
barely wilted and still bright green,
about 2 minutes. Set the spinach aside
to cool slightly; then squeeze dry.
Chop the spinach coarsely and

squeeze out any remaining liquid. Place the spinach in the bowl with the scallions. Stir in the egg, farfel, salt and pepper.

4. Preheat the broiler. Place about 4 yards of kitchen string in a small bowl of water to soak. Cut two of the carrots lengthwise into sticks about ¼ inch wide. Slice the remaining carrots into ¼-inch rounds and set aside. Place half of the carrot sticks in the brisket pocket in a layer going against the grain of the meat. Spread the spinach stuffing on top of the carrots and arrange the remaining carrot sticks on top of the stuffing. Using the kitchen string, tie the brisket at 1-inch intervals in both directions to secure the stuffing.

5. Place the brisket in a roasting pan and broil until browned on top, about 5 minutes. Turn and brown the other side. Reduce the oven temperature to 325°. Remove the brisket from the pan and pour off any fat. Scatter the sliced onions and carrot rounds over the bottom of the pan. Place the brisket on top of the vegetables, pour on the wine and stock and cover the pan tightly with the top or seal well with aluminum foil. Place the brisket in the oven and roast until the meat is fork tender, 3 to 3½ hours. Transfer the meat to a carving board, cover loosely with foil and let rest for about 20 minutes.

6. Meanwhile, strain the cooking liquid from the pan. If there is less than ¾ cup, add additional stock or water. Place the carrots and onions in a food processor. Add the cooking liquid and puree until smooth. Reheat the sauce in a small saucepan and season with additional salt and pepper to taste. Slice the brisket against the grain and serve with the sauce on the side.

—*Susan Grodnick*

MARINATED SIRLOIN WITH SHERRY VINAIGRETTE

In this recipe, the roasted sirloin must marinate overnight in the refrigerator.
F&W BEVERAGE SUGGESTION California Zinfandel, such as Louis M. Martini

10 TO 12 SERVINGS
4-pound sirloin steak, cut about 2½ inches thick, trimmed of excess fat
1 bottle (1 liter) sweet vermouth
3 garlic cloves, smashed
2 bay leaves
1 tablespoon plus 1 teaspoon salt
1½ teaspoons freshly ground pepper
1 can (6 ounces) tomato paste
¼ cup sherry wine vinegar
1 large shallot, minced
⅓ cup safflower oil
¼ cup extra-virgin olive oil
1 large cucumber—peeled, halved lengthwise, seeded and cut crosswise into ¼-inch slices
2 tablespoons minced parsley

1. Preheat the oven to 425°. In a roasting pan, roast the sirloin for 35 minutes, without turning, until the internal temperature registers 120° to 125° on a meat thermometer for rare. Remove the meat from the oven and transfer to a heatproof glass dish.

2. In a medium noncorrodible saucepan, combine the vermouth, garlic, bay leaves, 1 tablespoon of the salt and 1 teaspoon of the pepper. Stir in the tomato paste and bring to a simmer over moderate heat.

3. Pour this hot marinade over the meat and let cool, turning the meat once or twice. Cover with plastic wrap

and refrigerate to marinate overnight.

4. In a medium bowl, combine the vinegar, shallot and the remaining teaspoon salt and ½ teaspoon pepper. Whisk in the safflower and olive oils.

5. About 1 hour before serving, remove the meat from the marinade and thinly slice crosswise on the diagonal. Arrange the beef in a large oval serving dish and garnish with the cucumber slices. Pour the dressing over all and sprinkle with the parsley. Serve at room temperature.

—*W. Peter Prestcott*

PFEFFERSTEAK MADAGASCAR

2 SERVINGS
2½ tablespoons unsalted butter
1 small shallot, minced
1 tablespoon red currant jelly
1 tablespoon red wine vinegar
2 tablespoons dry red wine or beef broth
Dash of fresh lemon juice
Dash of hot pepper sauce
Freshly ground black pepper
2 slices of filet mignon, cut about 1½ inches thick (about 8 ounces each)
¼ teaspoon salt
Flour, for dredging
1 tablespoon Cognac or brandy
1 tablespoon drained green peppercorns

1. In a small saucepan, melt ½ tablespoon of the butter. Add the shallots and cook over moderately low heat until translucent, 2 to 3 minutes. Add the currant jelly, vinegar, wine, lemon juice, hot sauce and a pinch of black pepper. Simmer for 1 minute. Set aside.

2. Season the steaks with the salt and ⅛ teaspoon black pepper. Dredge in flour and shake off the excess.

3. In a large skillet, melt the remaining 2 tablespoons butter over moderately high heat. Add the steaks and sauté, turning once, until cooked to the desired doneness; 9 to 11 minutes for rare, 14 to 16 minutes for medium. Add the Cognac and ignite. When the flames die down, add the green peppercorns and cook for 1 minute. Transfer the steaks and peppercorns to 2 plates. Reheat the sauce and strain over the steaks.

—*Kaiserhof Restaurant, San Diego, California*

MESQUITE-GRILLED RIBLETS OF BEEF

These short ribs seasoned with a Chinese marinade taste best grilled over American mesquite, though you can broil the ribs indoors as well. The ribs must marinate overnight before cooking, so plan accordingly.

F&W BEVERAGE SUGGESTION
Barbaresco

2 SERVINGS
2 pounds short ribs, separated and cut crosswise into 2-inch lengths (ask your butcher to do this for you)
2 tablespoons dark brown sugar
2 tablespoons light soy sauce*
1 tablespoon medium-dry sherry
1 tablespoon Oriental sesame oil
2 tablespoons unhulled sesame seeds*
2 medium garlic cloves, minced
1 teaspoon minced fresh ginger
2 scallions, thinly sliced
¼ teaspoon freshly ground pepper
*Available at Oriental markets

1. Trim the fat and gristle from each riblet. Score each piece three times on each side. Place in a shallow baking dish in a single layer.
2. In a small bowl, combine the brown sugar, soy sauce, sherry, sesame oil, sesame seeds, garlic, ginger, scallions and pepper. Pour over the ribs. Turn the ribs to coat with mari-

nade all over. Cover and refrigerate, turning the ribs occasionally, for 24 hours.
3. *To cook outdoors:* Remove the ribs from the refrigerator. Soak two handfuls of mesquite wood or chips for 1 hour in water to cover. After the mesquite has soaked for 30 minutes, light a charcoal fire. Let the coals burn for 30 to 40 minutes, until they are covered with white ash. Remove the grill rack and place the drained mesquite on the burning coals. Replace the rack and put the ribs on the grill. Cover, if possible, and grill with the vents wide open for 10 minutes. Turn the ribs over and grill for 10 minutes longer, or until slightly charred outside and cooked through and tender.

To cook indoors: Remove the ribs from the refrigerator. Preheat the broiler for 20 minutes. Place the ribs on a rack in a broiling pan. Broil the ribs 2 to 3 inches from the heat for 10 minutes. Turn the ribs over and broil for 10 minutes longer, or until slightly charred outside, cooked through and tender.

—*Karen Lee & Alaxandra Branyon*

GRILLED RIB STEAK

A good piece of beef should be cooked rare or medium-rare to develop the full range of its flavor and tenderness. To test for doneness, press the surface of the steak with your finger. In its raw state, it will be soft to the touch and will retain the impression of your finger. As it cooks, it will become firmer. Rare is still soft, but offers a little resistance. Medium-rare feels springy to the touch, and well done is firm. (Do this test with all the meat you cook and you will soon become an expert at telling when meats

are done by touch. This is the standard test for doneness used by professional chefs.)

F&W BEVERAGE SUGGESTION
A flavorful red, such as Côtes du Rhône or California Zinfandel

6 SERVINGS
3 rib steaks with the bone, cut about 1½ inches thick and trimmed of fat (see Note)
Salt and freshly ground pepper
1 bunch of watercress, for garnish

1. The grill should be hot and the rack close to the coals before the meat is placed on it. With the grill registering 500°, or when the coals are red hot, cook the steaks 4 to 5 minutes per side with the lid down. If your grill doesn't have a lid, increase the cooking time by 3 to 4 minutes. Halfway through the cooking on each side, I lift and rotate the meat 90 degrees to create the traditional crosshatch grill marks, which enhance both the flavor and appearance. Once the meat has been turned over to the second side, salt and pepper the top. Check the firmness of the meat from time to time, noticing the changes that occur. If you see juices beginning to pool on the surface, the steak has reached medium-rare and is approaching medium. Remove the steak from the heat immediately.
2. To serve, I set the steaks on a large carving board and surround them with watercress. At the table I bone the steaks and slice them across the grain on the diagonal to form broad, thin slices. By serving 3 to 4 thin slices per person, and 2 or 3 slices when they request seconds or thirds, you will find that each steak serves two people. If you have carved especially well, you may even have some leftovers for a sandwich the next day.
NOTE: There is a considerable amount of fat on the rib, and it is

always a challenge to remove as much as possible without losing the shape of the steak. It is equally important that the bone be trimmed of fat. After trimming, leave the steaks out for about an hour to come to room temperature. Just before cooking, pat dry with paper towels.

—*Richard Grausman*

MUSLIM (MUSSAMAN) CURRY

This is one of the great curries of the world, uniting the flavors of India and Thailand in a harmonious mixed marriage, ruled by the Chinese dictum or the balance of flavor values: sweet, sour, salty, hot and bitter.

6 SERVINGS

2 pounds beef chuck or round, trimmed of fat and cut into ½-inch dice
2 medium all-purpose potatoes, peeled and cut into 1-inch cubes
½ cup roasted, salted peanuts
4 cups Thick Coconut Milk (p. 232)
3 tablespoons fish sauce (nam pla, nuoc mam or patis)*
½ cup Mussaman Curry Paste (p. 238)
1 cinnamon stick
8 whole cardamom pods
2 tablespoons fresh lime juice
1 tablespoon instant tamarind concentrate* dissolved in 3 tablespoons hot water or 1 tablespoon molasses dissolved in 3 tablespoons fresh lime juice
3 tablespoons dark brown sugar
*Available at Southeast Asian and some Chinese markets

1. In a wok or large flameproof casserole, combine the beef, potatoes, peanuts, coconut milk and fish sauce. Bring to a boil over moderately high heat. (The mixture will probably ap-

pear curdled at this point.) Reduce the heat to low and simmer, stirring occasionally, until the beef and potatoes are tender, 20 to 25 minutes.

2. Using a slotted spoon, transfer the beef, peanuts and potatoes to a bowl. Increase the heat to moderately high, bring the liquid to a boil and reduce by half, about 15 minutes.

3. Blend in the curry paste and return the beef, peanuts and potatoes to the wok. Add the cinnamon stick and cardamom pods. Reduce the heat to low and simmer for 5 minutes.

4. Stir in the lime juice, tamarind and sugar. The gravy should now be thick. Remove the cinnamon stick and transfer the curry to a serving bowl.

—*Jennifer Brennan*

OLD-FASHIONED BEEF STEW

🍷 F&W BEVERAGE SUGGESTION
Rioja, such as C.U.N.E.

4 TO 6 SERVINGS

2½ pounds boned beef shank, rump or brisket—trimmed and cut into 2-inch cubes
1½ tablespoons vegetable oil
2 large onions
1 cup beer or dry red wine
½ teaspoon thyme
2 imported bay leaves
2 teaspoons tomato paste
3 carrots, cut into ¼-inch rounds
1 pound waxy boiling potatoes, peeled and cut into ½-inch dice
1 cup frozen baby peas, thawed
½ teaspoon salt
¼ teaspoon freshly ground pepper

1. Pat the pieces of meat dry with paper towels. In a large skillet, heat 1 tablespoon of the vegetable oil over moderately high heat. Add a batch of the meat cubes, leaving plenty of space between each for good browning. Brown well on all sides, about 15 minutes. Remove to a large flame-

proof casserole. Using about ½ tablespoon more oil, brown the remaining meat and add to the casserole.

2. Coarsely chop one of the onions. Add it to the skillet and sauté over moderate heat until softened, 2 to 3 minutes. Add the beer and boil for 2 minutes over high heat.

3. Add the onion and beer to the casserole. Add 1½ cups of water, the thyme, bay leaves and tomato paste. Bring to a bare simmer and cook, covered, maintaining a simmer, until the meat is tender, about 5 hours.

4. Cut the remaining onion into eighths and add it to the casserole along with the carrots and potatoes. Continue to cook, uncovered, stirring occasionally, until the carrots and potatoes are tender, about 1 hour.

5. Add the peas and cook to warm through, about 2 minutes. Season with the salt and pepper.

—*Anne Disrude*

BRAD OGDEN'S CHILI CON CARNE

When it's cold, I often make chili because it's so easy and can be made ahead. In fact, chili *should* be made ahead to give the savory flavors a chance to blend.
🍷 F&W BEVERAGE SUGGESTION
Dark beer, such as Guinness

8 TO 10 SERVINGS

2 tablespoons olive oil
3 pounds beef chuck, coarsely ground
3 medium onions, chopped
3 tablespoons minced garlic
1 Anaheim chile—roasted, peeled, seeded and pureed—or canned hot green chile, seeded and pureed

⅓ cup chili powder
1 can (35 ounces) Italian plum
    tomatoes, coarsely chopped, with
    their liquid
½ cup tomato sauce
2 cups beef stock or water
1 can (12 ounces) beer
3 tablespoons red wine vinegar
1 tablespoon coarse (kosher) salt
2 teaspoons freshly ground pepper
2 teaspoons paprika
½ teaspoon ground cumin
⅛ teaspoon hot pepper sauce
3 cups cooked kidney beans or
    canned, drained and rinsed
Shredded Cheddar cheese, chopped
    sweet onion, sour cream, chopped
    fresh coriander and/or hot salsa, for
    garnish

1. In a large heavy skillet, heat the oil. Add the beef and sauté over high heat, stirring, until lightly browned, about 10 minutes. Drain the meat, reserving 3 tablespoons of the fat.

2. Return the reserved fat to the skillet, add the onions and cook over moderate heat until lightly browned, about 8 minutes. Add the garlic and cook for 1 minute.

3. In a large flameproof casserole, combine the beef, onions and garlic with the pureed Anaheim chile, chili powder, tomatoes with liquid, tomato sauce, stock, beer, vinegar, salt, pepper, paprika, cumin and hot sauce. Simmer over moderately high heat, stirring frequently and skimming off excess grease, for 35 minutes.

4. Add the beans and cook for 10 minutes longer. Remove the chili from the heat and let stand uncovered at room temperature for 3 to 4 hours so that the flavors can develop. (**The chili can be made ahead and refrigerated overnight.** It is better the second day.)

5. To serve, reheat the chili and adjust the seasonings if necessary. Serve with an assortment of garnishes.
—*Bradley Ogden*

COUNTRY-STYLE TERRINE

Menu suggestion: To start, a green salad with goat cheese and French bread; with the terrine, Potato Salad à l'Orange with Roasted Sweet Peppers (p. 139); for dessert, Apple, Prune and Apricot Compote (p. 215), sugar cookies and coffee.

F&W BEVERAGE SUGGESTION
California Zinfandel, such as Kendall-Jackson

10 TO 12 SERVINGS
1 pound chicken livers, halved and
    trimmed
⅓ cup Cognac or brandy
1 pound ground beef chuck
1 pound ground pork shoulder
¼ pound fresh pork fat, finely diced
½ cup fresh bread crumbs
1 tablespoon salt
2 teaspoons freshly ground pepper
½ teaspoon allspice
2 tablespoons unsalted butter
¼ pound mushrooms, chopped
2 eggs
1 tablespoon plus 1 teaspoon dried
    tarragon
1 garlic clove, minced
14 thin slices of bacon (about ½
    pound)

1. Pick out half of the chicken livers, choosing the plumpest and most perfect. Soak them in the brandy in a small bowl for 30 minutes. Drain the livers, reserving the brandy.

2. In a large bowl, combine the beef, pork, pork fat, bread crumbs, salt, pepper and allspice. Mix well.

3. In a large skillet, melt 1 tablespoon of the butter over high heat. When the foam subsides, add the marinated chicken livers and sauté turning once, for about 30 seconds on each side, or until lightly browned around the edges. Transfer to a plate and set aside.

4. Melt the remaining 1 tablespoon butter in the skillet. Add the mushrooms and sauté over high heat until they are browned, about 5 minutes. Scrape them into the bowl of meats.

5. In a blender or food processor, puree the remaining raw chicken livers with the eggs, tarragon, garlic and reserved brandy. Add to the meat mixture and mix until well blended.

6. Preheat the oven to 375°. Line a 9-cup (11½-by-4-inch) terrine with crosswise strips of bacon; line the ends of the terrine with lengthwise strips of bacon, allowing the ends to overhang. Evenly spread half the filling in the mold. Arrange the sautéed chicken livers in a row down the center and top with the remaining meat mixture. Smooth the top and fold the bacon ends over the mixture. Cover the terrine tightly with aluminum foil and place in a large roasting pan in the oven. Add enough warm water to the pan to reach halfway up the sides of the terrine.

7. Bake for 1½ hours. Using a bulb baster, remove any melted fat from the top of the terrine.

8. Carefully transfer the terrine to a baking sheet or larger pan. Cut out a piece of cardboard to fit inside the terrine, cover it with foil and place it on top of the meat. Weigh down with about 5 pounds of weights or heavy cans. Let cool, then refrigerate, still weighted, overnight. The terrine improves with flavor as it stands, refrigerated, for up to 3 days. Unmold before serving if desired.
—*Diana Sturgis*

MEAT

BARBECUED BEEF BUNS

These wondrous buns require a little time, so it might be a good idea to double the recipe. They freeze well. The beef is marinated overnight in the refrigerator, so plan accordingly.

MAKES 12
BARBECUED BEEF:
1 pound boneless beef chuck steak or rump
1½ tablespoons hoisin sauce*
1 tablespoon ketchup
½ tablespoon dark brown sugar
1 tablespoon soy sauce

DOUGH:
¼ cup sugar
½ cup warm water (105° to 115°)
1 envelope (¼ ounce) active dry yeast
2 eggs
2¼ cups bread flour
¼ cup lard, melted and cooled to room temperature

SAUCE FOR FILLING:
3 tablespoons oyster-flavored sauce*
1 tablespoon soy sauce
2 teaspoons Oriental sesame oil
1 tablespoon hoisin sauce*
1½ tablespoons granulated sugar
1½ tablespoons cornstarch
1 tablespoon vegetable oil
1 tablespoon chopped fresh ginger
3 scallions, chopped
Pinch of crushed hot pepper
*Available at Oriental markets

1. *Make the barbecued beef:* Divide the chuck steak into sections according to the muscle structure. Trim off the connective tissue and fat. Cut the meat into strips about 5 inches long and 2 inches wide.

2. In a bowl large enough to hold the meat, stir together the hoisin sauce, ketchup, brown sugar and soy sauce. Add the beef strips and toss to coat well. Cover and marinate overnight in the refrigerator, tossing the beef occasionally.

3. Preheat the oven to 400°. Line a large baking pan with aluminum foil. Place a rack in the pan and place the beef strips on the rack. Baste with the marinade and roast on the top shelf of the oven for 15 minutes. Turn, baste the second side and roast for 15 minutes longer. Remove and let cool on the rack; cut the beef into ¼-inch dice. (**The beef can be kept well wrapped and refrigerated for a week or frozen for 6 weeks.** Let return to room temperature before proceeding.)

4. *Make the dough:* In a small bowl, combine the sugar and water. Sprinkle the yeast on top of the liquid and let sit for about 30 minutes, until it becomes very foamy. In another small bowl, beat one of the eggs.

5. In a larger bowl, measure out 2 cups of the flour and make a well in the center. Add the yeast mixture, the beaten egg and the lard. With a fork, beat together the liquid ingredients and then stir them into the flour. When the liquid is well incorporated, turn the dough out onto a floured surface and knead until smooth and springy, about 15 minutes. Use as much of the remaining ¼ cup flour as is necessary to prevent sticking.

6. Oil a medium bowl and place the dough in it. Turn it over so that dough is lightly oiled all over. Cover with a towel, place in a warm spot and let rise until doubled in bulk, 2 to 3 hours.

7. *Meanwhile, make the sauce:* In a small bowl, combine the oyster sauce, soy sauce, sesame oil, hoisin sauce and granulated sugar. In a second small bowl, mix the cornstarch with 2 tablespoons of cold water.

8. Heat a wok over high heat for 1 minute. Pour in the vegetable oil around the sides. When it begins to smoke, add the ginger, scallions and hot pepper. Stir-fry for about 30 seconds, until aromatic.

9. Add the beef and stir-fry for about 1 minute, until warmed through. Add the sauce mixture and stir-fry for 1 minute. Stir the cornstarch mixture again, add to the wok and stir until the mixture thickens, about 30 seconds. Pour into a bowl and let cool to room temperature.

10. When the dough has risen once, divide it into 12 equal pieces. Form each into a ball, then flatten into a 3-inch disk. Use your fingers to stretch thin the edges and enlarge the disk to a 4-inch circle. (Leaving the center of the circle thicker is important to keep the filling from leaking out.)

11. Place 1 tablespoon of barbecued beef filling on each circle. Stretch and pull the edges up around the filling and press them together. When all the edges have been gathered, pinch and twist to firmly close. With your hands, shape the buns into even rounds and place them on a greased cookie sheet. Cover with a kitchen towel, place in a warm spot and let rise until doubled, 1 to 2 hours.

12. Preheat the oven to 350°. Lightly spray each bun with water. Beat the remaining egg with 1 tablespoon of water. With a pastry brush, brush the tops of the buns with the egg wash. Bake for 15 minutes, turning the sheet halfway through baking for even browning.

13. Serve hot. Or let cool to room temperature, wrap well and freeze. To reheat, thaw and then wrap the buns in foil and heat them in a 350° oven for 10 minutes.

—Anne Disrude

PANHANDLE ROAST BEEF HASH

Although traditional roast beef hash often features a bit of ketchup, my use of barbecue sauce produces a more interesting result. Select a good-quality, fairly thick sauce, preferably one with a bit of hot spice and smoke to it. As for accompaniments, if you'd like a vegetable, stick to something simple, such as green beans and red onions in a plain vinaigrette. A quick batch of buttermilk biscuits would also make supper special indeed. As for the poached eggs, I love them on hash, but to use them or not is up to you.

6 TO 8 SERVINGS

2 pounds boiling potatoes, peeled and cut into ½-inch dice
1 tablespoon salt
4 tablespoons unsalted butter
1 medium onion, chopped
1½ pounds leftover roast beef or pot roast (you can use deli roast beef if you wish), trimmed of fat and cut into ½-inch dice
¾ cup barbecue sauce, preferably one labeled "smoky" and "spicy"
1½ cups beef stock or canned broth
Freshly ground pepper
6 to 8 poached eggs (optional)

1. Place the potatoes in a large saucepan. Add cold water to cover and the salt. Bring to a boil, reduce the heat and simmer, stirring occasionally, until the potatoes are tender but still hold their shape, about 5 minutes after the water returns to a boil. Drain immediately and reserve.

2. In a large skillet, melt the butter over moderate heat. Add the onion and cook, stirring occasionally, until it just begins to brown, about 15 minutes. Add the diced beef, potatoes, barbecue sauce and beef stock. Simmer for 5 minutes, stirring frequently. Season with salt and pepper to taste. **(The recipe can be prepared to this point up to 2 hours ahead.** Reheat gently before proceeding.)

3. Preheat the broiler. Spoon the hot hash into 6 to 8 individual shallow gratin dishes or into one large (12-inch) gratin. Broil until the beef and potato cubes are crisp and brown on top, about 2 minutes.

4. If you like hash with eggs, make a shallow depression in the center of each portion with the back of a spoon. Set a poached egg in each depression and serve at once.

—*Michael McLaughlin*

WHOLE STUFFED CABBAGE IN BRODO

F&W BEVERAGE SUGGESTION
Beaujolais or California Gamay

8 TO 10 SERVINGS
1 chicken, about 3 pounds
2 medium onions
1 carrot, cut into large chunks
1 celery rib, cut into large pieces
12 parsley stems
2 plum tomatoes, chopped
3 cans (13¾ ounces each) chicken broth
1 large head of cabbage (about 3 pounds)
1 pound ground pork
2 tablespoons unsalted butter
2 medium garlic cloves, minced
½ cup minced parsley
2 imported bay leaves
2 teaspoons fennel seeds
¼ teaspoon cinnamon
½ teaspoon whole peppercorns
2 teaspoons thyme
¼ teaspoon freshly grated nutmeg
1 teaspoon imported sweet paprika
1½ teaspoons salt
2 eggs

1. Preheat the oven to 400°. Remove the chicken breasts and the large pieces of meat from the thigh and leg; set aside. Cut the carcass into pieces and put in a roasting pan; include the skin from the breasts and legs, the bones, fat and all the giblets except the liver. Roast in the oven, turning occasionally, until very brown, about 45 minutes.

2. Transfer the browned chicken bones and rendered fat to a large saucepan. Pour 1 cup of water into the roasting pan. Bring to a boil over high heat, scraping up all the browned bits that cling to the bottom of the pan. Pour this liquid into the saucepan.

3. Quarter 1 onion with the peel on. Add to the saucepan along with the carrot, celery, parsley stems, tomatoes, chicken broth and 5 cups of water. Simmer uncovered for 2 hours; do not let boil. Strain the broth and skim off the fat.

4. Remove the 3 or 4 toughest outer leaves of the cabbage and discard. Cut out a broad deep core. Place the cabbage in a large pot of boiling water and cook, removing the leaves with tongs as they loosen, until only a small center remains (2 to 3 inches wide), remove that and use elsewhere or discard. Return all the remaining leaves to the pot and cook until tender and translucent, 15 to 20 minutes. Drain and let cool. Trim off the tough central rib end on each leaf.

5. Meanwhile, partially freeze the reserved chicken, then finely grind in a food processor. Remove any tendons that won't grind. Combine with the pork and set aside.

6. Mince the remaining onion. In a medium skillet, melt the butter over moderate heat. Add the onion, garlic and ¼ cup of the minced parsley and sauté until the onion has softened, about 5 minutes. Remove from the heat and let cool.

7. In a spice grinder, pulverize the

105

MEAT

bay leaves with the fennel seeds, cinnamon, peppercorns, thyme, nutmeg, paprika and salt.

8. Reserve 1 teaspoon of the spice mixture. Beat the remainder with the eggs. Add to the ground meats along with the cooled onion mixture and mix thoroughly.

9. To assemble, line a 2-quart bowl with a large double-thickness of cheesecloth, allowing about a 6-inch overhang.

10. Set out the reserved cabbage leaves according to size, from large to small. Arrange the large leaves overlapping in the bottom of the bowl, core end toward the center, and spread liberally with meat mixture. Continue with all the leaves in order of size, using all the meat.

11. Pull the corners of the cheesecloth together and twist to shape the stuffed cabbage into a large ball. Tie the ends of the cheesecloth securely with kitchen string.

12. Dissolve the remaining 1 teaspoon spice mixture in the broth. Place the cabbage in a large, deep saucepan that just holds the bundle. Pour the broth over the cabbage.

13. Bring to a simmer over high heat, reduce the heat to low and poach the cabbage for 2 hours, or until the internal temperature reaches 140° on an instant-reading thermometer. (**The recipe can be made ahead to this point.** In fact, the flavor improves. Let the cabbage cool in the broth; then cover and refrigerate overnight. To reheat, gently simmer in the broth until heated through, about 1 hour.)

14. Remove the cabbage from the broth and let rest for 30 minutes; reserve the broth. Remove the cheesecloth. Cut the stuffed cabbage into 8 to 10 wedges and place in soup plates. Add the remaining ¼ cup minced parsley to the broth; ladle over the wedges.

—*Anne Disrude*

106

OLD-FASHIONED STUFFED CABBAGE

🍷 F&W BEVERAGE SUGGESTION
British ale

4 TO 6 SERVINGS
1 large head of cabbage (about 3 pounds)
2 tablespoons unsalted butter
1 medium onion, chopped
1 small green bell pepper, chopped
⅓ pound ground veal
⅓ pound ground pork
⅓ pound ground beef
1 cup cooked white rice
1 egg
1½ teaspoons salt
¾ teaspoon freshly grated nutmeg
¼ teaspoon freshly ground black pepper
1 can (28 ounces) plum tomatoes, drained and sieved
1 cup beef or chicken stock or canned broth
2 teaspoons tomato paste
3 tablespoons fresh lemon juice
¼ cup raisins
2 tablespoons brown sugar

1. Remove and discard the 3 or 4 toughest outer leaves of the cabbage. Cut out a broad, deep core. Cook the cabbage in a large pot of boiling water until you can remove 10 of the largest leaves with tongs. Remove the remaining cabbage and reserve for another use. Return the 10 leaves to the pot and boil until tender and translucent, about 15 to 20 minutes. Drain, let cool and pat dry. Cut away the tough end of the central rib on each leaf.

2. Melt the butter in a medium skillet over moderate heat. Add the onion and bell pepper and sauté over moderately low heat until the onion is translucent and excess moisture has evaporated, about 15 minutes. Transfer to a bowl and let cool.

3. Add the meats, rice, egg, 1 teaspoon of the salt, the nutmeg and black pepper to the onion mixture. Mix to blend well. Scoop about ⅓ cup of the meat and rice filling onto the bottom of each cabbage leaf. Fold up the bottom edge, fold in the sides and roll up.

4. In a large deep skillet or flameproof casserole, combine the tomatoes, stock, tomato paste, lemon juice, raisins, brown sugar and remaining ½ teaspoon salt. Bring to a simmer and add the cabbage rolls, seam-side down. Simmer gently, uncovered, for 2½ hours, or until the cabbage is tender.

5. Remove the stuffed cabbage to a platter. Bring the sauce to a boil and boil to thicken a little if desired. Add more brown sugar or lemon juice to taste. Pour the sauce over the rolls.

DILLED CABBAGE ROLLS: Prepare the stuffed cabbage as above, but omit the nutmeg and add ⅓ cup minced fresh dill to the meat and rice stuffing. Reduce the lemon juice in the sauce to 1½ tablespoons. At the end of Step 4, melt 2 tablespoons butter in a large skillet over moderate heat. Remove the cabbage rolls from the sauce and cook in the butter, turning, until browned, about 20 minutes. Remove to a platter. Add the sauce to the skillet and bring to a boil, scraping up any browned bits on the bottom of the skillet. Pour over the rolls and serve hot.

—*Anne Disrude*

MEAT

ROASTED PORK SHOULDER WITH AN ORIENTAL GRAVY

Tea is a subtle substitute for stock in this unusual, Oriental-flavored dish. Serve with fine noodles tossed with a film of sesame oil.

❑ F&W BEVERAGE SUGGESTION
Belgian beer, such as Duvel, or California Gewürztraminer, such as Winery Lake

8 TO 10 SERVINGS
½ pound Swiss chard leaves (1 pound chard)
10 scallions
6 large garlic cloves
1 tablespoon vegetable oil
1 tablespoon minced fresh ginger plus 4 slices (¼-inch-thick)
Zest of 1 navel orange, cut in fine strips
½ teaspoon salt
5-pound whole boned pork shoulder, bones reserved
3 tablespoons soy sauce
⅛ teaspoon freshly ground pepper
2 tablespoons rice wine or dry sherry
1 tablespoon rice wine vinegar
1 tablespoon Szechuan chili paste*
1½ cups brewed black tea
2 teaspoons cornstarch (optional)
*Available at Oriental markets

1. Blanch the chard leaves in a large pot of lightly salted boiling water for 2 to 3 minutes, until tender. Run under cold water until cool enough to handle. Squeeze out excess moisture. Coarsely chop. Set aside.
2. Mince 5 of the scallions and 3 of the garlic cloves. In a medium skillet, heat the oil. Add the minced scallions, minced garlic and minced ginger and sauté over moderate heat until softened, about 3 minutes. Toss with the chard. Add half the orange zest strips and ¼ teaspoon of the salt. Let cool to room temperature.

3. Preheat the oven to 350°. Spread out the pork shoulder fat-side down. Paint with 1 tablespoon of the soy sauce. Spread the filling evenly over the top. Roll and tie the roast. Sprinkle the remaining ¼ teaspoon salt and the pepper over the roast. Place in a roasting pan.
4. Trim the remaining 5 scallions to 5 inches in length; reserve the green ends for the sauce. Cut the scallions crosswise in half and add to the roasting pan. Halve the remaining 3 garlic cloves. Add to the roasting pan with the ginger slices and pork bone.
5. In a small bowl, combine the remaining 2 tablespoons soy sauce, the rice wine, rice wine vinegar, chili paste and tea. Pour ½ cup of this basting liquid over the roast and place in the oven.
6. Roast for about 2½ hours, or until a thermometer registers 150°, basting frequently with the basting liquid. Turn off the oven. Transfer the roast to a platter, loosely cover with foil and return to the oven. Let rest for 30 minutes.
7. Strain the liquid from the roasting pan. Skim off the fat. Blot up any extra fat in the pan with a paper towel. Return the strained liquid to the roasting pan and add any remaining basting liquid. Bring to a boil. Reduce the heat to moderately low and simmer for 10 to 15 minutes, scraping up any browned bits from the sides and bottom of the pan.
8. Strain the gravy into a small saucepan and add any accumulated juices from the roast. If a thicker sauce is desired, dissolve the cornstarch in 1 tablespoon of water. Stir into the gravy, bring to a boil and cook stirring, for 1 to 2 minutes, until thickened.
9. Chop enough of the reserved scallion greens to measure ¼ cup. Add to the gravy along with the remaining orange zest.
10. Cut the string from the roast.

Carve the roast at a slight angle into slices ¼ inch thick. Drizzle the sauce over the top or serve on the side.
—Anne Disrude

RAPINI WITH ITALIAN SAUSAGE

I once enjoyed a delicious Italian lunch at Manducatis, a casual restaurant on a bleak, unfashionable avenue in Long Island City across the East River from Manhattan. The homestyle meal consisted of a wide variety of fresh, simple dishes, including a ridiculously easy-to-prepare, traditional dish with only two ingredients—a satisfying juxtaposition of bitter green rapini (broccoli raab) and spicy, rich sausage. When served with pasta or potatoes, you have a whole meal.
❑ F&W BEVERAGE SUGGESTION
Chianti, such as Frescobaldi

4 SERVINGS
1¾ pounds sweet or hot Italian sausage
2 pounds broccoli raab, peeled or trimmed

1. Prick the sausages all over with a knife tip or a needle. Arrange them in a wide skillet in a scant ⅛ inch of water. Cook over high heat at first, then gradually reduce the heat, turning the sausages often, until well browned, about 15 minutes.
2. Meanwhile, cut the broccoli raab stems into 2-inch pieces; keep the leaves whole.
3. Drain off most of the fat from the sausages. Add the stems of the broccoli raab and 2 tablespoons of water to the skillet. Cover and cook over moderate heat until barely tender, about 3 minutes. Add the leaves, cover and cook until the leaves wilt, about 3 minutes. Serve at once.
—Elizabeth Schneider

SOMEWHAT ENLIGHTENED SAUSAGES

Slice the sausages and serve them hot with a simple beurre blanc on a bed of briefly sautéed spinach. Or serve cold on a chiffonade of salad greens and drizzled with a low-acid vinaigrette dressing. For a well-bound texture, it's important to have all the stuffing ingredients and equipment well chilled.

MAKES ABOUT 2 POUNDS

5 feet of salt-packed hog casings (see Note)
1 ounce dried morel mushrooms
½ pound pork with some fat, trimmed of all sinew and cut into 1-inch pieces
½ pound skinless, boneless chicken breasts, trimmed of all sinew and fat and cut into 1-inch pieces
1 cup heavy cream
2 egg whites, chilled
2 tablespoons cold unsalted butter
1¼ teaspoons salt
¼ teaspoon freshly ground white pepper
¼ pound Black Forest ham, cut into ⅛-inch dice
⅓ cup minced chives (2 large bunches)

1. Rinse the casings to remove excess salt. Soak for 30 minutes in cold water. Run cold water through the casings to flush them out and set aside in a bowl of fresh water until ready to use.

2. Place the morels in a small bowl and cover with 1½ cups hot water. Let stand until softened, 15 to 20 minutes. Drain the mushrooms, reserving the soaking liquid and squeezing excess liquid out of the mushrooms back into the bowl. Rinse the mushrooms in several changes of cold water until the water is clear. Squeeze excess mois-

ture from the mushrooms. Trim any sandy pieces from the stem ends and coarsely chop the mushrooms.

3. Strain the reserved soaking liquid through several layers of dampened cheesecloth. Place it and the chopped mushrooms in a small saucepan and boil over high heat until the liquid evaporates, 10 to 15 minutes. Put the mushrooms in the refrigerator to chill.

4. Spread the pork and chicken on a large plate in a single layer. Cover and place in the freezer until the pieces just begin to stiffen, 45 to 60 minutes. At the same time, put the cream and a food processor bowl with lid and steel blade in the freezer.

5. Place the pork and chicken in the chilled processor bowl. Process with quick on/off motions until the mixture starts to form a ball, about 2 minutes. Scrape the sides of the bowl. Add the egg whites, butter, salt and white pepper. Process, scraping the sides occasionally, until the mixture is light and smooth, another 2 minutes. Transfer the sausage mixture to a bowl set in a larger bowl of ice water.

6. Gradually stir in the cream, 1 or 2 tablespoons at a time. Fold in the morels, ham and chives. Cover the mixture and let rest in the refrigerator for 2 hours or overnight.

7. Drain the casings and flush with cold water again to remove even more salt. Squeeze out excess water.

8. Use a small pastry bag fitted with a ½-inch plain tip that has been lightly coated with oil. Slip one end of a 1½-foot length of casing onto the pastry tip. Gently gather the casing up onto the tip, leaving a 3-inch overhang.

9. Fill the pastry bag one-third full with the sausage mixture. Gently squeeze the pastry bag, holding the casing in place on the tip. When the casing begins to fill and the air has been forced out, tie a knot in the casing end. Continue squeezing to fill the casing fairly tight (not much room is

needed for expansion), moving the casing off the tip as it fills.

10. Form the sausage into 5-inch links, twisting each link twice and in the opposite direction from the previous one to prevent unwinding. Prick the sausage all over with a needle. Refrigerate for at least 2 hours, and up to overnight, before cooking. Repeat with the remaining ingredients.

11. To cook, bring a large pot of water to a simmer over high heat. Reduce the heat to moderately low, add the sausages and cook at a simmer, turning once, until firm and opaque throughout, 22 to 25 minutes. Do not boil.

12. The sausages can be held in the hot water, covered, with the heat off, until ready to serve, or removed, lightly covered, refrigerated until chilled and served cold.

NOTE: Sausage casings are sold by length, not weight. The smallest package you can buy is about 45 feet, but the casings will keep very nicely in the freezer. Ask your specialty butcher to order them for you or order direct from The Sausagemaker, 177 Military Rd., Buffalo, NY 14207; 716-876-5521.

SAUSAGE VARIATIONS:

#1: Omit the morels, ham and chives. In Step 6 add ¼ teaspoon finely grated nutmeg, 2 teaspoons fennel seeds and 1 teaspoon thyme, all finely ground together in a spice mill or mortar and pestle.

#2: Omit the morels and chives. In Step 9, along with the diced ham, add ¼ cup pistachios, skinned and coarsely chopped, and ½ teaspoon freshly cracked black pepper.

—*Anne Disrude*

Huevos Rancheros New York Style (p. 48) with a fresh tomato salsa.

Clockwise from upper left: Oriental Fried Feta Dumplings (p. 16), Chèvre Mousse (p. 17) and Four-Cheese Tart (p. 51).

COUNTRY PORK AND VEGETABLE STEW

One of the few Thai curries that does not require coconut milk, this curry is a favorite of farm people in the northeast of Thailand.

6 SERVINGS
6 dried Chinese black mushrooms*
1 cup broccoli florets
½ cup green beans, cut on the diagonal into 2-inch lengths
¼ cup vegetable oil
¼ cup Red Curry Paste (p. 237)
1 pound lean pork, cut into 2-by-½-inch julienne strips
3 tablespoons fish sauce (nam pla, nuoc mam or patis)*
Grated zest of 1 lime (about 2 teaspoons)
1 inch of fresh ginger, peeled and shredded
5 fresh green serrano peppers, seeded and cut into thin slivers
10 cherry tomatoes
1 teaspoon instant tamarind concentrate* dissolved in 2 tablespoons hot water or
1 teaspoon molasses dissolved in 2 tablespoons fresh lime juice
1 tablespoon sugar
1 teaspoon freshly ground black pepper
¼ teaspoon salt
¼ cup fresh mint leaves, for garnish
*Available at Southeast Asian and some Chinese markets

1. In a small bowl, soak the dried mushrooms in hot water until soft, about 15 minutes. Discard the stems and cut the mushroom caps into thin julienne strips.

2. Meanwhile, blanch the broccoli florets and green beans in a large saucepan of boiling water for 2 minutes. Drain, rinse under cold running water and set aside.

3. Set a wok over moderately high heat and add the oil. When a haze forms over the oil, add the curry paste and cook, stirring constantly, until the paste darkens and the sharp odor mellows, about 3 minutes.

4. Stir in the pork, fish sauce, lime zest and shredded ginger and stir-fry for 5 minutes.

5. Add the mushrooms, broccoli and beans to the wok. Stir-fry for 5 minutes longer. Stir in the serrano peppers and tomatoes and fry for 1 minute.

6. Stir in the tamarind, sugar, black pepper and salt. Transfer the curry to a serving dish and sprinkle with the mint leaves.

—Jennifer Brennan

GRILLED LEG OF LAMB

Rack, saddle and leg of lamb are all wonderful when grilled. The rack and saddle are delicate in flavor and require little seasoning. A bit of thyme, salt and pepper is all that is needed. The leg—stronger in flavor—can support the more robust seasonings of mustard, rosemary, garlic, curry and ginger.

Last summer I developed a terrific marinade by combining a cup of aïoli I had made earlier in the week, with some Dijon mustard, a bit of thyme and chopped fresh ginger. Everyone coming into the house asked what smelled so good. Cooked medium-rare and thinly sliced, the leg of lamb served 6, and we had delicious leftovers for sandwiches the next day.

We began the meal with cheese and a robust red wine from Spain, which was continued with the lamb. I accompanied the lamb with an easy vegetable dish, a sauté of zucchini, onion and tomatoes, as well as a salad. Mango sorbet and blueberries with almond *tuiles* (cookies) completed the dinner—a meal I am sure to repeat this summer.

6 TO 8 SERVINGS
6- to 7-pound leg of lamb—boned, butterflied and trimmed of all fat
Thyme, preferably fresh
Rosemary, preferably fresh
Freshly ground pepper and salt

1. A butterflied leg of lamb, boned and cut to lie flat, cooks well on a grill, although some parts are thicker than others, making even cooking and carving a little difficult. To remedy this, after the butcher has boned, trimmed and butterflied the leg for me, I trim it of any remaining fat. When the fat and connective tissues are cut away, the meat naturally separates into individual muscles that can be grilled like steaks to produce perfectly cooked meat.

2. Season the individual pieces of lamb with thyme, rosemary and pepper to taste. Add salt just before cooking (or after turning), so as not to

Herbed Italian Skillet Bread (p. 159).

MEAT

extract any moisture or toughen the meat.

3. Cook the lamb pieces over hot coals, turning once, until medium-rare, that is, springy to the touch (see the test for doneness in Grilled Rib Steak, page 101), 3 to 5 minutes per side, depending on the thickness of the muscle.

NOTE: The lamb can also be marinated with a strong seasoning, such as the Aïoli-Mustard Marinade on page 229. Coat the lamb with the marinade and let it stand, covered, at room temperature for several hours before cooking.

—*Richard Grausman*

ROASTED LEG OF LAMB WITH MINT AND WHITE BEANS

Broiled tomato halves topped with bread crumbs seasoned with garlic and herbs make a colorful garnish.

F&W BEVERAGE SUGGESTION
Bordeaux, such as 1979 Château Talbot, or California Cabernet, such as 1981 Jekel Private Reserve

6 TO 8 SERVINGS

1 whole leg of lamb (about 7 pounds), hip bone removed
1 pound shallots, peeled and halved if large
10 whole fresh mint leaves plus ¼ cup finely chopped fresh mint
½ teaspoon salt
¼ teaspoon freshly ground pepper
⅓ cup cider vinegar
½ cup plus 3 tablespoons chicken stock or canned broth
2 cans (15½ ounces each) white kidney beans, rinsed and well drained
1 tablespoon chopped parsley

1. Preheat the oven to 350°. If the lamb is not trimmed, remove all the fat from the underside of the leg. Place in a large roasting pan, meaty-side up.

2. Cut 1 or 2 shallots into 10 thin slices. Make about 10 incisions in the leg of lamb with a sharp pointed knife and insert a whole mint leaf and a slice of shallot in each. Season with the salt and pepper.

3. Roast for 30 minutes, baste once with the fat in the pan and scatter the remaining shallots around the lamb. Roast an additional 30 to 40 minutes, or to 120° to 125° on an instant-reading thermometer for rare. Roast for a total of 1 hour 20 minutes, or to 137° for medium; or for 1¾ hours, to 155°, if you like your meat well done. The meat will continue to cook for about 15 minutes as it rests after roasting.

4. Remove the lamb to a warm serving platter, cover loosely with foil and let rest 20 to 30 minutes.

5. Meanwhile, make the sauce. Remove the shallots with a slotted spoon and chop coarsely; set aside. Pour off all the fat from the roasting pan. Add the vinegar to the pan and bring to a boil, scraping up the browned bits from the bottom of the pan. Stir in ½ cup of the chicken stock and any lamb juices that have collected on the platter with the roast. Simmer about 1 minute, or until heated through. Strain into a small saucepan and keep warm.

6. In a medium saucepan, toss the chopped shallots with the beans and the remaining 3 tablespoons chicken stock. Cover and simmer for 5 minutes, or until heated through. Season with additional salt and pepper to taste. Top with the chopped parsley.

7. To serve, carve the leg of lamb into thin slices. Pour any juices from the carving board into the hot sauce. Stir in the chopped mint and season with salt and pepper to taste. Pass the sauce and beans separately.

—*Diana Sturgis*

MARINATED ROAST SADDLE OF LAMB WITH RED WINE

The lamb should marinate overnight, and the sauce base takes 5 hours to make, so plan accordingly.

F&W BEVERAGE SUGGESTION
1979 Château Cos d'Estournel or 1979 Simi Cabernet Sauvignon Reserve

8 SERVINGS

1 bottle dry white wine
½ cup olive oil
1 tablespoon thyme
1 tablespoon peppercorns
2 bay leaves, crumbled
1 saddle of lamb (7 pounds), boned and tied, bones reserved
1 medium onion
1 medium carrot
½ teaspoon fennel seeds
Salt and freshly ground pepper
2 teaspoons arrowroot
2 cups California Cabernet Sauvignon or other dry red wine
1 stick (4 ounces) cold unsalted butter, cut into tablespoons

1. In a shallow noncorrodible pan, combine the white wine, oil, thyme, peppercorns and bay leaves. Add the lamb and turn to coat well. Marinate overnight in the refrigerator, turning frequently when possible.

2. Preheat the oven to 400°. Place the reserved lamb bones in a large roasting pan and bake in the oven, turning once or twice, until browned, about 1 hour. Transfer the bones to a stockpot. Pour 2 cups of cold water into the roasting pan and bring to a boil over high heat, scraping up any browned bits from the bottom of the pan. Add to the pot. Add the onion, carrot, fennel seeds and enough water to cover. Bring slowly to a boil over low heat and simmer for 2 hours. Strain out the solids and simmer the broth until reduced to 4 cups, about 2 hours longer. Set the demiglace aside. **(The recipe can be prepared to this point up to 1 day ahead.)**

3. About 1 hour before serving, remove the lamb from the marinade and let return to room temperature. Preheat the oven to 400°. Set the lamb in a shallow roasting pan, season lightly with salt and pepper and roast for 40 minutes for rare or 50 minutes for medium rare. For medium, reduce the oven temperature to 325° after 50 minutes and continue to roast for another 20 minutes. Transfer the lamb to a platter and cover loosely with foil to keep warm while you finish the sauce.

4. In a small bowl, combine the arrowroot and red wine; whisk to blend well. Set the roasting pan over high heat, add the reserved demiglace and bring to a boil, scraping up any browned bits from the bottom of the pan. Stir in the wine-arrowroot mixture and cook, stirring constantly, until the sauce thickens, about 3 minutes longer. Strain the sauce into a medium saucepan and set over low heat. Gradually whisk in the butter, 1 tablespoon at a time. (Do not let the sauce boil.) Season with salt and pepper to taste and keep warm.

5. To serve, carve the lamb into ½-inch-thick slices. Spoon a little of the sauce over the lamb and pass the remainder separately.

—*Molly O'Neill*

BLACKENED LAMB CHOPS

Cajun chef Paul Prudhomme gave me this recipe. It's a way of cooking lamb chops that's similar to his famous blackened redfish. This rendition employs a mixture of aromatics called Cajun Magic for Meat. Paul gave me the approximate proportions, so readers can make it up for themselves.

He suggests serving these chops with a mint jalapeño jelly softened with a touch of vanilla.

IMPORTANT: Please do not attempt this recipe indoors unless you have a fanned vent over your stove. You can do it outdoors on a gas grill, but Paul warns that charcoal will not get the pan anywhere near hot enough.

2 SERVINGS
1 teaspoon onion powder
1 teaspoon cayenne pepper
¾ teaspoon garlic powder
½ teaspoon thyme
½ teaspoon powdered mustard
½ teaspoon freshly ground black pepper
½ teaspoon freshly ground white pepper
½ teaspoon salt
4 loin lamb chops, cut about 1 inch thick
1 stick (4 ounces) unsalted butter, clarified
Mint Jalapeño Jelly (p. 241)

1. Over a very high flame, heat a cast-iron skillet for 15 to 20 minutes,

until you see a faint white ash on the inside bottom of the skillet.

2. Meanwhile, in a small bowl, combine the onion powder, cayenne pepper, garlic powder, thyme, powdered mustard, black pepper, white pepper and salt.

3. Brush the lamb chops with the clarified butter. Sprinkle both sides of each chop with the seasoning mixture, patting gently so that the spices will adhere.

4. Fry the chops (see Note), uncovered, over high heat, turning once, for 1 to 2 minutes on each side, or until charred on the outside and rare inside. Serve with mint jalapeño jelly.

NOTE: Because this dish works only if the pan is very hot, it's best to cook no more than 2 large or 4 small chops at a time in a single skillet. To cook more, use a second cast-iron pan.

—*Paula Wolfert*

SPICY GREEK LAMB STEW

4 SERVINGS
6 tablespoons unsalted butter
2 medium onions, chopped
2 garlic cloves, minced
1 tablespoon olive oil
2 pounds boneless lamb shoulder, trimmed of fat and cut into 1-inch cubes
½ teaspoon salt
¼ teaspoon freshly ground pepper
2 imported bay leaves
1 cinnamon stick, broken in half
3 whole cloves
½ teaspoon rosemary
1 can (8 ounces) whole tomatoes in juice
1 cup dry white wine
½ pound macaroni
¼ pound feta cheese, crumbled

MEAT

1. In a large heavy noncorrodible skillet or flameproof casserole, melt 2 tablespoons of the butter over low heat. Add the onions and garlic and cook until softened, about 3 minutes.

2. Add 2 more tablespoons of the butter and the oil to the skillet and increase the heat to moderate. Toss the lamb with the salt and pepper and add to the skillet. Cook, stirring frequently, until the lamb has lost its red color, about 3 minutes.

3. Add the bay leaves, cinnamon stick, cloves, rosemary, tomatoes with their juice and wine. Stir to combine. Bring to a simmer, partially cover and reduce the heat to low. Cook until the lamb is tender, 1½ to 2 hours. If the sauce is not thick enough to coat a spoon lightly, uncover and boil to reduce slightly.

4. In a large pot of boiling salted water, cook the macaroni until tender but still slightly firm to the bite, 8 to 10 minutes. Drain in a colander. Arrange half of the hot macaroni on a heated platter. Crumble half of the feta cheese on top. Add the remaining macaroni and crumble on all except 1 tablespoon of the remaining cheese. Melt the remaining 2 tablespoons butter and pour over the macaroni.

5. Pour the lamb stew over the macaroni. Top with the remaining 1 tablespoon cheese and serve hot.

—*James Villas*

MIDDLE EASTERN LAMB STEW WITH FETA CHEESE

At Square One this stew is served in individual dishes and topped with a phyllo dough lid. Chef Joyce Goldstein suggests adding some sautéed chopped fresh spinach to the finished stew. The lamb must marinate overnight, so plan accordingly.

4 SERVINGS

*2 pounds well-trimmed boneless lamb
  shoulder, cut into 1-inch cubes*
¾ cup olive oil
*1 tablespoon plus 2 teaspoons
  cinnamon*
1 tablespoon plus 1 teaspoon oregano
2 medium onions, chopped
6 garlic cloves, minced
*1 can (35 ounces) Italian plum
  tomatoes—drained, diced and
  liquid reserved*
2 cups chicken stock or canned broth
½ teaspoon salt
¼ teaspoon freshly ground pepper
½ pound feta cheese, crumbled

1. In a medium bowl, toss the lamb with ½ cup of the olive oil, 1 tablespoon of the cinnamon and 1 teaspoon of the oregano; rub the spices into the meat. Cover and refrigerate overnight.

2. In a large flameproof casserole, heat the remaining ¼ cup olive oil. Add the lamb cubes in batches and sauté over moderately high heat until browned on all sides, 5 to 7 minutes. Remove the meat and set aside.

3. Add the onions to the casserole and sauté until translucent, about 4 minutes. Stir in the garlic, remaining 1 tablespoon oregano and 2 teaspoons cinnamon and cook for 3 minutes.

4. Return the lamb to the casserole and add the tomatoes with their liquid and the stock. Bring to a boil over high heat. Reduce the heat to moderate and simmer, uncovered, until the meat is tender, about 1½ hours.

5. Skim any excess fat from the stew and season with the salt and pepper. Ladle the stew onto warmed plates and top with crumbled feta cheese. (**This stew can be prepared up to 2 days ahead.**)

—*Joyce Goldstein, Square One,
San Francisco, California*

MOROCCAN LAMB TAGINE WITH GREEN CRACKED OLIVES

This stew, or *tagine*, adapted from my Moroccan cookbook, *Couscous and Other Good Food from Morocco*, is a lamb version of a famous chicken dish. The spicing is very special, and the long, slow cooking allows the combined flavors to penetrate the meat. In fact, this *tagine* is excellent reheated, and sometimes tastes even better the second or third day. The lamb is cooked until it is falling off the bone, important not only from the point of view of texture, but also because a Moroccan dish is eaten with the fingers along with Moroccan bread. I suggest that you try my recipe for quick Moroccan Bread (p. 159) because I believe the combination of anise-flavored bread and this particular sauce is special.

 F&W BEVERAGE SUGGESTION
Chilled rosé of Cabernet Sauvignon, such as Firestone Vineyards

4 TO 6 SERVINGS
*3 pounds meaty lamb necks, cut into
  1½-inch chunks*
Pinch of powdered saffron
1 teaspoon ground ginger

1 teaspoon finely ground pepper
½ teaspoon ground cumin
½ teaspoon paprika
3 garlic cloves, minced
1 teaspoon salt
2 tablespoons olive oil
¾ cup grated onion, rinsed and
  squeezed dry
½ cup minced parsley
½ cup minced fresh coriander
1 pound cracked green olives (see
  Note), drained and pitted if desired
3 tablespoons fresh lemon juice

1. Trim the lamb of excess fat. With a mortar and pestle or in a blender, make a paste of the saffron, ginger, pepper, cumin, paprika, garlic, salt and oil.

2. In a large flameproof casserole, toss the lamb with the spice paste over low heat for 2 minutes. Stir in the onion, parsley, coriander and 3 cups of water. Bring to a boil over high heat, reduce the heat to low and simmer, covered, for 2 hours, or until the meat is very tender and almost falling off the bones. Remove from the heat and let cool. (**The recipe can be prepared to this point up to 2 days in advance.** Cover and refrigerate.) Skim off all the fat that rises to the surface.

3. In a medium saucepan, combine the olives with cold water to cover. Bring to a boil over high heat and cook for 30 seconds; drain.

4. About 30 minutes before serving, preheat the oven to 450°. With a slotted spoon, remove the lamb from the casserole, cut the meat from the bones and place in a shallow ovenproof serving dish. Bake on the upper shelf of the oven for 15 to 20 minutes, or until the meat is lightly crisped.

5. Meanwhile, add the olives to the juices in the casserole. Boil over high heat until the juices are reduced to a thick gravy, about 10 minutes. Stir in the lemon juice, season with salt if necessary and pour over the lamb. Serve with Moroccan bread.

NOTE: Use Greek green cracked olives sold in jars in Greek groceries and in supermarkets under the labels Fantis, Krinos or Peloponnesus.
—*Paula Wolfert*

CHOPPED LAMB STEAK AU POIVRE WITH GARLIC CLOVES

A delectable and hearty treat for lamb and garlic lovers.
▌BEVERAGE SUGGESTION
Merlot, such as Rutherford Hill, or Cabernet, such as Jordan

4 SERVINGS

2 pounds chopped or ground lamb
  shoulder
1¼ teaspoons salt
3½ tablespoons coarsely cracked
  black peppercorns
32 medium garlic cloves, peeled
1 sprig of fresh thyme
1 medium tomato—peeled, seeded and
  minced
1 cup loosely packed fresh mint
  leaves
3 tablespoons unsalted butter

1. In a large bowl, break up the lamb and lightly mix in 1 teaspoon of the salt. Shape the meat into 4 large steaks, 1½ inches thick; do not pack tightly.

2. Coat both sides of the lamb steaks with the cracked peppercorns and let stand at room temperature for 1 hour.

3. Meanwhile, in a medium saucepan, combine 2 cups of water with the garlic cloves, thyme and remaining ¼ teaspoon salt. Bring to a boil and sim-

mer over moderate heat until the garlic is tender, about 25 minutes.

4. Using a slotted spoon, transfer the garlic to a small bowl. Discard the thyme sprig and boil the garlic water over high heat until reduced to ⅓ cup, about 10 minutes; reserve.

5. Blanch the mint in boiling water for 15 seconds. Drain and pat dry on paper towels. Mince and set aside.

6. Set a large heavy skillet over moderately high heat until very hot. Add the lamb steaks and sear for 2 minutes on each side. Reduce the heat to moderate and cook for 2 minutes longer on each side, until medium-rare. Transfer the steaks to a warmed platter.

7. Pour off any fat from the pan. Add the reserved garlic water, minced tomato and mint. Cook over high heat, scraping up any browned bits from the bottom of the pan, until the sauce reduces slightly, about 1 minute. Whisk in the butter, 1 tablespoon at a time. Season with salt to taste. Add the reserved garlic cloves to the sauce to reheat. Serve the lamb steaks on hot plates, surrounded by the garlic cloves and drizzled with the sauce.
—*Jeremiah Tower*

VEGETABLES

VEGETABLES

ROAST ASPARAGUS

Roasting fresh asparagus spears brings out their flavor in a whole new way and maintains a pleasingly firm texture. Treating asparagus in this fashion was first suggested to me by Johanne Kileen and George Germon, chef/owners of Al Forno in Providence, Rhode Island.

3 TO 4 SERVINGS
1 pound fresh asparagus, trimmed and peeled halfway up from the bottom
1 tablespoon extra-virgin olive oil
1 lemon, cut into wedges
Freshly ground black pepper

Preheat the oven to 500°. Place the asparagus in a single layer on a baking sheet or shallow pan. Drizzle with the olive oil. Roast the asparagus in the middle of the oven, turning the spears occasionally for even cooking and to avoid browning, for 8 to 10 minutes, depending on the thickness of the stalks. Serve hot with lemon wedges and pass a pepper mill at the table.

—Richard Sax

BAKED BEANS WITH SALSA

Fresh tomato salsa is the perfect lightener for baked beans. It introduces a clean acidity that balances the beans' sweet unctuous character. Cow peas hold their shape after cooking and so lighten the texture of the dish.

6 TO 8 SERVINGS
1 pound dried cow peas or black-eyed peas, rinsed and picked over
½ pound slab bacon, cut into 2-inch cubes
6 unpeeled garlic cloves
1 medium onion, halved
3 imported bay leaves

1 dried hot red pepper
½ cup unsulphured molasses
10 ripe plum tomatoes—peeled, seeded and cut into ½-inch chunks
1 cup thinly sliced scallions (about 1 bunch)
¼ cup minced fresh coriander
2 jalapeño peppers, seeded and minced
1 tablespoon olive oil
1 tablespoon red wine vinegar
1 tablespoon fresh lime juice
1 teaspoon oregano
½ teaspoon ground cumin
1 to 1½ teaspoons salt
½ teaspoon freshly ground black pepper
Cayenne pepper

1. In a large saucepan, cover the cow peas with 6 inches of water and soak overnight; or bring to a boil, cover, remove from the heat and let stand for 1 hour. Drain and rinse the beans.
2. Preheat the oven to 325°. In a large heavy flameproof casserole, combine the beans, bacon, garlic, onion, bay leaves, hot pepper and molasses. Add 3 to 4 cups of water to cover and bring to a boil over high heat. Cover, place in the oven and bake for 4 to 5 hours, or until the beans are tender. Check every hour and add additional water if necessary.
3. When the beans are done, if there is more than enough liquid to generously coat them, boil over moderately high heat to evaporate the excess. Remove and discard the bacon, onion, garlic and bay leaves. (The beans can be made up to 5 days ahead. Cover and refrigerate, but let return to room temperature before proceeding.)
4. Make the salsa 1 to 3 hours in advance. In a large bowl, combine the tomatoes, scallions, coriander, jalapeños, olive oil, vinegar, lime juice,

oregano, cumin, ½ teaspoon of the salt, ¼ teaspoon of the black pepper and cayenne to taste.
5. Combine the beans (warm or at room temperature) with the salsa. Add the remaining ¼ teaspoon black pepper, ½ to 1 teaspoon salt (depending on the saltiness of the bacon used) and more cayenne to taste. Serve at room temperature.

—Anne Disrude

BOSTON BAKED BEANS WITH MAPLE AND ROSEMARY

This delicious version of Boston baked beans from Frank McClelland—a variation on his grandmother's recipe—uses three types of beans for variety of texture and flavor.

4 TO 6 SERVINGS
1½ cups assorted dried beans (navy, red kidney, pinto)
1 teaspoon salt
1 teaspoon baking soda
1 teaspoon Dijon-style mustard
1½ tablespoons pure maple syrup
2 tablespoons dark unsulphured molasses
½ pound salt pork, cut into ½-inch dice
2 sprigs of fresh rosemary or 1 teaspoon dried

1. In a medium casserole, combine the beans with 6 cups of water. Let the beans soak overnight. Alternatively, cover the beans with 6 cups of cold water and bring to a boil over high heat. Boil for 2 minutes, turn off the heat and let the beans soak, covered, for 1 hour.
2. Preheat the oven to 250°. Leave the beans in their soaking water and bring to a boil over high heat. Stir in the salt, baking soda, mustard, maple syrup, molasses, diced salt pork and rosemary.

3. Cover the casserole and bake the beans for 8 hours.

—*Frank McClelland, Country Inn at Princeton, Princeton, Massachusetts*

BAKED BEANS WITH ONIONS AND ORANGE MARMALADE

The caramelized onions, marmalade and thyme give ordinary canned baked beans a sweetly delicious and unusual flavor. Serve these beans warm with a main dish of sautéed ham, steaks or frankfurters.

4 SERVINGS
2 tablespoons unsalted butter
2 medium onions, thinly sliced
¼ cup orange marmalade
1 teaspoon thyme
1 can (18 ounces) brick-oven baked beans
1 tablespoon Dijon-style mustard
⅛ teaspoon freshly ground pepper
4 slices of crisply cooked bacon, coarsely chopped

1. In a large heavy skillet, melt the butter over moderately low heat. Add the onions and cook, stirring occasionally, until very soft and lightly browned, 25 to 30 minutes.

2. Scrape the onions to one side of the pan, add the marmalade and cook until melted, 1 to 2 minutes. Stir together the onions and marmalade.

3. Increase the heat to moderate. Add the thyme, beans, mustard, pepper and bacon and cook until heated through, 1 to 2 minutes.

—*Diana Sturgis*

FRENCH-STYLE WHITE KIDNEY BEANS

The flavor of garlic and olive oil and the crunch of baby string beans will take you straight to the Mediterranean. Serve this warm dish, French style, with broiled or sautéed lamb steaks.

2 TO 3 SERVINGS
¼ pound young string beans, preferably haricots verts, trimmed
¼ cup extra-virgin olive oil
1 large garlic clove, crushed
¼ teaspoon thyme
1 can (19 ounces) white kidney beans, rinsed and drained
Salt and freshly ground pepper

1. Place the string beans in a medium saucepan of boiling salted water. Cook, uncovered, until the beans are crunchy but still tender and bright green, 2 to 3 minutes. Drain and set aside.

2. In a heavy medium saucepan, combine the olive oil and garlic. Cook over low heat for 10 minutes, without browning the garlic, to infuse the oil with flavor. Discard the garlic.

3. Add the thyme and kidney beans to the oil in the saucepan. Cook over low heat for 5 minutes. Add the string beans and toss gently. Season with salt and pepper to taste. Serve warm or at room temperature.

—*Diana Sturgis*

BOK CHOY WITH APPLE AND GINGER

A basic dish that can stand plenty of adjustment and substitution, this is a useful addition to the repertoire. If you like to work in a wok, ignore the skillet directions. If you want to double the recipe, fine.

3 SERVINGS
1 pound bok choy
1 medium apple
1 tablespoon peanut oil
1½ ounces thinly slivered Smithfield ham, country ham or fatty prosciutto (¼ cup) (see Note)
1 tablespoon plus 1 teaspoon coarsely grated fresh ginger
¼ teaspoon salt
¼ teaspoon freshly ground pepper

1. Trim off the heavy base from the bok choy (if very fresh, slice and include along with the stalks). Discard any blemished or tough leaves. Break the stalks from the base, as you would celery. Cut the leaves neatly from the stalks, leaving as little green as possible on the stalks. Slit the thick end of the stalks in half lengthwise, then cut the whole stalk crosswise on the diagonal into ½-inch slices. Halve the leaves lengthwise, then cut crosswise into ½-inch slices.

2. Quarter and core the apple (do not peel). Cut each quarter crosswise into ⅛-inch slices.

3. In a large skillet, heat the oil. Add the ham and toss over moderately high heat for 1 minute. Add the bok choy stems, apple and ginger, and toss until the vegetables are tender, about 5 minutes.

4. Add the bok choy leaves and toss over high heat until they are tender and most of the liquid has evaporated, about 1 minute. Season with the salt and pepper.

NOTE: If you can't get the Smithfield ham, country ham or prosciutto called for above, add 1 tablespoon of bacon fat to the skillet in Step 2.

—*Elizabeth Schneider*

GLAZED BRUSSELS SPROUTS WITH PINE NUTS

8 SERVINGS
1½ pounds brussels sprouts
4 tablespoons unsalted butter
½ cup pine nuts
Salt and freshly ground pepper

1. Remove the outer leaves from the brussels sprouts and cut a small cross in the stem ends. Steam the brussels sprouts over well-salted water until tender, 8 to 10 minutes. Drain and rinse under cold water. **(The recipe can be prepared to this point up to 1 day ahead.** Cover and refrigerate.)

2. Shortly before serving, melt the butter in a large skillet. Add the pine nuts and toast lightly over moderate heat until golden, 3 to 4 minutes. Add the brussels sprouts and toss gently until warmed through. Season with salt and pepper to taste.

—*Molly O'Neill*

STUFFED CABBAGE CAKE WITH BACON

4 TO 6 SERVINGS
1 large head of cabbage (about 3 pounds)
½ pound good-quality slab bacon, cut into ¼-inch strips
1 large onion, chopped
½ teaspoon caraway seeds, crushed
¼ teaspoon salt
¼ teaspoon freshly ground pepper
1 large baking potato, peeled and finely grated
1 egg, lightly beaten
2 tablespoons unsalted butter

1. Remove and discard the 3 or 4 toughest outer leaves of the cabbage. Cut out a deep core so that the leaves

will separate. Place the head in a large pot of boiling water. As the leaves begin to loosen, remove the next 6 to 7 to a bowl. Keep boiling until another 10 leaves can be removed. Take out the head. Return the 10 leaves to the boiling water and cook until tender and translucent, 15 to 20 minutes. Drain. Coarsely chop the first 6 to 7 outer leaves plus enough of the cabbage from the whole head to equal 6 cups (about 1 pound).

2. In a large skillet, cook the bacon over moderate heat until brown and crisp, about 15 minutes. Pour off all but 2 tablespoons of bacon fat. Add the onion, chopped cabbage, caraway seeds, salt and pepper. Cook over moderate heat until the cabbage begins to brown, about 30 minutes. Remove from the heat and let cool to room temperature.

3. Add the potato and egg to the cabbage and mix well.

4. Melt 1 tablespoon of butter in a large skillet, preferably nonstick. Cut away the thickest part of the ribs from the reserved cabbage leaves. Line the skillet with the leaves, placing the rib ends toward the center and letting the leaves overlap the sides of the pan. Fill in the center with a whole leaf.

5. Fill the leaves with the cabbage-bacon mixture. Press to fill any pockets and smooth the top. Fold over the overhanging leaves. Lay additional leaves on top to completely cover.

6. Pour 2 tablespoons of water around the edge of the pan. Cover and cook over moderate heat until browned on the bottom, about 20 minutes. Slide onto a plate. Melt the remaining 1 tablespoon butter in the skillet. Invert the pancake onto another plate and slide back into the skillet. Cook until browned on the second side, about 20 minutes. To serve, slide onto a plate and cut into wedges.

—*Anne Disrude*

CHINESE CABBAGE WITH MUSHROOMS, NOODLES AND ALMONDS

This homey dish of soft, slightly sweet cabbage, chewy noodles and crunchy almonds can be a vegetarian main dish or the accompaniment to roast duck, pork or chicken.

3 MAIN-COURSE OR
5 TO 6 SIDE-DISH SERVINGS
1¾ pounds Chinese cabbage (see Note)
½ pound wide egg noodles, preferably thick-cut
4 tablespoons unsalted butter
½ pound small mushrooms, quartered
1 teaspoon sugar
⅔ cup beef stock or canned broth
3 tablespoons dry sherry
2 teaspoons cornstarch
½ teaspoon salt
¼ teaspoon freshly ground white pepper
½ cup roasted and salted almonds, coarsely chopped
1 scallion green, thinly sliced

1. Cut off any dry or dark green leaves from the cabbage. Separate the remaining leaves from the base; rinse them well. Stack a few at a time and cut into 1½-inch squares or diamonds. Cut the core/base into thin rounds.

2. In a large pot of boiling, salted water, cook the noodles until tender, about 4 minutes.

3. Meanwhile, in a large skillet, heat 2 tablespoons of the butter over high heat. Add the mushrooms and toss until lightly browned, about 1 minute. Add another 1 tablespoon butter, the cabbage and sugar. Toss over very high heat until the juices evaporate and the cabbage is lightly browned, about 4 minutes.

4. In a bowl, add the beef broth and sherry to the cornstarch and stir to blend. Add to the skillet and bring to a boil, stirring. Reduce the heat to low.

5. Drain the noodles. Add them to the skillet with the remaining tablespoon butter and stir to mix well. Season with the salt and pepper, then transfer to a serving dish. Top with the almonds and scallion greens.

NOTE: There are two very similar varieties of Chinese cabbage commonly available. One is rounder and fuller with paler leaves and fleshier ribs, and the other is taller and looks somewhat more like a head of celery. Use the shorter, rounder variety in this recipe.

—Elizabeth Schneider

ROASTED CHESTNUTS

Preheat the oven to 350°. Using a sharp paring knife, cut a small x into the flat side of each chestnut, cutting through the woody outer shell; try not to cut into the meat. Place the chestnuts in a shallow pan in a single layer. Roast in the oven until a knife tip inserted through the x meets little resistance, 25 to 30 minutes. Peel off the shell and the tough inner skin while the chestnuts are still hot. The cooked chestnuts should be slightly resistant on the surface and soft and creamy within. They can be served on their own or in combination with other vegetables, or grated or pureed and used as a base for soups, sauces, soufflés, cakes and mousses. One pound of fresh chestnuts yields 2½ cups peeled.

PEELED CHESTNUTS

Peeled chestnuts are usually called for in recipes that require further cooking by another method. Prepare the chestnuts as for Roasted Chestnuts (at left), but roast only until the x opens slightly, about 10 minutes.

Once peeled and cooled, store chestnuts in the refrigerator in an airtight container for up to three days, or freeze for up to one year; do not thaw before using. One pound of fresh chestnuts yields 2½ cups peeled.

SAVORY CHESTNUT PUREE

A delightful accompaniment for duck, pork and furred and feathered game.

6 SERVINGS
2 cups Roasted Chestnuts (at left)
1 cup beef stock or canned broth
1 tablespoon heavy cream
Salt and freshly ground white pepper

In a food processor, puree the chestnuts to a stiff paste. Add the beef stock and cream and puree until smooth. Season to taste with salt and pepper and puree once more until blended. For an extra smooth puree, pass the mixture through a fine-mesh sieve.

—John Robert Massie

BRAISED CHESTNUTS WITH BRUSSELS SPROUTS

6 TO 8 SERVINGS
4 tablespoons unsalted butter
1 pound Peeled Chestnuts (above)
1½ cups beef stock or canned broth
1 pound brussels sprouts, trimmed
Salt and freshly ground pepper

1. In a large skillet, melt 2 tablespoons of the butter over moderately high heat. Add the chestnuts and toss to coat with butter.

2. Add the beef stock and bring to a boil. Reduce the heat to low, cover and simmer until the chestnuts are tender, 20 to 25 minutes.

3. Meanwhile, in a large pot of boiling salted water, cook the brussels sprouts until just tender, 7 to 10 minutes. Drain and rinse under cold running water; drain well.

4. When the chestnuts are tender, uncover and increase the heat to moderately high. Add the brussels sprouts and cook until the liquid reduces to a glaze, about 10 minutes. Swirl in the remaining 2 tablespoons butter and season with salt and pepper to taste.

—John Robert Massie

SAVORY CRANBERRY TARTLETS

These make a wonderful accompaniment to roast poultry or meat. They were originally designed to go with Marinated Roast Saddle of Lamb with Red Wine (p. 114).

MAKES 8 TARTLETS
THYME PASTRY:
2 cups all-purpose flour
½ teaspoon salt
¼ teaspoon freshly ground pepper
2 teaspoons fresh thyme or 1 teaspoon dried
1 stick (4 ounces) unsalted butter
3 tablespoons lard or solid vegetable shortening
5 tablespoons ice water

CRANBERRY COMPOTE:
3 tablespoons vodka
2¼ teaspoons sugar
¾ cup fresh or frozen cranberries

1. *Make the pastry:* In a medium bowl, combine the flour, salt, pepper and thyme. Cut in the butter and lard until the mixture resembles coarse meal. Stir in the ice water, 1 tablespoon at a time, until the dough can be formed into a ball. Wrap well and chill for at least 1 hour.

2. *Meanwhile, make the cranberry compote:* In a small saucepan, bring the vodka, sugar and ¾ cup of water to a boil over high heat. Reduce the heat to moderate and add the cranberries. Simmer, stirring occasionally, until the compote is thick, about 15 minutes. Set aside to cool.

3. To assemble the tartlets, preheat the oven to 350°. On a lightly floured board, roll out the pastry ¼ inch thick. Using a 2-inch cookie cutter, stamp out 8 rounds and place on a baking sheet. Mound 1 tablespoon of the cranberry compote onto each round. Bake for 25 to 30 minutes, or until the pastry is golden. Transfer the tartlets to a rack to cool. (**These tartlets can be prepared 1 day ahead.** Let cool completely; store in an airtight container in a cool place. Reheat in a 350° oven for 7 to 10 minutes before serving.)

—*Molly O'Neill*

SAUTEED DAIKON SLICES

2 SERVINGS
1 tablespoon vegetable oil
¾ pound firm, slender daikon, cut
    into ¼-inch slices (if the radish is
    wide, halve lengthwise)
½ teaspoon sugar
¼ teaspoon salt
1 tablespoon minced parsley
2 teaspoons minced fresh chives or
    dill

1. Heat a wok over moderately high heat, pour the oil around the edge and tip to distribute. Add the daikon and toss to coat all the slices.

Add the sugar and salt and stir-fry until the daikon has lost its raw crunch, about 5 minutes.

2. Scoop into a heated serving dish. Toss with the parsley and chives.

—*Elizabeth Schneider*

EGGPLANT IN GARLIC SAUCE

By using the French technique of removing excess water from the eggplant (salting it and weighing it down), you use only about one-fourth the amount of oil you would otherwise need to fry the eggplant in this Chinese version of ratatouille. (Many other Chinese recipes for eggplant in garlic sauce call for anywhere from one-half to one cup of oil. In this recipe only three tablespoons are used.) This dish tastes better if made a day in advance and served at room temperature. It keeps for up to a week in the refrigerator, and can be served as an appetizer or part of a multicourse Chinese dinner.

6 SERVINGS
6 small dried black Chinese
    mushrooms*
⅓ cup chicken stock or canned broth
1 medium eggplant, 1 to 1¼ pounds
2 teaspoons salt
1 teaspoon dried shrimp*
¼ cup American bottled chili sauce
2 tablespoons medium-dry sherry
1 tablespoon dark soy sauce*
1 tablespoon red wine vinegar
1 teaspoon sugar
½ to 1 teaspoon Szechuan chili paste
    with garlic*
3 tablespoons rendered poultry fat or
    peanut oil
2 garlic cloves, minced
2 scallions, sliced
1 medium red bell pepper, cut into
    1-inch squares or triangles
1 medium yellow or green bell pepper,
    cut into 1-inch squares or triangles
Available at Oriental markets

1. Rinse the mushrooms under cool water. Put in a small bowl, cover with about 1 cup of cold water and soak until soft, about 1 hour.

2. Remove the mushrooms from their soaking water. Squeeze the mushrooms over the bowl to extract as much liquid as possible. Reserve the soaking water. Cut off and reserve the mushroom stems. Leave the caps whole.

3. In a small saucepan, simmer the mushroom water and stems over low heat until the liquid is reduced to 2 tablespoons, about 20 minutes. Strain the mushroom stock through a sieve lined with a double thickness of dampened cheesecloth; discard the stems. Combine the mushroom stock and the chicken stock.

4. Trim off the ends of the eggplant. Cut the unpeeled eggplant lengthwise into 1-inch slices. Cut the slices into 1-inch cubes. Sprinkle with the salt. Place the eggplant on a cookie sheet lined with paper towels. Cover the eggplant with more paper towels. Place a heavy flat object such as a chopping block on top of the paper towels. Let stand for 30 minutes. Rinse, drain and dry the eggplant cubes well.

5. Rinse the shrimp, drain and place in a small bowl. Cover with boiling water and let stand for 15 minutes. Drain and mince.

6. In a bowl, combine the chili sauce, sherry, soy sauce, vinegar, sugar and chili paste. Set the seasoning sauce aside.

7. Place a wok over high heat for 1 minute. Add the poultry fat and heat until hot but not smoking. Add the eggplant. Cook over high heat, stirring and pressing lightly, until lightly browned, about 3 minutes.

8. Add the minced dried shrimp, garlic and scallions to the wok. Stir-fry for 30 seconds.

9. Add the mushroom caps and peppers. Stir-fry until the peppers just begin to soften, about 1 minute.

10. Stir the seasoning sauce and then add it to the wok. Cook, stirring, for 1 minute.

11. Add the chicken and mushroom stock and cook until the juices thicken, 1 to 2 minutes. Transfer to a serving dish. Let cool to room temperature before serving.

—*Karen Lee & Alexandra Branyon*

BRAISED EGGPLANT AND TOMATO WITH SAGE

Serve this as a side dish or as a first course with grilled bread brushed with olive oil and rubbed with garlic.

2 SERVINGS
2 small eggplants (about ½ pound each)
¾ teaspoon salt
¼ cup plus 2 tablespoons extra-virgin olive oil
½ pound plum tomatoes, halved
6 fresh sage leaves
3 garlic cloves, halved
Pinch of crushed hot pepper

1. Trim the stem ends from the eggplant. Halve lengthwise. Sprinkle the eggplant with ½ teaspoon of the salt and let stand for 30 minutes. Gently squeeze excess liquid from the eggplant and blot dry with paper towels.

2. In a large skillet, heat ¼ cup of the oil. Add the eggplant in a single layer, cut-side down. Distribute the tomatoes, sage leaves and garlic on top. Sprinkle with the remaining ¼ teaspoon salt and the hot pepper.

Cover and cook over moderate heat for 20 minutes.

3. Add the remaining 2 tablespoons oil. Turn the eggplant, cover and cook until soft, 10 to 15 minutes longer.

4. Place 2 pieces of eggplant in each of 2 warmed shallow soup plates and top with tomatoes and the juices. (If you wish, slip off the tomato skins.)

—*Anne Disrude*

BRAISED FENNEL WITH PROSCIUTTO AND PARMESAN CHEESE

8 SERVINGS
8 medium fennel bulbs, halved lengthwise, stalks and tops discarded
3 tablespoons fresh lemon juice
¼ teaspoon freshly ground pepper
2 cups chicken stock or canned broth
8 thin slices of prosciutto, halved crosswise
1 cup (4 ounces) freshly grated imported Parmesan cheese
1 stick (4 ounces) unsalted butter

1. Preheat the oven to 350°. Toss the fennel with the lemon juice and arrange in a large, well-buttered flameproof gratin dish in a single layer.

2. Sprinkle with the pepper. Pour the stock into the dish. Bring to a boil over high heat. Cover the gratin dish with a buttered sheet of waxed paper.

3. Transfer to the oven and bake, turning the fennel halves occasionally, for about 1 hour, until tender. (**The recipe can be prepared to this point a day ahead.** Let cool; then cover and refrigerate. Reheat in a low oven before proceeding.)

4. With a slotted spoon, transfer the fennel to an ovenproof platter. Cover with foil and keep warm in a 200° oven.

5. Boil the broth in the gratin dish over high heat until reduced to about ⅓ cup of syrupy glaze. Pour into a bowl.

6. Preheat the broiler. Return the fennel to the gratin dish, rounded-side up. Spoon a little of the glaze over each half. Arrange a slice of prosciutto over each piece. Sprinkle 2 teaspoons of the cheese over the top of each. Dot each piece with ½ tablespoon butter. Broil for 1 to 2 minutes, until the cheese is melted and lightly browned. Serve hot. Pass the remaining cheese on the side.

—*Arthur Gold & Robert Fizdale*

ROASTED GARLIC

6 TO 8 SERVINGS
2 large heads of garlic
1 tablespoon olive oil
Salt and freshly ground pepper

1. Preheat the oven to 350°. Peel off the outer layer of skin on the heads to expose the cloves, but do not peel the cloves. Rub the whole heads with the oil and place in a small shallow roasting pan. Add enough water to reach halfway up the heads.

2. Bake the garlic until very tender but not brown, 1½ to 2 hours. Remove from the pan and let cool. Peel the cloves and season with salt and pepper to taste. (**The garlic can be cooked 1 day ahead.** Once cool, cover and store at room temperature. Reheat the cloves in olive oil on top of the stove before serving.)

—*Molly O'Neill*

VEGETABLES

COLLARDS WITH CORNMEAL DUMPLINGS AND BACON

For this adaptation of a Southern classic, the collards are long-cooked until soft and succulent with smoky sweet bacon and a topping of light, fluffy dumplings.

4 SERVINGS
2 pounds collard greens, well washed
½ pound slab bacon, in one piece
1 tablespoon plus 1 teaspoon sugar
½ cup all-purpose flour
¾ cup yellow cornmeal, preferably coarse and stone-ground
1½ teaspoons baking powder
¼ teaspoon salt
¼ teaspoon crushed hot pepper
¼ cup sliced scallion greens
1 egg
Pepper vinegar or hot pepper sauce

1. Strip the leaves from the stems of the collard greens and discard the stems. Cut the leaves into thin slivers. In a large noncorrodible saucepan, combine the slivered leaves with water to almost cover. Add the bacon and 1 tablespoon of the sugar. Keep at a slow boil over moderately high heat, partly covered, until the collards are very, very soft, 2 hours or more. Add water, as needed, to maintain the same level throughout cooking. Once the greens are cooked, uncover and boil briefly to concentrate the liquid.

2. Remove the bacon and cut off and discard the rind, if any. Cut the bacon into strips about 1 inch long and ¼ inch wide. Cook the bacon in a medium skillet over moderate heat, covered, until browned, about 10 minutes. Reserve the fat and the bacon separately.

3. In a medium bowl, whisk together the flour, cornmeal, baking powder, salt, hot pepper and remaining 1 teaspoon sugar. Blend thoroughly.

4. In a small bowl, combine the scallions, egg and 1 tablespoon of the reserved bacon fat; stir in ½ cup of the collard cooking liquid. Pour this mixture into the dry ingredients and mix just enough to blend, no more.

5. Bring the greens to a boil over high heat. Drop tablespoons of the dumpling batter over the greens, leaving small spaces in between; there should be about 10 dumplings. Reduce the heat to moderate, cover and boil gently for 10 minutes. Uncover and boil a few minutes longer, until the dumplings are dried on top.

6. Sprinkle the reserved bacon over the dumplings and serve immediately, with pepper vinegar or hot sauce.

—Elizabeth Schneider

CREAMED TURNIP GREENS

This standard treatment for turnip greens is also one of the simplest and most successful. Creamed turnip greens are a lovely accompaniment to broiled or roast lamb, pork or turkey.

4 SERVINGS
1½ pounds turnip greens, well washed
1 tablespoon unsalted butter
½ cup minced onion
1 cup stock or canned broth
1 tablespoon all-purpose flour
½ cup milk
¼ to ½ cup heavy cream, to taste
Salt and freshly ground pepper

1. Strip the leaves from the stems of the turnip greens and discard the stems. Drop the leaves into a large pot of boiling water; return to a boil. Drain the leaves well and chop them fine.

2. In a large noncorrodible skillet, melt the butter over moderately high heat. Add the onions and cook until slightly softened, 2 to 3 minutes. Add the chopped turnip greens and stock and simmer, partly covered, until the greens are tender, 20 to 25 minutes.

3. Uncover and cook over high heat to evaporate most of the moisture. Reduce the heat to moderate, sprinkle on the flour and cook, stirring, for 2 minutes. Add the milk and ¼ cup of the cream and bring to a simmer, stirring. Cover and cook over very low heat, adding more cream if you like, until you have the desired consistency and flavor, 5 to 10 minutes. Season with salt and pepper to taste and serve hot.

—Elizabeth Schneider

PAPILLOTE OF LEEKS WITH PARMESAN CHEESE

Leeks are a grand enough vegetable to be served as a first course.

1 SERVING
½ tablespoon vegetable oil
2 teaspoons unsalted butter, softened
3 small or 2 medium leeks, trimmed to 6 inches of white and tender green
¼ cup heavy cream
1½ tablespoons freshly grated Parmesan cheese
2 sprigs of fresh thyme or ⅛ teaspoon dried
Salt and freshly ground pepper

1. Preheat the oven to 400°. Fold a 15-by-20-inch sheet of butcher's paper, parchment or aluminum foil in half crosswise to make a 15-by-10-inch rectangle. Using scissors, cut the rectangle into a heart shape with the fold running vertically down the center. Open up the heart and brush with the

oil. Spread the softened butter over the middle of half the papillote.

2. Cut the small leeks in half lengthwise and rinse well. (If using medium leeks, cut lengthwise into quarters.) Place on top of the butter, cut-sides up.

3. Pour the cream over the leeks and sprinkle with the Parmesan cheese. Remove some of the leaves from the thyme sprigs and sprinkle on top. Add the sprigs with the remaining leaves. Season lightly with salt and pepper.

4. Fold the paper over the leeks and beginning at the top of the heart, make a series of tight overlapping folds to seal the papillote.

5. Place the papillote on a cookie sheet and bake 20 minutes. Serve hot.

—Anne Disrude

SAUTE-BRAISED SHIITAKE MUSHROOMS

4 SERVINGS

1 pound fresh shiitake (Golden Oak) mushrooms
1 cup beef, turkey, chicken or duck stock or canned broth
3 tablespoons unsalted butter
2 tablespoons minced shallots
1/3 cup dry white wine or dry vermouth
1/4 teaspoon salt
1/4 teaspoon freshly ground pepper
Minced fresh parsley, thyme, lemon thyme or rosemary, for garnish (optional)

1. Cut the shiitake caps from the stems and then cut the stems into thin slivers. In a small saucepan, simmer the stems in the stock, covered, until tender, about 15 minutes.

2. Wipe the caps with a damp cloth and break into large bite-size pieces—or leave whole if small. In a large skillet, melt the butter over moderate

heat. Add the shallots and cook, stirring, for 20 seconds. Add the mushroom caps and sauté until barely softened, about 2 minutes.

3. Add the stock and stems, increase the heat to moderately high and cook until most of the liquid evaporates, about 4 minutes. Add the wine and toss over high heat until most of the liquid evaporates, about 3 minutes. Season with the salt and pepper and serve, sprinkled with fresh herbs.

—Elizabeth Schneider

SWEET PEPPER CHARLOTTE WITH TOMATOES AND CURRANTS

8 SERVINGS

3 tablespoons sherry wine vinegar
3 tablespoons currants or raisins
6 large red bell peppers
3/4 cup extra-virgin olive oil
1 large onion, chopped
3 garlic cloves, chopped
1 1/2 teaspoons oregano
1 can (14 ounces) Italian peeled tomatoes, drained and crushed
18 slices of firm-textured white bread, crusts removed
3/4 teaspoon salt
1/4 teaspoon coarsely ground black pepper
1 egg, beaten

1. In a small noncorrodible saucepan, bring the vinegar and currants to a boil. Remove from the heat and let stand until the currants plump up and soften, about 15 minutes.

2. Meanwhile, roast the peppers over a gas flame or under the broiler, turning frequently, until completely charred, 10 to 15 minutes. Place in a paper bag to steam for 10 minutes.

3. Peel the peppers under running water. Core them and remove the

membranes and seeds over a bowl to catch the juices. Coarsely chop the peppers. Strain the juices into a large bowl.

4. In a large skillet, heat 1/4 cup of the oil. Add the onion, garlic, chopped roasted peppers, oregano and currants with vinegar. Cook over moderately high heat, stirring frequently, until the onions and peppers are slightly browned, about 30 minutes. Add the tomatoes and cook for 5 minutes longer. Set aside.

5. Cut 9 slices of bread into 1 1/2-by-3-inch rectangles; reserve the trimmings. Cut 8 slices into two triangles each. Cut the remaining slice of bread and all trimmings into 1/2-inch pieces, add to the bowl of reserved pepper juices and toss. Add the pepper-tomato mixture, salt, black pepper, egg and 1/4 cup of the oil. Mix lightly to blend.

6. Preheat the oven to 350°. Lightly oil a 9-inch round cake pan at least 2 inches deep. Brush one side of all the bread pieces liberally with the remaining 1/4 cup oil. Placing the oiled side against the pan, line the bottom with the triangles, tips pointing inward. (There will be a little space between the triangles.) Line the sides of the pan with rectangles. Fill with the pepper mixture, packing lightly with a spatula. (**The recipe can be prepared to this point a day ahead.** Cover and refrigerate. Let return to room temperature before baking.)

7. Bake the stuffing in the lower third of the oven for 45 minutes, or until the bread is well browned. Invert onto a large round platter and serve hot or at room temperature.

—Anne Disrude

VEGETABLES

CREAMED PARSLEY AND SHALLOTS

This somewhat unusual vegetable dish was inspired by a Fredy Girardet recipe. Cleaning and trimming such a large amount of parsley takes time, so you may want to do this job a day or two ahead. Store the prepared parsley in plastic bags in the refrigerator.

8 SERVINGS
4 pounds flat-leaf Italian parsley—
well rinsed and dried, trimmed to
leaves and small stems only
6 tablespoons unsalted butter
1 pound shallots, sliced
1 cupe crème fraîche or heavy cream
1½ teaspoons salt
¼ teaspoon sugar
¼ teaspoon freshly ground pepper

1. Bring a large pot of water to a boil. Add the parsley to the water in batches, allowing each to wilt to make room for the next batch. When the water returns to a boil, cook the parsley until tender, about 6 minutes. Drain into a colander and rinse under cold running water to cool. Squeeze dry. Coarsely chop the parsley.

2. In a large skillet, melt the butter over moderate heat. Add the shallots and sauté until softened but not browned, about 5 minutes.

3. Add the crème fraîche, parsley, salt, sugar and pepper and cook, stirring, until the parsley absorbs the cream, about 5 minutes. Serve hot.

—Anne Disrude

RATATOUILLE WITH GOAT CHEESE

I usually serve this colorful ratatouille warm with toasted French bread as an appetizer, but it also makes a savory vegetable to accompany a simple roast or to toss with pasta.

8 SERVINGS
1 tablespoon plus 1 teaspoon coarse
(kosher) salt
1 pound eggplant, cut into ½-inch
dice
About ¼ cup fruity olive oil
2 medium onions, sliced
¾ pound red bell peppers, cut into
½-inch squares
¾ pound yellow bell peppers, cut into
½-inch squares
2 medium tomatoes—peeled, seeded
and cut into ½-inch dice
1 medium zucchini, cut into ½-inch
dice
2 garlic cloves, minced
1 tablespoon minced fresh tarragon
¼ teaspoon freshly ground black
pepper
Cayenne pepper
¼ pound Bucheron or other soft goat
cheese

1. Sprinkle 1 tablespoon of the salt over the eggplant; toss and let drain in a colander for 30 minutes. Rinse under cold running water and pat dry.

2. Heat ¼ cup oil in a large flame-proof casserole. Add the onions and sauté over moderate heat until just beginning to color, 3 to 5 minutes. Add the red and yellow peppers and cook, stirring frequently, until slightly softened, about 5 minutes. Add the eggplant and sauté, adding additional oil if necessary to prevent sticking, until it loses that whitish raw look,

about 10 minutes. Finally add the tomatoes, zucchini, garlic and tarragon; season with the remaining 1 teaspoon salt, the black pepper and cayenne to taste. Cover and cook for 20 minutes, stirring frequently to prevent sticking.

3. Uncover the pan and cook until the liquid is reduced to a syrupy consistency, about 10 minutes. Crumble the goat cheese over the ratatouille, remove the pan from the heat, cover and let stand for 5 minutes to allow the cheese to melt.

—Lydie Marshall

BASILICO POTATOES

These are the "bas'lacol' potatoes" that my friend Mick's mother used to make years ago. "She'd toss them with basil from our garden," he remembers, "for special summer suppers with barbecued steaks and sliced ripe tomatoes." They're wonderful, like crisp french fries flavored with the gutsy punch of fresh basil and plenty of fruity olive oil.

3 TO 4 SERVINGS
⅓ cup extra-virgin olive oil
3 to 4 medium baking potatoes,
peeled and sliced ¼ inch thick
1½ teaspoons salt
½ teaspoon freshly ground pepper
½ cup chopped fresh basil

1. Preheat the broiler. Line a baking sheet with heavy-duty aluminum foil. Drizzle the foil with 2 tablespoons of the olive oil. Arrange the potato slices in the pan, overlapping as little as possible. Drizzle the remaining olive oil over the potatoes and season with the salt and pepper. Turn the potatoes to coat generously all over.

2. Broil the potatoes 5 to 6 inches from the heat until golden brown, about 12 minutes. Carefully turn the potatoes over to avoid tearing the foil.

Broil about 12 minutes longer, until golden brown, checking during the last few minutes to prevent burning. Remove the pan from the oven and sprinkle the basil over the potatoes. Toss lightly and serve at once.

—*Richard Sax*

TURNIP-SHALLOT COMPOTE

6 SERVINGS
1½ pounds shallots, peeled
6 tablespoons unsalted butter
¾ teaspoon salt
½ teaspoon freshly ground pepper
1½ pounds turnips, peeled and cut into 1-inch cubes
¼ cup red wine vinegar
3½ cups White Veal Stock (p. 225), Duck Stock (p. 225) or chicken stock
2 tablespoons chopped parsley

1. Blanch the shallots in boiling salted water for 2 minutes; drain.
2. In a large skillet, melt the butter. Add the shallots, salt and pepper and sauté over moderately high heat until lightly browned, about 10 minutes. Add the turnips and sauté until lightly browned, about 10 minutes longer.
3. Add the vinegar and 1 cup of the stock and cook over moderate heat, adding more stock when the pan is almost dry, until the vegetables are a deep glazed brown and very tender, about 1½ hours. Season with more salt and pepper to taste and sprinkle with the parsley before serving.

—*Deirdre Davis & Linda Marino*

TURNIP, APPLE AND PEAR PUREE

This puree is a delicious accompaniment to pork and game dishes. If you prefer a finer puree, pass the mixture through the fine disk of a food mill.

6 SERVINGS
2 tablespoons unsalted butter
2 pounds turnips, peeled and coarsely chopped
2 tart green apples, such as Granny Smith—peeled, cored and coarsely chopped
1 Bartlett pear—peeled, cored and coarsely chopped
1 tablespoon fresh lemon juice
Pinch of freshly grated nutmeg
½ teaspoon salt
¼ teaspoon freshly ground white pepper

1. In a large skillet or heatproof casserole, melt the butter over moderately high heat. Add the turnips, apples and pear and sauté, tossing frequently, until softened but not browned, about 5 minutes.
2. Add enough water to barely cover (about 1½ cups) and cook, covered, over moderate heat until very tender, about 45 minutes. (If the mixture looks dry during cooking, add more water.)
3. Using a fork, mash the mixture to remove any lumps. (If the puree seems thin, cook over moderate heat, stirring constantly, until reduced to the desired consistency.) Blend in the lemon juice, nutmeg, salt and white pepper.

—*Frank McClelland, Country Inn at Princeton, Princeton, Massachusetts*

BAKED YAMS WITH AMARETTI CRUMBLE TOPPING

8 SERVINGS
5 pounds yams or sweet potatoes (about 10 large)
1½ sticks (6 ounces) unsalted butter
¼ to ½ cup brown sugar, to taste
¼ cup amaretto liqueur or dark rum
¼ cup orange marmalade
2 teaspoons ground ginger (omit if using gingersnaps, below)
½ teaspoon salt
24 amaretti cookies (Italian almond macaroons) or 20 gingersnaps

1. Preheat the oven to 375°. Bake the yams for 1 to 1½ hours, until very tender. Let stand until cool enough to handle.
2. Peel the yams. Mash well with 4 tablespoons of the butter, the brown sugar, liqueur, marmalade, ginger and salt.
3. Pulverize the cookies in a food processor or blender. Add the remaining 8 tablespoons butter and process until well mixed. (**The recipe can be prepared to this point 1 day ahead.** Refrigerate the yams and amaretti toping separately, covered).
4. Preheat the oven to 400°. Generously butter a large shallow baking dish. Spread the mashed yams evenly in the dish.
5. Pinch or cut the cookie topping into small pieces and scatter evenly over the yams.
6. Bake for about 30 minutes, until the yams are heated through and the topping is melted. Transfer to the broiler and cook for 1 to 2 minutes to crisp and brown the topping.

—*Arthur Gold & Robert Fizdale*

SALADS

SALADS

MUSTARD GREENS AND AVOCADO WITH SWEET-HOT DRESSING

Boiling hot, sweetened dressing is poured over the greens to soften the texture and modify the bitterness. Although both Southerners and Pennsylvania Dutch include greens and sweet dressings in their culinary repertoires, this sweet-hot sauce is lighter than either.

Mustard greens, with their strong earthy-flowery perfume, respond in a delightful way to the dressing, becoming more tender and mellow. If they are still too ferocious for your taste, combine them with lettuce and/ or other greens, such as dandelion, kale and Swiss chard, for a milder flavor.

4 SERVINGS
6 cups (firmly packed) cleaned and slivered mustard greens, or mixed greens (about 1 pound before cleaning)
4 scallion greens, thinly sliced
1/3 cup cider vinegar
2 tablespoons brown sugar
1 tablespoon corn oil
1/2 teaspoon Worcestershire sauce
1/4 teaspoon hot pepper sauce
1 large avocado, cut into 1/2-inch dice

1. In a large serving bowl, combine the greens and scallions.
2. In a small noncorrodible saucepan, combine the vinegar, brown sugar, corn oil, Worcestershire and hot sauce. Bring to a boil over high heat, stirring constantly.
3. Pour the dressing over the greens and toss quickly. Add the avocado, toss gently and serve at once, seasoned with additional Worcestershire and hot sauce as desired.
—Elizabeth Schneider

PEAR AND BLUE CHEESE SALAD WITH PARMESAN

This dish serves as both the salad, and the cheese and fruit courses. When buying Parmesan cheese, choose a piece of cheese that is moist rather than dry and flaky.

4 SERVINGS
1 lemon
1/2 cup sugar
20 black peppercorns
4 small Seckel or Forelle pears, peeled
3 tablespoons extra-virgin olive oil
1 tablespoon fresh lemon juice
1/4 teaspoon salt
1/8 teaspoon coarsely ground pepper
1 small head of curly endive, torn into 1/2-inch pieces
2 small Belgian endive, cut crosswise into 1/2-inch lengths
1/4-pound wedge of Roquefort cheese, cut lengthwise into 4 thin slices
2 ounces Parmesan cheese, finely grated into small curls

1. Using a vegetable peeler, remove the zest from the lemon; then squeeze out the juice. Place the lemon zest and juice in a medium noncorrodible saucepan. Add the sugar, peppercorns and 2 cups of water.
2. Add the whole pears to the saucepan and cook over high heat until the liquid comes to a boil. Reduce the heat to moderate and cook until the pears are tender and can be pierced easily with the tip of a knife, 10 to 20 minutes.
3. Set the pears aside to cool in the poaching liquid, about 2 hours.
4. In a small bowl, whisk together the oil, lemon juice, salt and pepper.
5. Divide the greens among 4 dinner plates and pour a quarter of the dressing over each. Arrange a pear, a slice of Roquefort and a spoonful of Parmesan over the greens on each plate.
—Christopher Idone

SALAD OF BITTER GREENS WITH GRAPEFRUIT VINAIGRETTE

6 SERVINGS
1 medium head of chicory or escarole, or 2 large bunches of arugula
2 Belgian endive, halved lengthwise and cored
Juice of 1 small grapefruit (about 1/2 cup)
1 1/2 teaspoons fresh lemon juice
1/4 teaspoon salt
1/8 teaspoon freshly ground pepper
6 tablespoons olive oil

1. Rinse the chicory under cold water. (Do not soak—it will become more bitter.) Dry thoroughly, tear into small pieces and place in a large bowl. Cut the endive lengthwise into 1/3-inch strips and add to the greens.
2. In a small bowl, combine the grapefruit and lemon juices with the salt and pepper. Gradually whisk in the oil. Pour the dressing over the greens and toss well.
—Deirdre Davis & Linda Marino

SICILIAN CITRUS SALAD

6 SERVINGS
5 medium navel oranges
1/2 cup olive oil, preferably extra-virgin
2 tablespoons fresh lemon juice
1/2 tablespoon peppercorns, coarsely cracked
2 tablespoons finely shredded lemon zest

1. Using a knife, peel the oranges; there should be no white membrane left. Slice the oranges crosswise into 1/4-inch rounds and arrange on 6 plates.

2. Drizzle the oil and lemon juice over the orange slices. Sprinkle with the cracked peppercorns and lemon zest. Cover the plates with plastic wrap and set aside to macerate at room temperature for 2 hours before serving.

—*Deirdre Davis & Linda Marino*

GREEN SALAD WITH LEMON AND FENNEL

To get most of the work for this salad out of the way ahead of time, rinse, dry and trim the greens up to six hours before serving. Wrap in a dampened kitchen towel and refrigerate. They will be nicely crisped by the time the salad is assembled.

8 SERVINGS
1 lemon
3 fennel bulbs
¼ cup safflower oil
¼ cup light olive oil
1 teaspoon crushed fennel seeds
½ teaspoon salt
¼ teaspoon coarsely cracked pepper
1 bunch of watercress, large stems removed
3 heads of Bibb lettuce, separated into leaves
1 head of Boston lettuce, torn into pieces

1. Remove the lemon zest in long strips with a vegetable peeler. Cut lengthwise into very thin strips. Wrap in plastic wrap to keep moist.

2. Remove and discard the green stalks of the fennel. Cut out the cores and remove any tough outer sections. Cut the bulbs lengthwise into thin strips. In a medium bowl, toss the fennel strips with the juice of half of the lemon. Cover with ice water and let stand until crisp, about 30 minutes. Drain and spin or pat dry.

3. In a small bowl, whisk together the safflower and olive oils, fennel seeds, salt, pepper and the strained juice of the remaining ½ lemon.

4. To assemble the salad, toss the fennel with 2 tablespoons of the dressing. In a separate bowl, combine the watercress and Bibb and Boston lettuce. Toss the greens with the remaining dressing.

5. Divide the greens among 8 large chilled plates. Place a small mound of fennel in the center. Top the fennel with lemon strips and an additional sprinkling of cracked black pepper.

—*Anne Disrude*

SALAD OF DANDELION AND FRESH GOAT CHEESE

🍷 F&W BEVERAGE SUGGESTION
California Sauvignon Blanc

4 TO 6 FIRST-COURSE SERVINGS
1 pound dandelion greens, well washed and dried
¼ pound fresh mild goat cheese, such as Montrachet, cut into ½-inch dice
1 small red onion, cut into ¼-inch dice
2 tablespoons sherry or red wine vinegar
2 tablespoons walnut or peanut oil
½ teaspoon sugar
3 to 4 tablespoons chopped walnuts, to taste

1. Cut off and discard the base of the dandelion stems. Cut each leaf into 2-inch pieces and pile into a large serving bowl. Intersperse the cheese cubes among the dandelion greens and sprinkle with the onion.

2. In a small saucepan, combine the vinegar, oil and sugar and bring to a boil, stirring, over high heat. Pour the dressing over the salad and toss lightly. Sprinkle with the walnuts and serve immediately.

—*Elizabeth Schneider*

ARUGULA AND WATERCRESS SALAD WITH SWISS CHEESE BEIGNETS

An unusual, refreshing change from the standard tossed salad with baked goat cheese, this one tops bitter greens, tossed with an herbal vinaigrette, with exceptionally light, hot cheese fritters.

6 TO 8 SERVINGS
2 bunches of arugula, tough stems removed
1 bunch of watercress, tough stems removed
½ cup Vinaigrette Dressing with Garlic and Fresh Herbs (p. 230)
Swiss Cheese Beignets (recipe follows)

1. Wash the salad greens. Dry in a salad spinner and then pat dry in a towel. Refrigerate until ready to toss the salad.

2. In a large bowl, toss the arugula and watercress with the dressing. Divide among 6 or 8 plates and top with the hot beignets.

—*Lydie Marshall*

SWISS CHEESE BEIGNETS

I found this recipe in my grandmother's papers labeled "how to use leftover egg whites"; it dates from the beginning of the century. What caught my attention was its simplicity and use of only egg whites, rather than whole eggs, which makes the beignets very light. If at all possible, beat the egg whites by hand in a copper bowl to ensure the most volume.

I love the combination of these crisp cheese tidbits with the tart-bitter salad greens, but they are marvelous all by themselves with cocktails or Champagne. Grate the cheese at the last minute. If grated ahead of time, the cheese tends to pack and the beignets are not as light.

MAKES ABOUT 1½ DOZEN
½ pound French Gruyère cheese
1 quart vegetable oil, for deep-frying
3 egg whites
Salt (optional)

1. With a fine shredding grater, flat or rotary, grate the cheese, keeping it as loosely packed as possible. In a large heavy saucepan or deep-fat fryer, heat the oil to 325°.

2. Meanwhile, beat the egg whites until they are stiff but not dry. Sprinkle about one-third of the grated cheese over the beaten egg whites and fold in. Sprinkle on half of the remaining cheese and fold in. Lightly fold in the remaining cheese just until it is evenly distributed. The mixture will remain lumpy.

3. Drop heaping tablespoons of the cheese-egg white mixture into the hot oil, frying in batches without crowding, until golden brown, about 5 minutes. As the beignets are added to the oil, they may stick together; separate carefully with 2 forks.

4. Drain the beignets on paper towels and sprinkle lightly with salt if desired. Serve hot.

—*Lydie Marshall*

TRICOLOR SALAD

A particularly effective presentation of this salad is to put everything in a glass bowl, keeping the red, white and green ingredients separate. Then at table, add the dressing and toss well.

8 SERVINGS
1 large bunch of arugula
1 large or 2 small heads of radicchio, torn into large pieces
3 to 4 Belgian endive, cut crosswise into ½-inch lengths

3 tablespoons extra-virgin olive oil
2 teaspoons red wine vinegar
Salt and freshly ground pepper

In a salad bowl, combine the arugula, radicchio and endive. Just before serving, pour the oil and vinegar over the salad. Season with salt and pepper to taste. Toss well to coat.

—*Arthur Gold & Robert Fizdale*

SUMMER TOSSED SALAD WITH MUSHROOMS AND FRESH AND PICKLED PEPPERS

6 SERVINGS
1 small head of red leaf lettuce
1 small head of Bibb lettuce
1 small bunch of arugula
¼ cup olive oil, preferably extra-virgin
1 medium red bell pepper, cut into thin strips
1 medium yellow bell pepper, cut into thin strips
6 medium mushroom caps, quartered
½ teaspoon salt
¼ teaspoon freshly ground black pepper
2 garlic cloves, minced
1 tablespoon minced fresh basil
4 pepperoncini (Tuscan pickled peppers in jars), quartered lengthwise and seeded
1 medium tomato, cut into 8 wedges
½ cup Vinaigrette Dressing with Garlic and Fresh Herbs (p. 230)
2 hard-cooked eggs, quartered lengthwise

1. Wash and dry the salad greens, tear into pieces and refrigerate, covered, until you toss the salad.

2. In a large skillet, heat the olive oil. Add the red and yellow peppers and stir-fry over moderately high heat until they begin to soften, about 3 minutes. Add the mushrooms, season

with the salt and black pepper and sauté for about 3 minutes, until the mushrooms soften slightly. Reduce the heat to moderately low and add the garlic and basil. Sauté for 2 minutes to combine the flavors. (**The recipe can be made to this point up to 2 hours ahead.** Reheat the vegetables before proceeding.)

3. Place the salad greens in a large bowl. Add the hot vegetables, pepperoncini, tomato wedges and dressing; toss. Arrange the salad on a large platter or individual plates and garnish with the eggs.

—*Lydie Marshall*

YELLOW PICKLED SALAD (ACHAR KUNING)

This salad should have four vegetables or more, with different colors and textures to add interest. Other vegetables that may be used to good account are carrots, in julienne strips; string beans, blanched and cut into 1-inch pieces, and sticks of Kirby cucumber.

6 SERVINGS
1 tablespoon corn or peanut oil
1 garlic clove, bruised
¼ teaspoon turmeric
¼ cup cider vinegar
2 teaspoons minced fresh ginger
2 teaspoons sugar
½ teaspoon salt
1 medium red or green bell pepper, cut into ¼-inch-wide strips
1 can (5 ounces) sliced bamboo shoots, rinsed and drained
1 can (15 ounces) baby corn, rinsed and drained
1 medium zucchini, cut into 2-by-⅜-inch julienne strips

1. In a wok or large skillet, heat the oil over moderately high heat. Add the garlic and turmeric and cook, stirring constantly, until the garlic is fra-

grant but not browned, about 1 minute. Add the vinegar, ginger, sugar, salt and ¼ cup of water. Simmer the dressing for 3 minutes.

2. Add the bell pepper, bamboo shoots, corn and zucchini. Increase the heat to high and cook, stirring, for 3 minutes. Turn out into a bowl. Let cool, then refrigerate, tossing occasionally, for at least 4 hours, and preferably overnight, to chill and develop the flavors. Serve chilled.

—*Copeland Marks*

CRISP GARLIC COLESLAW

The key to this simple coleslaw is to cut the cabbage into long fine shreds, crisp them in ice water and then spin dry before dressing. It's best if made as soon as possible before serving.

4 TO 6 SERVINGS
1¼ pounds green cabbage (½ head)
¼ cup extra-virgin olive oil
2 tablespoons balsamic vinegar
2 garlic cloves, crushed through a
   press
1 teaspoon coarse (kosher) salt
¼ teaspoon coarsely ground pepper

1. Cut the cabbage into two wedges and remove the core and thick rib sections. For easier shredding, separate the wedges into layers 1 inch thick. Using a large chef's knife, cut the cabbage into very fine long shreds.

2. Place the shredded cabbage in a large bowl of ice and water. Crisp for 15 minutes to several hours.

3. In a small bowl, whisk together the olive oil, vinegar, garlic, salt and pepper.

4. Drain the cabbage and spin dry in a salad dryer. Place in a large serving bowl, pour the garlic dressing on top and toss well to coat the shreds. For the crunchiest texture, serve the coleslaw immediately.

—*Anne Disrude*

MIXED SALAD WITH PINEAPPLE (ASINAN)

4 TO 6 SERVINGS
2 medium carrots, cut into julienne
   strips
2 firm Chinese bean curd cakes
1 can (8 ounces) unsweetened
   pineapple chunks, drained and
   ¼ cup of the juice reserved
3 tablespoons cider vinegar
2 tablespoons crunchy peanut butter
2 teaspoons sugar
½ teaspoon salt
1 to 2 teaspoons crushed hot pepper,
   to taste
3 Kirby cucumbers, cut into ½-inch
   dice
1 bunch of watercress, tough stems
   removed (about 4 cups)

1. In a medium saucepan of boiling salted water, blanch the carrots until crisp-tender, about 2 minutes. Drain and rinse under cold running water; drain well.

2. In a large saucepan of water, simmer the bean curd for 10 minutes. Remove with a slotted spoon, wrap in a kitchen towel and let drain for 15 minutes. Cut into ½-inch dice. (**The recipe can be made ahead to this point.** Wrap the carrots and bean curd separately and refrigerate.)

3. In a small bowl, mix the pineapple juice, vinegar, peanut butter, sugar, salt and hot pepper.

4. To assemble, combine the carrots, bean curd, pineapple, cucumber and watercress in a small salad bowl; toss lightly. Pour the dressing over the salad and toss again to mix. Serve at room temperature or slightly chilled.

—*Copeland Marks*

MIXED VEGETABLE SALAD WITH COCONUT (URAB URAB)

4 TO 6 SERVINGS
½ pound bean sprouts (about 3 cups)
¼ pound green beans, cut into 2-inch
   pieces
2 teaspoons instant tamarind or
   tamarind paste* (see Note)
1 garlic clove, crushed through a
   press
1 fresh hot red chile, seeded and
   minced, or 1 teaspoon crushed hot
   pepper
½ teaspoon sugar
½ teaspoon salt
½ bunch of watercress, tough stems
   removed (about 2 cups)
¼ cup dried unsweetened coconut*
*Available at Oriental markets and
   health food stores

1. Place the bean sprouts in a large heatproof bowl. Cover with boiling water and let stand for 2 minutes. Drain and rinse in cold water. Drain; let dry on paper towels. Wrap and refrigerate.

2. In a medium saucepan of boiling salted water, blanch the green beans until just tender, about 3 minutes. Drain and rinse under cold water; drain well.

3. In a small bowl, mix the tamarind, garlic, chile, sugar and salt to make the dressing.

4. Toss the bean sprouts, green beans and watercress together. Add the dressing and coconut and toss again to mix. Serve the salad at room temperature.

NOTE: If using tamarind paste, measure 2 teaspoons and soak in 2 tablespoons of water for 30 minutes. Strain through a sieve and discard the pulp.

—*Copeland Marks*

SALADS

SIMPLE PEPPER SALAD WITH SESAME SEEDS (TIMOR ACHAR)

This salad makes a fine accompaniment to grilled steak or chicken.

4 TO 6 SERVINGS
¼ pound snow peas
1 small red onion, thinly sliced
¼ cup cider vinegar
1 teaspoon sugar
½ teaspoon salt
2 tablespoons sesame seeds
1 small green bell pepper, cut into julienne strips
1 small red bell pepper, cut into julienne strips
1 large tomato, cut into wedges

1. Pull the strings off the snow peas; cut lengthwise into julienne strips. Cover with cold water; refrigerate for about 30 minutes to crisp. Drain well.
2. Rinse the onion in cold water, dry with paper towels.
3. In a small bowl, mix the vinegar, sugar and salt, stirring to dissolve the sugar. Set the dressing aside.
4. In a small skillet, toast the sesame seeds over moderate heat, tossing until nut brown, about 5 minutes.
5. In a large bowl, toss the vegetables with the vinegar dressing. Transfer to a serving dish. Sprinkle with the sesame seeds. Serve at once or refrigerate for up to 1 hour.

—Copeland Marks

MINTED ZUCCHINI AND APPLE SALAD

12 TO 16 SERVINGS
½ cup currants
¼ cup ruby port or sweet vermouth
2 pounds zucchini, cut into 3-by-¼-inch julienne strips
3 pounds Granny Smith apples, unpeeled, cut into 3-by-¼-inch julienne strips
½ cup fresh lemon juice
1 pound Jarlsberg cheese, cut into 3-by-¼-inch julienne strips
2 medium red onions, minced
½ cup extra-virgin olive oil
¼ cup sherry wine vinegar
1½ tablespoons salt
¼ cup minced fresh mint

1. In a small bowl, soak the currants in the port for at least 2 hours or overnight; drain.
2. In a large bowl, toss the zucchini and apple strips with the lemon juice. Add the cheese and onions and toss well to combine.
3. In a medium bowl, whisk together the olive oil, vinegar and salt. Stir in the currants and mint and pour this dressing over the salad. Toss gently but thoroughly. Serve the salad at room temperature.

—W. Peter Prestcott

HEARTS OF PALM, BEET AND ENDIVE SALAD

12 TO 16 SERVINGS
3½ pounds fresh beets
1 pound radishes, sliced into ¼-inch rounds
1 can (16 ounces) hearts of palm, drained and cut into ¼-inch rounds
1½ pounds celery (about 2 bunches), cut crosswise into ¼-inch slices
2 pounds firm, ripe tomatoes—halved, seeded and cut into ½-inch dice
7 scallions, minced (about 1 cup)
2½ cups minced fresh dill
½ cup safflower oil
¼ cup walnut oil
¼ cup extra-virgin olive oil
¼ cup sherry wine vinegar
3 tablespoons fresh lemon juice
2½ teaspoons salt
1½ teaspoons coarsely cracked pepper
2 pounds Belgian endive, leaves separated

1. Preheat the oven to 400°. Wrap the beets in aluminum foil, about 3 to a package. Bake the beets in the middle of the oven for 1¼ to 1½ hours, or until tender when pierced with a skewer or knife tip. Remove from the oven and open the packets of foil. When the beets are cool enough to handle, peel them under cold running water; pat dry. Slice into ¼-inch rounds and let cool completely.
2. In a large bowl, toss the radishes, hearts of palm, celery, tomatoes and scallions with 2 cups of the dill.
3. In a medium bowl, whisk together the safflower, walnut and olive oils, the vinegar, lemon juice, salt and pepper. Pour ½ cup of this dressing over the radish mixture and toss well.
4. In a medium bowl, toss the beets with half of the remaining dressing. In another bowl, toss the endive spears with the remaining dressing.
5. On a large round or oval platter, make a bed of the radish mixture. Arrange alternating rows of overlapping beets and endive spears. Sprinkle with the remaining ½ cup dill. Serve at room temperature.

—W. Peter Prestcott

FRESH AND SUN-DRIED TOMATOES WITH ZUCCHINI AND BALSAMIC VINEGAR

4 SERVINGS

1 pound tomatoes, cut into thin
  wedges
½ pound zucchini, cut into 2-by-
  ¼-inch julienne strips
6 sun-dried tomato halves (in oil), cut
  into thin strips
2 tablespoons extra-virgin olive oil
2 teaspoons balsamic vinegar
½ teaspoon salt
¼ teaspoon freshly ground pepper

Toss all of the ingredients together
and let marinate at room temperature
for 30 to 60 minutes.

—Anne Disrude

PELOPONNESE SALAD

6 TO 8 SERVINGS

1 cup extra-virgin olive oil
⅓ cup red wine vinegar
2 teaspoons salt
1 teaspoon freshly ground black
  pepper
2 tablespoons fresh thyme, chopped,
  or 1½ teaspoons dried
2 pounds tomatoes (about 8 medium),
  cut into 8 wedges each
1 red bell pepper, cut into ⅛-inch
  strips
1 green bell pepper, cut into ⅛-inch
  strips
2 small red onions, thinly sliced
½ pound imported black olives,
  pitted
½ pound feta cheese, coarsely
  crumbled

In a large bowl, combine the oil,
vinegar, salt, black pepper and
thyme. Add the tomatoes, bell peppers, onions, olives and cheese; toss
well. Cover and refrigerate for at least
1 hour. Toss before serving.

—Molly O'Neill

GAZPACHO ICE

8 SERVINGS

2 teaspoons sherry wine vinegar
1 tablespoon olive oil
1 teaspoon salt
½ teaspoon freshly ground black
  pepper
2 tablespoons minced fresh coriander
¼ teaspoon minced fresh hot green
  chile or hot pepper sauce
1 small green bell pepper, minced
1 small red bell pepper, minced
1 small red onion, minced
4 large tomatoes—peeled, seeded and
  minced
1½ cups tomato juice
2 tablespoons vodka

1. In a large bowl, combine the vinegar, oil, salt, black pepper and coriander. Add the hot pepper, green and
red bell peppers, onion, tomatoes and
tomato juice; stir well to blend.
2. Freeze the mixture in an ice
cream maker according to the manufacturer's instructions until still slightly slushy; add the vodka and freeze
until firm.

—Molly O'Neill

FRIED BEAN CAKE AND BEAN SPROUT SALAD (TAHU GORENG)

If you've never eaten fried bean curd,
the meaty, chewy texture may surprise you. Even people who are not
particularly fond of bean curd often
love it prepared this way. Hot, spicy
peanut sauce provides the perfect
counterpoint to the crisp, cool bean
sprouts.

4 SERVINGS

⅓ pound bean sprouts (about 2 cups)
4 firm Chinese bean curd cakes
¼ cup corn or peanut oil
3 tablespoons kecap manis* or
  homemade Indonesian Sweet Soy
  Sauce (p. 236)
1 tablespoon fresh lime or lemon juice
1 tablespoon smooth peanut butter
1 small fresh hot red chile, seeded and
  very thinly sliced (about 2
  teaspoons), or ½ teaspoon crushed
  hot pepper
1 garlic clove, crushed through a
  press
1 teaspoon sugar
2 scallions, thinly sliced
*Available at Oriental markets

1. Place the bean sprouts in a large
heatproof bowl. Cover with boiling
water and let stand for 2 minutes.
Drain and rinse in cold water; drain
well. Dry on paper towels. Refrigerate
for 15 minutes or overnight.
2. Dry the bean curd cakes on a
paper towel. Cut into 12 (1-inch)
cubes. Heat the oil in a wok or large
skillet. Fry the cubes in two or three
batches over moderate heat, tossing,
until light brown all over, 5 to 7 minutes. Remove with a slotted spoon
and drain on paper towels.
3. In a small bowl, combine the kecap manis, lime juice, peanut butter,
chile, garlic and sugar. Stir to blend
the dressing well.
4. To assemble the salad, place the
bean sprouts on a serving platter.
Cover with the fried bean curd. Pour
the sauce over all. Garnish with the
scallions. Serve at room temperature.

—Copeland Marks

SALADS

CABBAGE SALAD WITH SHRIMP (ACHAR UDANG)

Tart and crisp, this salad makes a refreshing light luncheon dish

4 SERVINGS
2 tablespoons fresh lime juice
2 tablespoons cider vinegar or distilled white vinegar
2 teaspoons salt
1 tablespoon plus 1 teaspoon sugar
2 teaspoons minced fresh ginger
2 cups finely shredded cabbage (about 5 ounces)
2 Kirby cucumbers, unpeeled and sliced
1 red bell pepper, cut into julienne strips
½ pound medium shrimp—cooked, shelled and deveined

1. In a large bowl, mix together the lime juice, vinegar, salt, sugar, ginger and 2 tablespoons of water.
2. Add the cabbage, cucumbers, bell pepper and shrimp. Toss with the dressing until well mixed. Let marinate at room temperature, tossing occasionally, for up to 2 hours. Serve at room temperature or slightly chilled.
—Copeland Marks

BEEFSTEAK TOMATOES WITH MINTED CRACKED WHEAT SALAD

4 SERVINGS
¼ cup plus 1 tablespoon olive oil
¾ cup bulgur wheat
¼ cup fresh lemon juice
2 tablespoons fresh lime juice
1 teaspoon salt
½ teaspoon freshly ground pepper
2 scallions, minced
2 tablespoons minced fresh mint
4 medium beefsteak tomatoes

1. In a medium skillet, heat ¼ cup of the olive oil. Add the bulgur and toss over high heat until coated with oil, about 1 minute; remove from the heat. Stir in ¾ cup of hot water, cover and soak until the water is absorbed and the bulgur is tender, at least 1 hour.
2. In a medium bowl, combine the lemon and lime juices with the salt and pepper. Add the scallions, mint, remaining 1 tablespoon oil and the soaked bulgur; toss well. Cover and refrigerate for 1 hour or longer.
3. Cut the tops from the tomatoes; hollow out the centers. Toss the bulgur salad well and spoon it into the tomatoes.
—Molly O'Neill

THE PARROT RESTAURANT'S PARROT SALAD

8 SERVINGS
8 strips of bacon
1¼ pounds spinach, stemmed
1 can (5 ounces) sliced water chestnuts, rinsed and drained
16 large mushrooms, sliced (about 1 pound)
½ pound bean sprouts
½ cup raspberry vinegar
3 tablespoons mango chutney
4 medium garlic cloves, minced
1 tablespoon grainy mustard
1 teaspoon coarsely cracked pepper
1 cup olive oil, preferably extra-virgin
1 cup (4 ounces) grated Monterey Jack cheese

1. In a medium skillet, fry the bacon over moderate heat until browned and crisp, about 8 minutes. Drain on paper towels.
2. On each of 8 individual plates, arrange the spinach, water chestnuts, mushrooms and bean sprouts. Crumble the bacon and distribute evenly among the plates.

3. In a food processor, combine the vinegar, chutney, garlic, mustard and pepper; process until smooth. With the machine on, add the olive oil and process until thickened.
4. Spoon some of the dressing over each serving and top with the grated cheese.
—The Parrot Restaurant, Frederick, Maryland

BLACK BEAN AND BELL PEPPER SALAD

This simple salad can be tossed together in no time at all and is perfect for last-minute preparations.

4 SERVINGS
1 can (16 ounces) black beans, rinsed and drained
1 large green bell pepper, diced
½ cup peeled, seeded and diced fresh tomato or drained and chopped canned tomato
2 scallions, thinly sliced
1 jalapeño pepper—seeded, deribbed and minced
1 tablespoon chopped fresh coriander
1 tablespoon corn oil
1 tablespoon fresh lime juice
¼ teaspoon salt
⅛ teaspoon freshly ground pepper

1. Place the beans in a medium bowl. Add the bell pepper, tomato, scallions, jalapeño pepper and coriander. Toss to mix.
2. In a small bowl, combine the corn oil, lime juice, salt and pepper. Pour the dressing over the bean mixture and toss well to coat.
—Diana Sturgis

THREE-BEAN MACARONI SALAD

Although this salad joins two classics, it doesn't use either of the traditional dressings. Instead, it is seasoned with orange zest and Chinese flavorings, such as star anise, ginger and sesame oil. Let the salad marinate at room temperature for at least one hour before serving to develop the flavors. Add the vinegar just before serving, so as not to discolor the green beans.

4 TO 6 SERVINGS

1½ teaspoons Szechuan peppercorns*
4 star anise pods*
1 small dried hot red pepper
⅓ cup safflower or other light
    vegetable oil
1 tablespoon Oriental sesame oil
6 scallions—white part minced, green
    part cut into 1½-by-⅛-inch
    julienne strips
2 tablespoons minced fresh ginger
1½ tablespoons minced garlic
Minced zest of 1 navel orange
3 tablespoons soy sauce
½ pound dry, shaped pasta, such as
    orecchiette or small shells
½ pound green beans, cut on the
    diagonal into ½-inch pieces
½ pound yellow wax beans, cut on
    the diagonal into ½-inch pieces
2 cups cooked small red or black
    beans, such as small kidney beans
    or turtle beans (from 1 cup dried)
    or canned
⅓ cup chopped fresh mint
3 tablespoons white wine vinegar
Salt
*Available at Oriental markets

1. In a small skillet, toast the Szechuan peppercorns over high heat, tossing, until fragrant, about 1 minute. Remove from the pan and let cool slightly.

2. In an electric spice grinder, grind the star anise, hot pepper and roasted Szechuan peppercorns to a fine pow-

der. If you do not have a spice grinder, use a large knife to coarsely chop the spices, then use the flat of the blade or a mortar and pestle to grind them to a powder.

3. In a small skillet, heat the safflower and sesame oils over moderately low heat. Add the minced scallion, ginger, garlic, orange zest and spice mixture. Cook over moderately low heat, stirring occasionally, until the garlic is softened but not browned, about 5 minutes. Stir in the soy sauce, remove from the heat and set aside. (**The flavored oil can be made several hours or even days ahead.** Cover and refrigerate.)

4. In a large pot of boiling salted water, cook the pasta until tender but still firm, 12 to 15 minutes. Drain well.

5. In a large pot of boiling salted water, cook the green and wax beans until crisp-tender, 3 to 5 minutes. Rinse under cold running water; pat dry.

6. At least 1 hour before serving, toss the red or black beans and the green and wax beans with the pasta, flavored oil and julienned scallion green. Let stand at room temperature for 1 to 2 hours to allow the flavors to develop. Just before serving, add the mint, vinegar and salt to taste.

—Anne Disrude

BEAN, CORN AND RICE SALAD WITH CHILI VINAIGRETTE

This spicy salad is a perfect accompaniment for grilled lamb or barbecued chicken. The flavors improve if the salad sits at room temperature for about an hour before serving.

6 TO 8 SERVINGS

3½ cups cooked converted rice, cooled
    (from 1 cup raw rice)
1 can (16 ounces) pink beans, rinsed
    and drained

1½ cups cooked fresh corn or 1 can
    (12 ounces) vacuum-packed corn
    niblets
⅓ cup chopped scallions
2 pickled jalapeño peppers—seeded,
    deribbed and minced
⅓ cup safflower or corn oil
2 tablespoons fresh lime juice
1 tablespoon cider vinegar
1 tablespoon (packed) brown sugar
1 teaspoon chili powder
1 teaspoon salt
½ teaspoon ground cumin

1. In a large bowl, combine the rice, beans, corn, scallions and jalapeño peppers. Toss to mix.

2. In a small bowl, combine the oil, lime juice, vinegar, brown sugar, chili powder, salt and cumin. Whisk until the sugar dissolves and the mixture is well blended.

3. Pour the dressing over the salad and toss to coat. Let stand at room temperature, tossing occasionally, for up to 4 hours before serving, or cover and refrigerate for up to 3 days.

—Susan Wyler

POTATO SALAD A L'ORANGE WITH SWEET PEPPERS

8 SERVINGS

2 pounds red bell peppers (about 6)
2½ pounds small red potatoes
1 tablespoon red wine vinegar
1 tablespoon fresh orange juice
1 teaspoon freshly grated orange zest
¾ teaspoon freshly ground black
    pepper
¾ teaspoon salt
⅓ cup safflower oil
1 cup thinly sliced scallions
1 tablespoon chopped parsley

SALADS

1. Broil the peppers about 3 inches from the heat, turning, until blackened all over, 15 to 20 minutes. Place them in a paper bag for about 10 minutes to loosen the skins. Peel off the blackened skins under running water.

2. Halve the peppers over a bowl to catch the juices. Remove the seeds, cores and ribs. Slice the peppers into strips about 2 by ½ inch. Strain and reserve 1 tablespoon of the juices.

3. Place the potatoes in a large saucepan and cover them with cold water. Bring to a boil and cook until tender, about 20 minutes. Drain, peel if desired and cut into ¼- to ⅜-inch-thick slices. Place in a large bowl.

4. In a medium bowl, whisk together the vinegar, orange juice, orange zest, reserved pepper juices, black pepper and salt. Gradually whisk in the oil.

5. Pour the dressing over the warm potatoes. Add the roasted peppers, scallions and parsley and toss to mix.
—Diana Sturgis

LIGHTENED POTATO SALAD

Use one, two or a mixture of the vegetables listed below to lighten this mayonnaise-dressed potato salad, but use a total of 6 cups. For a less traditional flavor, add a good handful of any minced fresh herb, such as basil, tarragon or coriander.

6 TO 8 SERVINGS
3 pounds waxy potatoes, peeled and
  cut into ½-inch dice
½ cup dry white wine
3 tablespoons cider vinegar
1½ teaspoons salt
½ teaspoon freshly ground pepper
4 jumbo eggs—hard-cooked, peeled
  and chopped
¾ cup mayonnaise, preferably
  homemade
2 cups julienned zucchini (1 by ⅛
  inch)

1 cup julienned jicama (1 by ⅛ inch)
1 cup julienned daikon radish (1 by
  ⅛ inch)
1 cup (packed) watercress leaves
  and small stems
1 cup slivered fresh water chestnuts
⅓ cup minced fresh basil, tarragon or
  coriander (optional)

1. Bring a large pot of salted water to a boil. Add the potatoes and cook, stirring occasionally, until easily pierced with a fork, about 10 minutes. Drain well and place in a large bowl.

2. In a small noncorrodible saucepan, combine the wine, vinegar, ½ teaspoon of the salt and ¼ teaspoon of the pepper. Bring just to a boil. Pour the hot dressing over the potatoes and toss to coat. Let the potatoes cool to room temperature, tossing occasionally.

3. Add the chopped hard-cooked eggs and the mayonnaise to the potatoes and toss to coat. Just before serving, add the vegetables, remaining 1 teaspoon salt and ¼ teaspoon pepper and the herbs. Season with additional salt and pepper to taste.
—Anne Disrude

LAYERED SALAD WITH SPICY PEANUT DRESSING (GADO-GADO)

Gado-gado is the premier Indonesian salad. It can serve as the centerpiece of an all-vegetable meal, as one of several dishes in an Asian-style meal or as a colorful addition to a buffet. Though the salad is traditionally layered, you can compose it to achieve a more dramatic effect.

6 TO 8 SERVINGS
½ pound red potatoes
2 cups cauliflorets (1-inch)

1 medium carrot, cut into 2-by-
  ¼-inch julienne strips
¼ pound green beans, cut into 2-inch
  pieces
2 cups shredded cabbage (about
  5 ounces)
1 cup jicama, sliced into 2-by-¼-inch
  julienne strips (optional)
1 firm Chinese bean curd cake
1 cup Thick Coconut Milk (p. 232) or
  canned unsweetened coconut milk*
⅓ cup crunchy peanut butter
1 large garlic clove, minced
3 tablespoons kecap manis* or
  homemade Indonesian Sweet Soy
  Sauce (p. 236)
3 tablespoons fresh lemon juice
1 square inch of lemon zest
2 tablespoons brown sugar
1 to 2 teaspoons crushed hot pepper
  or 1 small fresh hot red chile, finely
  chopped
½ teaspoon salt
2 scallions, thinly sliced
2 hard-cooked eggs, sliced
6 cherry tomatoes
*Available at Oriental markets

1. In a medium saucepan of boiling salted water, cook the potatoes until tender, 12 to 20 minutes, depending on size; drain. When cool enough to handle, peel and slice.

2. In another saucepan of boiling salted water, cook the cauliflower until just tender, about 3 minutes. Remove with a slotted spoon and rinse under cold water; drain well.

3. In the same boiling water, repeat this process with the carrot, then the green beans and finally the cabbage. (The jicama is not cooked.)

4. In a medium saucepan of simmering water, poach the bean curd for 10 minutes. Remove with a slotted spoon, wrap in a kitchen towel and let

drain for at least 15 minutes. Cut into ½-inch cubes.

5. To make the sauce, in a medium saucepan, combine the coconut milk, peanut butter, garlic, *kecap manis*, lemon juice, lemon zest, brown sugar, hot pepper, salt and 2 tablespoons of water. Bring to a boil over moderate heat, stirring frequently. Reduce the heat to moderately low and simmer until thickened, about 10 minutes. Keep warm over very low heat until ready to use.

6. Arrange the vegetables in layers in a large salad bowl. Scatter the bean curd and scallions on top. Garnish with the egg and tomatoes. Pour the warm peanut butter sauce over all. Serve at room temperature.

—*Copeland Marks*

CHICKEN CAESAR SALAD

4 TO 6 SERVINGS
1 cup olive oil
4 garlic cloves, minced
1 tablespoon minced parsley
½ teaspoon salt
¼ teaspoon coarsely cracked pepper
4 skinless, boneless chicken breast halves
6 slices of stale French bread, cut into ½-inch cubes
3 anchovy fillets, rinsed and patted dry
1½ tablespoons fresh lemon juice
1 tablespoon red wine vinegar
1 egg yolk
1 medium head of romaine lettuce, torn into pieces
½ cup freshly grated Parmesan cheese
Freshly ground pepper

1. In a shallow dish, combine ¼ cup of the oil, 1 minced garlic clove, the parsley, ¼ teaspoon of the salt and the cracked pepper. Add the chicken and turn to coat well. Cover and marinate at room temperature for 1 hour, turning occasionally.

2. In a large skillet, heat ¼ cup of the oil. Add the bread cubes and fry over moderate heat, tossing, until crisp and golden, about 5 to 7 minutes. Add 2 minced garlic cloves and fry, tossing, for 1 minute longer. Using a slotted spoon, transfer the croutons to paper towels to drain.

3. Preheat the broiler and a broiler pan. In a small bowl, mash the anchovies to a paste with the remaining minced garlic clove and ¼ teaspoon salt. Add the lemon juice, vinegar and egg yolk. Gradually whisk in the remaining ½ cup oil. Set aside.

4. Remove the chicken from the marinade and place on the heated broiler pan. Broil about 3 inches from the heat, turning once, for 3 minutes on each side. Remove the chicken from the pan and let cool to room temperature. Halve each breast crosswise and cut lengthwise into ½-inch-wide strips. Toss with ⅓ cup of the dressing.

5. In a large bowl, toss together the romaine, croutons, ¼ cup of the Parmesan and the remaining dressing. Divide the salad among 4 to 6 large plates. Top with the chicken strips, sprinkle on the remaining ¼ cup cheese and season with a few gridings of pepper.

—*Frank Stitt, Highlands: A Bar & Grill, Birmingham, Alabama*

CHICKEN AND CANADIAN BACON SALAD WITH TOASTED PECANS

🍷 **F&W BEVERAGE SUGGESTION**
Chianti Classico

12 TO 16 SERVINGS
6 whole boneless chicken breasts, with the skin intact (about 4½ pounds)
3 tablespoons peanut oil
½ pound pecan halves (2⅓ cups)
2 teaspoons ground cumin
2 packages (10 ounces each) frozen baby peas
2 pounds Canadian bacon or lean ham, cut into ½-inch dice
2 pounds mushrooms, cut into ½-inch dice
⅓ cup fresh lemon juice
2 cups thinly sliced scallions (about 2 bunches)
1½ cups plain yogurt
1½ cups sour cream
¼ cup Dijon-style mustard
2 tablespoons salt
2 teaspoons freshly ground pepper

1. Place the chicken breasts in a large wide saucepan or heatproof casserole with water to cover. Bring to a simmer over moderate heat. Reduce the heat to very low and poach the chicken at a bare simmer until firm to the touch, about 45 minutes. Remove from the heat and let cool in the poaching liquid. Drain the chicken, remove the skin and cut the meat into ½-inch cubes.

2. Meanwhile, in a large skillet, heat the oil. Add the pecans, sprinkle with the cumin and sauté over moderately high heat, tossing constantly, until aromatic and lightly toasted, about 4 minutes. Transfer the pecans to paper towels to drain.

3. Blanch the peas in boiling salted water for 30 seconds; drain and let cool.

4. In a large bowl, combine the chicken, pecans, Canadian bacon and mushrooms. Add the lemon juice and toss until coated. Add the scallions and all but ⅓ cup of the peas.

5. In a medium bowl, combine the yogurt, sour cream, mustard, salt and pepper and mix well. Pour the dressing over the salad and toss to coat.

6. Transfer the salad to a large decorative serving bowl or platter and garnish with the remaining peas. Serve at room temperature.

—*W. Peter Prescott*

WARM TURKEY AND BACON SALAD

A not-too-sweet fruit or vegetable bread would be a perfect accompaniment for this hearty salad.

6 SERVINGS
½ *pound sliced bacon, cut crosswise into ½-inch pieces*
1 *pound fresh mushrooms, coarsely chopped*
2 *cups coarsely shredded cooked turkey*
⅓ *cup balsamic vinegar*
1 *teaspoon salt*
½ *teaspoon freshly ground pepper*
1 *medium head of romaine lettuce, coarsely shredded*
1 *bunch of arugula or watercress, stemmed and coarsely shredded*

1. In a large skillet, cook the bacon over moderate heat until lightly browned and crisp, about 10 minutes. Transfer the bacon to paper towels to drain.

2. Add the mushrooms to the fat in the skillet and cook over very low heat until soft, about 15 minutes, stirring from time to time.

3. Add the turkey and bacon and cook over moderately low heat until warmed through, about 5 minutes. Add the vinegar, salt and pepper and toss well.

4. Place the lettuce and arugula in a large salad bowl. Add the turkey mixture and toss quickly and thoroughly. Serve immediately.

—*Molly O'Neill*

SEAFOOD AND SHORT-GRAIN RICE SALAD WITH ORIENTAL FLAVORS

In this method for cooking short- (or medium-) grain rice, the rice is sautéed in oil so that the grains will remain relatively separate in the finished product. The dish is at its best when the rice is warm or at room temperature, as the kernels harden, if chilled. For warm rice, the dish can be prepared ahead through Step 4; for room temperature, through Step 7.

6 TO 8 FIRST-COURSE OR 4 MAIN-COURSE SERVINGS
½ *teaspoon salt*
½ *pound medium shrimp, in their shells*
¼ *pound sea scallops, quartered*
1 *pound small squid, cleaned and cut into bite-size pieces*
¼ *pound snow peas, strings removed and cut lengthwise into thin strips*
1 *tablespoon sugar*
½ *cup rice vinegar*
1 *tablespoon Oriental sesame oil*
1½ *tablespoons peanut oil*
1 *cup short-grain white rice*
1 *piece (2-by-1-inch) of fresh ginger— peeled, sliced paper thin and cut into julienne strips*
1 *tablespoon hulled sesame seeds*
½ *cup chopped red radishes*
2 *tablespoons very thinly sliced scallion green*

1. In a medium saucepan, bring 1½ cups of water and ¼ teaspoon of the salt to a boil over high heat. Add the shrimp, scallops and squid and return to a simmer, stirring. Immediately remove from the heat, cover and let stand for 10 minutes.

2. Meanwhile, into another saucepan of boiling salted water, drop the snow pea strips and cook just until they lose their raw taste, about 1½ minutes. Drain and drop into a bowl of ice water to chill. Drain and refrigerate, covered.

3. In a bowl, combine the sugar, vinegar and the remaining ¼ teaspoon salt. Stir until the crystals dissolve, then add the sesame oil.

4. Drain the seafood and reserve the broth. Peel the shrimp and halve them lengthwise. In a medium bowl, combine the shrimp, squid, scallops and ¼ cup of the vinegar mixture. Toss and refrigerate.

5. In a heavy, medium saucepan, heat the peanut oil. Add the rice and cook over moderate heat, stirring, until the kernels are opaque, 3 to 4 minutes. Meanwhile, strain the reserved broth into a small saucepan and bring to a boil. Pour the broth over the rice, cover and cook over very low heat for 15 minutes. Remove the rice from the heat and let stand, covered, for 10 minutes.

6. In a small bowl, toss the ginger with 1 tablespoon of the vinegar mixture. Toast the sesame seeds in a small skillet over low heat, stirring, until golden. Let cool.

7. Using a rubber spatula, fluff the rice into a medium bowl and toss gently, until lukewarm. Gradually add the remaining ¼ cup vinegar mixture, tossing continuously. When cooled to room temperature, drain and add the ginger; toss. Fold in the radishes.

8. Mound the rice attractively on a serving platter. Drain the seafood, toss with the scallions and arrange around the rice. Scatter the snow peas over all and garnish with the sesame seeds.

—*Elizabeth Schneider*

JAMBALAYA SALAD

This satisfying, colorful salad is a takeoff on one of the South's best-known dishes. Ease of serving is a real advantage; it's all there on one plate, needing nothing more as a go-with than some French bread. The salad, gently spiced, pairs perfectly with a cold beer or a tall, minted iced tea.

6 SERVINGS
1 large egg plus 2 egg yolks
⅓ cup sherry wine vinegar
3 tablespoons whole-grain mustard
1½ teaspoons salt
2 teaspoons freshly ground black pepper
2¼ cups olive oil
1 medium onion, finely chopped

½ teaspoon crushed hot pepper
1 teaspoon thyme
2 imported bay leaves
2 cups chicken stock or canned broth
1 cup long-grain white rice
3 celery ribs, cut crosswise on the diagonal into ½-inch pieces
1 small green bell pepper, cut into 1-inch pieces
1 small red bell pepper, cut into 1-inch pieces
4 scallions, thinly sliced
1½ cups diced cooked chicken (about ¾ pound skinless, boneless chicken)
1½ cups diced cooked ham (about ¾ pound)
1 large head of iceberg lettuce, coarsely shredded (about 6 cups)
2 medium tomatoes, cut into 6 wedges each, or 12 cherry tomatoes
18 large cooked shrimp—shelled and deveined, with tails left on

1. In a food processor, combine the whole egg, egg yolks, vinegar, mustard, ½ teaspoon of the salt and the black pepper. Process for 1 minute. With the machine on, pour in 2 cups of the olive oil in a steady stream. Cover and refrigerate until serving time.

2. In a medium saucepan, heat 3 tablespoons of the olive oil. Add the onion and cook, stirring, over moderate heat until tender but not brown, about 5 minutes.

3. Add the hot pepper, thyme and bay leaves and cook, stirring, for 2 to 3 minutes, until fragrant. Stir in the stock, remaining 1 teaspoon salt and the rice. Increase the heat to moder-

ately high and bring to a boil. Reduce the heat to low, cover the pan and cook undisturbed for 20 minutes, or until the rice is tender and all the liquid is absorbed. Remove from the heat and let stand, covered, for 5 minutes. Scrape the rice into a large bowl, remove the bay leaves and let stand, stirring occasionally, until cool.

4. Add the celery, green and red bell peppers, scallions, chicken, ham and remaining 1 tablespoon olive oil. Toss well to mix. (**The recipe can be made to this point up to a day ahead.** Let return to room temperature.)

5. To serve, line 6 large plates with shredded lettuce, mound about 1½ cups of the rice salad on each plate of lettuce. Garnish with 2 tomato wedges and 3 shrimp each. Drizzle with some of the dressing and serve with additional fresh pepper. Pass the remaining dressing separately.

—*Michael McLaughlin*

STIR-FRIED SCALLOP AND RED PEPPER SALAD

I can't tell you how much leftover Chinese food I have eaten in my life. But knowing that if Chinese food is rewarmed, the vegetables will become soggy and the meat overcooked, I always eat the remains at room temperature. One day I put some leftover scallops in ginger sauce on a bed of lettuce leaves and discovered that the cooled scallops made a great salad.

The following dish is traditionally served hot, but if you make it a few hours in advance and let it cool to room temperature, you'll enjoy an exciting main-course salad.

4 TO 6 SERVINGS
1 tablespoon water chestnut powder* or cornstarch
3 tablespoons medium-dry sherry

1 egg white
1 pound bay scallops or quartered sea
  scallops
1½ tablespoons dark soy sauce*
1 tablespoon chicken stock or water
1 tablespoon demiglace (optional)
1 teaspoon red wine vinegar
1 teaspoon sugar
½ to 1 teaspoon Szechuan chili paste
  with garlic*
1 cup peanut oil
2 tablespoons minced fresh ginger
2 scallions, sliced
1 garlic clove, minced
1 red bell pepper, cut into 1-inch
  squares or triangles
2 ounces snow peas, strings removed
  and cut in half crosswise on the
  diagonal (about ¾ cup)
¼ pound peeled water chestnuts,
  preferably fresh,* thinly sliced
  (about ¾ cup)
2 teaspoons Oriental sesame oil
*Available at Oriental markets

1. In a medium bowl, dissolve the water chestnut powder in 1 tablespoon of the sherry. Whisk in the egg white until blended. Add the scallops and toss to coat evenly. Cover and refrigerate for at least 1 hour, or up to 12 hours.

2. In a small bowl, mix the remaining 2 tablespoons sherry with the soy sauce, chicken stock, demiglace, vinegar, sugar and chili paste. Set the seasoning sauce aside.

3. Place a wok over high heat until it smokes; this will take about 2 minutes. Add the peanut oil and heat to 325°, or until shimmering.

4. Stir the scallops and marinade. Carefully add to the hot oil all at once, stirring with a pair of chopsticks in a circular motion for about 1 minute, or until the scallops turn white. Turn off the heat and drain the oil and scallops into a colander. Shake to remove as much oil as possible.

5. Return the wok to high heat. In the oil that sticks to the wok, stir-fry the ginger, scallions, garlic and red pepper for 1 minute. Return the scallops to the wok and add the snow peas and water chestnuts. Toss briefly over the heat to mix.

6. Add the seasoning sauce and stir-fry for 30 seconds. Turn off the heat. Add the sesame oil. Toss to mix. Transfer to a platter and let cool to room temperature. (**The salad can be made up to a day ahead and refrigerated, covered.** Let return to room temperature before serving.)
—*Karen Lee & Alaxandra Branyon*

MUSSEL AND RED BEAN SALAD

This salad makes a perfect light meal. All you need to add is a loaf of bread and a good bottle of wine.
▌F&W BEVERAGE SUGGESTION
  California Sauvignon Blanc, such
  as Cakebread Cellars

6 SERVINGS
3 pounds mussels, preferably
  cultivated, scrubbed and debearded
2 tablespoons unsalted butter
3 medium shallots, minced
½ cup dry white wine
2 cans (19 ounces each) red kidney
  beans (4 cups), rinsed and drained
¼ cup olive oil
2 tablespoons sherry wine vinegar
½ teaspoon Dijon-style mustard
¼ teaspoon freshly ground pepper

Salt
¼ cup chopped parsley

1. Soak the mussels in a bowl of cold salted water to remove any sand, about 10 minutes.

2. In a large heavy saucepan, melt the butter over moderate heat. Add the shallots and sauté until softened, 3 to 4 minutes. Add the wine, increase the heat to high and bring to a boil. Add the mussels, cover and cook, shaking the pan occasionally, until the mussels have opened, about 5 minutes.

3. Remove the mussels from the pan with a slotted spoon. Discard any that have not opened. Increase the heat to high and boil the cooking liquid until reduced by half, about 10 minutes.

4. Remove the mussels from their shells and place in a large bowl. Add the beans and toss.

5. In a small bowl, whisk together the oil, vinegar, mustard, pepper and ½ cup of the reduced mussel cooking liquid. Season with salt to taste. Pour the dressing over the beans and mussels, add the parsley and toss to combine. Serve at room temperature.
—*John Robert Massie*

Tricolor Salad (p. 134).

*Clockwise from upper right: Simple
Pepper Salad with Sesame Seeds (p. 136),
Yellow Pickled Salad (p. 134) and
Cabbage Salad with Shrimp (p. 138).*

SCALLOP AND SWEET PEPPER SALAD WITH AVOCADO

If you would like a little more color in your salad, use half yellow bell pepper and half red.

4 SERVINGS

1 pound bay scallops
Salt and freshly ground black pepper
1 red bell pepper, cut lengthwise into thin strips
½ small onion, thinly sliced
1 tomato—peeled, seeded and chopped
2 tablespoons sherry wine vinegar
⅓ cup plus 1 tablespoon olive oil
1 large garlic clove, crushed through a press
10 to 12 large fresh basil leaves, finely shredded
1 large avocado
2 tablespoons fresh lime juice
Fresh coriander or Italian flat-leaf parsley leaves, for garnish

1. Bring 1½ inches of water to a boil in a large saucepan. Carefully insert a steamer basket and add the scallops. Cover tightly and steam until the scallops just turn opaque but are still soft, 3 to 5 minutes; do not overcook. Transfer the scallops to a bowl, season with salt and black pepper and toss with the bell pepper strips and onion.

2. In a food processor, puree the tomato. Add the vinegar, ⅓ cup of the olive oil and the garlic and blend well. Season to taste with salt and pepper. Pour the dressing over the scallops, add the shredded basil and toss well. Chill the salad for at least 45 minutes.

3. To serve, peel the avocado and slice it lengthwise into 16 pieces. Arrange 4 slices decoratively on each

---

Top, Layered Salad with Spicy Peanut Dressing (p. 140). Bottom, Boston Baked Beans with Maple and Rosemary (p. 120) and Corn and Okra Fritters (p. 155).

plate. Sprinkle with the lime juice and the remaining 1 tablespoon olive oil. Season lightly with salt. Mound the scallop salad on the plate and garnish with fresh coriander or Italian parsley leaves. Serve with crusty French bread.

—*Perla Meyers*

TUSCAN-STYLE WHITE BEAN SALAD

While this dish can serve as accompaniment to almost any simple meat, I like to offer it as the centerpiece of a compose-your-own salad for a long, lazy summer lunch. I present the beans, surrounded by ripe red tomato wedges, with an assortment of tasty and colorful components for each guest to choose according to individual taste: Italian tuna packed in olive oil, good black olives, crisp greens, scallions, sliced cucumbers and the like. Set out a cruet of extra-virgin olive oil, lemon wedges and a pepper mill for seasoning. Serve with crusty loaves of Italian bread and a chilled, light-bodied wine.

6 TO 8 SERVINGS

2 cups dried cannellini (about 12 ounces), Great Northern white or cranberry beans (see Note)
1 small yellow onion
2 garlic cloves
4 sprigs of fresh sage or thyme or ¼ teaspoon dried thyme
4 fresh plum tomatoes
2½ teaspoons salt
1 teaspoon freshly ground pepper
1 small red onion, chopped
1 small celery rib with leaves, cut into ¼-inch dice
¼ cup thinly sliced scallion green
2 tablespoons shredded fresh basil
1 tablespoon chopped parsley
⅓ cup extra-virgin olive oil
3 tablespoons fresh lemon juice

1. Either soak the dried beans overnight in cold water to cover by 4 inches or place in a large saucepan with several inches of water to cover and bring to a boil. Boil, covered, for 2 minutes, then remove from the heat and let stand for 1 hour. Drain the beans.

2. Place in a large saucepan and cover with 4 inches of fresh cold water. Cover and bring to a boil over high heat. Tuck the yellow onion, garlic and 2 sprigs of the sage in with the beans. Simmer over low heat until the beans are tender but not mushy, about 1½ hours. Drain the beans; discard the onion, garlic and sage.

3. Core and seed one of the tomatoes and cut it into ½-inch dice. Cut the remaining 3 tomatoes lengthwise into 6 wedges each and set aside. Finely chop the remaining 2 sprigs of sage.

4. Place the beans in a large mixing bowl and season with the salt and pepper. Add the chopped tomato and sage, the red onion, celery, scallion greens, basil, parsley, olive oil and lemon juice. Toss gently with 2 rubber spatulas to combine the ingredients without crushing the beans. Cover and set aside for at least 1 hour at room temperature to blend the flavors. **(The recipe can be prepared a day in advance up to this point and refrigerated, covered.)**

5. Transfer to a serving bowl or platter and surround with the tomato wedges. Serve at room temperature.

NOTE: If *fresh* cranberry beans are available, use 3 pounds (weighed in the pod), shelled. Begin at Step 2, but cook the beans for only about 20 minutes, until tender. If you prefer to use canned beans, use 2 cans (19 ounces each) cannellini. Simply rinse and drain, then proceed to Step 3.

—*Richard Sax*

PASTA, RICE & BREADSTUFFS

PASTA, RICE & BREADSTUFFS

SPICY PASTA WITH ZUCCHINI, GOAT CHEESE AND OLIVES

The following concoction is colorful, zesty and entirely satisfying. Prepare the tomato sauce in advance if you want supper to be truly casual. It can be refrigerated for several days or frozen for weeks. The remaining steps proceed quickly, and the results—curly pasta coated with a spicy, chunky sauce, topped with browned slices of zucchini, with the soft surprise of melting goat cheese beneath the surface—is a marvel of flavors and textures. A green salad would go well here, as will a crusty Italian bread and a light red wine, such as Collavini Refosco.

6 TO 8 SERVINGS
¼ cup olive oil
1 large onion, chopped
1 to 1½ teaspoons crushed hot
   pepper, to taste
6 garlic cloves, minced
1½ teaspoons basil
1 teaspoon oregano
½ teaspoon thyme
1 bay leaf
1 can (35 ounces) Italian peeled
   tomatoes, with their juices
1½ teaspoons salt
5 small zucchini (about 1⅔ pounds),
   trimmed and sliced into ½-inch
   rounds
¼ teaspoon freshly ground black
   pepper
1 pound fusilli (corkscrew pasta)
24 Calamata olives
12 ounces fresh goat cheese—rindless,
   well chilled and cut into ½-inch
   chunks
¾ cup finely chopped parsley
1 cup freshly grated Parmesan cheese

1. In a large flameproof casserole, heat 2 tablespoons of the olive oil. Add the onion and hot pepper and cook, uncovered, over moderate heat, stirring occasionally, until tender and lightly browned, 10 to 15 minutes.

2. Add the garlic, basil, oregano, thyme and bay leaf and cook until the garlic is softened, about 3 minutes.

3. Stir in the tomatoes, crushing them with a wooden spoon, and their juices. Add the salt and bring to a boil. Reduce the heat, cover and simmer, stirring occasionally, until the sauce is thick and chunky, about 40 minutes. (**The sauce can be prepared several days in advance.** Let cool, then cover and refrigerate.)

4. In a large skillet, preferably nonstick, heat the remaining 2 tablespoons oil over moderate heat. Add the zucchini, season with additional salt and the black pepper, and cook, turning occasionally until well browned, 7 to 10 minutes. Drain on paper towels.

5. In a large pot of boiling salted water, cook the pasta until tender but still slightly firm to the bite, 8 to 10 minutes. Drain well.

6. Reheat the tomato sauce in the casserole over moderate heat. Add the pasta and cook, stirring, until the pasta absorbs most of the liquid, about 5 minutes. Stir in the olives and cook for 1 minute longer. Remove from the heat and stir in the goat cheese and parsley; cover and let stand for 1 minute. Serve topped with the browned zucchini. Pass the grated Parmesan on the side.

—Michael McLaughlin

BUTTERED SPAETZLE WITH SPINACH

8 SERVINGS
3¾ cups all-purpose flour
1¾ teaspoons salt
¼ teaspoon freshly ground pepper
¼ teaspoon freshly grated nutmeg
6 eggs
1 cup milk
1 cup heavy cream
2 tablespoons vegetable oil
6 tablespoons unsalted butter
½ pound spinach, stemmed and
   finely shredded

1. In a large bowl, combine the flour with ¾ teaspoon of the salt, the pepper and the nutmeg. Form a well in the flour and add the eggs and ½ cup of the milk. Beat the eggs with a fork to blend with the milk, then stir in the flour, pulling it into the center from the sides of the well. Whisk until smooth. Gradually whisk in the remaining ½ cup milk and the cream, ½ cup at a time. Cover and let stand at room temperature for 30 minutes.

2. Bring a large pot of salted water to a boil. Place a large bowl of cold water next to the boiling water. To cook the spaetzle, hold a colander over the boiling water and pour in about 1 cup of the batter. Use a rubber spatula to force the batter through the holes.

3. When the spaetzle float to the top of the water, scoop them out with a slotted spoon, or a skimmer or small strainer, and transfer to the cold water. Repeat with the remaining batter.

4. When all the spaetzle are cooked, drain well. Put in a large bowl; add the oil and toss well to coat. (**The recipe can be made to this point up to a day in advance.** Cover and refrigerate.)

5. To finish the spaetzle, divide the butter between 2 large skillets, preferably nonstick. Melt over high heat. When the butter separates, add the spaetzle and sauté over moderate heat, tossing frequently, until heated through and golden, about 10 minutes. Season with the remaining 1 teaspoon salt and additional pepper to taste. Add half the spinach to each skillet and toss with the spaetzle just until wilted, about 1 minute.

—*Anne Disrude*

AROMATIC RICE WITH COCONUT, DATES, FRESH CORIANDER AND LEMON

Use any of the long-grain aromatic white rice varieties to make this unusual dish (if the imported *basmati* is your choice, wash it first). This combination of flavors and textures works well as a side dish, to accompany a richly sauced curry or creamy stew. Its light, fluffy, rather dry texture provides a perfect foil for a spicy, soupy partner.

6 SERVINGS

1 coconut
1¾ cups long-grain aromatic rice
½ teaspoon salt
¾ cup thinly sliced pitted dates
1½ teaspoons freshly grated lemon zest
¼ teaspoon fennel seeds, crushed in a mortar
About 3 tablespoons fresh lemon juice
¾ cup chopped fresh coriander

1. Preheat the oven to 325°. Using a screwdriver and hammer or mallet, puncture two of the coconut "eyes." Strain and reserve the liquid. Set the coconut on a shelf in the oven and bake for 15 minutes. Crack the shell around the equator with a few hard taps of the hammer. Pry out the coconut meat from the shell in chunks.

2. Using the thinnest slicing blade of a food processor, make very thin slivers of coconut; stop when you have 1 cup. (Wrap and freeze the remaining coconut for another use.) Add enough water to the reserved coconut liquid to equal 2⅔ cups.

3. In a heavy 2-quart saucepan, combine the rice with the coconut liquid and bring to a full boil over high heat. Add the salt. Reduce the heat to very low, cover, and cook for 15 minutes. Remove from the heat and let stand, covered, for 10 minutes.

4. Fluff the rice into a hot serving dish. Toss with the dates, coconut, lemon zest, fennel seeds and lemon juice to taste. When well combined, add the coriander, toss lightly and serve.

—*Elizabeth Schneider*

RISOTTO WITH SPRING VEGETABLES

4 TO 6 SERVINGS

4 cups rich chicken stock or unsalted canned broth
½ cup fresh peas
½ cup sugar snap peas
8 medium asparagus spears, trimmed and cut diagonally into thin slices
3 baby carrots—peeled, trimmed and cut diagonally into ¼-inch slices
4 tablespoons unsalted butter
¼ cup minced onion
1 cup Arborio rice
Pinch of saffron threads
½ cup freshly grated Parmesan cheese
Salt and freshly ground white pepper
½ bunch of chives, trimmed

1. In a medium saucepan, bring the stock to a boil. Add the peas and cook until crisp-tender, about 3 minutes.

2. Remove the peas with a slotted spoon, rinse under cold water and drain well; set aside. Repeat this procedure with the snap peas, asparagus and carrots. Reserve the hot stock.

3. In a heavy medium saucepan, melt the butter over moderate heat. Add the minced onion and sauté until it is translucent but not browned, about 3 minutes.

4. Add the rice and stir until coated with butter. Cook, stirring constantly, for 2 minutes. Reduce the heat to moderately low. Add ½ cup of the hot stock and cook, stirring, until the liquid is absorbed, 3 to 4 minutes.

5. Continue to cook, stirring constantly and adding the stock, ½ cup at a time, until all the liquid is absorbed, 20 to 30 minutes. Fold in the saffron and the blanched vegetables. Turn off the heat and fold in ¼ cup of the Parmesan cheese. (The rice should be tender but still firm to the bite with a creamy sauce between the grains. Adjust the consistency, if necessary, by adding additional stock.)

6. Season with salt and white pepper to taste and garnish the top of each portion with the chives. Pass the remaining ¼ cup Parmesan cheese separately.

—*Christopher Idone*

SHORT-GRAIN BROWN RICE WITH SPICY LENTILS

For vegetable lovers, this simple Indian-style combination of spicy-creamy-tart lentils over chewy brown rice makes an easy everyday meal. It keeps well for several days and can also be made with medium-grain brown rice.

4 TO 6 SERVINGS

1 cup lentils (about 8 ounces)
1½ cups apple juice
2 tablespoons unsalted butter

PASTA, RICE & BREADSTUFFS

1½ teaspoons chopped garlic
1 teaspoon salt
2 teaspoons ground coriander
1½ teaspoons ground ginger
½ teaspoon turmeric
1 cup plain whole-milk yogurt
1 tablespoon cumin seeds
6 cups cooked short- or medium-grain
   brown rice, reheated if necessary
2 or 3 small apples—peeled, cored
   and diced
4 scallion greens, thinly sliced, for
   garnish

1. In a medium saucepan, combine the lentils, apple juice and 1½ cups of water. Bring to a simmer and cook, covered, until the lentils are tender, about 25 minutes (timing will vary).

2. In a small saucepan, melt the butter over moderately high heat. Add the garlic and sauté until lightly golden. Add the salt, coriander, ginger and turmeric and stir for 1 minute. Add 1 cup of the lentils and their liquid and stir to blend. Reduce the heat to very low, cover and cook for 10 minutes, stirring occasionally.

3. Pour the spiced lentils into a food processor or blender and puree until smooth. Season with salt to taste. Add the yogurt and blend. Combine this mixture with the cooked lentils. (This improves with reheating, so you can refrigerate when cooled, if you prefer.)

4. In a small ungreased skillet, heat the cumin seeds over moderately high heat, stirring constantly, until they smell toasty and just begin to smoke. Immediately transfer them to a spice mill and let cool. Then grind coarsely.

5. Spoon the hot rice into serving bowls and ladle the lentils over the rice. Top each portion with apples and scallions, then sprinkle generously with the toasted cumin.

—Elizabeth Schneider

SHRIMP PILAU

Rice-based pilaus are a staple of the southern Low Country, where they are spelled a dozen different ways (including purlow and perlew) but are pronounced per-low.

6 SERVINGS
½ pound sliced bacon, finely diced
1½ cups long-grain white rice
2 medium onions, finely chopped
2¼ cups chicken stock or canned
   broth
3 medium tomatoes—peeled, seeded
   and finely chopped
2 teaspoons fresh lemon juice
1½ teaspoons Worcestershire sauce
1 teaspoon salt
¾ teaspoon freshly grated nutmeg
¼ teaspoon freshly ground black
   pepper
¼ teaspoon cayenne pepper
2 pounds medium shrimp, shelled and
   deveined
¼ cup minced parsley

1. Preheat the oven to 350°. In a large heavy skillet, sauté the bacon over moderately high heat until crisp, about 5 minutes. Drain on paper towels and reserve 3 tablespoons of the melted fat.

2. In a fine sieve, rinse the rice well under cold running water; drain.

3. In a large heatproof casserole, heat the reserved bacon fat. Add the onions and sauté over moderate heat until softened, about 3 minutes. Add the rice and stir to coat with the fat. Add the chicken stock, tomatoes, lemon juice, Worcestershire sauce, salt, nutmeg, black pepper and cayenne. Bring to a boil. Cover and transfer the casserole to the oven.

4. Bake for 20 minutes. Remove the casserole from the oven and stir in the shrimp and bacon. Return to the oven and bake, uncovered, for 15 minutes. Let stand at room temperature for 10 minutes. Fluff up the pilau with a fork, adjust seasoning, if necessary, and sprinkle the parsley on top.

—James Villas

BAKED CHEESE GRITS

Serve as a breakfast dish or as an accompaniment to a baked ham dinner.

6 TO 8 SERVINGS
1 cup quick grits
2 teaspoons salt
2 cups milk
4 eggs
½ cup grated extra-sharp Cheddar
   cheese
1 teaspoon Worcestershire sauce
¼ teaspoon freshly ground pepper
1 stick (4 ounces) unsalted butter, cut
   into pieces.

1. Preheat the oven to 325°. In a large saucepan, bring 4 cups of water to a boil. Stir in the grits and salt. Return to a boil, reduce the heat to moderate and cook, stirring frequently, until thick, about 5 minutes.

2. Stir in the milk and return to a boil over high heat; reduce the heat to moderate and cook, stirring occasionally, until thick, about 5 minutes.

3. In a medium bowl, beat the eggs with the Cheddar cheese, Worcestershire sauce and pepper until blended. Add the butter. Pour this mixture into the grits. Turn off the heat and stir until the butter and cheese melt.

4. Pour into a buttered shallow 2-quart baking dish. Set in a larger roasting pan and pour in enough hot water to reach halfway up the baking dish. Bake for 35 to 40 minutes, until a knife inserted two-thirds of the way in from the rim of the dish comes out clean.

5. Remove from the oven and let rest in the water bath for 15 minutes before serving.

—James Villas

CORN AND OKRA FRITTERS

Frank McClelland serves these delicious corn and okra fritters with Boston baked beans.

4 TO 6 SERVINGS
Oil, for deep-frying
2 cups fresh corn kernels (from 3 ears)
  or 1 package (10 ounces) frozen
  kernels, thawed
2 eggs, separated
½ cup sifted cake flour
½ teaspoon salt
1½ teaspoons baking powder
1 teaspoon sugar
6 ounces fresh okra, cut into ¼-inch
  rounds (about 1 cup)
Warm maple syrup

1. In a large heavy saucepan, heat 3 inches of oil to 400°. In a food processor, puree 1½ cups of the corn kernels until smooth. Scrape the puree into a medium bowl and add the remaining ½ cup corn kernels. Blend in the egg yolks.

2. In a small bowl, combine the cake flour with the salt, baking powder and sugar. Sift the dry ingredients into the corn mixture and stir until blended.

3. Beat the egg whites until soft peaks form. Fold the beaten egg whites into the corn mixture. Stir in the okra.

4. Drop heaping tablespoons of the batter into the hot oil and fry, turning once, until well browned, 30 to 40 seconds. Drain on paper towels; serve hot, drizzled with warm maple syrup.

—Frank McClelland, Country Inn at Princeton, Princeton, Massachusetts

DOUBLE-FRIED HUSH PUPPIES

Dipping the hush puppies in egg white and cornmeal and frying for a second time produces a crisp crust so that they don't become limp as they sit and no longer have to be served "immediately."

MAKES ABOUT 4 DOZEN
1 cup cornmeal
¾ cup cake flour
2 teaspoons sugar
2 teaspoons baking powder
¾ teaspoon salt
1¼ cups cooked fresh or frozen corn
  kernels
½ cup milk
2 egg yolks, at room temperature
6 scallions, chopped
Oil, for deep-frying
5 egg whites
2 teaspoons ground cumin mixed with
  2 teaspoons salt (optional)

1. Into a medium bowl, sift together ¼ cup of the cornmeal, the cake flour, sugar, baking powder and salt.

2. In a food processor or blender, puree 1 cup of the corn with the milk. Mix in the egg yolks. Form a well in the dry ingredients, pour in the corn puree and stir to combine. Stir in the remaining ¼ cup corn kernels and the scallions.

3. In a deep-fat fryer or large heavy saucepan, heat 4 inches of oil to 385°. Beat 2 of the egg whites until soft peaks form and fold them into the batter.

4. Working in batches, drop the batter by teaspoons into the hot oil without crowding. Fry, turning occasionally, until well browned all over, about 5 minutes. Remove with a slotted spoon and drain on paper towels. Remove any bits of fried batter from the oil to keep it clean as you work.

5. Place the remaining ¾ cup cornmeal in a large paper bag. In a large bowl, beat the remaining 3 egg whites lightly with a fork until just frothy. Again working in batches, coat the drained fried hush puppies in the egg white. Then place in the paper bag, close and shake to coat with the cornmeal. Shake off any excess and return to the hot oil. Fry for about 3 minutes, turning, until when tapped with a spoon, they sound as if a hard shell has been formed. Drain the hush puppies on paper towels.

6. Sprinkle with a little salt or cumin-salt if desired. Serve hot, warm or at room temperature.

—Anne Disrude

CORN CAKES GRILLED WITH FONTINA AND BASIL

4 SERVINGS
½ cup yellow cornmeal
2 tablespoons all-purpose flour
½ teaspoon baking powder
½ teaspoon salt
½ cup plus 2 tablespoons milk
3 to 4 tablespoons vegetable oil
2 ounces Italian Fontina cheese,
  shredded
2 tablespoons minced fresh basil

1. In a bowl, combine the cornmeal, flour, baking powder and salt. Toss to mix well. Make a well in the center, add the milk and stir to blend.

2. In a large heavy skillet or on a griddle, heat 1½ tablespoons of the oil over moderately high heat until shimmering. Spoon tablespoons of the batter into the skillet to make 4 or 5 pancakes. Fry on the first side until brown around the edges, 4 to 5 min-

utes. Turn and fry until brown and crisp, about 4 minutes. Transfer to paper towels to drain and repeat with the remaining oil and batter.

3. Preheat the broiler. Place the corn cakes on a broiler pan. Top with the cheese. Broil about 6 inches from the heat until the cheese melts, about 2 minutes. Sprinkle with the basil.

—Anne Disrude

FRUITED COUSCOUS DRESSING

This innovative side dish—a light combination of quick-cooking couscous, prunes, lemon zest, pine nuts and apples—makes a great match for either sausage or lamb.

MAKES ABOUT 8 CUPS
2 cups chicken stock or 1 cup canned broth diluted with 1 cup water
1 cup chopped pitted prunes (8 ounces)
½ cup chopped parsley
1 teaspoon freshly grated lemon zest
½ teaspoon cinnamon
½ teaspoon ground cumin
½ teaspoon freshly ground pepper
1⅔ cups instant couscous
½ cup pine nuts (2½ ounces)
½ pound slab bacon, cut into ¼-inch dice
6 tablespoons unsalted butter
2 medium onions, chopped
2 medium tart green apples—peeled, cored and chopped (about 1½ cups)

1. In a medium saucepan, combine the stock, prunes, parsley and lemon zest. Slowly bring to a boil over low heat. Simmer, covered, for 5 minutes. Add the cinnamon, cumin and pepper and stir in the couscous. Remove from the heat and let stand, covered, until the couscous absorbs all the liquid, about 15 minutes.

2. Meanwhile, in a large heavy skil-

let, cook the pine nuts over moderate heat, tossing, until lightly toasted, about 3 minutes. Place the nuts in a large bowl.

3. Preheat the oven to 350°. Add the bacon to the skillet and sauté over moderately high heat, stirring, until golden brown, about 3 minutes. With a slotted spoon, add the bacon to the nuts; discard the fat in the pan.

4. Add the butter to the skillet and melt over high heat. Add the onions and apples and cook until softened but not browned, about 5 minutes. Scrape the mixture into the bowl.

5. Fluff up the couscous with a fork and add it to the bowl. Toss well to combine. Turn the mixture into a buttered large shallow baking dish. (**The recipe can be prepared to this point a day ahead.** Cover and refrigerate. Let the dressing return to room temperature before baking.)

6. Bake the dressing, covered, until heated through, about 20 minutes. Fluff with a fork before serving.

—Diana Sturgis

BRIOCHE AND OYSTER PUDDING

This side dish has a creamy, pudding-like consistency and a fabulous flavor. It also provides a delicious repast by itself, coupled with a steamed artichoke or a salad and perhaps a glass of chilled white wine.

8 SERVINGS
6 tablespoons unsalted butter, softened
1 medium leek (white and tender green), chopped
¼ cup chopped celery
4 ounces smoked ham, coarsely chopped

12 parsley stems
1 sprig of fresh thyme or ⅛ teaspoon dried
1½ cups milk
1 cup heavy cream
6 brioche rolls (about 10 ounces total), ends trimmed, sliced lengthwise ⅜ inch thick
2 whole eggs
3 egg yolks
2 tablespoons minced fresh chives
1½ tablespoons minced parsley
½ teaspoon salt
4 to 5 drops hot pepper sauce, to taste
1 dozen oysters, shucked and coarsely chopped, liquor reserved

1. In a large skillet, melt 1 tablespoon of the butter. Add the leek, celery, ham, parsley stems and thyme and cook over moderate heat until the leek softens, about 5 minutes. Add the milk and cream and cook at a bare simmer for 45 minutes.

2. Meanwhile, preheat the oven to 350°. Lightly butter both sides of the brioche slices using 4 tablespoons of the butter. Place on a cookie sheet and bake for about 15 minutes, turning once, until lightly browned. (Leave the oven on.)

3. Use the remaining 1 tablespoon butter to grease a 9-inch springform pan. Arrange the toasted brioche slices in the pan in 3 overlapping rows.

4. Strain the flavored milk and cream, pressing the solids to extract as much liquid as possible. (**The recipe can be prepared to this point a day ahead.** Cover and refrigerate. Reheat the milk before proceeding.)

5. In a medium bowl, beat together the whole eggs and egg yolks. Slowly whisk in 1 cup of the hot milk, then whisk in the remainder. Add the chives, parsley, salt, hot sauce and oysters with their liquor.

6. Wrap the outside of the springform pan in a double layer of aluminum foil. Pour the oyster mixture into the pan, distributing the oysters evenly if necessary. Place the springform in a roasting pan and set in the oven. Pour in enough hot water to reach one-third up the sides of the springform pan. Bake for 35 to 40 minutes, or until a knife inserted 3 inches from the center comes out clean.

7. Transfer to a rack and let rest for 10 minutes. Run a knife around the edge and remove the outer ring of the pan. Using a large spatula, carefully slide the pudding onto a large round platter. Serve the pudding warm or at room temperature.

—*Anne Disrude*

SPICY CORNBREAD AND PUMPKIN SEED STUFFING

Not all stuffings come baked in a bird. This hearty, wholesome casserole, full of rich tastes—chorizo, pumpkin seeds, coriander seeds—teams particularly well with roasted pork.

MAKES ABOUT 8 CUPS
1 pound Mexican-style soft-cured
  chorizo, casings removed
1 tablespoon whole coriander seeds
½ teaspoon ground coriander
¼ cup hulled, unsalted pumpkin seeds
  (pepitas)*
1 cup chicken stock or canned broth
2 eggs
Cornbread for Stuffing (recipe
  follows), cut into 1-inch cubes
  (about 8 cups)
Pumpkin Seed Puree (p. 17)
*Available at health food stores and
  Mexican markets

1. In a large skillet, fry the chorizo over moderately high heat, breaking up the meat with a spoon, until lightly browned, about 10 minutes. Stir in the whole and ground coriander seeds and set aside.

2. Preheat the oven to 375°. In a small dry skillet, toast the pumpkin seeds over moderately high heat, tossing frequently, until they begin to brown and pop, 2 to 3 minutes. Transfer to a small bowl.

3. In a large bowl, lightly whisk together the stock and eggs. Add the cornbread, chorizo and 1 cup of the pumpkin seed puree; toss well. Add the toasted pumpkin seeds and toss again. Scrape the stuffing into a large buttered baking dish. (**The recipe can be prepared to this point 1 day ahead.** Cover and refrigerate. Let return to room temperature before baking.)

4. Bake the stuffing for 40 minutes, or until the top is crisp. To serve, garnish the top of the stuffing with the remaining pumpkin seed puree.

—*John Robert Massie*

CORNBREAD FOR STUFFING

This recipe produces a rich but very dry cornbread, making it ideal as a poultry stuffing or as an ingredient in baked dishes, such as our Spicy Cornbread and Pumpkin Seed Stuffing (above).

MAKES ONE 13-BY-9-INCH SHEET
1½ cups yellow cornmeal
½ cup all-purpose flour
1 tablespoon baking powder
1 teaspoon salt
3 eggs
1¼ cups milk
1 tablespoon sugar
4 tablespoons unsalted butter, melted

1. Preheat the oven to 400°. Lightly grease a 13-by-9-inch baking dish.

2. In a large bowl, sift together the cornmeal, flour, baking powder and salt. In another bowl, beat the eggs with the milk and sugar. Add the egg mixture to the dry ingredients and mix thoroughly. Stir in the melted butter and pour the batter evenly into the prepared pan.

3. Bake the cornbread for 15 to 18 minutes, or until a toothpick inserted in the center comes out clean.

—*John Robert Massie*

DOUBLE RICE AND MUSHROOM DRESSING

This earthy tasting baked side dish requires turkey or chicken livers and is a natural with poultry. It can be prepared in advance and heated along with the main course.

MAKES ABOUT 8 CUPS
½ pound turkey and/or chicken livers,
  trimmed
½ cup milk
1 stick (4 ounces) unsalted butter
½ cup chopped pecans
¾ cup chopped cooked ham (about 4
  ounces)
1 pound mushrooms, chopped
8 large scallions, chopped (about 1½
  cups)
4 cups chicken stock or 2 cups canned
  broth diluted with 2 cups water
¾ cup brown rice
¾ cup wild rice, well rinsed
1½ teaspoons thyme
1 teaspoon salt
½ teaspon freshly ground pepper

1. Place the livers in a small bowl and cover with the milk. Refrigerate for 30 minutes, or overnight.

2. In a large heavy saucepan, melt 2 tablespoons of the butter over high heat. Add the pecans and sauté until fragrant, about 2 minutes. Using a slotted spoon, transfer the nuts to a bowl.

3. Add the ham to the saucepan and sauté until lightly browned, about 2 minutes. Transfer to the bowl with the sautéed pecans.

4. Drain the livers and pat dry. In the same pan, melt 2 tablespoons of the butter over high heat. Add the livers and sauté, tossing, until browned on the outside, about 2 minutes. Transfer to a plate.

5. Melt the remaining 4 tablespoons butter in the pan. Add the mushrooms and sauté over moderately high heat, stirring occasionally, until most of their juices have evaporated, about 15 minutes. Stir in the chopped scallions and cook until wilted, about 2 minutes.

6. Stir in the chicken stock and brown rice and bring to a boil. Reduce the heat to moderately low, cover and simmer for 20 minutes.

7. Stir in the wild rice, thyme, salt and pepper. Simmer, covered, until tender, 20 to 25 minutes.

8. Preheat the oven to 350°. Cut the livers into ½-inch pieces. Add to the hot rice. Stir in the ham and pecans and turn the mixture into a large well-buttered casserole. **(The recipe can be prepared to this point a day ahead.** Cover and refrigerate. Let return to room temperature before baking.)

9. Bake the dressing, covered, until heated through, about 30 minutes. Fluff up with a fork before serving and season with more salt if desired.

—Diana Sturgis

BREAD CRACKERS

For a different look, instead of putting the seeds *in* the dough, sprinkle them on the top before baking. Start by painting the dough with an egg glaze (1 egg yolk beaten with 1 tablespoon of water) and then sprinkle with the seeds—or coarse salt and cracked pepper, or all three.

MAKES 20 VERY LARGE CRACKERS
1 envelope (¼ ounce) active dry yeast
1 tablespoon sugar
1½ cups warm water (105° to 115°)
3 to 3½ cups all-purpose or whole wheat flour (or three parts all-purpose to one part rye, buckwheat, corn or oat flour)
2 teaspoons salt
¼ cup vegetable oil
1 tablespoons crushed caraway, fennel or cumin seeds

1. In a small bowl, dissolve the yeast and sugar in the water.

2. In a medium bowl, blend the flour and salt. Make a well in the center of the dry ingredients and add the vegetable oil and caraway seeds. Add the yeast mixture and stir the dry ingredients into the wet ingredients.

3. Remove the dough to a lightly floured board and knead a few times until smooth. Transfer to an oiled bowl, turn the dough to grease it; let rise until doubled in bulk, about 1 hour.

4. Preheat the oven to 350°. Punch the dough down and cut into 20 pieces. Roll each piece into a ball and press into a disk. Roll one disk of dough out as thin as possible, by hand or with a pasta machine (see Note), into a round or oblong.

5. Place 2 to 4 crackers (however many will fit) on a lightly oiled baking sheet and prick with a fork at 2-inch intervals. Bake until lightly browned around the edges, about 15 minutes. Remove to a rack and allow to cool and finish drying out. Store in an airtight tin. Repeat with the remaining balls of dough.

NOTE: To roll crackers out with a pasta machine, set the rollers at the widest setting and run a piece of dough through. Change to the next thinner setting and run the dough through again. Keep running the dough through at successively thinner settings until it is as thin as possible without falling apart.

—Anne Disrude

MUFFIN CRACKERS

This dough should be neither too wet nor too dry. If it seems to be crumbly or falls apart when rolled out, sprinkle some more milk over the dough and work it in with your fingers. If it's too wet, use extra flour when you roll it out. The dough can also be made in a food processor.

MAKES 16 LARGE CRACKERS
2¼ cups all-purpose or whole wheat flour (or half all-purpose and half rye or corn flour)
2 tablespoons sugar
2 teaspoons baking powder
1 teaspoon salt
¼ cup vegetable oil
¼ cup milk
1 egg, beaten
2 teaspoons crushed caraway, fennel or cumin seeds or cracked black pepper (optional)

1. Preheat the oven to 350°. In a medium bowl, blend the flour, sugar, baking powder and salt.

2. Make a well in the dry ingredients and add the vegetable oil, milk, egg and caraway seeds. Stir the dry ingredients into the wet ingredients.

3. Remove to a lightly floured board and knead a few times until smooth. Cut into 16 pieces. Roll each piece into a ball and press into a disk. Roll one disk of dough out as thin as possible, by hand or in a pasta machine (see Note) into a round or large oblong. Use extra flour to prevent sticking.

4. Place 2 to 4 crackers (however many will fit) on a lightly oiled cookie sheet and prick with a fork at 2-inch intervals. Bake until lightly browned around the edges, about 15 minutes. Remove to a rack and allow to cool and finish drying out. Store in an airtight tin. Repeat with the remaining dough.

NOTE: To roll crackers out with a pasta machine, set the rollers at the widest setting and run a piece of dough through. Change to the next thinner setting and run the dough through again. Keep running the dough through at successively thinner settings until it is as thin as possible without falling apart.

—Anne Disrude

QUICK MOROCCAN BREAD

This heavy-textured, fragrant bread from Morocco needs only one rising.

MAKES 2 ROUND LOAVES
1 envelope (¼ ounce) active dry yeast
¼ teaspoon sugar
¼ cup warm water (105° to 115°)
3½ cups bread flour

1 cup whole wheat flour, preferably coarse
1 tablespoon coarse (kosher) salt
1 tablespoon anise seeds
1 teaspoon vegetable oil
2 tablespoons cornmeal

1. In a small bowl, combine the yeast and sugar with the water. Let stand for 5 minutes, or until it foams.

2. In a large mixing bowl, combine the bread flour, whole wheat flour and salt. Add the yeast mixture and enough lukewarm water (about 1½ cups) to form a stiff dough. Turn the dough out onto a lightly floured work surface and knead for 15 minutes, or until smooth and elastic. (If using a mixer with a dough hook, knead for 8 minutes at a low speed.) Knead in the anise seeds.

3. Divide the dough in half, shape into 2 balls and let stand for 5 minutes. Lightly oil the surface of each ball of dough and flatten into a disk 1 inch thick and 5 to 6 inches in diameter. Cover with a dampened kitchen towel and let rise in a warm place for 2 hours, or until a hole poked in the dough with your finger remains deeply indented. Prick each loaf deeply 6 or 7 times with a fork to release the gas. Preheat the oven to 400°.

4. Place each loaf on a baking sheet sprinkled with cornmeal. Bake for 12 minutes. Reduce the oven temperature to 300° and bake for 40 minutes longer, or until the bottom of the bread sounds hollow when tapped. Let cool before slicing into wedges.

—Paula Wolfert

SWEDISH LIMPA BREAD

MAKES 2 LOAVES
5½ cups all-purpose flour
2 cups rye flour
2 envelopes (¼ ounce each) active dry yeast
2 teaspoons salt
2 teaspoons caraway seeds
1 tablespoon finely grated orange zest
2⅔ cups very warm water (115°)
2 tablespoons unsalted butter, softened

1. In a large mixing bowl, stir together 4½ cups of the all-purpose flour, the rye flour, yeast, salt, caraway seeds and orange zest.

2. Form a well in the dry ingredients. Pour in the water and butter and blend well. Add just enough of the reserved flour to make a soft dough.

3. Turn the dough out onto a lightly floured surface and knead for 8 to 10 minutes, until springy, smooth and satiny. Transfer to a well-greased bowl, turn to coat all surfaces and cover with plastic wrap. Let rise in a warm place until doubled in bulk, about 1 hour.

4. Punch down the dough, divide in half and shape into 2 balls. Transfer to a large greased cookie sheet. Cover with plastic wrap. Let rise until doubled in bulk, about 1 hour.

5. Preheat the oven to 400°. Make 2 slashes across the top of each loaf with a razor blade. Bake for 30 to 40 minutes, or until the loaves sound hollow when thumped on the bottom. Let cool on a rack before slicing.

—James Villas

PASTA, RICE & BREADSTUFFS

HERBED ITALIAN SKILLET BREAD

MAKES 2 ROUND FLAT LOAVES
1 tablespoon sugar
1½ cups warm water (105° to 115°)
1 envelope (¼ ounce) active dry yeast
3¼ to 3¾ cups bread flour
1 tablespoon coarse (kosher) salt
1 teaspoon coarsely cracked pepper
1 teaspoon finely chopped fresh or
  dried rosemary
½ cup olive oil, preferably extra-
  virgin
4 garlic cloves, thinly sliced
4 sprigs of rosemary, for garnish

1. In a medium bowl, dissolve the sugar in ½ cup of the water. Sprinkle the yeast on top. Set aside until foamy, about 5 minutes.

2. In a large bowl, combine 3¼ cups of the flour with 2 teaspoons of the salt, ½ teaspoon of the pepper and the chopped rosemary.

3. Stir ¼ cup of the olive oil and the remaining 1 cup water into the yeast mixture. Make a well in the flour and add the liquid ingredients. Stir until well mixed.

4. Turn the dough out onto a floured surface and knead until smooth and elastic, about 15 minutes. Use as much additional flour as necessary to prevent sticking and to form a slightly soft dough.

5. Form the dough into a ball and place in a large oiled bowl. Turn to coat with oil. Cover the bowl with plastic wrap and a towel. Place in a warm spot and let the dough rise until doubled in bulk, about 1 hour. Punch the dough down and let rise until doubled in bulk again, about 1 hour.

6. Preheat the oven to 400°. Place a 12- to 14-inch cast-iron skillet in the oven to heat.

7. Divide the dough in half. Return half the dough to the bowl, cover and refrigerate while you make the first loaf. (If you'd prefer to make only one loaf, the other half of the dough can be frozen and baked at a later time.) Roll the dough out to a ½-inch-thick round. With a sharp knife, score lightly in a crisscross pattern.

8. Remove the skillet from the oven and coat the bottom and sides with 1 tablespoon of the oil. Place the dough in the skillet. Press down around the edges to even the thickness. Distribute 2 of the sliced garlic cloves over the bread and top with 2 broken sprigs of rosemary if desired. Drizzle the bread with 1 tablespoon of the oil. Sprinkle with ½ teaspoon of the salt and ¼ teaspoon of the pepper.

9. Bake for 25 to 30 minutes, until browned. Repeat with the remaining dough and ingredients for the second loaf. Serve the bread warm or at room temperature.

—*Anne Disrude*

CALZONE MARGHERITA

Use only red, ripe and meaty tomatoes for this filling. In winter, plum tomatoes are especially good. For a truly authentic Italian taste, look for freshly made mozzarella or imported water buffalo mozzarella.

F&W BEVERAGE SUGGESTION
1982 Chianti Classico, such as Ruffino

MAKES 4
Calzone Dough (p. 161)
1 pound ripe tomatoes—peeled,
  seeded and finely diced
½ teaspoon salt
8 ounces mozzarella cheese, finely
  diced
¼ cup freshly grated Parmesan cheese
2 tablespoons olive oil, preferably
  extra-virgin
2 medium garlic cloves, finely
  chopped
8 fresh basil leaves, minced, or
  ½ teaspoon dried basil
½ teaspoon oregano
⅛ teaspoon freshly ground pepper

1. While the calzone dough is rising, make the filling: Place the tomatoes in a colander, sprinkle with the salt and let drain for 30 minutes.

2. In a medium bowl, combine the mozzarella and Parmesan cheeses, the oil, garlic, basil, oregano and pepper. Add the tomatoes to the cheese mixture and toss to mix.

3. Punch the dough down and turn out onto a lightly floured surface. Divide into 4 equal pieces. One at a time, roll out into four 10-inch circles. If you have time, wrap the dough in kitchen towels and plastic wrap and let it rest for 30 minutes; it will yield a more tender dough. If time is of the essence, proceed to Step 4.

4. Preheat the oven to 450°. Arrange the dough circles on a large greased baking sheet with half of each circle off the edge of the sheet. Place about ½ cup filling on the half of each circle that is on the sheet, leaving a 1-inch border around the rim. Fold the dough over to cover the filling and form a semicircle. Press the edges together to seal. Crimp decoratively by folding the lower edge up and over the top edge at ¾-inch intervals.

5. Bake on the lowest rack of the oven for 20 to 25 minutes, or until brown and puffed. Transfer the calzone to a rack and let rest for 10 minutes before serving.

—*Michele Scicolone*

CALZONE SICILIANO

Oregano, anchovies and olives with onion are a favorite flavor combination in Palermo, Sicily.

F&W BEVERAGE SUGGESTION
Sicilian white wine, such as Baronessa Anca Donnafugata

MAKES 4

Calzone Dough (recipe follows)
3 tablespoons olive oil, preferably extra-virgin
2 medium onions, thinly sliced
1 can (35 ounces) Italian peeled tomatoes, drained and chopped
1½ teaspoons oregano
Pinch of salt
⅛ teaspoon freshly ground pepper
1 can (2 ounces) flat anchovy fillets, drained
⅓ cup Calamata or oil-cured black olives, pitted and chopped

1. While the calzone dough is rising, make the filling: In a large skillet, heat the oil. Add the onions and sauté over moderate heat until tender and golden, 10 to 15 minutes. Add the tomatoes, oregano, salt and pepper. Simmer, stirring occasionally, until the tomato juices have evaporated and the sauce is thickened, about 20 minutes. Let the filling cool to room temperature.

2. Roll out, fill and bake as in Steps 3 through 5 of Calzone Margherita. To fill the calzone, spread the cooled onion-tomato mixture over half of each circle of dough. Arrange the anchovies on top and dot with the olives.

—Michele Scicolone

CALZONE CON SALSICCIA

Better than a sausage and pepper hero! These savory calzone, individually wrapped, make great picnic fare.

F&W BEVERAGE SUGGESTION
Montepulciano d'Abruzzo such as Casal Thaulero

MAKES 4

Calzone Dough (recipe follows)
4 links (about ¾ pound) Italian sweet or hot sausage
3 tablespoons olive oil, preferably extra-virgin
4 medium green bell peppers (about 1 pound), thinly sliced
3 medium onions, thinly sliced
½ to 1 teaspoon salt, depending on the saltiness of the sausage
⅛ teaspoon freshly ground black pepper

1. While the calzone dough is rising, make the filling: Prick the sausages all over with a fork. Place in a medium skillet with ½ inch of water. Cover and simmer over moderate heat until the water evaporates, about 20 minutes. Uncover and cook, turning occasionally, until the sausages are browned. Let cool; then cut into ¼-inch slices.

2. In a large skillet, heat the olive oil. Add the bell peppers and cook over moderate heat for 5 minutes. Add the onions, salt and black pepper. Cook until the peppers are soft and the onions are lightly browned, 15 to 20 minutes. Remove from the heat and let cool before assembling the calzone.

3. Roll out, fill and bake as in Steps 3 through 5 of Calzone Margherita. To fill the calzone, arrange the sausage slices over half of each circle of the dough. Top with the green peppers and onions.

—Michele Scicolone

CALZONE DOUGH

MAKES ENOUGH FOR 4

1 envelope (¼ ounce) active dry yeast
1 cup warm water (105° to 115°)
¼ cup olive oil, preferably extra-virgin
2½ to 3 cups all-purpose flour
1½ teaspoons salt

1. In a small bowl, sprinkle the yeast over the warm water; let stand for 5 minutes, or until the yeast is completely dissolved. Stir in the olive oil.

2. Hand method: In a large bowl, combine 2½ cups flour and the salt. Add the yeast mixture and stir until well blended. Turn out onto a lightly floured surface. Knead until smooth and elastic, 8 to 10 minutes, adding more flour if needed; the dough should remain slightly soft.

Food processor method: Combine the flour and salt in a food processor fitted with the metal blade. With the machine on, add the yeast mixture through the feed tube and process until the dough is smooth and cleans the sides of the bowl. Turn the dough out onto a lightly floured surface and knead briefly, adding more flour if needed.

Heavy-duty mixer method: In the large bowl of an electric mixer fitted with a dough hook, combine the flour and salt. With the mixer on low speed, gradually add the yeast mixture. Knead until the dough masses on the hook and becomes smooth and elastic, adding more flour as needed.

PASTA, RICE & BREADSTUFFS

3. Place in a lightly oiled bowl; turn to coat. Cover with plastic wrap and let rise in a warm place until doubled in volume, about 1 hour.

4. Roll out and fill the dough as directed in Steps 3 and 4 of Calzone Margherita. (If making the dough ahead of time, punch down, divide into 4 equal pieces, wrap tightly and store in the freezer for up to 1 month. Let the dough return to room temperature before proceeding.)

—*Michele Scicolone*

TOASTED LOBSTER SANDWICH

This elegant sandwich can be varied by adding hot bacon or caviar.

BEVERAGE SUGGESTION
Champagne or a full-bodied Chardonnay, such as Phelps

4 SERVINGS
1 tablespoon olive oil
1½ teaspoons fresh lemon juice
¾ pound cooked lobster meat (from two 1¾-pound lobsters), cut into 1- to 1½-inch pieces
½ cup mayonnaise, preferably homemade
1 tablespoon minced fresh chervil or flat Italian parsley mixed with ½ teaspoon dried tarragon
Salt and freshly ground pepper
8 slices of brioche or egg bread
2 tablespoons unsalted butter, melted
1 medium tomato—peeled, seeded and minced
12 sprigs of chervil or parsley, for garnish

1. Preheat the broiler. In a medium bowl, combine the olive oil and lemon juice. Add the lobster and toss well.

2. In a small bowl, combine the mayonnaise and chervil. Add to the lobster mixture and toss to coat. Season with salt and pepper to taste.

3. Brush the bread with the melted butter and place on a baking sheet. Broil 5 to 6 inches from the heat, turning once, for about 1½ minutes per side, until lightly toasted.

4. Mound ½ cup of the lobster mixture on half the bread slices. Garnish each sandwich with 1 tablespoon of the minced tomato, 3 sprigs of chervil and a grinding of pepper. Top with the remaining bread and serve.

—*Jeremiah Tower*

HERBED GOAT CHEESE AND ROASTED PEPPER SANDWICH WITH OLIVES AND WATERCRESS

For this colorful sandwich, the goat cheese is marinated overnight in olive oil and fresh herbs.

F&W BEVERAGE SUGGESTION
California Zinfandel, or California Sauvignon Blanc, such as Robert Pepi

4 SERVINGS
½ cup extra-virgin olive oil
½ cup sliced black olives, preferably oil cured
1 tablespoon fresh rosemary or 1 teaspoon dried
1 tablespoon fresh thyme or 1 teaspoon dried
1 log (11 ounces) of goat cheese, such as Montrachet, cut into ½-inch slices
½ teaspoon freshly ground pepper, or to taste
1 loaf of crusty French or Italian bread
2 medium red bell peppers—roasted, peeled, seeded and cut into thin strips
½ bunch of watercress, tough stems removed

1. In a shallow noncorrodible dish, combine the oil, olives, rosemary and thyme. Add the cheese in a single layer and spoon the herbed oil over each slice. Sprinkle with the pepper, cover and refrigerate overnight.

2. To assemble the sandwich, return the cheese to room temperature. Slice the bread in half lengthwise, brush the cut sides evenly with the herbed oil, and sprinkle with the sliced olives. Layer the bottom half of the loaf with the roasted peppers, goat cheese and watercress. Cover with the top of the loaf and slice crosswise into 4 sections.

—*Molly O'Neill*

LAMB AND ROASTED EGGPLANT SANDWICHES WITH GARLIC AND ONION JAM

Cold roast beef can be substituted for the lamb in these sandwiches.

4 SERVINGS
1 medium eggplant, sliced crosswise into ¼-inch rounds
2 tablespoons olive oil, preferably extra-virgin
8 slices of firm-textured white bread, lightly toasted
½ cup Garlic and Onion Jam (p. 239)
¾ pound thinly sliced cold, roasted lamb
1 cup shredded bitter greens, such as arugula, radicchio or watercress

1. Preheat the oven to 400°. Arrange the eggplant slices on a baking sheet in a single layer. Brush the slices with the olive oil and bake on the upper shelf of the oven for about 20 minutes, or until soft and golden brown.

2. To assemble the sandwiches, spread each slice of toast with 1 tablespoon of the garlic and onion jam. Layer 4 of the toast slices with equal amounts of eggplant, lamb and shredded greens. Top with the remaining toast and cut the sandwiches in half on the diagonal.

—Molly O'Neill

MINTED CHICKEN AND RAW ARTICHOKE PITAS

The unusual addition of raw artichoke gives these sandwiches a special flavor and texture. If you like, warm the pita in a low oven before stuffing.

4 SERVINGS
¼ *cup fresh lemon juice*
⅓ *cup minced fresh mint leaves*
½ *teaspoon salt*
½ *teaspoon freshly ground pepper*
¼ *cup extra-virgin olive oil*
1 large artichoke
¾ *pound cooked chicken, cut into*
    1-inch pieces (about 3 cups)
⅓ *cup finely chopped or coarsely*
    grated Parmesan cheese (about
    1½ ounces)
½ *cup mayonnaise, preferably*
    homemade
4 loaves of pita bread, 6 inches
    in diameter

1. In a large mixing bowl, combine the lemon juice, mint, salt and pepper. Gradually whisk in the oil.

2. Using a sharp knife, remove the tough outer leaves from the artichoke. Peel the stem. Cut the artichoke into quarters and, using a teaspoon, remove the hairy choke and the purple inner leaves. Using a very sharp stainless steel knife, thinly slice the artichoke quarters crosswise. Alternatively, slice the artichoke quarters, stem-end down, in a food processor fitted with a slicing disk. (You should have about 1½ cups.)

3. Immediately toss the artichoke with the lemon mixture. Add the chicken and Parmesan and mix well. Stir in the mayonnaise and blend the ingredients thoroughly. Cut a 1-inch slice from the top of each pita and stuff the pockets with the salad.

—Molly O'Neill

GRILLED SMOKED TURKEY AND CHEDDAR SANDWICH WITH HOT PEPPER JELLY

This grilled combination is one I particularly like. A colorfully crunchy coleslaw seems the perfect mate, along with a glass of good beer or a light white wine, such as Chenin Blanc.

MAKES 1 LARGE SANDWICH
4 tablespoons unsalted butter
2 thick slices of sourdough or
    country-style white bread, sliced ½
    inch thick, from an oval loaf about
    7 inches across
4 tablespoons hot pepper jelly
4 ounces sharp white Cheddar cheese,
    thinly sliced
½ *pound sliced smoked turkey, skin*
    and fat removed

1. In a small saucepan, melt the butter over low heat. Set aside.

2. Spread 1 side of each of the bread slices with 2 tablespoons of the pepper jelly. Lay the sliced cheese over the jelly, dividing evenly between the two slices of bread. Fold each slice of turkey in half and arrange the slices, overlapping slightly, over the cheese on one slice of bread. Invert the remaining cheese-covered bread slice on top of the turkey.

3. Heat a medium griddle or cast-iron skillet over moderate heat until just warm. Generously brush half the melted butter over the top surface of the sandwich. Invert the sandwich butter-side down onto the heated griddle. Brush the remaining butter over the top of the sandwich.

4. Cook, covered, until the bread is crisp and golden brown on the bottom and the cheese is beginning to melt, about 5 minutes. With a wide spatula, turn and brown the other side.

5. Transfer the sandwich to a cutting board and with a serrated knife, cut in half. Serve at once.

—Michael McLaughlin

BREAD BASKET WITH ASSORTED TEA SANDWICHES

This festive bread basket, filled to the brim with a variety of two-bite sandwiches, will be a decorative centerpiece for your tea table. The sandwiches are simple to assemble and can be prepared in advance. Creamy fillings—such as the Roquefort, Walnut and Cognac or Smoked Salmon and Dill or Goat Cheese and Fresh Herb (recipes follow)—should be softened before spreading so they won't tear the bread.

MAKES ABOUT 30 SANDWICHES
1 round, rectangular or oval loaf of
    bread, 2½ to 3 pounds

163

PASTA, RICE & BREADSTUFFS

1½ cups assorted sandwich spreads (recipes follow), at room temperature
Minced parsley and/or sweet paprika (optional)
Curly lettuce leaves, to line basket
Sliced or carved vegetables and/or sprigs of fresh herbs, for garnish

1. Using a long, sharp serrated knife, cut off the top inch from the loaf of bread; set the top aside.

2. Holding the knife vertically, cut completely around the inside of the loaf, leaving a ¼- to ⅜-inch-thick wall of crust; be careful not to slice through the bottom crust.

3. Using a small sharp knife, make 4 incisions at even intervals, parallel to and about ¼ inch above the bottom crust. Insert the large knife into one of the incisions and, keeping the blade parallel to the bottom crust, swivel the knife side to side to detach the center of the bread; try not to enlarge the cuts. Repeat with the other incisions to completely detach the inside of the bread from the bottom crust.

4. Carefully lift out the center of the bread in one piece. Wrap well in plastic and freeze until partially frozen but not hard, about 1 hour. Meanwhile, prepare the sandwich spreads.

5. Unwrap the partially frozen bread and, using a sharp knife, trim to an even shape. Cut the bread into slices that are about ⅛ inch thick.

6. Spread a layer of filling over half the bread slices; top with the remaining bread. Cover the sandwiches with a damp towel and plastic wrap and chill for at least 30 minutes.

7. Unwrap the sandwiches and arrange on a work surface in a single layer. With a very sharp knife, cut the sandwiches into small squares, rectangles, triangles or diamonds. Cut straight down with the knife to keep the edges of the sandwiches smooth and clean. Assemble the basket as described in Step 8, or cover the sandwiches with a damp towel and plastic wrap and refrigerate until 20 minutes before serving.

8. To assemble the bread basket, place the reserved bread top inside the basket, cut-side down; this will make a raised shelf to prop up the sandwiches. Dip the edges of the sandwiches in parsley or paprika if desired. Line the inside of the basket with curly lettuce leaves. Fill the basket with the sandwiches and garnish with fresh vegetables. Serve immediately or cover with a damp towel and plastic wrap and refrigerate until 20 minutes before serving.

—Diana Sturgis

SMOKED SALMON AND DILL SANDWICH SPREAD

Though this spread makes an excellent sandwich, it can also be piped into cucumber cups, cherry tomatoes, hardcooked egg halves or small pastry puffs.

MAKES ABOUT 1½ CUPS
1 stick (4 ounces) unsalted butter, softened
3 ounces cream cheese, softened
¼ cup sour cream
5 ounces smoked salmon, chopped
3 tablespoons minced fresh dill
2 teaspoons fresh lemon juice
⅛ teaspoon freshly ground white pepper

In a medium bowl, combine the butter, cream cheese and sour cream; blend thoroughly. Stir in the smoked salmon, dill, lemon juice and white pepper. Use immediately or cover and refrigerate. Let the spread soften for about 30 minutes before using.

—Diana Sturgis

GOAT CHEESE AND FRESH HERB SANDWICH SPREAD

While this filling is tempting on its own, it's fabulous with a slice of ham. For 30 tea sandwiches, you'll need about ¼ pound of ham, thinly sliced; lightly spread the top slice of bread with softened butter so that the ham will adhere.

MAKES ABOUT 1½ CUPS
1 stick (4 ounces) unsalted butter, softened
5 ounces mild, soft goat cheese, such as Bucheron, softened
¼ cup minced parsley
1 tablespoon minced fresh tarragon or 1 teaspoon dried

In a medium bowl, combine the butter and goat cheese; blend thoroughly. Stir in the parsley and tarragon. Use immediately or cover and refrigerate. Let the spread soften for about 30 minutes before using.

—Diana Sturgis

ROQUEFORT, WALNUT AND COGNAC SANDWICH SPREAD

MAKES ABOUT 1½ CUPS
1 stick (4 ounces) unsalted butter, softened
4 ounces Roquefort cheese, softened
3 ounces cream cheese, softened
⅓ cup finely chopped walnuts
2 tablespoons Cognac or brandy

In a medium bowl, combine the butter, Roquefort and cream cheese; blend thoroughly. Stir in the walnuts and Cognac. Use immediately or cover and refrigerate. Let the spread soften for about 30 minutes before using.

—Diana Sturgis

PIES, CAKES & COOKIES

PIES, CAKES & COOKIES

PECAN CREAM PIE

8 SERVINGS

PASTRY:
1 cup all-purpose flour
1½ tablespoons sugar
¼ teaspoon salt
5 tablespoons unsalted butter
½ egg, lightly beaten (see Note)

FILLING:
1¼ cups heavy cream
1½ teaspoons unflavored gelatin
2 tablespoons unsalted butter
½ cup (packed) dark brown sugar
⅔ cup sour cream
3 eggs, at room temperature,
    separated
1 teaspoon vanilla extract
1 cup pecans, toasted and chopped
1 tablespoon granulated sugar
1 tablespoon bourbon

1. *Make the pastry:* In a medium bowl, combine the flour, sugar and salt. Cut in the butter until the mixture resembles coarse meal. Gradually add the egg, stirring with a fork until the dough begins to mass together. Add a few drops of cold water if necessary. Gently pat into a ball and flatten into a 6-inch disk. Wrap in waxed paper and chill for at least 1 hour. **(Tightly wrapped, the pastry will keep for up to 3 days in the refrigerator and for up to 3 months in the freezer.)**

2. Preheat the oven to 400°. Grease a 9-inch pie pan. Roll out the pastry between two sheets of generously floured waxed paper to form an 11- to 12-inch round. Without stretching the pastry, gently fit it into the pan. Trim the overhang to ½ inch. Fold the edges under and crimp decoratively. With a fork, lightly prick the dough all over. Refrigerate for 15 minutes.

3. Line the pastry shell with aluminum foil and fill with dried beans, rice or pie weights. Bake for 12 minutes. Remove the foil and weights, reduce the heat to 350° and bake for 8 minutes longer. Let the pastry shell cool completely.

4. *Make the filling:* Pour ¼ cup of the heavy cream into a small bowl, sprinkle on the gelatin and set aside to soften for 5 minutes.

5. In a small saucepan, melt the butter over moderate heat. Add the brown sugar and stir until completely dissolved. Add the gelatin mixture and stir to combine. Blend in the sour cream and egg yolks. Cook, stirring constantly, until the mixture thickens, 2 to 3 minutes. (Do not let it boil.)

6. Pour the mixture into a medium bowl and stir in the vanilla. Refrigerate, stirring frequently and scraping the sides of the bowl with a rubber spatula, until chilled and thickened but not set, 20 to 30 minutes. Stir in two-thirds of the pecans.

7. Beat the egg whites until stiff peaks form. Stir one-fourth of the whites into the gelatin mixture to lighten it, then fold in the remaining whites. Spoon the mixture into the cooled pie shell and refrigerate until set, about 45 minutes.

8. Whip the remaining 1 cup heavy cream until thick. Add the granulated sugar and bourbon and beat until stiff peaks form. Spread the cream over the chilled pie and refrigerate for 30 minutes longer. Sprinkle the remaining pecans on top before serving.

NOTE: For ½ egg, lightly beat 1 egg and measure out 1½ tablespoons.

—*Elizabeth Terry, Elizabeth on 37th,
Savannah, Georgia*

PUMPKIN CHEESECAKE PIE IN A GINGERSNAP CRUST

12 SERVINGS

½ cup pecans
2 tablespoons granulated sugar
1 cup gingersnap crumbs (from about
    20 cookies)
5 tablespoons unsalted butter, melted
1 pound cream cheese, at room
    temperature
⅔ cup (packed) brown sugar
½ cup sour cream, at room
    temperature
1 cup canned solid-pack pumpkin
3 eggs, at room temperature
1 teaspoon cinnamon
Pinch of ground cloves
Pinch of ground ginger
Pecan halves, for garnish

1. Preheat the oven to 325°. Place the ½ cup pecans and the granulated sugar in a food processor and process until finely chopped, about 20 seconds. Pour into a large bowl, add the gingersnap crumbs and mix. Pour in the butter and stir well to combine. Turn the mixture into a 10-inch pie dish and press evenly against the bottom and sides of the dish to form a crust. Bake for 10 minutes. Set aside to cool. (Leave the oven on.)

2. In a large bowl, beat the cream cheese and brown sugar until soft and well blended. Stir in the sour cream and pumpkin. Gradually beat in the eggs, 1 at a time, and the cinnamon, cloves and ginger.

3. Place the pie dish on a baking sheet and pour in the filling. Bake in the middle of the oven for 45 minutes, or until the filling is set. Let cool on a rack. Arrange the pecan halves around the edge of the pie. (**The pie can be made a day ahead if desired.** Refrigerate, covered.)

—*Diana Sturgis*

166

OLD-FASHIONED PUMPKIN PIE

Molasses is the secret ingredient that helps flavor this traditional pumpkin pie. Light textured when freshly made, the pie will be denser, with a deeper flavor, if it is refrigerated overnight.

8 TO 10 SERVINGS

PIE CRUST:
1 cup plus 2 tablespoons all-purpose flour
¼ teaspoon baking powder
¼ teaspoon salt
6 tablespoons unsalted butter, chilled and cut into pieces
1 tablespoon sugar
1 egg yolk
1 tablespoon ice water

FILLING:
1⅓ cups canned solid-pack pumpkin
3 whole eggs
1 cup sour cream
½ cup heavy cream
½ cup light unsulphured molasses, such as Grandma's by Mott's
1 teaspoon ground ginger
1 teaspoon allspice
1 teaspoon cinnamon

ACCOMPANIMENT:
½ cup heavy cream, chilled
2 teaspoons sugar
1 egg white
Cinnamon

1. Make the crust: In a large bowl, mix together the flour, baking powder and salt. Cut in the butter until the mixture resembles coarse meal. Mix in the sugar. Add the egg yolk and ice water and stir to form a dough. Pat the dough into a 6-inch disk; wrap and refrigerate until chilled, about 20 minutes.

2. On a lightly floured sheet of waxed paper, roll out the dough into an 11-inch circle. Invert the pastry into a buttered 9-inch metal pie pan and peel off the paper. Fit the pastry evenly in the pan, trim away any excess and decoratively crimp the edge. Refrigerate the pie shell while you make the filling. **(The crust can be made a day ahead.)**

3. Make the filling: Preheat the oven to 400°. In a large bowl, lightly beat the pumpkin, eggs, sour cream, heavy cream, molasses, ginger, allspice and cinnamon to blend well.

4. Place the pie pan on a baking sheet and pour the filling into the prepared pie shell. Bake in the middle of the oven for 20 minutes. Reduce the oven temperature to 325° and continue to bake for 25 to 30 minutes, until the pie is set but slightly wobbly in the center. Let cool on a rack. Serve at room temperature or chilled.

5. As accompaniment: In a large bowl, beat the heavy cream with 1 teaspoon of the sugar until stiff. In another bowl, beat the egg white until soft peaks form. Whisk in the remaining 1 teaspoon sugar and beat until stiff peaks form. Fold the beaten egg white into the whipped cream. **(The cream can be prepared and refrigerated 2 hours before serving.)** Serve a bowlful of the cream dusted lightly with cinnamon on the side.

—Diana Sturgis

GLAZED GUAVA TARTS

These tarts must bake for only about 5 minutes, as the guava should be tender but not soft.

MAKES 4 INDIVIDUAL TARTS
Rich Pastry Dough (recipe follows)
3 to 4 guavas, peeled and cut crosswise into 1/16-inch-thick rounds (you should have 48 rounds)
2 teaspoons sugar
2 tablespoons guava jelly

1. Preheat the oven to 400°. Line a cookie sheet with aluminum foil.

2. On a lightly floured surface, roll out the pastry dough to 1/16 inch thick. Using a 4-inch round cutter or a sharp paring knife, cut out 4 circles of dough.

3. Transfer the dough circles to the cookie sheet and score the edges decoratively if desired. Refrigerate the dough for 10 minutes.

4. Bake the pastry circles for 12 minutes, or until lightly browned around the edges.

5. Arrange 12 rounds of guava in a circular pattern on each dough circle (the smaller rounds can be placed in the center). Sprinkle ½ teaspoon of sugar over the top of each tart.

6. Place the tarts on the top rack of the oven and bake for 5 minutes, or until the pastry is crisp and the guava is tender but not soft. Transfer the tarts to a rack to cool.

7. In a small saucepan, melt the guava jelly over moderately low heat. Brush the jelly evenly over the top of each tart to glaze.

—Marcia Kiesel

RICH PASTRY DOUGH

1 cup all-purpose flour
1 tablespoon sugar
¼ teaspoon salt
5 tablespoons unsalted butter, cut into tablespoons
1 egg yolk
2 tablespoons ice water

1. In a food processor, combine the flour, sugar, salt and butter. Turn the machine on and off until the mixture resembles coarse meal. Add the egg yolk and ice water and process just until the dough begins to form a ball.

2. Turn the dough out onto a work surface and gather it into a ball. Flatten the dough into a disk and wrap in plastic. Refrigerate for at least 30 minutes before rolling out.

—Marcia Kiesel

MINIATURE BERRY AND CHERRY TARTLETS

These tiny, not-too-sweet tartlets should be served after dinner with coffee. For this recipe you will need 2-inch tartlet molds.

MAKES ABOUT 16 SMALL TARTLETS

1 cup all-purpose flour
1 tablespoon sugar
Pinch of salt
6 tablespoons cold unsalted butter, cut into pieces
2 tablespoons ice water
1 pint berries (strawberries, raspberries, blueberries, fraises des bois or cherries)
¼ cup apricot jam

1. In a medium bowl, mix together the flour, sugar and salt. Cut in the butter until the mixture resembles coarse meal.

2. Add the ice water while tossing with a fork and mix until the dough pulls away from the sides of the bowl.

3. Form the dough into a ball, flatten to a 6-inch disk, cover with plastic wrap and refrigerate for at least 20 minutes.

4. On a lightly floured surface, roll out the dough ⅛ inch thick. Using a 3-inch biscuit cutter, cut out as many circles of dough as possible. Place a round in each 2-inch tartlet mold and gently press it into shape.

5. Place the tartlet shells on a cookie sheet and refrigerate for 30 minutes before baking.

6. Preheat the oven to 350°. Line each tartlet shell with foil and fill with pie weights or dried beans. Bake the tartlets for 10 to 12 minutes, until golden brown. Remove the foil and weights.

7. Let the shells cool to room temperature, then carefully remove from the molds. (The tartlet shells can be prepared up to 1 day ahead.)

8. Up to 1 hour before serving, decoratively arrange a few berries in each tartlet shell.

9. In a small saucepan, combine the apricot jam with 2 tablespoons of water and cook over moderately high heat, stirring, until the jam melts, 3 to 5 minutes. Spoon a small amount of the warm glaze over the fruit in each tartlet.

—Christopher Idone

PUFFED APPLE TARTS

Store-bought puff pastry works beautifully in these free-form tarts. If you're feeling extremely indulgent, serve them à la mode with vanilla ice cream.

MAKES 2

1 small tart apple, such as Granny Smith—peeled, cored and sliced ¼ inch thick
1 tablespoon sugar
1 tablespoon unsalted butter
¼ teaspoon vanilla extract
½ pound puff pastry, chilled
1 tablespoon apricot jam, melted and cooled
1 egg white, beaten

1. In a small saucepan, combine half the apple slices with the sugar, ½ tablespoon of the butter and the vanilla. Cover and cook over moderate heat until the apple is soft, about 5 minutes. Let cool.

2. Meanwhile, on a lightly floured surface, roll the puff pastry into an 8-by-8-inch square ⅛ inch thick. Using a 4-inch biscuit cutter, stamp out four rounds. Set 2 of the rounds on a baking sheet, prick all over with a fork; brush with the apricot jam. Using a rolling pin, enlarge the 2 remaining rounds by ½ inch; set aside.

3. Preheat the oven to 400°. Mash the cooked apple and spoon the mixture onto the glazed pastry rounds; spread to within ¼ inch of the edges. Cover with the remaining apple slices and dot with the remaining ½ tablespoon butter. Moisten the edges of the pastry with water and top with the reserved pastry rounds. Use the tines of a fork to seal the edges. Brush the tarts lightly with the egg white. Using a sharp knife, make a small slit in the top of each one. Bake the tarts for 30 minutes, until golden. Serve warm.

—Molly O'Neill

CHOCOLATE ALMOND TARTLETS

Whether trimmed with whipped cream rosettes, dusted with toasted almonds or served plain straight from the fridge, these are sweets that will please anyone who adores chocolate. My preference is to serve them at room temperature when they're at their creamiest.

MAKES 12 TARTLETS

½ recipe Cream Cheese Dough (recipe follows)
1⅓ cups heavy cream
8 ounces bittersweet chocolate, preferably Lindt or Tobler, finely chopped

¼ cup amaretto liqueur
½ cup whole blanched almonds,
   toasted and finely chopped

1. Remove the dough from the refrigerator and let stand for about 10 minutes, until malleable. Meanwhile, lightly butter twelve 3-inch fluted tartlet molds.

2. On a lightly floured work surface, roll out half the dough about ⅛ inch thick. Using a 3½-inch round cookie or biscuit cutter, cut out 6 circles of dough. Fit the dough into the tartlet molds without stretching. Place in the freezer for at least 30 minutes, or until firm. Meanwhile, repeat with the remaining dough.

3. Preheat the oven to 400°. Line each frozen tartlet with aluminum foil and fill with pie weights or dried beans. Bake for 15 minutes. Remove the foil and weights and bake for 2 to 3 minutes longer, until golden brown. Remove from the oven and let cool in the tins on a rack; then unmold. (**The recipe can be prepared ahead to this point.** Refrigerate the pastry shells in an airtight container for up to 3 days or freeze for up to 1 month. Defrost before proceeding.)

4. In a small saucepan, bring ⅔ cup of the heavy cream to a boil. Remove from the heat, add the chocolate and stir until completely melted, smooth and glossy. Mix in 2 tablespoons of the amaretto and set aside to cool to room temperature, stirring occasionally. Do not refrigerate.

5. To finish the tartlets, fill with the chocolate-almond cream. Sprinkle with chopped almonds and refrigerate for at least 30 minutes until set.

6. Whip the remaining ⅔ cup cream with the remaining 2 tablespoons amaretto and pipe onto the tartlets. Serve them chilled or at room temperature.

—*Dorie Greenspan*

CREAM CHEESE DOUGH

While this easy dough can be made by hand or with an electric mixer (see Note), it is a perfect job for the food processor. The machine turns out an excellent, very smooth dough in less than a minute.

MAKES ABOUT 1½ POUNDS
½ pound cream cheese
2 sticks (½ pound) unsalted butter
2 cups all-purpose flour

1. Cut the cream cheese into 8 pieces and let stand at room temperature for 10 minutes.

2. Cut the butter into tablespoons and let stand at room temperature for 10 minutes.

3. Put the flour into a food processor. Scatter the cream cheese and butter over the flour and process, turning the machine quickly on and off 6 to 8 times. Then let the machine run until the dough resembles large curds, stopping to scrape down the sides of the bowl once, about 15 seconds; do not let the dough form a ball on the blade.

4. Turn the dough out onto a work surface and gather into a ball. Divide the dough in half and shape each piece into a 4-by-5-by-1-inch rectangle. Wrap the dough tightly in plastic wrap and refrigerate for at least 2 hours before using. (**The dough can be refrigerated for up to 3 days or frozen for 1 month.**)

NOTE: To make the dough by hand or with a mixer, first cream together the butter and cream cheese. Then blend in the flour to form a smooth dough.

—*Dorie Greenspan*

CIDER APPLE TURNOVERS

MAKES ABOUT 3 DOZEN
¾ cup dried apples, coarsely chopped
⅓ cup golden raisins
¾ cup apple cider
1 medium firm apple, such as Granny
   Smith, Stayman or Golden
   Delicious, finely diced
⅓ cup chopped pecans
⅓ cup plus 1 tablespoon unsweetened
   apple butter
Flaky Pastry (recipe follows)
1½ tablespoons unsalted butter
1 egg
¼ cup sugar

1. In a small heavy saucepan, combine the dried apples, raisins and cider. Bring to a boil over moderately high heat and cook, stirring frequently, until the liquid is absorbed, 3 to 4 minutes. Scrape the mixture into a bowl, stir in the diced apple, nuts and apple butter and let cool, about 20 minutes.

2. Working with a quarter of the dough at a time, remove it from the refrigerator and set aside until malleable, about 10 minutes. On a lightly floured surface, roll out the dough ⅛ inch thick. Using a biscuit cutter, cut out as many 4-inch rounds as possible. Collect the scraps and chill for rerolling.

3. Place 1 tablespoon of the filling in the center of each round and add a dot of butter. Moisten the edges of the dough with water and fold one side of the circle over the filling. Pinch the pastry together and crimp the edges with the tines of a fork. Refrigerate for at least 30 minutes or up to 24 hours. Repeat with the remaining dough and filling. (**The turnovers can be made ahead to this point and frozen, tightly wrapped, for up to 1 month. Bake without defrosting.**)

4. Preheat the oven to 425°. Place

the turnovers on a greased baking sheet. In a small bowl, beat the egg with 1 teaspoon of cold water. Brush the egg glaze over the turnovers and sprinkle each with ¼ teaspoon sugar. Cut 2 small steam vents in the top of each pastry or prick with a fork. Bake for about 18 minutes, until the turnovers are golden and the filling is bubbly. (Frozen turnovers will take about 5 minutes longer.)

—Dorie Greenspan

FLAKY PASTRY

MAKES ENOUGH FOR 3 DOZEN TURNOVERS

4½ cups all-purpose flour
3 tablespoons sugar
1 teaspoon salt
3 sticks (¾ pound) unsalted butter, cut into 16 pieces
About ½ cup ice water

1. In a food processor, combine the flour, sugar and salt. Pulse twice.

2. Add the butter and turn the machine on and off about 10 times, until the mixture resembles coarse meal.

3. Gradually add the ice water 1 tablespoon at a time, pulsing until the mixture resembles ground almonds and holds together when pressed between your fingers. (You may need slightly more or less than ½ cup ice water.)

4. Turn the dough out onto a lightly floured surface and divide into 4 equal pieces. Shape each piece into a ball, flatten into a 6-inch disk and wrap in plastic. Refrigerate for at least 30 minutes before using. Let the dough rest at room temperature until malleable, about 10 minutes, before rolling.

—Dorie Greenspan

STRAWBERRY-CREAM CHEESE GALETTE

To time this easy brioche-based tart for a dinner party, prepare the yeast dough two to three hours before company arrives. After two risings, the dessert bakes in only 20 minutes and is best eaten slightly warm.

Two tablespoons of large crystallized sugar can be substituted for the granulated sugar in Step 6. It will add a touch of glitter to this otherwise homey dessert.

6 TO 8 SERVINGS

1 tablespoon active dry yeast
¼ cup warm water (105° to 115°)
½ cup plus 2 tablespoons sugar
1¼ cups all-purpose flour
½ teaspoon salt
1 egg
5 tablespoons unsalted butter, at room temperature
¼ cup plus ⅓ cup heavy cream, chilled
1½ cups small fresh strawberries
1 tablespoon framboise (raspberry eau-de-vie) or kirsch
¼ pound fresh cream cheese, at room temperature

1. In a large mixing bowl, combine the yeast with the warm water. Let stand for about 5 minutes, until the yeast is completely dissolved.

2. In a medium bowl, combine 2 tablespoons of the sugar with the flour and salt.

3. Add the egg to the yeast and beat in 4 tablespoons of the butter and ¼ cup of the cream with a wooden spoon. Gradually beat in the flour mixture about 1 tablespoon at a time. (At first, the butter may remain lumpy, but as you add more flour, it will blend in.) When all the flour is incorporated, beat the batter against the sides of the bowl for 1 to 2 minutes. The more beating, the lighter the dough will become; it should be very

soft. Clean the sides of the bowl with a rubber spatula. Cover the bowl with plastic wrap and let stand in a warm place until the dough is doubled in size, about 1½ hours.

4. Meanwhile, in a medium bowl, combine the strawberries with 2 tablespoons of the sugar and the framboise. Set aside and let marcerate for about 1 hour.

5. Grease an 11-inch tart pan with a removable bottom. Press the dough into the prepared pan and even the top with a rubber spatula. Drain the strawberries (discard the marinade or reserve for fruit salad). Scatter the berries over the dough, leaving a ½-inch margin all around the edge. Let the cake rise until the dough fills the pan, about 1 hour. Meanwhile, preheat the oven to 375°.

6. In a medium bowl with an electric mixer, beat the cream cheese with ¼ cup of the sugar until smooth. Slowly beat in the remaining ⅓ cup cream and beat until smooth and thick. Spoon the cream cheese mixture over the risen cake, again leaving a ½-inch margin of plain dough. Sprinkle the remaining 2 tablespoons sugar over the top and dot with the remaining 1 tablespoon butter.

7. Bake in the center of the oven for about 20 minutes, or until the edges of the dough are golden brown. Serve warm or at room temperature.

—Lydie Marshall

STRAWBERRY-PEACH COBBLER

6 TO 8 SERVINGS

3 pounds fresh peaches—peeled, pitted and cut into ½-inch slices— or 3 pounds frozen sliced peaches (about 6 cups)
2 cups (1 pint) ripe, but firm, strawberries, hulled and halved

170

⅔ cup plus 2 teaspoons sugar
2 tablespoons unsalted butter
2 cups all-purpose flour
1 tablespoon baking powder
1 teaspoon salt
¼ cup cold vegetable shortening
1 cup heavy cream
Vanilla ice cream

1. In a medium bowl, toss the peaches and strawberries with ⅔ cup of the sugar. Spoon the fruit into a shallow 10-cup baking dish. Dot with butter.

2. Preheat the oven to 400°. Sift the flour, baking powder, salt and remaining 2 teaspoons sugar into a mixing bowl. Cut in the shortening until the mixture resembles coarse meal. Gradually stir in the cream with a wooden spoon until the dough forms a ball.

3. Turn out the dough onto a floured sheet of waxed paper. Roll out ¼ inch thick and trim as necessary to fit the baking dish. Place the dough over the fruit. Crimp the edges. Bake for 30 minutes, or until the pastry is golden brown.

4. Let the cobbler cool about 15 minutes. Serve warm topped with a spoonful of vanilla ice cream.

—*James Villas*

CHESTNUT TORTA

8 TO 10 SERVINGS
4 eggs, separated
1 cup sugar
10 tablespoons unsalted butter, at
    room temperature
1 teaspoon vanilla extract
1 pound Roasted Chestnuts (p. 123)
½ cup pine nuts, toasted (see Note)
4 ounces semisweet chocolate

1. Preheat the oven to 350°. Butter an 8-inch springform pan and line the bottom with parchment or waxed paper. Butter the paper and flour the pan.

2. In a large mixer bowl, beat the egg yolks and sugar until the mixture is pale and thick enough to leave a ribbon, 2 to 3 minutes. Beat in 8 tablespoons of the butter and the vanilla.

3. Using a rotary grater, grate the chestnuts and pine nuts. Stir the grated nuts into the egg mixture.

4. In a large bowl, beat the egg whites until soft peaks form. Fold the whites into the chestnut mixture.

5. Turn the batter into the prepared pan and bake for 35 to 40 minutes, or until the cake is firm and a cake tester inserted into the center comes out clean. Set the pan on a rack to cool for 15 minutes. Remove the sides of the pan and let cool completely.

6. Meanwhile, in a double boiler or a microwave oven, melt the chocolate with the remaining 2 tablespoons butter, stirring frequently until smooth.

7. Invert the cake onto a platter. Remove the base of the pan and peel off the parchment paper. Pour the warm chocolate glaze over the cake and spread evenly over the top and sides.

NOTE: To toast pine nuts, cook in a small ungreased skillet over moderately high heat, tossing frequently until lightly browned, about 2 minutes.

—*John Robert Massie*

GINGER-MOLASSES
SKILLET CAKE

8 SERVINGS
1¾ cups all-purpose flour
1 teaspoon baking powder
¼ teaspoon baking soda
2 teaspoons ground ginger
½ teaspoon salt
½ teaspoon coarsely ground pepper
¼ teaspoon ground cloves
¼ teaspoon allspice
¼ teaspoon cinnamon
1 cup (packed) dark brown sugar
1 stick (4 ounces) unsalted butter
⅔ cup plus 2 tablespoons light
    unsulphured molasses
⅔ cup milk
½ teaspoon vanilla extract
¼ cup pine nuts
1 cup heavy cream, chilled
½ cup sour cream, chilled

1. Preheat the oven to 350°. In a large bowl, blend the flour, baking powder, baking soda, ginger, salt, pepper, cloves, allspice and cinnamon together.

2. In a small saucepan, combine ¾ cup of the brown sugar, 6 tablespoons of the butter and ⅔ cup of the molasses. Stir over moderate heat until melted and well combined. Stir in the milk and vanilla and set aside.

3. Place the remaining ¼ cup brown sugar, 2 tablespoons butter and 2 tablespoons molasses in a 12-inch cast-iron skillet. Place the skillet in the oven to melt the butter and sugar and also to heat the skillet. Stir to combine.

4. Stir the brown sugar and milk mixture into the dry ingredients. Beat just until smooth. Pour the batter into the skillet. Sprinkle the pine nuts on top and bake for 25 to 30 minutes, until a tester inserted in the center of the cake comes out clean.

5. Beat the heavy cream until soft peaks form. Add the sour cream and continue beating until stiff. Serve the cake warm from the skillet. Pass the whipped cream separately.

—*Anne Disrude*

PIES, CAKES & COOKIES

APPLE UPSIDE-DOWN CAKE

6 SERVINGS

1 stick (4 ounces) unsalted butter, softened

½ cup sugar

3 tart cooking apples, such as Granny Smith or Greening—peeled, cored and each sliced into about 12 wedges

½ cup all-purpose flour

½ teaspoon baking powder

½ teaspoon ground cardamom

1 egg

½ teaspoon vanilla extract

2½ tablespoons milk

1. Spread 4 tablespoons of the butter over the bottom and sides of a heavy 8-inch ovenproof skillet, preferably cast iron. Sprinkle ¼ cup of the sugar over the butter. Packing them as closely as possible and trimming if necessary, arrange the apples (rounded-side down) in concentric circles in the skillet.

2. Cook over moderate heat, shaking and rotating the skillet occasionally, until the butter and sugar are lightly caramelized and turn a honey color, about 20 minutes. Remove from the heat. Rearrange the apples, if necessary, and let cool for at least 30 minutes before proceeding. (**The recipe can be prepared to this point several hours ahead.** Cover the skillet loosely and set it aside at room temperature).

3. Preheat the oven to 350°. In a medium bowl, sift together the flour, baking powder and cardamom.

4. In a large bowl, cream together the remaining 4 tablespoons butter and ¼ cup sugar until light and fluffy. Beat in the egg and the vanilla. Stir in half of the dry ingredients, then the milk and finally the remaining dry ingredients until blended. Spoon the batter evenly over the apples. (It will make a thin layer.)

5. Place the skillet on a baking sheet to catch any drips and bake until the cake is golden brown and a cake tester inserted in the center comes out clean, about 30 minutes. Remove from the oven. Run a knife around the sides of the skillet and invert the cake onto a serving platter. If any apples stick to the pan, scrape them off with the knife and rearrange them on top of the cake.

—*Dorie Greenspan*

APPLE-STREUSEL COFFEE CAKE

8 TO 12 SERVINGS

1 large tart green apple (Greening or Granny Smith), peeled and cut into ⅜-inch dice

2 teaspoons cinnamon

1 tablespoon fresh lemon juice

½ cup (packed) light brown sugar

1¼ cups coarsely chopped walnuts (about 5 ounces)

6 egg yolks

1 cup sour cream

1½ teaspoons vanilla extract

3 cups sifted cake flour

1½ cups granulated sugar

¾ teaspoon baking powder

½ teaspoon baking soda

1 teaspoon salt

3 sticks (12 ounces) unsalted butter, softened to room temperature

1. Preheat the oven to 350°. Spray a 9-by-13-inch aluminum baking pan with Baker's Joy, or grease and flour the pan. (Note: If using glass or dark metal, reduce the oven to 325°.)

2. In a small bowl, toss the apple with ½ teaspoon of the cinnamon and the lemon juice; set aside.

3. In a medium bowl, combine the brown sugar, walnuts and remaining 1½ teaspoons cinnamon; set this streusel mixture aside.

4. In another medium bowl, combine the egg yolks, sour cream and vanilla; beat lightly to blend.

5. In a large mixing bowl, stir together the cake flour, granulated sugar, baking powder, baking soda and salt. Add the butter and half the egg mixture and beat at medium-high speed for 1 minute, scraping down the sides of the bowl once. Add the remaining egg mixture to the batter in three parts, scraping down the sides of the bowl and beating for 20 seconds after each addition. Fold in the apple mixture.

6. Spoon half of the cake batter (about 3 cups) into the prepared pan; smooth the surface with a spatula. Sprinkle evenly with half of the streusel mixture and top with the remaining batter. Smooth the surface and sprinkle with the remaining streusel.

7. Bake for 35 minutes, or until the cake springs back when pressed lightly in the center and a tester inserted in the cake comes out clean. Let the cake cool completely in the pan on a rack before serving. Cut out squares directly from the pan.

—*Rose Levy Beranbaum*

LEMON POPPY SEED POUND CAKE

This is the triumphant result of 30 trials to achieve what in cake baking is an apparent contradiction: a buttery pound cake with a texture that is dense yet at the same time meltingly tender.

8 TO 12 SERVINGS

2 cups sifted cake flour

1½ cups sugar, preferably superfine

1 teaspoon baking powder

¾ teaspoon salt

¼ cup milk

4 eggs, at room temperature

2 teaspoons vanilla extract

2 sticks (8 ounces) plus 2 tablespoons
  unsalted butter at room
  temperature, cut into pieces
¼ cup poppy seeds (2 ounces)
1 tablespoon freshly grated lemon
  zest
⅓ cup fresh lemon juice

1. Preheat the oven to 325°. Spray a 9-by-5-by-3-inch loaf pan with Baker's Joy, or grease and flour the pan.

2. In a large mixer bowl, combine the flour, 1 cup of the sugar, the baking powder and the salt; blend well. In a medium bowl, combine the milk, eggs and vanilla and beat lightly. Add half of this mixture together with the butter to the dry ingredients and beat at medium speed for 1 minute, scraping down the sides of the bowl once or twice. Add the remaining egg mixture to the batter in two parts, beating at the same speed for 20 seconds after each addition and scraping the sides of the bowl. Beat in the poppy seeds and lemon zest.

3. Spoon the batter into the prepared pan and smooth the surface with a spatula. (The pan will be more than three-quarters full.) Bake for 60 minutes, or until a cake tester inserted in the center comes out clean and the cake springs back when pressed lightly in the center.

4. Prepare a lemon glaze shortly before the cake is done: In a small saucepan, heat the remaining ½ cup sugar and the lemon juice over low heat, stirring until the sugar dissolves.

5. Brush three-quarters of the glaze onto the top of the hot cake still in the pan. Let cool on a rack for 10 minutes. Loosen the sides with a narrow spatula and invert onto a greased wire rack. Brush the bottom and sides of the cake with the remaining glaze, turn right-side up and let cool completely. (**The cake can be refrigerated, wrapped, for up to 5 days.** Let return to room temperature before serving.)
—Rose Levy Beranbaum

ORANGE CHIFFON CAKE

Because the oil used in the batter does not harden on chilling, this cake can be served slightly chilled or at room temperature. The cake can also be wrapped and refrigerated for up to one week.

🍷 F&W BEVERAGE SUGGESTION
California Muscat, such as
Quady's Essensia

12 TO 16 SERVINGS
2¼ cups sifted cake flour
1½ cups sugar
1 tablespoon baking powder
1 teaspoon salt
½ cup safflower oil
6 egg yolks, at room temperature
¾ cup fresh orange juice
1 teaspoon vanilla extract
2 tablespoons freshly grated orange
  zest
8 egg whites, at room temperature
½ teaspoon cream of tartar
Confectioners' sugar, for garnish

1. Preheat the oven to 325°. In the large bowl of an electric mixer, combine the flour, all but 2 tablespoons of the sugar, the baking powder and the salt; blend well. Make a well in the center. Add the oil, egg yolks, orange juice, vanilla and orange zest; beat on medium speed until the batter is smooth, about 1 minute.

2. In a large bowl, beat the egg whites until frothy. Add the cream of tartar and continue beating until soft peaks form. Beat in the remaining 2 tablespoons sugar and continue beating until the whites are stiff but not dry. Gently fold the beaten egg whites into the batter until just blended. (A large balloon wire whisk or slotted skimmer is ideal for this.)

3. Pour into an ungreased 10-inch tube pan with removable bottom and bake for 55 minutes, or until a cake tester inserted in the center comes out clean and the cake springs back when pressed lightly in the center.

4. Invert and let the cake cool completely in the pan, about 1½ hours. When cool, loosen the sides of the cake with a long metal spatula and lift out the center of the pan with the cake on it. Carefully loosen the bottom of the cake and central core with a spatula or thin, sharp knife. (A wire cake tester works well around the center core.) Invert onto a greased wire rack and invert right-side up onto a serving plate.

5. Sprinkle with confectioners' sugar. To serve, cut with a serrated knife.
—Rose Levy Beranbaum

CELESTIAL LEMON ROLL

This lighter-than-air lemon roll has only 165 calories per serving.

8 SERVINGS
LEMON FILLING:
3 tablespoons cornstarch
⅓ cup granulated sugar
1 teaspoon freshly grated lemon zest
⅓ cup fresh lemon juice
1 jumbo egg yolk
1 tablespoon unsalted butter

ANGEL FOOD CAKE ROLL:
4 jumbo egg whites
⅛ teaspoon salt
⅛ teaspoon cream of tartar
½ cup sifted superfine sugar
½ cup sifted cake flour
2 teaspoons fresh lemon juice
½ teaspoon vanilla extract
¼ teaspoon almond extract
3 tablespoons confectioners' sugar
Lemon zest, sprigs of lemon verbena
  or lemon geranium, for garnish

PIES, CAKES & COOKIES

1. *Make the lemon filling:* In a small heavy saucepan, combine the cornstarch and granulated sugar. Whisk in the lemon zest, lemon juice and ¾ cup of water. Cook, stirring, over moderate heat until the mixture boils and is thick and smooth, about 3 minutes. Blend a little of the hot mixture into the egg yolk and scrape the warmed yolk back into the pan. Cook over low heat, stirring constantly, for 1 minute. Remove from the heat and stir in the butter. Let cool to room temperature, stirring often to prevent a skin from forming, cover and refrigerate. (**The filling can be made a day ahead.** Cover and refrigerate. Return to room temperature and stir to restore to a spreading consistency before proceeding.)

2. *Make the cake roll:* Preheat the oven to 300°. Spray a 15½-by-10½-by-1-inch jelly-roll pan lightly with nonstick vegetable spray and line the bottom and sides of the pan with parchment or waxed paper. Grease the paper lightly with the nonstick spray.

3. In a large bowl, beat the egg whites with the salt and cream of tartar until the egg white bubbles are tiny and of even size and will mound when turned with a spatula, about 1 minute. Do *not* overbeat to soft peaks.

4. With a rubber spatula, gently fold in the superfine sugar, 2 tablespoons at a time. Sift the flour, about 2 tablespoons at a time, over the egg whites and fold in gently. When all of the flour has been incorporated, fold in the lemon juice, vanilla and almond extract.

5. Spread the batter into the prepared pan, smoothing it evenly into the corners. Bake on the middle rack until springy to the touch, 20 to 25 minutes. The cake will be pale; do not overcook.

6. Meanwhile, spread a kitchen towel on the counter and sift the confectioners' sugar over it to cover an area approximately the size of the cake.

7. As soon as the cake is removed from the oven, invert it onto the sugared towel and peel off the paper at once. Using a knife with a serrated edge, cut off any crisp edges that might crack as the cake is rolled. With one of the short ends toward you, roll the cake up in the towel. Let the cake cool in the towel for about 35 minutes.

8. Unroll the cake, spread it evenly with the filling, leaving ½-inch margins all around, then reroll, jelly-roll style and let stand, covered by the towel, 20 minutes longer. Remove the towel and sift any loose confectioners' sugar over the roll. Ease the roll onto a platter and garnish with lemon zest, sprigs of lemon verbena or lemon geranium.

—*Jean Anderson*

PUMPKIN WALNUT RING

A little walnut oil is added to the vegetable oil in this cake to intensify the nut motif. The pumpkin imparts a subtle earthy flavor.

6 TO 8 SERVINGS
1 cup plus 2 tablespoons cake flour
1 teaspoon baking soda
1 teaspoon cinnamon
½ teaspoon freshly grated nutmeg
½ teaspoon ground cloves
¼ teaspoon salt
½ cup coarsely chopped walnuts
2 eggs, at room temperature
¾ cup plus 2 tablespoons (packed) light brown sugar
6 tablespoons safflower or corn oil
2 tablespoons walnut oil
1 cup solid-pack canned pumpkin
Chocolate Walnut Glaze (optional; recipe follows)

1. Preheat the oven to 350°. Spray the inside of a 6-cup bundt pan or savarin ring with Baker's Joy, or grease and flour the pan.

2. In a medium bowl, combine the flour, baking soda, cinnamon, nutmeg, cloves, salt and walnuts; whisk together to blend.

3. In a mixer on medium speed, beat together the eggs, brown sugar, safflower oil and walnut oil until very smooth, 2 to 3 minutes. Beat in the pumpkin until combined. Add all of the dry ingredients and beat just until incorporated.

4. Scrape the batter into the prepared pan and bake in the middle of the oven for 30 minutes, or until a cake tester inserted in the thickest part of the cake comes out clean.

5. Let cool in the pan on a rack for 10 minutes. Unmold onto the rack and let cool completely. This cake keeps especially well. To store, wrap tightly in plastic and foil and keep at room temperature overnight; refrigerate for up to 5 days or freeze for up to 3 months. Let the cake return to room temperature and drizzle with glaze, if desired, before serving.

—*Rose Levy Beranbaum*

CHOCOLATE WALNUT GLAZE

MAKES ABOUT ⅓ CUP
1 ounce semisweet chocolate (I use Tobler Tradition)
1 ounce milk chocolate (I use Lindt)
1 tablespoon walnut oil

In a small saucepan melt the semisweet and milk chocolates with the walnut oil over hot—not simmering—water, stirring constantly.

—*Rose Levy Beranbaum*

CREAM CAKE WITH HONEY BUTTERCREAM

A cross between the lightness of genoise and the moistness and richness of a sponge, this cake is mellower, tenderer and more buttery than either. (Unfrosted, it also makes a perfect base for strawberry shortcake.)

6 TO 8 SERVINGS
1½ cups sifted cake flour
¾ cup sugar
1¼ teaspoons baking powder
½ teaspoon salt
1 stick (4 ounces) plus 3 tablespoons unsalted butter, softened to room temperature
½ cup heavy cream
3 egg yolks
1 teaspoon vanilla extract
Honey Buttercream (recipe follows)

1. Preheat the oven to 350°. Spray a 9-by-2-inch round cake pan or springform with Baker's Joy, or grease the pan, line the bottom with a circle of parchment or waxed paper and grease the paper; dust the pan with flour.

2. In a large mixing bowl, combine the flour, sugar, baking powder and salt; mix well. Add the butter and about 2 tablespoons of the cream and beat at medium-high speed for 1½ minutes, scraping down the sides of the bowl once or twice.

3. In a small bowl, lightly beat the remaining cream, the egg yolks and vanilla. Beat into the batter in three additions, beating for 20 seconds after each addition and stopping occasionally to scrape down the sides of the bowl.

4. Scrape the batter into the pan; smooth with a spatula. Bake for 25 minutes, or until the top is golden and springs back when pressed lightly in the center and a cake tester inserted near the middle comes out clean.

5. Let the cake cool in the pan on a rack for 10 minutes. Loosen the sides with a knife and invert onto a greased wire rack. Remove the parchment paper and invert right-side up to cool completely. Frost the top and sides with the honey buttercream.

—*Rose Levy Beranbaum*

HONEY BUTTERCREAM

MAKES ABOUT 1¼ CUPS
2 egg yolks
2 tablespoons honey
1 stick (4 ounces) plus 2 tablespoons unsalted butter, softened to room temperature

1. In a mixer bowl, beat the egg yolks until pale, about 3 minutes.

2. Meanwhile, in a small saucepan, bring the honey to a rolling boil over moderate heat. With the mixer on, drizzle the hot honey into the egg yolks in a thin stream. Beat until the outside of the bowl is completely cool.

3. On low speed, gradually beat in the butter until smooth and creamy, 5 to 7 minutes. (The mixture may separate at some point, but beating will smooth it out.)

—*Rose Levy Beranbaum*

CHOCOLATE WALNUT CAKE

12 SERVINGS
6 ounces semisweet chocolate, coarsely chopped
½ cup safflower oil
1½ cups (6 ounces) walnuts, toasted and cooled (see Note)
¾ cup sugar
½ teaspoon cinnamon

2 cups fresh bread crumbs (made from about 6 slices of firm-textured white bread)
6 eggs, separated
⅓ cup Cognac or brandy
Mocha-Walnut Buttercream (recipe follows)
Chocolate Glaze (recipe follows)
Chocolate Leaves (recipe follows) or chopped walnuts, for garnish

1. Preheat the oven to 350°. Grease an 8-by-3-inch springform pan. Dust with flour; tap out any excess.

2. In a small heavy saucepan, melt the chocolate with the safflower oil over low heat until just warm. Stir to blend and let the chocolate mixture cool to room temperature.

3. In a food processor, combine the walnuts and 2 tablespoons of the sugar. Process briefly until just ground, 10 to 12 seconds. In a large bowl, combine the ground nuts, cinnamon and bread crumbs and toss well to combine.

4. In another bowl, beat the egg yolks lightly. Gradually whisk in ½ cup of the sugar, beating until the mixture is pale and thick, about 5 minutes.

5. In a large bowl, beat the egg whites until soft peaks form. Gradually add the remaining 2 tablespoons sugar and continue to beat until stiff, glossy peaks form.

6. Fold the cooled chocolate mixture and the Cognac into the beaten egg yolks. Pour over the bread crumb mixture and fold together until blended. Stir one third of the beaten whites into the mixture to lighten it. Fold in all of the remaining egg whites until no white streaks remain.

7. Quickly scrape the batter into the prepared cake pan and bake in the middle of the oven for 45 to 50 minutes, or until the surface is covered with small cracks and a cake tester inserted in the center comes out clean.

8. Transfer the cake to a wire rack

and let cool for 10 minutes. Remove the sides of the pan and let cool completely. (**The cake can be made to this point up to a day ahead.** Wrap well.)

9. Invert the cake and carefully remove the springform bottom. With a long serrated knife, split the cake in half horizontally into 2 equal layers. Spread the mocha-walnut buttercream over one cut cake layer and sandwich the cake together again.

10. Place the cake, flat-side up, on a rack over a jelly-roll pan. Pour the warm chocolate glaze over the cake. Using a metal spatula, spread it evenly over the top and sides. Refrigerate until the glaze sets, about 30 minutes.

11. Using a metal spatula (your fingers may melt the chocolate), arrange the leaves decoratively on top of the cake.

NOTE: To toast walnuts, place them on a baking sheet and bake in a 350° oven until they are fragrant, about 10 minutes.

—*Diana Sturgis*

MOCHA-WALNUT BUTTERCREAM

MAKES ABOUT 1¼ CUPS
1 tablespoon instant coffee powder
1 ounce semisweet chocolate, coarsely chopped
1 stick (4 ounces) unsalted butter, at room temperature
1 cup confectioners' sugar
1 egg yolk
½ cup toasted walnuts, cooled and chopped (see Note, above)

1. In a small bowl, dissolve the coffee in 2 teaspoons of water.
2. In a small heavy saucepan, melt the chocolate with the coffee over

very low heat, stirring until smooth. Remove from the heat and let cool to room temperature.

3. In a food processor, combine the butter, confectioners' sugar, egg yolk and cooled chocolate mixture. Process until smooth, about 30 seconds. Turn the mixture into a small bowl and stir in the nuts. (**The buttercream can be made one day in advance.** Cover and refrigerate. Let return to room temperature before spreading.)

—*Diana Sturgis*

CHOCOLATE GLAZE

MAKES ABOUT ⅔ CUP
4 ounces semisweet chocolate, coarsely chopped
3 tablespoons unsalted butter

In a small heavy saucepan, melt the chocolate and the butter over low heat. Stir until smooth and use the glaze while it's still warm.

—*Diana Sturgis*

CHOCOLATE LEAVES

3 ounces semisweet chocolate
Large, smooth nontoxic leaves (lemon or rose are a good choice), washed and well dried

1. In a small heavy saucepan, melt the chocolate over very low heat. Do not let it get too hot.
2. Using a flat pastry brush, paint

the underside of each dry leaf with a layer of melted chocolate.

3. Place the leaves, chocolate-side up, in a single layer on a tray, and refrigerate until set, about 10 minutes.

4. Brush with a second coat of chocolate and refrigerate once again until set.

5. Place a leaf, chocolate-side down, on a cool surface. Starting at the stem end, peel the leaf up and away from the chocolate. (Use the tip of a knife rather than your fingers to separate the leaf from the chocolate. The warmth of your fingers is enough to melt the chocolate.)

6. As each leaf is finished, carefully transfer it back to the tray with a large metal spatula and refrigerate until ready to use.

—*Diana Sturgis*

BEST AMERICAN CHOCOLATE LAYER CAKE

This cake has an exceptionally soft, tender texture and full, rounded chocolate flavor without the usual bitter edge that baking soda imparts. Baker's Joy is a vegetable oil spray that contains flour; I find it offers a quick, easy alternative to greasing and flouring the cake pan.

🍷 F&W BEVERAGE SUGGESTION
Cold glass of milk

8 TO 10 SERVINGS
1 cup boiling water
½ cup plus 1 tablespoon Dutch processed cocoa powder (I use Poulain)
2¼ teaspoons vanilla extract
3 eggs
2¼ cups plus 2 tablespoons sifted cake flour

1½ cups sugar
1½ tablespoons baking powder
1 teaspoon salt
1½ sticks (6 ounces) unsalted butter,
   at room temperature
Perfect Fudge Frosting (recipe
   follows)

1. Preheat the oven to 350°. Grease the bottom of two 9-inch round cake pans. Line with a round of parchment or waxed paper; then spray the pan with Baker's Joy or grease and dust with flour.

2. In a small bowl, gradually whisk the boiling water into the cocoa until smooth. Let the cocoa cool to room temperature.

3. In another small bowl, beat the vanilla into the eggs. Whisk in one-fourth of the cooled cocoa mixture.

4. In a large mixing bowl, combine the flour, sugar, baking powder and salt; mix well. Add the remaining cocoa-water mixture and the butter to the dry ingredients and beat at medium-high speed for 1½ minutes, stopping the machine once or twice to scrape the sides of the bowl. Add the egg-cocoa mixture in 3 parts, scraping down the sides of the bowl and beating for 20 seconds after each addition.

5. Pour the batter into the prepared cake pans and bake for 20 to 25 minutes, or until the cakes spring back when lightly pressed in the center and a cake tester inserted near the center comes out clean; the cakes should not yet have begun to pull away from the sides of the pan.

6. Let the cakes cool in the pans on a rack for 10 minutes. Loosen the sides with a spatula and invert onto lightly greased racks to finish cooling. When completely cool, fill and frost with Perfect Fudge Frosting. Refrigerate for about 1 hour to set up the frosting before serving.

—*Rose Levy Beranbaum*

PERFECT FUDGE FROSTING

This is, quite simply, the easiest and most delicious chocolate frosting I know. Perfectly smooth and glossy, its flavor depends entirely upon the quality of chocolate used, and the maximum flavor of the chocolate is retained because it is never placed over direct heat. The quickest and easiest way to prepare this frosting is with a food processor or blender.

MAKES ABOUT 2 CUPS
12 ounces semisweet chocolate (I use
   Lindt or Tobler), coarsely chopped
1 cup heavy cream
1 tablespoon Cognac (optional)

1. In a food processor, process the chocolate until finely chopped.

2. Scald the cream over moderate heat, until bubbles appear around the edge of the pan. With the machine on, pour the hot cream through the feed tube in a steady stream. Process until smooth. Blend in the Cognac. Let cool at room temperature to thicken. It is preferable not to stir during cooling in order to achieve a thick, fudgy consistency.

—*Rose Levy Beranbaum*

APPLESAUCE SPICE BARS

MAKES ABOUT 24 BARS
1¼ cups all-purpose flour
1 teaspoon baking powder
¼ teaspoon baking soda
1 teaspoon cinnamon
¼ teaspoon allspice

1 stick (4 ounces) plus 2½
   tablespoons unsalted butter
1⅓ cups (packed) light brown sugar
2 eggs
½ cup unsweetened applesauce,
   preferably homemade
1½ teaspoons vanilla extract
1 tablespoon applejack or brandy
1 baking apple, such as Rome or
   Cortland—peeled, cored and cut
   into ¼-inch dice
½ cup raisins
½ cup chopped pecans
2½ tablespoons heavy cream
1 teaspoon light corn syrup

1. Preheat the oven to 350°. Butter a 9-by-12-inch baking pan. Line the bottom of the pan with waxed paper or parchment; butter the paper. Dust the pan with flour and tap out any excess.

2. In a bowl, sift together the flour, baking powder, baking soda, cinnamon and allspice.

3. In a heavy medium saucepan, melt 1 stick of the butter over low heat. Whisk in 1 cup of the brown sugar and continue to stir until the sugar is melted and the mixture is smooth, about 1 minute. Remove from the heat.

4. Gradually whisk in the eggs, one at a time, until well blended. Blend in the applesauce, 1 teaspoon of the vanilla and the applejack until smooth. Add the dry ingredients in two parts and stir until well mixed. Stir in the diced apple, raisins and nuts. Pour the batter into the prepared pan; smooth the top with a spatula.

5. Bake until the cake begins to pull away from the sides of the pan and a toothpick inserted in the center comes out clean, about 25 minutes. Let the cake cool in the pan for 10 minutes.

6. Meanwhile, make a glaze by combining the cream and corn syrup with the remaining ⅓ cup brown sugar and 2½ tablespoons butter in a small saucepan. Bring to a boil over moderately high heat and cook, whisking frequently, for 5 minutes. Remove from the heat and stir in the remaining ½ teaspoon vanilla.

7. Run a blunt knife around the edges of the partially cooled cake and invert it onto a rack. Turn the cake right-side up and pour the hot glaze over it, spreading if necessary to coat evenly. Let the cake cool completely before cutting into bars about 4½ by 1 inch.

—*Dorie Greenspan*

RASPBERRY SNAILS

Chocolate, which is a traditional companion to raspberry, seems pleasantly surprising in these small packages with intense flavor.

MAKES 3 DOZEN
½ recipe Cream Cheese Dough (p. 169)
⅔ cup seedless raspberry jam
¼ cup sugar
½ teaspoon cinnamon
¼ cup currants
⅔ cup mini-chocolate chips or
   chopped semisweet chocolate
1 egg

1. Remove half the dough from the refrigerator and let rest at room temperature until malleable, about 10 minutes. Meanwhile, in a small saucepan, melt the raspberry jam over low heat, stirring frequently. Remove from the heat and let cool while you shape the dough.

2. On a lightly floured surface, roll out the dough into a 10-inch square. Using a pastry brush, spread a thin coating of jam over the dough.

3. Combine 2 tablespoons of the sugar with the cinnamon and sprinkle half of the mixture evenly over the dough. Scatter half the currants and chocolate over the dough. Cover the dough with a sheet of waxed paper and, using your hands, gently press the ingredients into the dough.

4. Mark the top and bottom edges of the dough at 2-inch intervals. Using these marks as guides, cut diagonally across to make a harlequin pattern. Then cut the dough in half crosswise to make 18 equal triangles (see diagram at right). There will be 2 odd pieces of dough at either end. These can be pieced together to make nibbles for the baker.

5. Starting at the wide base of each triangle, roll up the dough. Place them on a buttered cookie sheet, preferably nonstick, with the points tucked underneath. Refrigerate the cookies for at least 30 minutes before baking. (**The cookies can be shaped well ahead of time and frozen.** Bake without thawing.) Repeat with the remaining dough, jam, cinnamon-sugar, currants and chocolate chips.

6. Preheat the oven to 350°. Beat the egg with 1 teaspoon of cold water to make a glaze. Brush the glaze over each cookie. Sprinkle with the remaining 2 tablespoons sugar.

7. Bake for 25 minutes, or until golden. (Frozen cookies will take 5 to 7 minutes longer.) Transfer to a rack and let cool before serving. The baked cookies can be stored in an airtight container for 2 to 3 days or frozen for up to 1 month.

—*Dorie Greenspan*

CINNAMON KNOTS

These are the cookies for which the "bet-you-can't-eat-just-one" wager was meant. Equally at home with coffee, tea or mugs of steaming cider, the knots may be made with ginger-sugar for a spicy change.

MAKES ABOUT 4 DOZEN
½ recipe of Cream Cheese Dough
   (p. 169)
1 cup sugar
¼ cup cinnamon

1. Remove half the dough from the refrigerator and let stand at room temperature for about 10 minutes, until malleable.

2. In a small bowl, combine the sugar and the cinnamon. Sprinkle about ¼ cup of the mixture on a work surface. Put the dough on the sugared surface and sprinkle with about 2 tablespoons of cinnamon sugar. Roll out the dough into a 13-inch square, sprinkling with more cinnamon sugar and turning the dough several times as you roll.

3. Trim the dough into a 12-inch square. Cut in half crosswise and, working with one half of the dough at a time, fold each piece lengthwise in half into a 12-by-3-inch rectangle. Cut crosswise at 1-inch intervals into 12 strips.

4. With the strips still folded, use a small paring knife to cut a slit down the center of each strip, cutting through the folded end but leaving a ½-inch margin at the free ends.

5. Holding the cookie by the folded end, fold back both layers of dough

and pull through the slit and back down to form a knot. Put the cookies on a buttered cookie sheet, preferably nonstick, and refrigerate for at least 30 minutes, until firm, before baking. Repeat with the remaining dough.

6. Preheat the oven to 400°. Bake the cookies in the middle of the oven for 10 to 12 minutes, until slightly puffed and golden. Transfer to a rack and let cool before serving. (After baking, the cookies can be frozen for up to 3 months.)

—Dorie Greenspan

SIENA ALMOND COOKIES

Although these crisp, light macaroons are traditionally patted into diamond shapes, they can also be simply dropped and baked into rounds.

MAKES ABOUT 2 DOZEN
¼ cup Passover cake meal
1¼ cups granulated sugar
2 tablespoons margarine
2 egg whites
Pinch of salt
2 teaspoons freshly grated orange zest
1 teaspoon almond extract
½ teaspoon vanilla extract
2 cups finely chopped blanched
  almonds
Confectioners' sugar

1. In a small bowl, mix together the cake meal and ¼ cup of the granulated sugar. Generously grease a large heavy cooking sheet with the margarine and sprinkle with the cake-meal mixture. Preheat the oven to 250°.

2. In a medium bowl, beat the egg whites and salt until stiff and dry. Gradually beat in the remaining 1 cup granulated sugar until the meringue is

the consistency of marshmallow. Stir in the orange zest, almond extract, vanilla and chopped almonds, mixing to form a stiff paste.

3. Scoop slightly mounded tablespoonfuls of cookie dough, and with greased hands, shape each into a diamond. Place the cookies about 1 inch apart on the prepared baking sheet and bake for 20 to 25 minutes, until the macaroons are white and dry throughout. Remove the cookies from the oven and dust with confectioners' sugar. Transfer to a rack to cool. Store the cookies in an airtight container at room temperature.

—Edda Servi Machlin

SALLY'S SESAME CRISPS

MAKES ABOUT 5 DOZEN
1 cup sesame seeds
1½ sticks (6 ounces) unsalted butter, melted and cooled to room temperature
¾ cup (packed) light brown sugar
1 egg
2 tablespoons dark rum
1¼ cups sifted all-purpose flour
¼ teaspoon baking powder
½ teaspoon freshly grated nutmeg
¼ teaspoon salt
⅛ teaspoon white pepper

1. Place the sesame seeds in a large skillet and cook over moderate heat, tossing frequently until light brown and toasted, about 5 minutes. Spread out on a plate and let cool.

2. Preheat the oven to 375°. In a

medium bowl, combine the butter, sugar, egg, rum and sesame seeds.

3. Combine the flour, baking powder nutmeg, salt and white pepper and sift over the butter mixture. Blend well.

4. Drop by rounded ½ teaspoon measures about 2 inches apart onto buttered cookie sheets. Bake in the middle of the oven for about 10 minutes, or until the cookies are golden brown with darker edges. Transfer to wire racks and let cool.

—Joanna Pruess

MOLASSES SPICE COOKIES

MAKES ABOUT 4 DOZEN
1½ sticks (6 ounces) unsalted butter
1½ cups sugar
¼ cup dark molasses
1 egg
2 cups sifted all-purpose flour
2 teaspoons baking soda
1 teaspoon cinnamon
¾ teaspoon ground ginger
½ teaspoon salt
¼ teaspoon ground cloves

1. In a medium saucepan, melt the butter over low heat. Set aside and let cool to room temperature.

2. Stir 1 cup of the sugar, the molasses and the egg into the butter.

3. Sift together the flour, baking soda, cinnamon, ginger, salt and cloves. Add to the butter mixture and mix well. Cover and chill the dough until stiff, about 45 minutes.

4. Preheat the oven to 375°. Shape the dough into balls 1 inch in diameter. Roll each ball in the remaining ½ cup sugar and place about 2 inches apart on greased cookie sheets. Bake in the middle of the oven for 8 to 10 minutes, or until the cookies are golden brown and the tops are cracked. Using a wide spatula, transfer the cookies to wire racks and let cool.

—*Joanna Pruess*

SWEET BEAN CRISPS

You'll be pleasantly surprised when you taste these crunchy bean cookies. Serve them for dessert alongside vanilla ice cream or fill the cookie jar and watch them disappear.

MAKES ABOUT 5 DOZEN
1¼ cups all-purpose flour
2 teaspoons baking powder
½ teaspoon cinnamon
½ teaspoon ground cloves
½ teaspoon salt
½ cup golden raisins
1 teaspoon freshly grated orange zest
½ cup sweet Marsala
1½ tablespoons Pernod
1 can (19 ounces) garbanzo beans—
   drained, rinsed and patted dry
1 cup milk
1 teaspoon vanilla extract
1 stick (4 ounces) unsalted butter,
   softened
¾ cup (packed) dark brown sugar
1 egg, at room temperature
Confectioners' sugar, for dusting

1. Preheat the oven to 375°. Sift together the flour, baking powder, cinnamon, cloves and salt.

2. In a small saucepan, combine the raisins, orange zest, Marsala and Pernod. Bring to a boil over high heat. Remove from the heat and let cool to room temperature.

3. In a food processor or blender, combine the beans, milk and vanilla. Puree until smooth, 4 to 5 minutes.

4. In a large bowl, cream together the butter and brown sugar until fluffy. Beat in the egg. Blend in the cooled raisin mixture and the bean puree. Add the dry ingredients and mix until thoroughly combined.

5. Spoon heaping teaspoonfuls of batter 2 inches apart onto lightly greased cookie sheets. Bake for 25 to 30 minutes, until the cookies are lightly browned around the edges. Transfer to wire racks and let cool completely. Dust lightly with confectioners' sugar.

—*Anne Disrude*

PECAN ICEBOX COOKIES

MAKES ABOUT 4 DOZEN
1 stick (4 ounces) unsalted butter,
   softened
1 cup (packed) dark brown sugar
1 egg
1 teaspoon vanilla extract
2½ cups all-purpose flour
½ teaspoon baking soda
½ teaspoon salt
½ cup chopped pecans

1. In a medium-size bowl, cream the butter and sugar together until light and fluffy. Beat in the egg and vanilla.

2. Combine the flour, baking soda and salt and sift into the butter mixture. Blend together thoroughly. Stir in the pecans.

3. Shape the dough into a roll 2 inches in diameter. Wrap tightly in plastic wrap and refrigerate overnight or for up to 1 week.

4. Preheat the oven to 350°. Using a sharp thin knife, cut the dough into ¼-inch slices and place on ungreased cookie sheets. Bake in the middle of the oven for about 15 minutes, or until lightly browned and set. Transfer to wire racks and let cool.

—*Joanna Pruess*

POGACHEL

These Hungarian cookies, plain as biscuits and not overly sweet, are especially good for dunking.

MAKES ABOUT 32
1 stick (4 ounces) unsalted butter,
   softened
¾ cup sugar
1 egg
2 tablespoons sour cream
2 cups all-purpose flour
2 teaspoons baking powder
½ teaspoon salt

1. Preheat the oven to 350°. In a medium bowl, cream the butter and sugar together until fluffy and light in color. Beat in the egg and the sour cream.

2. Combine the flour, baking powder and salt. Sift these dry ingredients over the butter mixture. Using your hands, knead the mixture to make a smooth dough.

3. Working on a lightly floured surface, carefully roll out the soft dough to an even thickness of slightly more than ¼ inch. Using a round cookie cutter about 2¼ inches in diameter, dipped in flour, cut out the cookies. Carefully transfer to a lightly floured cookie sheet using a spatula dipped in flour. Gather the scraps, reroll them and continue. Prick the center of each cookie in two places with a fork. Bake in the middle of the preheated oven for 18 to 20 minutes or until lightly browned around the edges. Transfer to wire racks to cool.

—*Joanna Pruess*

Frozen Gin and Tonic (p. 212).

Celestial Lemon Roll (p. 173).

At left, top to bottom: Cream Cake with Honey Buttercream (p. 175) and Creamy Raspberry Swirl Cheesecake (p. 206). Above, Sweet Bean Crisps (p. 180).

Vanilla Lover's Vanilla Ice Cream (p. 208) with a raspberry puree.

Preserved Ginger Ice Cream (p. 210) with fresh fruit.

PIES, CAKES & COOKIES

TULIP CUPS

Tulip batter is simple to make, but expect a few misshapen cups before you have 12 perfect tulips. Any remaining cookies may be left flat or rolled into cigar shapes and served another time. Tulips can be stored for a day or two in an airtight tin. They lose their crispness on a humid day.

MAKES ABOUT 12
⅔ *cup sugar*
½ *cup all-purpose flour*
1 whole egg
2 egg whites
½ *teaspoon vanilla extract*
4 tablespoons unsalted butter, melted

1. In a medium bowl, place the sugar, flour, whole egg, egg whites and vanilla. Beat with a wooden spoon until well mixed. Stir in the butter and 1 tablespoon of water; the batter will be thin. (**The recipe can be made to this point 1 day ahead.** Refrigerate, tightly covered.) Stir before using and add up to 1 tablespoon additional water, if necessary, to restore the batter's consistency.

2. Preheat the oven to 425°. Butter a large heavy cookie sheet. Using a tablespoon measure, drop 4 separate tablespoons of the batter onto the sheet, allowing plenty of room for each one to spread. Using the back of a spoon, spread the batter into 4-inch circles, leaving about 1 inch in between.

3. Bake in the lower third of the oven until the cookies have a golden-brown border about 1 inch wide, 6 to 8 minutes. Meanwhile, cut four 4-inch-square pieces of aluminum foil and set 4 narrow glass jars (such as 2-inch-diameter spice jars) bottom-side up on the work surface.

Clockwise from lower right: Gingered Brown Betty (p. 195), Applesauce Spice Bars (p. 177) and Cider Apple Turnovers (p. 169) ready to be baked.

4. Remove the cookies from the oven. Working quickly, scrape a cookie from the sheet with a wide metal spatula and invert it over the spice jar. Cover with a square of foil to protect your hands and mold the cookie into a tulip shape. Repeat with the remaining cookies. If they should harden on the sheet, return to the oven for 30 seconds to restore pliability. Remove the shaped tulip cups from their molds.

5. Scrape the cookie sheet clean and repeat Steps 2 through 4.
—*Diana Sturgis*

SWEETHEART COOKIES

MAKES ABOUT 2 DOZEN
1½ *sticks (6 ounces) unsalted butter, softened*
½ *cup sugar*
1 egg yolk
½ *teaspoon freshly grated lemon zest*
1½ *cups all-purpose flour*
¼ *teaspoon salt*
About 2 tablespoons raspberry jam

1. In a medium bowl, cream the butter and sugar until fluffy and light. Beat in the egg yolk and lemon zest.

2. Combine the flour and salt and sift into the butter mixture. Stir until well blended. Cover and refrigerate the dough until firm, 2 to 3 hours.

3. Preheat the oven to 350°. Shape the dough into balls 1¼ inches in diameter and place them on ungreased cookie sheets. With your fingertip or the end of a wooden spoon, make a small depression in the center of each cookie. Fill each hollow with ⅛ to ¼ teaspoon raspberry jam.

4. Bake in the middle of the oven for 15 minutes, or until the cookies are lightly browned around the edges. Transfer to wire racks and let cool.
—*Joanna Pruess*

BUTTER WALNUT CRESCENTS

MAKES ABOUT 2½ DOZEN
1 stick (4 ounces) unsalted butter, softened
½ *cup confectioners' sugar*
1 teaspoon vanilla extract
½ *cup finely ground walnuts*
1 cup all-purpose flour
½ *teaspoon salt*
Confectioners' sugar, for dusting

1. Preheat the oven to 350°. In a medium bowl, cream the butter until light and fluffy. Stir in ½ cup confectioners' sugar. Add the vanilla extract and ground walnuts and mix well.

2. Combine the flour and salt and sift over the butter mixture. Stir until smooth.

3. Shape a rounded teaspoon of dough into a ball 1 inch in diameter. Roll each ball between your hands to shape it into an elongated cylinder; pinch the ends to taper. Form into crescents and place on a lightly floured cookie sheet.

4. Bake the cookies in the middle of the oven for about 13 minutes, or until the edges are browned. Transfer to wire racks and let cool to room temperature. Dust with additional confectioners' sugar.

—*Joanna Pruess*

DESSERTS

APRICOT SUZETTES

MAKES ABOUT 20 CREPES

1 cup all-purpose flour
2 tablespoons sugar
1¾ cups milk
1 teaspoon almond extract
4 eggs, lightly beaten
6 tablespoons unsalted butter, melted
½ pound dried apricots (about 1 cup)
1 cup orange juice
1 cup apricot brandy
¼ cup safflower oil
½ cup apricot jam
½ pound cream cheese, softened
¾ cup finely chopped hazelnuts
Whipped cream (optional)

1. In a large bowl, sift together the flour and sugar. Add the milk and almond extract and whisk until smooth. Stir in the eggs and 2 tablespoons of the melted butter. (The batter should be the consistency of heavy cream. If it is too thick, add a little water or club soda.) Cover and set aside for at least 1 hour.

2. Meanwhile, in a small saucepan, combine the dried apricots and orange juice. Bring to a boil over moderate heat. Reduce the heat and simmer until soft, about 20 minutes. Drain the apricots and place in a bowl. Add the apricot brandy, cover and set aside at room temperature for 45 minutes.

3. Place an 8-inch crêpe pan over moderately high heat. Brush with a little of the safflower oil. When the oil just begins to smoke, pour 2 tablespoons of the crêpe batter into the center of the pan and swirl to cover the bottom evenly. Cook until the bottom of the crêpe is slightly golden, about 20 seconds. Turn the crêpe over and cook until spotted, 6 to 8 seconds. Slide the crêpe onto a plate and repeat until the batter is used up, stacking the finished crêpes as you go.

4. Drain the apricots, reserving the soaking liquid, and chop coarsely.

5. In a heavy medium saucepan, melt the jam over low heat. Add the apricots and the reserved liquid; simmer until the alcohol taste is gone and the liquid is syrupy, about 5 minutes.

6. Preheat the oven to 375°. Spread 1 tablespoon of the apricot mixture over the lower half of 1 crêpe. Dot with 2 to 3 teaspoons of the cream cheese. Roll up tightly. Place the rolled crêpe in a heatproof serving dish. Repeat with the remaining crêpes and filling.

7. Pour the remaining 4 tablespoons melted butter over the crêpes and sprinkle with chopped nuts. Bake for 10 minutes, or until the jam starts bubbling at the edges. Serve warm, with whipped cream if desired.

—W. Peter Prestcott

SWEET RICE WITH RASPBERRIES AND CREAM

This East-West hybrid shows off the special properties of sticky rice—its gumdroplike texture and moldability. The simple flavors do not hide the delicacy of the rice.

4 SERVINGS

1 cup sweet (glutinous, sticky) rice*
¼ cup plus 2 tablespoons honey
¼ cup boiling water
Pinch of salt
3 tablespoons framboise (raspberry eau-de-vie)
½ pint (1 cup) raspberries
½ cup heavy cream
*Available at Oriental markets

1. Pour the rice into a sieve set in a bowl of cold water. Swish the grains together vigorously to rub off the starch. Drain the water and repeat the process until the water runs clear. Pour the rice into a quart measure and add fresh cold water to cover by several inches. Soak until the rice almost doubles in volume, about 2 hours. Drain well.

2. Pour the rice onto a plate set in a steamer. Cover and steam the rice, tossing every 10 minutes, until tender but not at all mushy, 40 to 60 minutes.

3. In a small bowl, combine ¼ cup of the honey, the boiling water and salt. Tossing the rice, gradually add half of this liquid. Re-cover and steam 10 minutes longer. Sprinkle in the remainder of the honey mixture, tossing. Steam 5 minutes longer and toss; steam 5 minutes more. Remove from the heat and toss the rice with 2 tablespoons of the framboise. Cover with a kitchen towel and let stand for 5 minutes; then toss gently until lukewarm.

4. Very lightly oil four ¾-cup custard cups. Using wet hands and dividing the rice evenly among the dishes, firmly press a little more than half into them to make nestlike shapes. Fill the depressions tightly with half the raspberries. Top each with a scant teaspoon of the honey. With wet hands, cover with the remaining rice. Press the rice and smooth the tops. Cover the cups with foil. (The recipe can be prepared to this point up to 12 hours ahead.)

5. Just before serving, set the covered cups in the steamer and steam until heated through, about 10 minutes. Meanwhile, combine the remaining berries with the remaining tablespoon each of framboise and honey.

6. Unmold the rice desserts onto individual plates. Pour about 2 tablespoons of the heavy cream around each, then scatter the berries over the cream. Serve at once.

—Elizabeth Schneider

DESSERTS

APPLE BREAD PUDDING

In this innovative bread pudding, apple juice concentrate and apple jelly replace some of the liquid in the custard, making a wonderfully light but intensely flavorful dessert. With sautéed apples and vanilla ice cream on top, this is the dish you wish your grandmother had made.

6 TO 8 SERVINGS

5 tablespoons unsalted butter, at
  room temperature
8 thin slices of stale, firm-textured
  white bread
6 eggs
¼ cup granulated sugar
½ teaspoon cinnamon
1 cup heavy cream
1 can (6 ounces) frozen unsweetened
  apple juice concentrate, defrosted
½ cup apple jelly
4 Golden Delicious apples
2 teaspoons confectioners' sugar
1 pint vanilla ice cream (optional)

1. Butter one side of the bread slices with 2 tablespoons of the butter. Cut each slice into quarters. Lightly butter a 6-cup baking dish with 1 tablespoon of butter. Lay the bread evenly in the dish, overlapping the slices.

2. In a large bowl, whisk together the eggs, granulated sugar and cinnamon until well blended.

3. In a medium saucepan, combine the cream, apple juice and apple jelly. Bring to a simmer over moderate heat. Gradually whisk the liquid into the eggs in a thin stream. Pour the custard over the bread and let stand, pushing the slices down once or twice, until the bread is saturated, about 15 minutes. (**The recipe can be prepared to this point up to 4 hours ahead**.)

4. Preheat the oven to 325°. Place the baking dish in a roasting pan and add enough warm water to reach halfway up the sides of the dish. Bake in the center of the oven for 45 to 50 minutes, until the custard is set.

5. Meanwhile, quarter, core and peel the apples. Cut each quarter into two wedges. In a large skillet, melt the remaining 2 tablespoons butter. Add the apples and sauté over moderately high heat, tossing occasionally, until browned, about 25 minutes.

6. Preheat the broiler. Broil the pudding about 4 inches from the heat until the top is browned, 1 to 2 minutes. Dust with 1 teaspoon of the confectioners' sugar, mound the sautéed apples on top and sprinkle with the remaining 1 teaspoon confectioners' sugar. Serve warm or at room temperature, with a scoop of vanilla ice cream.

—Diana Sturgis

BRIOCHE BREAD PUDDING

6 SERVINGS

¼ cup currants
¼ cup orange liqueur, such as Grand
  Marnier
3 tablespoons unsalted butter,
  softened
8 ounces brioche or challah,
  preferably stale, cut into ½-inch
  slices
2½ cups milk
1 vanilla bean
2 whole eggs
3 egg yolks
1 cup sugar
Heavy cream (optional)

1. In a small bowl, combine the currants and orange liqueur. Let stand for 30 minutes.

2. Preheat the oven to 350°. Butter both sides of each slice of brioche. Place in the preheated oven and bake,

turning once, until lightly toasted, about 5 minutes; set aside. Leave the oven on.

3. Butter a shallow, 8-inch square baking dish. Overlap the slices of brioche in the dish. Drain the currants, reserving the orange liqueur, and sprinkle them over the brioche.

4. In a medium saucepan, bring the milk with the vanilla bean to a simmer over moderate heat. Remove from the heat and add the reserved liqueur.

5. In a large bowl, beat the whole eggs and egg yolks with the sugar until thickened and light colored.

6. Remove the vanilla bean from the milk and gradually pour into the egg-sugar mixture, stirring constantly. Pour over the brioche.

7. Place the baking dish in a roasting pan and add enough warm water to reach halfway up the sides of the dish. Bake in the center of the oven for 30 to 35 minutes, or until the custard is set. Remove from the oven and let cool to room temperature before serving. (**The recipe can be prepared ahead to this point.** Refrigerate overnight, covered; the flavors will improve.) Let return to room temperature and serve with a pitcher of heavy cream if desired.

—John Robert Massie

GOOD OLD-FASHIONED
BREAD PUDDING

6 SERVINGS

⅓ cup raisins
12 slices of stale French, Italian or
  other firm-textured white bread, cut
  ½-inch thick (6 ounces)
2 to 3 tablespoons unsalted butter,
  softened
3 whole eggs
2 egg yolks
½ cup sugar

193

½ teaspoon freshly grated nutmeg
1 cup heavy cream
1¼ cups milk
Apricot Sauce (p. 232) or maple syrup

1. Lightly butter a shallow 6- to 8-cup baking dish. Sprinkle half of the raisins over the bottom. Spread the bread with the butter and arrange in the dish, overlapping as necessary. Scatter the remaining raisins on top.

2. In a large bowl, whisk together the whole eggs, egg yolks, sugar and nutmeg until well blended.

3. In a medium saucepan, combine the cream and milk and bring to a simmer. Gradually whisk the hot liquid into the eggs in a thin stream. Pour the custard over the bread and let stand until the bread is saturated, about 15 minutes. **(The recipe can be prepared to this point up to 4 hours ahead.)**

4. Meanwhile, preheat the oven to 350°. Place the baking dish in a roasting pan and add enough warm water to reach halfway up the sides of the dish. Bake in the center of the oven for 30 to 35 minutes, or until the custard is set. Serve warm or at room temperature with apricot sauce or maple syrup.

—*Diana Sturgis*

CHOCOLATE BREAD PUDDING

Quick, easy and foolproof, this rich pudding has a chocolate lover's bitter edge, which is nicely set off by the velvety custard sauce. Neither heavy nor sweet, the pudding resembles a chocolate mousse cake when chilled.

12 SERVINGS
⅔ cup plus 1 tablespoon sugar
1 cup heavy cream
8 ounces semisweet chocolate, coarsely chopped
5 eggs, separated

1 stick (4 ounces) unsalted butter, cut into pieces
1 tablespoon vanilla extract
2 cups fresh bread crumbs, made from about 5 slices of firm-textured white bread
Custard Sauce (p. 233) or lightly sweetened whipped cream
12 strawberries and 12 sprigs of mint, for garnish

1. Preheat the oven to 350°. Butter an 8-inch square baking pan or 8-by-3-inch soufflé dish or cake pan and dust with 1 tablespoon of the sugar.

2. In a medium saucepan, bring the cream to a simmer. Meanwhile, place the chocolate in the food processor and chop finely, 15 to 20 seconds.

3. With the machine on, pour in the hot cream. As soon as the mixture is smooth, add ⅓ cup of the sugar and the egg yolks, 1 at a time. Add the butter and vanilla. Process just until smooth.

4. In a large bowl, combine the bread crumbs and the chocolate mixture. Stir until well blended.

5. Beat the egg whites until soft peaks form. Gradually beat in the remaining ⅓ cup sugar and continue to beat until the whites are glossy and stand in stiff peaks.

6. Stir one-third of the egg whites into the chocolate mixture to lighten it. Fold in the remaining whites until no white streaks remain. Turn into the prepared baking pan.

7. Place the baking pan in a roasting pan and add enough warm water to reach halfway up the sides of the baking pan. Bake in the center of the oven for 45 to 50 minutes, or until the pudding is set and a cake tester plunged into the center emerges with only a few crumbs clinging to it. Re-

move and let cool on a rack for 10 minutes, then invert onto a serving platter. Serve warm, with custard sauce. Garnish with strawberries and mint sprigs.

—*Diana Sturgis*

APPLE PANDOWDY

This homey apple dessert tastes even better when topped with ice cream or whipped cream.

8 SERVINGS
3 pounds tart cooking apples, such as Granny Smith or Stayman—peeled, cored and sliced into ½-inch wedges
1 tablespoon fresh lemon juice
1 teaspoon freshly grated lemon zest
½ cup (packed) light brown sugar
2 teaspoons cinnamon
⅛ teaspoon mace
6½ tablespoons unsalted butter, chilled
2 cups all-purpose flour
3 tablespoons granulated sugar
1 tablespoon baking powder
¾ cup plus 1 tablespoon heavy cream

1. In a large bowl, toss together the apples, lemon juice, lemon zest, brown sugar, cinnamon and mace.

2. Lightly butter a 7- to 8-cup deep dish pie pan. Spoon the apples into the dish and dot with 1½ tablespoons of the butter.

3. Sift together the flour, granulated sugar and baking powder. Cut the remaining 5 tablespoons butter into small bits and cut into the flour until the mixture resembles coarse meal.

4. Add ¾ cup of the cream and quickly incorporate it into the butter-flour mixture. Knead the dough lightly until smooth, about 45 seconds.

5. Preheat the oven to 425°. On a lightly floured surface, roll out the

dough ¼ inch thick. Trim to a circle about ½ inch larger than the diameter of the pie pan and cut a small steam vent in the center. Carefully place the crust over the apples in the pie dish. (Do not press the dough into the edges of the pan.) Collect the scraps of dough, roll them out to a ⅛-inch thickness and cut out decorations. Brush these lightly with water and attach them to the crust. Brush the top of the pandowdy with the remaining 1 tablespoon cream.

6. Bake the pandowdy for 10 minutes. Reduce the oven temperature to 350° and continue baking, 35 to 45 minutes, until the crust is golden brown and the filling bubbly. To serve, cut a piece of the crust, place it upside down in a bowl and top with apples and juice.

—*Dorie Greenspan*

GINGERED BROWN BETTY

Keep in mind that this must be refrigerated overnight before baking.

6 SERVINGS
5 cups coarsely cubed brioche, challah or other rich egg bread, crusts removed (1-pound loaf)
1 stick (4 ounces) plus 2 tablespoons unsalted butter, melted
⅓ cup sugar
2 teaspoons ground ginger
1½ pounds baking apples, such as Cortland—peeled, cored and thinly sliced
Crème fraîche, whipped cream or vanilla ice cream, as accompaniment

1. Generously butter a 6-cup charlotte mold or soufflé dish. Line the bottom of the mold with a circle of waxed paper. Butter well.

2. Place the bread cubes in a large bowl and drizzle with the melted butter while tossing to moisten.

3. In another large bowl, combine the sugar and ginger. Add the apple slices and toss to coat evenly.

4. Place a quarter of the bread cubes in the bottom of the mold so that they cover the base in an even layer. Distribute a third of the apple slices over the bread. Repeat twice more, ending with a layer of bread. Cover with aluminum foil, fit a plate or piece of cardboard cut to size inside the mold and weight with a 2-pound can. Refrigerate, weighted, overnight.

5. Preheat the oven to 375°. Remove the weights and the plate or cardboard from the dessert and bake, still wrapped in foil, for 25 minutes. Remove the foil and bake until the top is nicely browned, about 30 minutes.

6. Let stand at room temperature for 5 minutes, then loosen the sides with a knife and invert onto a large plate. Peel off the waxed paper and serve warm with cream or ice cream.

—*Dorie Greenspan*

MAPLE APPLE CRISP

I like this dessert warm, with a big scoop of vanilla ice cream.

6 SERVINGS
3 pounds tart, firm apples such as Granny Smith—peeled, cored and sliced into ½-inch wedges
1 tablespoon fresh lemon juice
¼ cup maple syrup
½ cup walnuts
½ cup all-purpose flour
½ cup whole wheat flour
¾ cup (packed) light brown sugar
1 tablespoon cinnamon
1½ sticks (6 ounces) unsalted butter, chilled and cut into 12 pieces

1. Preheat the oven to 375°. Lightly butter an 8-inch square baking pan. In a large bowl, toss together the apples, lemon juice and maple syrup.

2. In a food processor or blender, combine the walnuts, all-purpose flour, whole wheat flour, brown sugar and cinnamon. Turn the machine on and off several times until the nuts are chopped and the ingredients are well mixed. Add the butter and turn the machine on and off until the mixture is crumbly, about 10 seconds.

3. Place 1 cup of the crumb mixture in the bottom of the baking pan and press it into an even layer. Bake for 10 minutes. Remove from the oven and arrange the apple slices on top of the baked crust, adding any liquid from the bowl. Sprinkle the remaining crumb mixture over the apples.

4. Bake the crisp 35 to 45 minutes, until the top is browned and the apples are bubbly and tender.

—*Dorie Greenspan*

CHESTNUT WAFFLES WITH CHESTNUT CREAM

MAKES ABOUT EIGHT 4-INCH WAFFLES
2 eggs, lightly beaten
5 tablespoons unsalted butter, melted and cooled to tepid
¾ cup milk
1½ cups chestnut flour* (see Note)
1 tablespoon sugar
1 tablespoon baking powder
Pinch of salt
1 cup heavy cream
1½ tablespoons sweetened chestnut puree*
*Available at specialty food stores

1. In a medium bowl, combine the eggs, melted butter and milk. Stir in

195

the chestnut flour, sugar, baking powder and salt.

2. In a large bowl, beat the cream until soft peaks form. Beat in the chestnut puree until blended. Cover and refrigerate until serving time.

3. Preheat a waffle iron. Pour enough batter into the waffle iron to fill it, close and cook until the waffles are well browned and crisp, 5 to 6 minutes. Repeat with the remaining batter. Serve the waffles with a dollop of the chestnut cream on top.

NOTE: You can buy pre-ground chestnut flour or you can make it yourself by grinding dried chestnuts (also available at specialty food stores) to a powder in a spice grinder.

—John Robert Massie

BANANA-PECAN WAFFLE ICE CREAM SUNDAE WITH PINEAPPLE SAUCE

---

10 TO 12 SERVINGS
½ cup all-purpose flour
¼ teaspoon cinnamon
Pinch of freshly grated nutmeg
¾ teaspoon baking powder
¼ teaspoon baking soda
Pinch of salt
1 teaspoon sugar
1 egg, separated
¼ cup sour cream
¼ cup plus 2 tablespoons milk
3 tablespoons plus 2 teaspoons
* unsalted butter, melted and cooled*
½ ripe banana, mashed
6 tablespoons chopped toasted pecans
½ gallon vanilla ice cream
Chunky Pineapple Sauce (p. 232)

1. In a medium bowl, sift together the flour, cinnamon, nutmeg, baking powder, baking soda, salt and sugar.

2. In another medium bowl, beat together the egg yolk, sour cream, milk, butter and banana. Stir in the pecans and the sifted dry ingredients and blend well.

3. Beat the egg white until stiff but not dry. Fold into the banana mixture until no white streaks remain.

4. Bake the batter in a preheated waffle iron according to the manufacturer's instructions. To serve, top each waffle with a scoop of ice cream and a large spoonful of the chunky pineapple sauce.

—Margaret Fox, Cafe Beaujolais, Mendocino, California

HAZELNUT SUCCES

This extremely elegant dessert can be made in stages. Once assembled, it keeps well in the refrigerator for up to 24 hours before serving.

F&W BEVERAGE SUGGESTION Vouvray, such as Philippe Chase, or a late-harvest California Riesling, such as Joseph Phelps

12 TO 16 SERVINGS
1 cup plus 2 tablespoons (5 ounces)
* lightly toasted and skinned*
* hazelnuts*
1 cup confectioners' sugar
6 egg whites, at room temperature
Pinch of cream of tartar
1 cup granulated sugar
Hazelnut Praline Buttercream, at
* room temperature (recipe follows)*
⅔ cup Powdered Hazelnut Praline
* (recipe follows)*
12 hazelnuts with skins on, for
* garnish*

1. Preheat the oven to 250°. Line 2 large cookie sheets with parchment paper and trace a 10-inch circle onto each piece of parchment.

2. Finely grate the toasted hazelnuts (a rotary nut grater works best) into a bowl. Sift in ¾ cup of the confectioners' sugar and toss to mix.

3. In a large mixer bowl, beat the egg whites and cream of tartar on low speed until foamy, about 2 minutes. Increase the speed to high and beat until the whites nearly double in volume and stiff peaks form. Gradually beat in the granulated sugar, 1 tablespoon at a time. Beat until the whites are dense and glossy and form stiff peaks.

4. With a large rubber spatula, lightly fold in the nut mixture until no white streaks remain.

5. Use a tiny amount of the nut meringue to anchor the corners of the parchment to the baking sheets. Spoon half of the meringue onto one of the circles and, with a thin metal spatula, spread into an even layer to fill the circle. Form a second circle with the remaining meringue on the other baking sheet.

6. Bake the nut meringues in the upper and lower thirds of the oven, switching positions once, until lightly browned and crisp throughout when tapped, 1 to 1½ hours. The amount of time it takes to dry out will depend on the humidity of the day. Let cool to room temperature. (**The recipe can be prepared to this point up to 2 days ahead.** Wrap the meringue layers, with the parchment still attached to the bottom, for stability, in a large sheet of foil to seal.)

7. To assemble the dessert, peel off the parchment paper from the meringue layers. Set one layer on a flat surface and spread evenly with 2 cups of the hazelnut praline buttercream. Place the second layer, flat-side up, on top of the buttercream and press gently. With a metal spatula, spread the remaining buttercream evenly on the top and sides of the cake.

8. To decorate the dessert, press the powdered hazelnut praline around the sides of the cake and sift the remaining ¼ cup confectioners' sugar evenly over the top. Garnish with the whole hazelnuts. Refrigerate uncovered for at least 1 hour, or up to 24 hours to firm up. Serve chilled.

—*Diana Sturgis*

HAZELNUT PRALINE BUTTERCREAM

MAKES ABOUT 3⅔ CUPS
¾ cup sugar
5 egg yolks
1 whole egg
3 sticks (12 ounces) unsalted butter, softened and lightly beaten
1⅔ cups Powdered Hazelnut Praline (recipe follows)

1. In a small heavy saucepan, combine the sugar with ½ cup of water. Bring to a boil over moderately high heat, stirring to dissolve the sugar. Boil without stirring until the syrup reaches the soft-ball stage, 244° on a candy thermometer, about 6 minutes.

2. Meanwhile, in a mixer bowl, beat the egg yolks and whole egg on high speed until pale, fluffy and quadrupled in volume, about 5 minutes.

3. Gradually beat the boiling syrup into the eggs in a thin steady stream. Beat until the mixture cools to room temperature, 6 to 8 minutes.

4. Gradually, beat in the butter, 4 tablespoons at a time, and continue to beat until the buttercream is fluffy.

5. Fold in the powdered hazelnut praline. Use at once or cover and refrigerate overnight. Remove from the refrigerator at least 1 hour before using, to return to room temperature.

—*Diana Sturgis*

POWDERED HAZELNUT PRALINE

MAKES ABOUT 2⅓ CUPS
1 cup plus 2 tablespoons (5 ounces) lightly toasted and skinned hazelnuts
1¼ cups granulated sugar

1. Lightly oil a baking sheet and place the nuts in a single layer in the middle of the tray.

2. In a heavy medium saucepan, place the sugar and ½ cup of water. Bring to a boil over moderately high heat, stirring to dissolve the sugar. Boil without stirring until the sugar turns golden, about 10 minutes.

3. Drizzle the boiling caramel over the nuts and set aside until hard and cool, about 20 minutes.

4. Break the nuts and caramel into chunks by hitting the bottom of the pan. Grind to a powder in a food processor, about 20 seconds. Use at once or store in an airtight container for up to 3 weeks.

—*Diana Sturgis*

ICE CREAM PUFFS WITH CHOCOLATE SAUCE

This recipe doubles easily.

6 SERVINGS
4 tablespoons unsalted butter, cut up
¼ teaspoon salt
½ cup unbleached all-purpose flour
2 whole eggs
1 egg yolk beaten with 1 teaspoon water, to make a glaze
1½ pints ice cream
Quick and Easy Chocolate Sauce (p. 234) or Hot Caramel Sauce (p. 234)

1. Preheat the oven to 375°. In a heavy medium saucepan, combine the butter and salt with ½ cup of water. Bring to a boil over moderate heat.

2. Remove from the heat and immediately add the flour all at once. Stir with a wooden spoon until the mixture forms a mass. Return to low heat and cook, stirring, until the mixture cleans the pan and forms a fairly smooth ball, about 1 minute. Remove from the heat and set aside to cool slightly for 1 to 2 minutes.

3. Stir briefly to break up the mass, add one of the whole eggs and beat vigorously with a wooden spoon. When you first begin to mix, the egg and dough will look separated and stringy; continue to beat and it will become smooth and satiny. Add the second egg and beat for 1 minute to incorporate as much air as possible.

4. Spoon heaping tablespoons of the pastry into 6 equal mounds on a lightly greased cookie sheet, spacing them about 3 inches apart.

5. Lightly brush the egg yolk glaze over the dough, without allowing it to drip onto the baking sheet, as this may retard the rising.

6. Bake the puffs for 40 to 45 minutes, until golden and quite dry all over. Remove from the oven and quickly split them horizontally with a serrated knife (see Note). Transfer to a rack and let cool to room temperature, about 15 minutes. **(The recipe can be prepared ahead to this point.)**

7. Just before serving, fill the bottoms of the puffs with scoops of ice cream. Cover with the pastry tops and drizzle with warm chocolate or caramel sauce. Serve at once.

NOTE: If your oven is slow and you find any large pieces of moist dough inside the puffs when you split them, just scoop out and discard.

—*Diana Sturgis*

CAPPUCCINO ICE CREAM CAKE WITH HOT CHOCOLATE SAUCE

Serve this delicate three-tiered oatmeal cake layered with our own cappuccino ice cream (easy to make and easy to spread) and a drizzle of hot chocolate sauce. We think your guests will be thankful. Everything—cake layers, ice cream and sauce—can be made ahead. The cake can be layered with the ice cream and frozen until 10 to 15 minutes before serving time. The sauce can be set aside and reheated. If you've made the ice cream ahead of time, be sure to let it soften slightly before trying to spread it in Step 4.

8 SERVINGS
¾ cup quick-cooking oats
⅔ cup granulated sugar
1 tablespoon all-purpose flour
1 teaspoon baking powder
7 tablespoons unsalted butter, melted
1 egg, at room temperature, lightly beaten
Cappuccino Ice Cream (p. 208)
2 tablespoons confectioners' sugar
Hot Chocolate Sauce (p. 233)

1. Preheat the oven to 375°. Line 3 baking sheets with parchment paper. Draw an 8-inch circle in the center of each sheet.
2. In a bowl, combine the oats, granulated sugar, flour and baking powder. Stir in the melted butter until well blended. Stir in the lightly beaten egg.
3. Spoon about one-third of the batter onto each circle on the baking sheets and spread to cover thinly and evenly with a spatula or the back of a spoon. Bake for about 8 minutes, or until lightly browned. (You may want to form and bake these one at a time, as they must be watched carefully so that they do not burn.) Remove at once and slide the parchment with the cake onto a rack to cool. Repeat with the remaining batter. When the cakes

are cool, peel off the parchment. Chill the layers before assembling.
4. To assemble, put one cake, flat-side down, on a chilled round platter. Working quickly, spoon half the ice cream over the cake. Spread into an even layer. Cover with the second cake and the remaining ice cream. Top with the third cake, flat-side up. Wrap the cake carefully in foil and put in the freezer immediately.
5. Transfer the cake from the freezer to the refrigerator 10 to 15 minutes before serving time to let the ice cream soften. Sprinkle with the confectioners' sugar, cut into wedges and serve with hot chocolate sauce on the side.

—Arthur Gold & Robert Fizdale

GRAND MARNIER SOUFFLE

6 SERVINGS
1 tablespoon unsalted butter, melted
1 tablespoon sugar, preferably brown granulated
1 cup milk
1 teaspoon vanilla extract
¼ cup cornstarch
½ cup granulated sugar
6 egg yolks
Pinch of salt
¼ cup all-purpose flour
¼ cup Grand Marnier
2 tablespoons freshly grated orange zest
4 egg whites
Confectioners' sugar, for dusting

1. Brush a 5-cup soufflé dish with the melted butter. Dust with the 1 tablespoon sugar; discard any excess. Refrigerate until ready to use.
2. In a heavy medium saucepan, bring ¾ cup of the milk and the vanilla to a boil over moderate heat. Remove from the heat and set aside.

3. In a small bowl, blend the cornstarch and the remaining ¼ cup milk until smooth. Add ¼ cup of the granulated sugar, 2 of the egg yolks and the salt. Stir until smooth. Gradually whisk this mixture into the warm milk. Cook over moderately low heat, whisking constantly, until thick, 3 to 4 minutes. Remove from the heat and let cool, about 10 minutes.
4. Beat in the remaining 4 egg yolks, one at a time. Sift the flour over the mixture in two batches, mixing well between additions.
5. Cook the mixture over moderately low heat, stirring constantly, until smooth, about 5 minutes. Remove from the heat. Stir in the Grand Marnier and orange zest. Scrape the custard into a medium bowl and set aside to cool.
6. Preheat the oven to 400°. In a large bowl, beat the egg whites until soft peaks form. Slowly add the remaining ¼ cup granulated sugar and continue beating until firm peaks form.
7. Fold the beaten egg whites into the cooled custard. Transfer the soufflé mixture to the prepared dish and bake for 20 minutes, until puffed and browned on top.
8. Dust the top of the soufflé with confectioners' sugar. Sprinkle each serving with additional Grand Marnier if desired.

—W. Peter Prestcott

PUMPKIN AND GINGER SOUFFLE

This low-calorie soufflé uses the complex tastes of pumpkin and ginger to give the dessert a sense of richness. If you divide the soufflé into slightly more modest portions, to serve 8, the calorie count drops from 200 per serving to 155.

6 SERVINGS
2 tablespoons granulated sugar

¼ cup cornstarch
½ cup superfine sugar
1 teaspoon cinnamon
½ teaspoon ground ginger
¼ teaspoon freshly grated nutmeg
1⅓ cups milk
1 cup solid-pack canned pumpkin
    puree or 1 cup cooked, pureed
    pumpkin, butternut or acorn
    squash, well drained
3 egg yolks, lightly beaten
¼ cup finely minced preserved stem
    ginger* plus 2 tablespoons syrup
    drained from the jar
1 teaspoon freshly grated orange zest
7 egg whites
¼ teaspoon salt
Pinch of cream of tartar
1 teaspoon confectioners' sugar
*Available at Chinese markets and
    specialty food shops

1. Generously spray the bottom and sides of a 14-inch oval gratin dish with nonstick vegetable spray. Coat the dish with the granulated sugar and tap out the excess.

2. In a heavy medium saucepan, combine 3 tablespoons of the cornstarch, ¼ cup of the superfine sugar, the cinnamon, ginger and nutmeg. Whisk in the milk and pumpkin. Cook, stirring, over moderate heat until thickened and smooth, about 3 minutes.

3. Whisk a little of the hot pumpkin mixture into the beaten egg yolks. Stir the warmed yolks back into the pan and cook, stirring constantly, for 1 minute; do not boil. Remove the pan from the heat and quick-chill in a large bowl of ice and water, whisking often to prevent a skin from forming.

4. Meanwhile, set an oven rack in the middle position, place a heavy baking sheet on the rack and preheat the oven to 375°.

5. Toss the minced preserved ginger with the remaining 1 tablespoon cornstarch. As soon as the pumpkin mixture has cooled to room

temperature, remove from the ice bath and stir in the minced ginger, ginger syrup and orange zest; set aside.

6. Beat the egg whites with the salt and cream of tartar until the whites are snowy, soft and billowy. Gradually beat in the remaining ¼ cup superfine sugar, 1 tablespoon at a time, until the whites just begin to form soft peaks. Stir about 1 cup of the beaten egg whites into the pumpkin mixture to lighten it, then fold in the remaining whites until no streaks of white remain.

7. Pour the soufflé mixture into the prepared gratin dish and set it on the baking sheet in the oven. Bake for 30 to 35 minutes, or until the top is puffed and nicely browned.

8. Quickly sift the confectioners' sugar on top of the soufflé, rush it to the table and serve.

—Jean Anderson

SPICY APPLE CHIFFON WITH LEMON-RUM GLAZE

Topped with ginger-spiked apples and a tart lemon-rum glaze, this airy dessert weighs in at only 180 calories per serving.

8 SERVINGS
APPLE CHIFFON:
½ cup heavy cream, chilled
1 envelope (¼ ounce) unflavored
    gelatin
⅓ cup plus 2 tablespoons superfine
    sugar
½ teaspoon ground ginger
½ teaspoon cinnamon
Pinch of ground cloves
Pinch of freshly grated nutmeg
1 cup milk
1 jumbo egg yolk, lightly beaten
3 large Golden Delicious apples—
    peeled, cored and sliced about ½
    inch thick
¼ cup fresh lemon juice

2 pieces (1½-inch cubes) of fresh
    ginger, peeled and bruised

GLAZE AND TOPPING:
2 tablespoons superfine sugar
1 tablespoon arrowroot or cornstarch
2 tablespoons fresh lemon juice
1 tablespoon light rum
3 tablespoons fine gingersnap crumbs

1. Make the apple chiffon: In a medium bowl, whip the cream until firm peaks form. In a small bowl, soften the gelatin in ¼ cup of water, about 5 minutes.

2. In a small heavy saucepan, combine ⅓ cup of the sugar, the ginger, cinnamon, cloves and nutmeg. Blend in the milk and bring just to a simmer over moderate heat, stirring occasionally. Add the softened gelatin and stir until completely dissolved.

3. Blend a little of the hot milk mixture into the beaten egg yolk, then whisk the warmed egg yolk back into the pan. Cook over low heat, stirring, for 1 minute; do not let boil. Remove the pan from the heat and quick-chill in a large bowl of ice and water, stirring often, until syrupy and cool. Transfer the custard to a medium bowl. Beat with an electric mixer on high speed until lightened in texture, about 2 minutes. Fold in the whipped cream and pour the chiffon into 8 half-cup ramekins or custard cups. Refrigerate the ramekins while you prepare the apples.

4. In a medium saucepan, combine the apples with 3 cups of water, the lemon juice and fresh ginger. Bring to a boil over high heat, reduce the heat and simmer until just tender, about 1½ minutes. Drain the apples well, discarding the ginger. Spread the apple slices out on several thicknesses of paper towels and top with more paper towels. Let cool for 5 minutes, then remove the top layer of towels and

sprinkle the remaining 2 tablespoons sugar evenly over the apples. Let cool to room temperature.

5. Arrange the apple slices artfully on top of the chiffon filling, pressing them in lightly.

6. *Make the glaze:* In a very small heavy saucepan, combine the sugar and arrowroot, pressing out all lumps. Blend in ½ cup of cold water and cook, stirring, over moderately low heat until very thick, about 3 minutes. Remove from the heat, blend in the lemon juice, rum and just enough additional cold water, if necessary, to make the mixture the consistency of corn syrup.

7. Gently drizzle the glaze over the apples. Refrigerate the desserts for several hours until well chilled. Just before serving, sprinkle each with 1 generous teaspoon of gingersnap crumbs.

—*Jean Anderson*

RICH LEMON MOUSSE

I first tasted this delicious and simple mousse at Ray's Boathouse Restaurant in Seattle, Washington.

6 TO 8 SERVINGS
5 eggs
1 cup sugar
1 stick (4 ounces) unsalted butter, melted and cooled
1 cup fresh lemon juice (4 to 5 lemons)
2 cups heavy cream, chilled
1 tablespoon freshly grated lemon zest (from 3 lemons)
Sprigs of fresh mint, for garnish

1. In a large bowl, combine the eggs and sugar. Using an electric mixer, beat at medium speed until pale, about 5 minutes. Beat in the melted butter in a thin stream. Add the lemon juice.

2. Pour the egg mixture into the top of a double boiler. Cook over moderate heat, whisking constantly, until the mixture has thickened, about 15 minutes.

3. Transfer the custard to a medium bowl and refrigerate for at least 1 hour, stirring once or twice.

4. In a large bowl, beat the heavy cream until it forms soft peaks. Fold the cream into the chilled custard. Fold in the lemon zest. Serve the mousse in chilled stemmed glasses, garnished with sprigs of mint.

—*W. Peter Prestcott*

PUMPKIN MOUSSE TULIPS

12 SERVINGS
3 eggs, separated
½ cup plus 1 tablespoon sugar
½ cup milk
1 envelope (¼ ounce) unflavored gelatin
1 tablespoon all-purpose flour
1½ teaspoons freshly grated orange zest
½ cup fresh orange juice
1 cup canned solid-pack pumpkin
½ teaspoon allspice
½ cup heavy cream
12 Tulip Cups (p. 189)
½ cup crème fraîche
12 small twists of orange zest

1. In a medium saucepan, place the egg yolks, ½ cup of the sugar, the milk, gelatin, flour and orange zest. Stir well to combine and cook, stirring, over moderate heat until the mixture comes to a boil.

2. Remove from the heat and stir in the orange juice, pumpkin and allspice. Strain into a large bowl and gradually whisk in the heavy cream.

3. In another large bowl, beat the egg whites until soft peaks form. Add the remaining 1 tablespoon sugar and beat until stiff. Stir one-fourth of the egg whites into the pumpkin mixture to lighten it. Fold in the remaining egg whites until no white streaks remain. Refrigerate the mousse, covered, until ready to assemble.

4. To serve, scoop about ¼ cup of the pumpkin mousse into each tulip cup and top with about 2 teaspoons of crème fraîche and a tiny twist of orange zest. Serve within 1 hour of filling to prevent the tulip cups from softening.

—*Diana Sturgis*

DELICATE COCONUT TULIPES WITH PAPAYA SORBET

These cookies make perfect containers for our papaya sorbet, but you can also fill them with ice cream or mousse.

MAKES ABOUT 15
1 cup grated fresh coconut or grated unsweetened coconut
⅔ cup sugar
⅓ cup all-purpose flour
1 whole egg, lightly beaten
2 egg whites
4 tablespoons unsalted butter, melted
Fresh Papaya Sorbet (p. 213)

1. Preheat the oven to 325°. In a medium bowl, combine the coconut, sugar and flour. Add the whole egg and egg whites and beat until well blended. Stir in the butter and 1 tablespoon of water.

2. Working in batches of 3 or 4 cookies, drop scant tablespoonfuls of batter, about 4 inches apart, onto a buttered cookie sheet. Using the back of a spoon, spread the batter into even circles, 3 inches in diameter. Bake in the lower third of the oven for

6 to 8 minutes, until the edges of the cookies are golden brown.

3. Meanwhile, cut several pieces of foil into 4-inch squares and set out several narrow glass jars (such as store-bought spice jars or other cylindrical containers 1½ to 2 inches in diameter).

4. Remove the cookies from the oven. Working quickly, slide a wide metal spatula under a cookie, pushing to separate from the sheet without tearing; the cookie will be soft. Invert the cookie and drape it over a jar. Place a square of foil on top to protect your fingers and mold the cookie around the jar into a tulip shape. Repeat with the remaining cookies. (If the cookies harden before they are molded, reheat them in the oven for about 30 seconds.) Repeat until all the batter is used.

5. To serve, scoop about ¼ cup fresh papaya sorbet into each tulip cup and serve at once.

—*Lisa Brainerd*

PASSION FRUIT-FILLED BEIGNETS

These bite-size beignets are dusted with confectioners' sugar and filled with a tart passion-fruit curd. Serve them warm for breakfast or as a mid-afternoon snack.

MAKES ABOUT 16 SMALL BEIGNETS
1½ teaspoons active dry yeast
¼ cup warm water (105° to 115°)
¼ cup warm milk (105° to 115°)
2 tablespoons honey
½ teaspoon salt
1 egg
1½ tablespoons unsalted butter, melted and cooled

½ teaspoon vanilla extract
1½ to 1¾ cups all-purpose flour
1½ quarts vegetable oil, for deep-frying
Passion Fruit Curd (recipe follows)
Confectioners' sugar, for dusting

1. In a large bowl, sprinkle the yeast over the water; set aside for 5 minutes.

2. Stir in the milk, honey, salt, egg, butter and vanilla. Stir in 1 cup of the flour and when fully incorporated, add enough of the remaining flour, ½ cup at a time, until the dough becomes stiff and difficult to mix.

3. Turn the dough out onto a lightly floured surface and knead in enough of the remaining flour to make the dough firm but still slightly sticky. Continue to knead for 3 to 4 minutes. Place the dough in a large lightly greased bowl, turn to coat with oil and cover with a damp towel. Set aside in a warm draft-free place until doubled in size, about 1½ hours.

4. Punch the dough down and divide in half. Using your hands, roll each piece of dough into a long cylinder 1 inch in diameter. Cut the cylinder into 1-inch pieces and roll each into a ball. Place 2 inches apart on a lightly floured baking sheet. Cover with a damp cloth and let rise in a warm, draft-free place until almost doubled in size, about 45 minutes.

5. Meanwhile, in a deep-fat fryer or deep wide saucepan, heat the oil to 350°. Fry the beignets in batches without crowding. Cook until golden brown on one side, about 2 minutes. Using a slotted spoon, turn the beignets and cook until golden brown, about 2 minutes longer. Transfer to a plate lined with paper towels to drain and cool slightly, 5 to 10 minutes.

6. Using a metal skewer or the tine of a fork, pierce a deep hole in the side of each beignet. Spoon the passion fruit curd into a pastry bag fitted

with a small plain tip. Place the tip of the pastry tube in the hole of each beignet and fill with fruit curd. Dust the beignets with some confectioners' sugar and serve them warm or at room temperature.

—*Marcia Kiesel*

PASSION FRUIT CURD

This slightly tart fruit curd can be used to fill doughnuts or small tarts or as a spread with scones or muffins.

MAKES ⅔ TO ¾ CUP
4 to 5 passion fruits
2 egg yolks
⅓ cup sugar
2 tablespoons unsalted butter, cut into 4 pieces

1. Cut the passion fruits in half and scrape the seeds and pulp into a fine strainer set over a medium bowl. Using a wooden spoon, press the passion fruit seeds against the strainer to extract all the juice. Measure out ¼ cup of juice and reserve any excess for another use.

2. In a small heavy noncorrodible saucepan, combine the passion fruit juice, the egg yolks and the sugar. Cook over low heat, stirring constantly, until the mixture begins to thicken, about 5 minutes. Add the butter and continue to cook, stirring, without boiling, for 1 minute.

3. Remove the mixture from the heat and pass it through a strainer set over a medium bowl. Let cool to room temperature. Refrigerate, covered, until ready to use. **(The fruit curd can be made up to 1 week ahead.)**

—*Marcia Kiesel*

DESSERTS

JOHN ASH & CO.'S LEMON CUSTARD

Chef John Ash suggests serving this custard in tart shells, on pound cake, in a jelly roll or as a conserve.

MAKES ABOUT 3½ CUPS
1½ teaspoons cornstarch
1 cup fresh lemon juice
1¼ cups sugar
6 egg yolks
4 whole eggs
1½ sticks (6 ounces) unsalted butter,
*   melted and cooled to tepid*
1 teaspoon freshly grated lemon zest
½ teaspoon salt

1. In the top of a double boiler, dissolve the cornstarch in 1 tablespoon of the lemon juice. Add the sugar, egg yolks, whole eggs, butter, lemon zest, salt and the remaining lemon juice. Whisk until the ingredients are thoroughly blended.

2. Cook over simmering water, stirring frequently with a wooden spoon, until the custard is thick enough to coat back of spoon heavily, 10 to 15 minutes. Remove from the heat and let cool completely.

—John Ash, John Ash & Co.,
Santa Rosa, California

COFFEE CREME BRULEE

6 SERVINGS
2⅔ cups heavy cream
2 tablespoons plus 2 teaspoons
*   instant coffee*
8 egg yolks
½ cup plus 3 tablespoons granulated
*   sugar*
6 tablespoons light brown sugar

1. Preheat the oven to 325°. In a heavy medium saucepan, warm the cream over moderate heat until the surface begins to shimmer, about 5 minutes. Using a wooden spoon, gently stir in the coffee. Remove from the heat.

2. In a large bowl, stir the egg yolks and sugar with a wooden spoon until blended. Gradually add the hot cream and stir gently to avoid forming air bubbles. Strain the custard into a large measuring cup or pitcher. Skim off any surface bubbles.

3. Place six ¾-cup ramekins in a roasting pan. Pour the custard into the ramekins, filling them up to the rim. Place the roasting pan in the oven and pour in enough warm water to reach halfway up the sides of the ramekins. Cover loosely with foil and bake for about 1 hour, or until firm around the edges. (It may still be wobbly at the center; it will firm up as it chills.)

4. Remove the ramekins from the water bath and let cool. Cover and refrigerate until cold, at least 3 hours. **(The custards can be prepared to this point up to 2 days ahead.** If small pools of liquid develop on the surfaces, blot with a paper towel before proceeding.)

5. Preheat the broiler or a salamander. Set the ramekins on a baking sheet and evenly sieve 1 tablespoon of the brown sugar over each custard. Spread to an even layer using a spatula or a knife. Broil the custards, as close to the heat as possible, until the sugar is caramelized, 30 to 60 seconds. Alternatively, caramelize the brown sugar using a salamander. Let cool and serve immediately or refrigerate for up to 4 hours (remove the custards from the refrigerator about 20 minutes before serving).

—John Robert Massie

LE CIRQUE'S CREME BRULEE

8 SERVINGS
4 cups heavy cream
1 vanilla bean
Pinch of salt
8 egg yolks
¾ cup plus 2 tablespoons granulated
*   sugar*
8 tablespoons light brown sugar

1. Preheat the oven to 300°. In a heavy medium saucepan, combine the cream, vanilla bean and salt. Warm over moderate heat until the surface begins to shimmer, about 5 minutes.

2. In a large bowl, stir the egg yolks and sugar with a wooden spoon until blended. Pour in the hot cream and stir gently to avoid forming air bubbles. Strain the custard into a large measuring cup or pitcher and skim off any surface bubbles. (Rinse the vanilla bean and reserve for another use.)

3. Place eight ¾-cup ramekins in a roasting pan. Pour the custard into the ramekins, filling them up to the rim. Place the roasting pan in the oven and pour in enough warm water to reach halfway up the sides of the ramekins. Cover loosely with foil and bake for 1 hour and 15 minutes, or until the custard is firm around the edges. (It may still be wobbly at the center; it will firm up as it chills.)

4. Remove the ramekins from the water bath and let cool. Cover and refrigerate until cold, at least 3 hours. **(The custards can be prepared to this point up to 2 days ahead.** If small pools of liquid develop on the surfaces, blot with a paper towel before proceeding.)

5. Preheat the broiler or a salamander. Set the ramekins on a baking sheet. Sieve 1 tablespoon of brown sugar over the top of each custard in a thin layer. Using a metal spatula or a

sharp knife, spread the sugar evenly. Broil the custards as close to the heat as possible until the sugar is caramelized, 30 seconds to 2 minutes; watch carefully. Alternatively, caramelize the brown sugar using a salamander. Let cool and serve immediately or refrigerate for up to 4 hours.

—*Le Cirque, New York City*

MAPLE WALNUT CREME BRULEE

In this recipe, we have replaced the traditional broiled brown sugar topping with one that is prepared on the stove by reducing maple syrup to the hard-crack stage.

6 SERVINGS
2⅔ cups heavy cream
½ cup walnut pieces
1½ cups pure maple syrup
8 egg yolks

1. In a heavy medium saucepan, combine the cream, walnuts and ½ cup of the maple syrup. Warm the mixture over moderate heat until the surface begins to shimmer, about 5 minutes. Reduce the heat to low, cover and let the mixture infuse for 30 minutes.

2. Preheat the oven to 325°. In a large bowl, lightly beat the egg yolks with a wooden spoon. Gradually add the maple walnut cream and stir gently to combine. Strain the custard into a large measuring cup or pitcher. Skim off any surface bubbles.

3. Place six ¾-cup ramekins in a roasting pan. Pour the custard into the ramekins, filling them up to the rim. Place the roasting pan in the oven and pour in enough warm water to reach halfway up the sides of the ramekins. Cover loosely with foil and

bake for about 1 hour, or until the custard is firm around the edges. (It may still be wobbly at the center; it will firm up as it chills.)

4. Remove the ramekins from the water bath and let cool. Cover and refrigerate until cold, at least 3 hours. **(The custards can be prepared to this point up to 2 days ahead.** If small pools of liquid develop on the surfaces, blot with a paper towel before proceeding.)

5. In a heavy medium saucepan, cook the remaining 1 cup maple syrup over high heat until reduced to ½ cup, 3 to 5 minutes. Pour the syrup over the custards and quickly rotate the ramekins to spread the syrup evenly. Let cool and serve immediately or refrigerate for up to 4 hours (remove the custards from the refrigerator about 20 minutes before serving).

—*John Robert Massie*

ORANGE CREME BRULEE

6 SERVINGS
2⅔ cups heavy cream
Zest of 2 medium navel oranges
½ cup plus 3 tablespoons granulated
    sugar
8 egg yolks
6 tablespoons light brown sugar

1. Preheat the oven to 325°. In a heavy medium saucepan, combine the cream with half of the orange zest. Warm the cream over moderate heat until the surface begins to shimmer, about 5 minutes. Reduce the heat to low, cover and let the mixture infuse for 10 minutes.

2. Meanwhile, in a food processor, combine the sugar and the remaining orange zest. Process, stopping to scrape down the sides of the bowl, until the zest is minced and the sugar is pale orange, about 1 minute.

3. In a large bowl, stir the egg yolks and the orange sugar with a wooden spoon until blended. Gradually add the orange cream, stirring gently to combine. Strain the custard into a large measuring cup or pitcher. Skim off any surface bubbles.

4. Place six ¾-cup ramekins in a roasting pan. Pour the custard into the ramekins, filling them up to the rim. Place the roasting pan in the oven and pour in enough warm water to reach halfway up the sides of the ramekins. Cover loosely with foil and bake for about 1 hour, or until firm around the edges. (It may still be wobbly at the center; it will firm up as it chills.)

5. Remove the ramekins from the water bath and let cool. Cover and refrigerate until cold, at least 3 hours. **(The custards can be prepared to this point up to 2 days ahead.** If small pools of liquid develop on the surfaces, blot with a paper towel before proceeding.)

6. Preheat the broiler or a salamander. Set the ramekins on a baking sheet and evenly sieve 1 tablespoon of the brown sugar over each custard. Broil the custards, as close to the heat as possible, until the sugar is caramelized, 30 to 60 seconds. Alternatively, caramelize the brown sugar using a salamander. Let cool and serve immediately or refrigerate them for up to 4 hours (remove the custards from the refrigerator about 20 minutes before serving).

—*John Robert Massie*

203

DESSERTS

BURNT ORANGE BAVARIAN

8 SERVINGS

6 egg yolks
⅔ cup sugar
2 tablespoons finely minced orange zest
2 cups warm milk
1 tablespoon unflavored gelatin
2 tablespoons fresh orange juice
2 cups heavy cream, chilled
Lightly whipped cream and thin strips of orange zest, for garnish

1. In a medium heatproof bowl, beat the egg yolks until light and thick.

2. In a heavy medium saucepan, combine the sugar and orange zest. Cook over moderate heat until the sugar melts and turns a deep brown, about 10 minutes. Reduce the heat to low and, stirring constantly, gradually add ½ cup of the warm milk—be careful because the caramel may splatter. Stir in the remaining 1½ cups milk.

3. Slowly beat the caramel milk into the beaten egg yolks. Return the mixture to the saucepan and cook over very low heat, stirring until the custard thickens slightly, about 5 minutes. (Do not let boil.) Remove from the heat.

4. In a small bowl, combine the gelatin and orange juice and set aside for 5 minutes to soften. Add to the warm custard and stir to blend. Strain the custard into a large bowl set over ice and stir frequently until cool.

5. In a large bowl, whip the cream until soft peaks form. Fold the cream into the cooled custard and pour the mixture into a lightly buttered 8-cup glass serving bowl or soufflé dish. Refrigerate the Bavarian until firm, about 3 hours. Just before serving, garnish with whipped cream and orange zest.

—*Molly O'Neill*

COCONUT BLANCMANGE WITH BITTERSWEET CHOCOLATE SAUCE

Blancmange is a cornstarch custard pudding that was originally made with rice, almond paste and gelatin.

4 SERVINGS

1 cup plus 1 tablespoon confectioners' sugar
⅓ cup cornstarch
1¼ cups *Thin Coconut Milk (p. 232)*
1½ cups *Thick Coconut Milk (p. 232)*
Dash of almond extract
1 tablespoon heavy cream
Bittersweet Chocolate Sauce (recipe follows)
Shavings of toasted coconut, for garnish

1. In a medium bowl, sift together the sugar and cornstarch. Whisk in ½ cup of the thin coconut milk.

2. In a medium noncorrodible saucepan, warm the remaining ¾ cup thin coconut milk over moderately low heat. Stir the warmed milk into the sugar mixture and return it to the saucepan. Cook over moderately low heat, stirring constantly, until the mixture thickens, about 5 minutes. Remove from the heat and stir in the thick coconut milk.

3. Strain the coconut mixture through a fine sieve set over a medium bowl. Stir in the almond extract and heavy cream. Divide the coconut cream among 4 lightly greased ½-cup ramekins. Cover each with plastic wrap and refrigerate until set, about 2 hours. **(The blancmange will keep for up to 2 days in the refrigerator.)**

4. To unmold the blancmange, run a paring knife around the edges of each ramekin, shake gently to loosen and invert onto dessert plates.

5. Spoon 1 tablespoon of bittersweet chocolate sauce around the base of each blancmange and garnish the top with a few shavings of toasted coconut.

—*Marcia Kiesel*

BITTERSWEET CHOCOLATE SAUCE

This recipe makes only the small amount of chocolate sauce needed to accompany the blancmange. If you wish to serve it with ice cream, simply triple the recipe.

MAKES ABOUT ¼ CUP

1 tablespoon unsweetened cocoa powder
2½ teaspoons sugar
2 tablespoons heavy cream
1 tablespoon milk
½ ounce bittersweet chocolate
Dash of brandy

1. In a small bowl, combine the cocoa and sugar. Add 2 tablespoons of hot water and stir until the sugar and cocoa are dissolved.

2. In a small saucepan, warm the cream and milk over low heat, about 2 minutes.

3. Stir in the cocoa mixture and simmer over low heat until well combined, about 1 minute.

4. Add the bittersweet chocolate and stir until melted. Remove from the heat and stir in the brandy. Serve warm or at room temperature.

—*Marcia Kiesel*

CHOCOLATE SILK

Dense, dark and delicious, this creamy dessert is a lightened version—just 160 calories per serving—of a classic *pots de crème au chocolat*. If you succumb and top it with the optional whipped cream and pistachios, it's still only 200 calories per serving.

DESSERTS

t dry. With a rubber spatula, fold
he-third of the egg whites into the
ocolate mixture. Then fold in the
maining egg whites.

4. Pour the chocolate fondant into a
ghtly oiled 4-cup loaf pan. Cover
ith plastic wrap and place in the
eezer for at least 1 hour. **(The recipe
n be made to this point a day or 2
ead.)**

5. In a small bowl, stir together the
maining ¼ cup sugar and the kirsch
til the sugar is partially dissolved.
dd the blueberries, toss to coat and
acerate at room temperature for at
ast 1 hour or longer. **(The blueber-
es can be refrigerated, covered,
vernight.)**

6. Unmold the fondant by passing
knife inside the edges of the pan.
vert and shake out onto a platter;
p briefly in hot water if necessary to
nmold. Let the fondant return to
om temperature before serving; this
n take anywhere from 30 minutes to
hours, depending on how long the
essert was in the freezer.

7. To serve, cut the chocolate fon-
nt into ½-inch-thick slices. Arrange
each plate and spoon some blue-
erries with their syrup over part of
e chocolate.

—*Lydie Marshall*

LIGHT STRAWBERRY CHEESECAKE

he cheesecake should be refrigerated
r at least 6 hours (or overnight) be-
re serving, so plan accordingly.
an, too, on just 175 calories per
rving!

12 SERVINGS
tablespoon honey
tablespoons unsalted butter or
   margarine
½ cups fine graham cracker crumbs
pound low-fat cottage cheese

2 ounces (4 tablespoons) cream cheese
¼ cup half-and-half
6 tablespoons sugar
3 jumbo eggs
1½ teaspoons vanilla extract
1 tablespoon fresh lemon juice
*1 pint strawberries, sliced about ¼
   inch thick*
*¼ cup sieved low-sugar strawberry
   jam (I used Smucker's)*

1. Preheat the oven to 325°. In a
small heavy saucepan, combine the
honey and butter and stir over low
heat until uniformly liquid, about 2
minutes. In a large bowl, combine the
graham cracker crumbs with the melted honey and butter. Toss well to
mix. Lightly spray a 9-inch springform pan with nonstick vegetable
spray. Pat the crumb mixture evenly
over the bottom and halfway up the
sides of the pan. Make the edges of
the crust as smooth and as even as
possible.

2. Place the cottage cheese, cream
cheese, half-and-half, sugar, eggs, vanilla and lemon juice in a food processor; blend for 15 seconds. Scrape the
sides down with a rubber spatula,
then mix until the filling is perfectly
smooth with no lumps visible, 15 to
20 seconds longer. Pour the filling
into the prepared crust.

3. Bake the cheesecake in the middle of the oven, uncovered, for 50
minutes, or until a toothpick inserted
midway between the rim and the center of the filling comes out clean. (The
filling may quiver slightly at this point
as you nudge the pan, but it will firm
up upon cooling.) Remove the cake
from the oven and let cool on a rack
for 30 minutes. Cover with plastic
wrap and refrigerate for at least 6
hours, or overnight, to chill.

4. Before serving, arrange the

strawberry slices on top of the cake in
concentric circles, with the points of
the berries aiming toward the center.

5. In a small heavy saucepan, heat
the strawberry jam over the lowest
heat, stirring, until just melted, about
2 minutes. Dip a pastry brush into the
melted jam and brush the tops of the
strawberries lightly with the glaze.
Remove the sides of the springform
pan and serve.

—*Jean Anderson*

CREAMY RASPBERRY SWIRL CHEESECAKE

The creamy richness of basic cheesecake blends perfectly with the sweet-
tartness of raspberry jam swirled
throughout the cake.

8 TO 12 SERVINGS
½ cup graham cracker crumbs
⅓ cup seedless raspberry jam
*2 packages (8 ounces each) cream
   cheese, softened*
1 cup sugar
1 tablespoon cornstarch
3 eggs, at room temperature
2 tablespoons fresh lemon juice
1½ teaspoons vanilla extract
¼ teaspoon salt
3 cups sour cream
Fresh raspberries, for garnish

1. Preheat the oven to 350°. Wrap
the outside of an 8-by-2½-inch springform pan in a double layer of aluminum foil to prevent seepage. Grease
the pan or spray with vegetable shortening. Sprinkle the graham cracker
crumbs over the bottom of the pan
and tap to distribute evenly.

2. Heat the raspberry jam over
moderately low heat, stirring, until
melted and smooth; set aside.

3. In a large mixer bowl, at medium
speed, beat together the cream cheese
and sugar until very smooth, about 3
minutes. Beat in the cornstarch. Add

06

6 SERVINGS
6 tablespoons sugar
¼ cup sifted unsweetened cocoa
    powder
2 tablespoons sifted cornstarch
1 teaspoon unflavored gelatin
1 cup half-and-half
1 cup evaporated skim milk
⅔ cup whole milk
2 jumbo egg yolks, lightly beaten
2 teaspoons vanilla extract

OPTIONAL TOPPING:
¼ cup heavy cream, whipped
1 tablespoon coarsely chopped
    blanched pistachio nuts or 6
    candied violets

1. In a large heavy saucepan, combine the sugar, cocoa, cornstarch and gelatin, pressing out all lumps. Add the half-and-half, evaporated skim milk and whole milk; whisk vigorously to blend. Set the pan over moderately low heat and cook, stirring constantly with a wooden spoon, until the mixture just boils and is thickened and smooth, about 10 minutes.
2. Blend a little of the hot mixture into the beaten egg yolks, then stir the warmed egg yolks back into the pan. Cook over moderately low heat, stirring constantly, for 3 to 4 minutes. The mixture must not boil or the eggs will scramble. Remove from the heat and stir in the vanilla. Set the saucepan on a rack to cool for 10 minutes, stirring frequently to prevent a skin from forming on the surface.
3. Ladle the mixture into 6 decorative 4-ounce *pot de crème* cups or white porcelain ramekins and let cool completely. Cover each cup with plastic wrap, then refrigerate at least 5 hours, or overnight.
4. Serve as is or top each serving with a little of the whipped cream and either a scattering of chopped pistachios or a single candied violet.
—*Jean Anderson*

POTTED CHOCOLATE

2 SERVINGS
2 ounces semisweet chocolate
1 tablespoon unsalted butter
1 tablespoon strongly brewed coffee
5 chocolate wafers, coarsely crushed
    (about ¼ cup crumbs)
1 egg white
1 tablespoon sugar
Whipped cream, for garnish

1. In a medium saucepan, combine the chocolate, butter and coffee. Cook over low heat, stirring frequently, until the mixture is melted and smooth, about 4 minutes. Remove from the heat and scrape the mixture into a medium bowl; let cool completely. Stir in the cookie crumbs.
2. Meanwhile, beat the egg white until frothy. Add the sugar and continue beating until stiff but not dry. Fold the beaten white into the melted chocolate.
3. Spoon the chocolate mixture into two 3-ounce ramekins and refrigerate for at least 2 hours, until set. Before serving, garnish the potted chocolate with a dollop of whipped cream or piped rosettes.
—*Molly O'Neill*

CHOCOLATE-DIPPED STRAWBERRIES

Dipped strawberries should be refrigerated just long enough to set the chocolate; they should not be stored in the refrigerator.

MAKES 12
3 ounces semisweet chocolate
1 tablespoon unsalted butter
12 large strawberries

1. In a double boiler
chocolate and butter
heat. Melt the mixture
quently, until smooth,
utes. Remove from the
2. Cover a small platt
plate with a sheet of
Holding on to the hull
berry halfway into the
place on the prepared
with the remaining berr
late. Refrigerate until
minutes. Store the dipp
cool place for up to 1 d

CHOCOLATE FOND FRESH BLUEBE

While chocolate and b
an unexpected combina
in fact, a heavenly ma
best-quality chocolate y
like bittersweet becaus
most intense chocolate f

6 SERVING
6 ounces bittersweet cho
    into small pieces
1 stick (4 ounces) unsalt
    softened
¼ cup plus 2 tablespoon
    sugar
3 eggs, separated
½ cup diced (¼-inch) gla
    (about 2½ ounces)
2 tablespoons kirsch
1 cup fresh blueberries

1. In a double boiler, m
olate over simmering wat
a microwave), stirring u
Remove from the heat an
2. In a large bowl, wit
mixer on medium speed
butter with 2 tablespoons
until light and fluffy. Beat
ed chocolate and the egg
the diced apricots.
3. Beat the egg whites u

the eggs, 1 at a time, beating well for about 30 seconds after each addition. Add the lemon juice, vanilla and salt and beat until well blended. Beat in the sour cream.

4. Pour about one-third of the cheese filling into the prepared cake pan. Drizzle half of the raspberry jam over the filling. Add another third of the filling and repeat with the remaining jam. Top with the remaining filling. Using a small spatula or knife, cut down through the batter and swirl to marble the jam throughout the filling, without cutting into the crumb crust.

5. Set the springform pan in a larger roasting pan and surround with about 1 inch of hot water. Bake for 45 minutes. Turn off the oven and let the cake continue to cook in the hot oven without opening the door for 1 hour longer. Remove the springform pan to a rack and let cool to room temperature, about 1 hour. Cover with plastic wrap, being careful not to touch the surface of the cheesecake, and refrigerate for at least 4 hours, or overnight, until completely chilled.

6. Run a thin metal spatula around the edge of the cake and remove the side of the springform. Use a spatula to smooth the sides of the cake if necessary. Refrigerate until serving time. Garnish with raspberries, if desired.

—*Rose Levy Beranbaum*

CREAM HEARTS WITH STRAWBERRY PUREE

If you like, the strawberry puree can be bolstered with additional sugar, a touch of liqueur, such as Triple Sec or Grand Marnier, or ½ teaspoon of good strawberry preserves.

MAKES 2
1 cup (½ pint) strawberries
2 tablespoons granulated sugar

2 ounces cream cheese, at room temperature
1½ teaspoons confectioners' sugar
¼ teaspoon vanilla extract
½ cup plus 1 tablespoon heavy cream, chilled

1. In a food processor or blender, combine the strawberries and granulated sugar; puree until smooth. Scrape the puree into a small bowl, cover and refrigerate.

2. In a medium bowl, combine the cream cheese, confectioners' sugar, vanilla and 1 tablespoon of the heavy cream. Using an electric mixer on medium speed, beat until the mixture is very smooth, about 8 minutes.

3. In another bowl, beat the remaining ½ cup heavy cream until stiff. Using a rubber spatula, gently fold the whipped cream into the cream cheese mixture.

4. Moisten two 4-by-4-inch pieces of cheesecloth and use them to line two ½-cup perforated heart-shaped porcelain molds. Mound the cheese mixture into the molds. Set the molds on a plate to drain and refrigerate for at least 3 hours before serving.

5. Unmold the hearts onto plates and peel off the cheesecloth. Stir the chilled strawberry puree and drizzle it over and around the hearts.

—*Molly O'Neill*

FROZEN MASCARPONE CREAM WITH CHUNKY MANGO SAUCE

This cool, rich and decadent ice cream is delicious plain or with just about any other fruit sauce.

6 SERVINGS
2 egg yolks
¼ cup sugar
4 ounces mascarpone cheese*, chilled
1 tablespoon rum or brandy
3 to 4 drops almond extract, to taste
¾ cup heavy cream

Chunky Mango Sauce (recipe follows)
*Available at fine Italian groceries and some cheese shops

1. In a large bowl, beat the egg yolks with an electric mixer on high speed, until light in color, about 5 minutes. Beat in the sugar and continue beating until pale and light. Blend in the mascarpone, rum and almond extract. Blend in the cream.

2. Pour into a lightly oiled 3-cup loaf pan and cover with plastic wrap. Freeze until firm, at least 2 hours.

3. To unmold, run a knife around the edges of the pan and invert the mascarpone onto a serving plate. Cut into ½-inch slices and serve with several spoonfuls of mango sauce.

—*Marcia Kiesel*

CHUNKY MANGO SAUCE

This chunky fruit sauce is simple to prepare and delicious served over ice cream.

MAKES ABOUT 1½ CUPS
1½ pounds whole mangoes, peeled and pitted
2 teaspoons sugar, or to taste, depending on ripeness of the fruit
1 teaspoon lemon juice, or to taste

1. Cut half of the mango pieces into ½-inch dice (there should be about ½ cup); set aside.

2. Place the remaining mango in a food processor and puree, about 1 minute. Spoon the mango puree into a medium bowl and fold in the reserved mango pieces. Add the sugar and lemon juice to taste.

—*Marcia Kiesel*

DESSERTS

FROZEN CHOCOLATE MASCARPONE CREAM WITH TOASTED HAZELNUTS

4 SERVINGS

½ cup hazelnuts
3 ounces bittersweet chocolate
2 eggs yolks, at room temperature
2 tablespoons sugar
6 ounces (¾ cup) mascarpone cheese*,
  at room temperature
¼ teaspoon vanilla extract
1 tablespoon coffee liqueur, such as
  Kahlúa or Tia Maria
½ cup heavy cream, chilled
*Available at fine Italian groceries
  and some cheese shops

1. Preheat the oven to 350°. Spread the hazelnuts on a small baking sheet and roast until the skins begin to crack and the nuts are browned, about 10 minutes. Transfer to a kitchen towel and rub off as much of the outer brown skin as possible. Let the nuts cool, then coarsely chop.

2. In a small saucepan over hot water or in a microwave oven, melt the chocolate, stirring until smooth.

3. In a medium bowl, beat the egg yolks lightly. Add 1 tablespoon of the sugar and beat with an electric hand mixer on medium speed for 1 minute. Add the remaining 1 tablespoon sugar and beat for 3 to 4 minutes, until thick and pale yellow.

4. Blend in the melted chocolate. Beat in the mascarpone, vanilla and coffee liqueur.

5. In another bowl, beat the cream until it stands in soft peaks. Stir one-fourth of the whipped cream into the chocolate mixture. Fold in the remaining whipped cream and the nuts.

6. Scrape into a small (3-cup) loaf pan or bowl, cover with plastic wrap and freeze for 3 hours or until firm.

7. To unmold, run a knife around the edges of the pan and invert the dessert onto a serving plate. Cut into ½-inch slices and serve.

—*Anne Disrude*

VANILLA LOVER'S VANILLA ICE CREAM

People who think vanilla ice cream is plain tend to skimp on the flavoring itself and overcompensate with too much sugar, cream and eggs. No wonder they don't love vanilla ice cream. This is for people who do.

MAKES ABOUT 1 QUART

2 cups heavy cream
1 cup milk
½ cup sugar
Pinch of salt
3 egg yolks
1 tablespoon plus 1 teaspoon vanilla
  extract

1. In a heavy medium saucepan, combine the cream, milk, sugar and salt. Cook over moderate heat, stirring frequently with a wooden spoon, until the sugar dissolves and the mixture is hot, 6 to 8 minutes.

2. In a large bowl, beat the egg yolks lightly. Gradually whisk in the hot cream in a thin stream. Return the mixture to the saucepan and cook over moderately low heat, stirring constantly, until the custard thickens enough to lightly coat the back of a spoon, 5 to 7 minutes. (Do not let the temperature exceed 180°.)

3. Strain the custard into a metal bowl. Set the bowl in a basin of ice and water and let stand, stirring occasionally, until cooled to room temperature. Stir in the vanilla. Cover and refrigerate for at least 4 hours, or until very cold.

4. Pour the custard into an ice cream maker and freeze according to the manufacturer's instructions.

—*Leslie Newman*

CAPPUCCINO ICE CREAM

This is a rather soft ice cream that can be quickly prepared, as the eggs do not have to be cooked.

MAKES ABOUT 1 QUART

3 cups heavy cream, chilled
¾ cup superfine sugar
3 egg yolks
2 tablespoons instant espresso
  powder
1 teaspoon unsweetened cocoa
  powder
½ teaspoon cinnamon
1 teaspoon coffee liqueur, such as
  Kahlúa or Tia Maria

1. In a large bowl, beat the cream until it begins to mound. Gradually beat in half the sugar and beat until soft peaks form.

2. In another bowl, beat the egg yolks with the remaining sugar until light in color. Stir in the powdered espresso, cocoa, cinnamon and coffee liqueur. Fold in the whipped cream.

3. Scrape the mixture into an ice cream maker and freeze according to the manufacturer's instructions. If you are making this ice cream for the Cappuccino Ice Cream Cake (p. 198), place the ice cream in the freezer for 20 to 30 minutes to firm up before assembling the cake.

—*Arthur Gold & Robert Fizdale*

DOUBLE ESPRESSO ICE CREAM

This is an easy no-cook ice cream with real flavor and texture appeal. Chocolate-covered espresso beans are available at candy and specialty shops. If you can't find them, your ice cream will still be wonderful. Do not substitute coffee bean-shaped candies, cof-

DESSERTS

fee-flavored chocolates or chocolate chips; they are much too sweet for a real espresso ice cream.

MAKES ABOUT 1 QUART

1 can (14 ounces) sweetened
   condensed milk
2 cups heavy cream
½ cup very strong espresso, cooled
1 teaspoon vanilla extract
½ cup (about 3 ounces) chocolate-
   covered espresso beans, coarsely
   crushed

1. In a medium bowl, combine the condensed milk, cream, espresso and vanilla. Stir well, cover and refrigerate for 4 hours, or until very cold.

2. In an electric mixer on medium speed, beat the chilled espresso cream until it is thick and custardlike, 6 to 8 minutes.

3. Pour the mixture into an ice cream maker and freeze according to the manufacturer's instructions until partially frozen. Stop the machine and quickly stir in the crushed chocolate-covered espresso beans. Continue churning until the ice cream is frozen.
—*Leslie Newman*

FRESH LIME ICE CREAM

This sophisticated ice cream has an intense lime flavor and is amazingly easy to prepare.

MAKES ABOUT 1½ QUARTS

½ cup plus 1 tablespoon fresh lime
   juice (from 3 to 4 medium limes)
1 tablespoon plus 1 teaspoon grated
   lime zest (from 3 to 4 medium
   limes)
2 cups sugar, preferably superfine
Pinch of salt
2 cups heavy cream
2 cups milk

1. In a large bowl, combine the lime

juice, lime zest, sugar and salt; stir to mix well.

2. Gradually stir in the cream and then the milk; stir gently until the sugar dissolves. Cover and refrigerate for at least 4 hours or overnight, if possible, to allow the flavor to develop fully.

3. Stir the mixture, pour it into an ice cream maker and freeze according to the manufacturer's instructions.
—*Leslie Newman*

ORANGE ICE CREAM

MAKES ABOUT 1 QUART

3 navel oranges
¾ cup sugar
3 cups heavy cream
1 cup milk
1 teaspoon vanilla extract
4 egg yolks
¼ cup Grand Marnier

1. Using a vegetable peeler, strip the zest from the 3 oranges. (Save the oranges for another use.) In a food processor, combine the sugar with one-third of the zest. Process until the zest is minced, about 1 minute.

2. Scrape the orange sugar into a medium saucepan. Add the cream, milk, vanilla and the remaining zest. Bring to a boil over moderate heat, stirring occasionally to dissolve the sugar. Set the cream mixture aside to steep for 10 minutes.

3. In a medium bowl, beat the egg yolks until thick and light. Whisk in the orange cream until well blended.

4. Pour the mixture back into the saucepan and cook over moderate heat, stirring constantly, until the custard thickens enough to coat the back of a spoon, about 4 minutes. Stir in the Grand Marnier.

5. Strain the custard into a stainless steel bowl set over a larger bowl of ice

and water. Stir until cool. Pour the custard into an ice cream maker and freeze according to the manufacturer's instructions.
—*l'Auberge de l'Ill, Illhaeusern, France*

REAL CARAMEL ICE CREAM

This is butterscotch for grown-ups, a homey sweet turned rich and tantalizing with the burnished edge of caramel. The taste is sophisticated, but the procedure is simple. Just be sure to allow an extra 10 or 15 uninterrupted minutes to prepare the caramel immediately after making the custard base, so that you can combine them while they are both still warm.

MAKES ABOUT 1¼ QUARTS

1 cup milk
2½ cups heavy cream
1¼ cups sugar
Pinch of salt
4 egg yolks
1 teaspoon lemon juice
1 teaspoon vanilla extract

1. In a heavy medium saucepan, combine the milk, 2 cups of the cream, ½ cup of the sugar and the salt. Cook over moderate heat, stirring frequently with a wooden spoon, until the sugar dissolves and the mixture is hot, 6 to 8 minutes.

2. In a large bowl, beat the egg yolks lightly. Gradually whisk in the hot cream in a thin stream. Return the mixture to the saucepan and cook over moderately low heat, stirring constantly, until the custard thickens enough to lightly coat the back of a spoon, 5 to 7 minutes. (Do not let the temperature exceed 180°.) Remove the custard from the heat and set aside.

3. In a small heavy saucepan, combine the remaining ¾ cup sugar with the lemon juice and 2 tablespoons of

209

water. Melt the sugar over moderately low heat, without stirring, brushing any sugar crystals from the sides of the pan with a wet brush. Let the sugar boil undisturbed until the syrup begins to color, about 15 minutes. Continue boiling, swirling the pan frequently, until the caramel is a deep, rich amber, about 5 minutes longer. (Do not let the syrup darken any further, or the caramel may develop a bitter, slightly burnt taste.) Remove from the heat and stir in the remaining ½ cup cream. Stir the caramel cream into the warm custard and mix thoroughly.

4. Strain the caramel custard into a metal bowl. Set the bowl in a basin of ice and water and let stand, stirring occasionally, until cooled to room temperature. Stir in the vanilla. Cover and refrigerate for at least 4 hours, or until very cold.

5. Pour the custard into an ice cream maker and freeze according to the manufacturer's instructions.
—Leslie Newman

PUMPKIN MAPLE ICE CREAM

8 SERVINGS
3 egg yolks
1 cup maple syrup
1 cup milk, scalded
1 cup canned solid-pack pumpkin
1½ teaspoons freshly grated nutmeg
1 cup heavy cream
Dark rum and chopped walnuts, for garnish

1. In a large bowl, blend the egg yolks and maple syrup well.

2. Gradually beat the hot milk into the eggs and syrup. Pour the mixture into a heavy medium saucepan and cook, stirring, over moderately low heat until it registers 180° on an instant-reading thermometer, about 15 minutes. Do not let boil.

3. Return the hot mixture to the bowl and blend in the pumpkin, nutmeg and cream. Pour the mixture into an ice cream maker and freeze according to the manufacturer's instructions. Transfer to a covered container and let the ice cream ripen in the freezer for at least 2 hours or overnight.

4. To serve, scoop into stemmed glasses. Top with a dash of rum and a sprinkling of chopped walnuts.
—Diana Sturgis

PRESERVED GINGER ICE CREAM

This exotic ice cream is surprisingly versatile. Serve it with fresh fruit salad after an Asian feast or perhaps with grilled peaches as a grand finale to any barbecue.

MAKES ABOUT 1 QUART
2 cups heavy cream
1 cup milk
½ cup sugar
Pinch of salt
3 egg yolks
⅓ cup minced preserved stem ginger*
    plus 2 tablespoons syrup from the jar
2 teaspoons vanilla extract
*Available at Chinese markets, specialty food shops and many supermarkets

1. In a heavy medium saucepan, combine the cream, milk, sugar and salt. Cook over moderate heat, stirring frequently with a wooden spoon, until the sugar dissolves and the mixture is hot, 6 to 8 minutes.

2. In a large bowl, beat the egg yolks lightly. Gradually whisk in the hot cream in a thin stream. Return the mixture to the saucepan and cook over moderately low heat, stirring constantly, until the custard thickens

enough to lightly coat the back of a spoon, 5 to 7 minutes. (Do not let the temperature exceed 180°.)

3. Strain the custard into a metal bowl. Set the bowl in a basin of ice and water and let stand, stirring occasionally, until cooled to room temperature. Stir in the minced ginger, ginger syrup and vanilla. Mix well, making sure the ginger doesn't clump together. Cover and refrigerate for at least 6 hours, or overnight, if possible, to allow the flavor to develop fully.

4. Pour the mixture into an ice cream maker and freeze according to the manufacturer's instructions.
—Leslie Newman

ARMAGNAC ICE CREAM

People who can't stand boozy ice cream won't be able to resist this scrumptiously subtle variation on vanilla. They'll put away two bowlfuls while they're wondering what's in it.

MAKES ABOUT 1 QUART
2 cups heavy cream
1 cup milk
½ cup sugar
Pinch of salt
3 egg yolks
1 teaspoon vanilla extract
3 tablespoons Armagnac

1. In a heavy medium saucepan, combine the cream, milk, sugar and salt. Cook over moderate heat, stirring frequently with a wooden spoon, until the sugar dissolves and the mixture is hot, 6 to 8 minutes.

2. In a large bowl, beat the egg yolks lightly. Gradually whisk in the hot cream in a thin stream. Return the mixture to the saucepan and cook over moderately low heat, stirring constantly, until the custard thickens enough to lightly coat the back of a metal spoon, 5 to 7 minutes. (Do not let the temperature exceed 180°.)

3. Strain the custard into a metal bowl. Set the bowl in a basin of ice and water and let stand, stirring occasionally, until cooled to room temperature. Stir in the vanilla and Armagnac. Cover and refrigerate for at least 4 hours, or until very cold.

4. Pour the custard into an ice cream maker and freeze according to the manufacturer's instructions.

—*Leslie Newman*

FROZEN BERRY YOGURT WITH CARDINAL SAUCE

A lovely low-calorie way to take the sizzle out of summer, this confection has only 190 calories per serving.

6 SERVINGS
1 package (10 ounces) frozen
*   raspberries in light syrup, partially*
*   thawed*
1 package (10 ounces) frozen
*   strawberries in light syrup,*
*   partially thawed*
2 cups low-fat plain yogurt
6 tablespoons superfine sugar
1 tablespoon Grand Marnier
¼ teaspoon freshly grated orange zest
Cardinal Sauce (recipe follows)
1 cup fresh red raspberries, for
*   garnish*
6 small fresh mint sprigs, for garnish

1. In a food processor, puree the partially thawed raspberries and strawberries. (If you wish to remove the seeds, strain the puree through a fine-mesh sieve and return the puree to the food processor.) Add the yogurt, sugar, Grand Marnier and orange zest and process for 20 seconds. Scrape the sides down and process until absolutely smooth, 30 to 40 seconds longer.

2. Spoon the mixture into a 9-by-9-by-2-inch baking dish or pan. Set in the freezer and freeze for 3 to 4 hours, or until soft-firm.

3. To serve the dessert, layer scoops of the berry yogurt and Cardinal Sauce alternately into 6 parfait glasses, ending with a drizzling of sauce. Tuck a few raspberries in and around the final scoop of frozen yogurt and garnish each portion with a sprig of mint.

—*Jean Anderson*

CARDINAL SAUCE

MAKES ABOUT 1½ CUPS
1 package (10 ounces) frozen
*   raspberries in light syrup, thawed*
¼ cup low-sugar strawberry jam (I
*   used Smucker's)*
1 tablespoon superfine sugar
1½ teaspoons cornstarch

1. Drain the thawed raspberries in a strainer set over a bowl; reserve the juices and set aside. In a food processor, process the drained raspberries and the strawberry jam until smooth, about 20 seconds. Strain the mixture through a fine-mesh sieve in a small bowl to remove the seeds and set the puree aside.

2. Measure out the reserved raspberry juice and, if necessary, add cold water to measure ½ cup. In a small heavy saucepan, combine the sugar and cornstarch, pressing out all lumps. Add the raspberry juice and cook over low heat, stirring constantly, until the mixture bubbles up and turns clear, about 2 minutes. Remove from the heat and blend into the raspberry puree. Cover and refrigerate until ready to serve.

—*Jean Anderson*

COCONUT FROST WITH CHOCOLATE ALMOND SAUCE

Do not use sweetened canned coconut milk in this recipe, as it will give the sorbet an off flavor and prevent it from freezing properly.

MAKES ABOUT 1 QUART
⅔ cup sugar
2 cans (14 ounces each) unsweetened
*   coconut milk* (see Note)*
4 teaspoons amaretto liqueur
Chocolate Almond Sauce (recipe
*   follows)*
*Available at Oriental and Latin
*   American markets*

1. In a small saucepan, combine the sugar with ⅔ cup of water. Cook over moderate heat, stirring, until the sugar dissolves, about 2 minutes. Bring to a boil and cook until the mixture is reduced to 1 cup, about 2 minutes longer. Set aside to cool.

2. Stir in the coconut milk and amaretto. (Do not chill the mixture before churning.) Pour the mixture into an ice cream maker and freeze according to the manufacturer's instructions. Turn into a chilled bowl, cover and freeze, or serve at once.

3. To serve, scoop the sorbet into dessert bowls and drizzle with the chocolate almond sauce.

NOTE: To make your own coconut milk, place 2 coconuts in a preheated 350° oven and bake until cracked, 25 to 30 minutes. Wrap the coconuts in 3 layers of kitchen towels and using a small hammer, pound them until they break open. Unwrap and discard any liquid inside. Pry the meat from the shell and using a vegetable peeler, scrape off the thin layer of skin. Cut the coconut meat into 1-inch chunks and process in a food processor until shredded. Pour 4½ cups of boiling water over the coconut and process

for 1 minute longer. Transfer the processed coconut to a strainer set over a bowl and press with a wooden spoon to extract as much coconut milk as possible.

—*Diana Sturgis*

CHOCOLATE ALMOND SAUCE

This rich sauce is delicious drizzled over the Coconut Frost and can be served warm or at room temperature.

MAKES ABOUT 1 CUP
6 ounces semisweet chocolate, coarsely chopped
½ cup milk
1 tablespoon sugar
2 tablespoons amaretto liqueur

1. In a small heavy saucepan, combine the chocolate, milk and sugar. Cook over low heat, stirring, until the chocolate is melted and the sauce is smooth, 3 to 5 minutes. Do not boil.

2. Set aside to cool for 10 minutes. Stir in the amaretto.

—*Diana Sturgis*

GREEN APPLE SORBET

This sorbet has a coarse texture and a wonderful apple flavor.

4 TO 6 SERVINGS
1½ pounds tart green apples, such as Granny Smith—peeled, cored and coarsely chopped
½ cup applejack or Calvados
½ cup sweet sparkling cider
3 tablespoons fresh lime juice
½ cup sugar
½ teaspoon cinnamon
4 lime slices

1. In a medium noncorrodible saucepan, combine the apples, applejack, cider, lime juice, sugar and cin-

namon. Cook over moderate heat until the apples soften, 5 to 8 minutes.

2. In a food processor or blender, puree the apple mixture until smooth; let cool completely.

3. Scrape the puree into an ice cream maker and freeze according to the manufacturer's instructions.

4. Serve the sorbet with a slice of lime and an additional splash of applejack or Calvados.

—*W. Peter Prestcott*

FROZEN GIN AND TONIC

This sorbet is delicious with bits of lime zest throughout, but if you'd rather have a perfectly smooth version, strain out the lime zest before freezing.

MAKES ABOUT 1 QUART
1 unblemished lime
½ cup sugar
⅓ cup gin
3 bottles (10 ounces each) tonic water

1. Place the lime in a colander and pour about 1 cup of boiling water over it to remove any wax or spray; pat dry. Using a vegetable peeler, remove the zest, making sure to scrape off any white pith that clings. Mince the zest (there will be about 2 teaspoons). Squeeze out 1 tablespoon of juice from the lime; reserve.

2. Place the zest and sugar in a small bowl and using a wooden spoon, crush them until well combined, about 3 minutes. Set aside for 30 minutes.

3. Transfer the sugar/zest mixture to a deep pitcher or bowl. Stir in the gin and reserved lime juice. Slowly pour in the tonic water and stir to

dissolve the sugar. Refrigerate, covered, until chilled, about 30 minutes. Strain if desired.

4. Pour the mixture into an ice cream maker and freeze according to the manufacturer's instructions. Turn into a chilled bowl, cover and freeze, or serve at once.

—*Diana Sturgis*

GRAPEFRUIT BLUSH

A small amount of Campari adds some extra flavor to this sorbet and gives it a wonderful pink blush.

MAKES ABOUT 1 QUART
5 large grapefruits
¾ cup sugar
2 tablespoons Campari

1. Place 1 of the grapefruits in a colander and pour about 1 cup of boiling water over it to remove any wax or spray. Rub the fruit dry. Using a vegetable peeler, remove all the zest, making sure to scrape off any white pith that clings. Chop the zest coarsely and place it in a food processor. Add the sugar and process until the zest is finely minced, about 2 minutes.

2. Squeeze the juice from all the grapefruits (there will be about 4 cups). Add the sugar/zest mixture to the juice; set aside, stirring occasionally, until the sugar dissolves and the zest flavor permeates the juice, about 30 minutes.

3. Pour the grapefruit juice through a fine strainer set over a medium bowl. Refrigerate until chilled, about 30 minutes. Stir in the Campari. Pour the mixture into an ice cream maker and freeze according to the manufacturer's instructions. Turn into a chilled bowl, cover and freeze, or serve at once.

—*Diana Sturgis*

PEACH VANILLA SORBET

This sorbet should be made with the ripest peaches you can find.

MAKES ABOUT 5 CUPS
¾ cup sugar
2 pounds ripe peaches (about 7
    peaches)
1 teaspoon vanilla extract

1. In a medium saucepan, combine the sugar and 1 cup of water. Bring to a boil over high heat, stirring until the sugar dissolves, about 2 minutes. Set aside to cool.

2. Drop the peaches, a few at a time, into a large saucepan of boiling water, and blanch for 20 seconds. Remove with a slotted spoon and peel off the skins. Cut the peaches into eighths and discard the pits.

3. Place the peach sections in the sugar syrup, return to a boil and simmer until just tender, 3 to 5 minutes. Remove from the heat and let the peaches cool to room temperature in the syrup. Stir in the vanilla.

4. In a food processor or blender, puree the peaches and syrup until smooth, about 30 seconds. Refrigerate, covered, until chilled, about 30 minutes. Scrape the mixture into an ice cream maker and freeze according to the manufacturer's instructions. Turn into a chilled bowl, cover and freeze, or serve at once.

—*Diana Sturgis*

STRAWBERRY SMOOTHIE

Adding a small amount of alcohol to sorbet prevents the churned mixture from becoming too hard when frozen.

MAKES ABOUT 1 QUART
½ cup sugar
6 cups strawberries (3 pints), halved
2 tablespoons vodka

1. In a medium saucepan, combine the sugar and 1 cup of water. Bring to a boil over high heat, stirring, until the sugar dissolves, about 2 minutes. Add the berries; return to a boil and simmer for 1 minute. Set aside to cool for about 30 minutes.

2. Pour the strawberry mixture into a food processor or blender and puree until smooth. Transfer to a fine-mesh sieve set over a medium bowl and using a wooden spoon, press the berry mixture through. Refrigerate until chilled, about 30 minutes.

3. Stir the vodka into the chilled berry puree. Pour the mixture into an ice cream maker and freeze according to the manufacturer's instructions. Turn into a chilled bowl, cover and freeze, or serve at once.

—*Diana Sturgis*

RASPBERRY SATIN

The addition of egg white lends a particularly satiny texture to sorbets. If you wish to omit the whites, the results will be flavorful, but not as smooth.

MAKES ABOUT 1 QUART
⅔ cup plus 1 tablespoon sugar
4 cups (2 pints) raspberries
1 tablespoon framboise (raspberry
    eau-de-vie) or vodka
1 egg white

1. In a medium saucepan, combine ⅔ cup of the sugar with 1 cup of water. Cook over moderate heat, stirring, until the sugar dissolves, about 2 minutes. Bring to a boil, add the raspberries and toss with the syrup. Return to a boil and simmer the raspberries and syrup for 2 minutes.

2. Pour the berries and syrup into a fine-mesh sieve set over a medium bowl. Using a rubber spatula, press the mixture through the sieve; or pu-

ree in a blender or food processor and strain. Discard the solids.

3. Stir the framboise into the raspberry liquid and refrigerate until chilled, about 30 minutes. Scrape the sorbet mixture into an ice cream maker and freeze according to the manufacturer's instructions, until the sorbet is light colored, thickened and partially frozen, about 25 minutes.

4. Meanwhile, beat the egg white until soft peaks form. Gradually beat in the remaining 1 tablespoon sugar until stiff peaks form. Add the beaten egg white to the ice cream maker and churn the sorbet until it freezes into a smooth, satiny mass, about 15 minutes. Transfer to a chilled bowl, cover and freeze or serve at once.

—*Diana Sturgis*

FRESH PAPAYA SORBET

This refreshing sorbet can certainly stand on its own, but it makes an elegant dessert when served in our Delicate Coconut Tulipes (p. 200).

MAKES ABOUT 3½ CUPS
¾ cup sugar
¼ cup fresh lime juice
2 cups pureed papaya (2 large
    papayas, peeled)

1. In a small saucepan, combine the sugar and ¾ cup of water. Cook over moderate heat, stirring constantly to dissolve the sugar, then bring just to a boil. Remove from the heat and let cool to room temperature.

2. Pour the syrup into a bowl set over a larger bowl of ice and stir until cool. Add the lime juice and pureed papaya. Scrape the mixture into an ice cream maker and freeze according to the manufacturer's instructions.

—*Lisa Brainerd*

DESSERTS

DELICE MAISON

During the summer months, my favorite dessert is always very simple. I find the best-looking fruits in the market and top them with a tangy fresh cheese and a sprinkling of sugar. Blueberries, strawberries and sour cherries are my favorites in June; blackberries and red currants in July; and peaches and plums, which I poach in a simple sugar syrup, in August.

6 TO 8 SERVINGS
½ pound fresh cream cheese
½ pound mascarpone* or 1 cup sour cream
¼ cup sugar
1 to 2 tablespoons heavy cream
About 1½ cups crème de cassis or crème de myrtilles
1 pint blueberries
1 pint strawberries
½ pint fresh or frozen sour cherries (optional)
*Available at fine Italian markets and some cheese shops

1. Beat the cream cheese and the mascarpone in a heavy mixer, until it thickens. Beat in the sugar and enough heavy cream to soften the cheese to the consistency of stiff whipped cream. Refrigerate until ready to serve.

2. To serve, ladle 2 to 3 tablespoons crème de cassis into each dish. Reserve enough berries and cherries for garnish; divide the rest among the serving dishes. Top with 2 spoonfuls of the cream cheese mixture and decorate with the reserved fruit. Pass a bowl of sugar on the side for guests to sprinkle as they please.

—Lydie Marshall

LAYERED SUMMER FRUITS WITH SOUR-CREAM YOGURT SAUCE

Choose fully ripe, naturally sweet fruits for this recipe and use as little sugar as possible to sweeten them. The calorie counts—183 for each of 12 servings or 157 calories for each of 14 servings—are for the full amount of sugar called for in the recipe. For each 1 tablespoon of sugar you subtract, reduce the calorie count by 3 for each of 14 servings and 4 for each of 12.

12 TO 14 SERVINGS
1 small very ripe pineapple (1½ to 2 pounds)
9 tablespoons superfine sugar or less, to taste
1 tablespoon coarsely chopped fresh mint
1 quart strawberries, sliced about ¼ inch thick; reserve 1 whole strawberry for garnish
1 tablespoon Cointreau or Grand Marnier
2 pounds very ripe peaches or nectarines—peeled, pitted and cut into slim wedges
1 tablespoon fresh lemon juice
1 cup sour cream
1 cup low-fat plain yogurt
1 teaspoon freshly grated orange zest
1 pound seedless green grapes, stemmed and halved lengthwise (about 3 cups)
1 pint fresh blueberries

1. Trim and peel the pineapple. Quarter the pineapple lengthwise, then halve each quarter lengthwise so that you have 8 long slim wedges. Slice the point off each wedge to remove the woody core. Finally, cut each wedge crosswise into slices about ⅛ inch thick and place in a large bowl. Taste and, if needed, add 1 tablespoon of the sugar. Add the mint and toss well.

2. Place the strawberries in another bowl and add the Cointreau. Taste the

fruit and, if needed, add up to 3 tablespoons of the sugar. Toss well.

3. Place the peaches in a third bowl and add the lemon juice. Taste the fruit and, if needed, add up to 3 tablespoons of the sugar. Toss well.

4. In a medium bowl, combine the sour cream, yogurt, 2 tablespoons of the sugar and the orange zest. Mix the sauce well.

5. To assemble the fruit bowl, place all the grapes in the bottom of a very large glass or crystal bowl. Add the peaches and about one-third of the sauce. Add half the blueberries and all of the pineapple and top with another one-third of the sauce, adding it as artfully as possible so that it trickles down over the fruits below and is visible through the bowl. Next add all the strawberries and cluster the remaining blueberries in the center. Spoon the remaining sauce on top and garnish with the whole strawberry.

—Jean Anderson

SUMMER FRUIT IN LIME CARAMEL

4 SERVINGS
1 banana, cut into ½-inch rounds
3 large peaches—peeled, pitted and sliced ½ inch thick
2 large plums, sliced ½ inch thick
½ cup seedless red grapes
½ cup seedless green grapes
3 tablespoons fresh lime juice
½ cup sugar

1. In a medium bowl, combine the banana, peaches, plums and red and green grapes. Add 1 tablespoon of the lime juice and toss to coat.

2. In a small heavy saucepan, combine the sugar with 3 tablespoons of water. Bring to a boil over high heat

and cook without stirring until the mixture turns nut brown, about 8 minutes.

3. Remove from the heat and immediately add 3 tablespoons of cold water. (Stand back; the mixture will splatter.) Cook over low heat, stirring, until the caramel is smooth. Add the remaining 2 tablespoons lime juice and let cool to room temperature.

4. Pour the caramel over the fruit and toss. Cover and refrigerate for up to 2 hours before serving.

—*Perla Meyers*

HONEY-SCOTCH BAKED APPLES

6 SERVINGS

½ cup honey
½ cup scotch whisky
3 tablespoons unsalted butter, softened
1½ tablespoons light brown sugar
6 large baking apples (Golden Delicious, York, Cortland or Rome Beauty), cored ¾ of the way through
⅓ cup dried apricots, finely chopped
2 tablespoons apricot jam
½ cup heavy cream

1. In a small bowl, combine the honey, scotch and ¼ cup of warm water. In another small bowl, cream together the butter and brown sugar.

2. Preheat the oven to 350°. Remove the peel from the top third of each apple. Stuff about 1 tablespoon of the apricots into the hollow center of each and top with a rounded teaspoon of the butter-sugar mixture. Place the apples in a baking pan large enough to allow a little space between each apple and pour ¼ cup of warm water into the bottom of the pan. Pour half of the honey-scotch mixture over the apples.

3. Bake the apples, basting every 15 minutes with the remaining honey-

scotch mixture, until they can be easily pierced with a knife, about 45 minutes. Remove the apples and set aside.

4. Pour the syrup from the baking dish into a small heavy saucepan. Bring to a boil over high heat and cook for 1 minute. Add the apricot jam and boil for 1 minute longer. Brush the apples lightly with some of this glaze.

5. Pour the heavy cream into the remaining hot glaze and return to a boil for 1 minute longer. Pass separately with the warm apples.

—*Dorie Greenspan*

APPLE, PRUNE AND APRICOT COMPOTE

8 SERVINGS

⅓ cup raisins
1 cup pitted prunes (6 ounces)
1 can (6 ounces) frozen apple juice concentrate
1 cup dried apricots (6 ounces)
2 whole cloves
1 cinnamon stick
1 tablespoon fresh lemon juice
3 tart green apples, such as Granny Smith
1 cup crème fraîche or sour cream

1. Place the raisins and prunes in a small saucepan, cover with water and bring to a boil. Reduce the heat, cover and simmer until the prunes are soft and plumped, about 20 minutes. Drain and place in a bowl.

2. Place the apple juice concentrate in a medium saucepan with 2 cups of water. Add the apricots, cloves and cinnamon and bring to a boil. Reduce the heat, cover and simmer, until the apricots are plumped and tender, about 20 minutes. Remove from the heat and with a slotted spoon, transfer the apricots to the bowl of prunes.

3. Add the lemon juice to the pan of apple juice. Peel, core and slice each apple into 8 wedges and as you work drop the pieces into the saucepan to prevent discoloration. Cover and simmer, stirring once or twice, until tender, 5 to 7 minutes.

4. Add the apples and their liquid to the bowl of fruit. Serve at room temperature or chilled, topped with crème fraîche or sour cream.

—*Diana Sturgis*

FLAMBEED MAPLE-RUM BANANAS

Use tiny finger bananas, if you find them in your market, for they work beautifully in this dish. However you'll need 10 of them, split lengthwise only.

10 SERVINGS

1 stick (4 ounces) unsalted butter
½ cup maple syrup
5 bananas, halved crosswise, then split lengthwise
½ cup dark rum
1 quart vanilla ice cream
⅓ cup chopped toasted pecans

1. In a large skillet, melt the butter over moderately high heat. Stir in the maple syrup and bring to a simmer.

2. Add the bananas and cook, basting them with the hot syrup in the pan, until hot, about 2 minutes.

3. Pour in the rum and ignite with a match. Ladle the sauce over the bananas as it flames.

4. To serve, place a scoop of ice cream in each dessert dish. Add 2 pieces of banana and a generous spoonful of the sauce. Garnish with pecans.

—*John Robert Massie*

DESSERTS

MELON MELBA

4 SERVINGS
¼ cup red currant jelly
2 to 3 tablespoons kirsch, to taste
1 tablespoon fresh lemon juice, or
    more to taste
1 pint strawberries, hulled
¼ to ⅓ cup superfine sugar
1 small cantaloupe
2 kiwi fruits, peeled and sliced
1 pint vanilla ice cream
4 sprigs of fresh mint, for garnish

1. In a small saucepan, melt the jelly over low heat. Remove from the
heat and add the kirsch and lemon
juice.
2. In a food processor, puree the
strawberries with ¼ cup of the sugar.
Add the jelly and process to blend
well. Taste and add more sugar if necessary. Cover and refrigerate until
ready to use. **(The sauce can be made
a day ahead.)**
3. Cut the melon lengthwise into
quarters. Remove and discard the
seeds and cut off the rind. Cut each
piece lengthwise into 3 slices. Cover
and refrigerate until serving time.
4. To serve, place 3 slices of melon
on each of 4 plates, connecting them
to form a circle. Garnish each circle
with slices of kiwi and spoon 2 tablespoons of the strawberry sauce into
the center. Place a scoop of ice cream
on the sauce and garnish each plate
with a mint sprig. Serve at once; pass
the remaining sauce separately.
—Perla Meyers

LAVENDER-PEPPER PEARS

For an intriguing dessert to round out
a light meal, try this perfumed fruit
with a wedge of Italian Fontina or other mild semisoft cheese.

2 SERVINGS
1 tablespoon fresh lemon juice
2 large ripe Bartlett pears, peeled
⅛ teaspoon lavender*, crumbled
½ teaspoon coarsely cracked black
    pepper
*Available at spice markets and
    specialty food shops

Sprinkle the lemon juice over the
pears. Combine the lavender and
pepper and sprinkle over the pears.
Serve on a plate with a knife and fork.
—Anne Disrude

PAPILLOTE OF PEARS WITH ORANGE AND VANILLA

2 SERVINGS
1 tablespoon clarified or melted
    butter
1 ripe pear—peeled, halved and cored
2 teaspoons fresh lemon juice
½ vanilla bean
1 tablespoon plus 1 teaspoon crème
    fraîche
2 teaspoons sugar
4 strips of orange zest, about 2 by ½
    inch
2 small scoops of vanilla ice cream

1. Preheat the oven to 400°. Fold
two 15-by-20-inch sheets of butcher's
paper, parchment or aluminum foil in
half crosswise to make 15-by-10-inch
rectangles. Using scissors, cut each
rectangle into a heart shape with the
fold running vertically down the center. Open up the hearts and brush
each with ½ tablespoon of the butter.

2. Brush the pear halves with the
lemon juice to prevent discoloration.
Cut each half crosswise on the diagonal into 6 slices and place on half of
each heart. Fan out slightly.
3. Scrape the seeds from the vanilla
bean and mix them with the crème
fraîche and sugar. Spoon over the
pears. Place 2 strips of orange zest on
top of each pear half and top with a
piece of the scraped vanilla bean.
4. Fold the paper over the pears
and beginning at the top of each
heart, make a series of tight overlapping folds to seal the papillotes.
5. Place the papillotes on a cookie
sheet and bake for 12 minutes. Open
at table and serve with a scoop of ice
cream. Serve at once.
—Anne Disrude

PEARS POACHED IN SAUTERNES

8 SERVINGS
6 large pears, such as Anjou—peeled,
    cored and quartered (about 3¼
    pounds)
2 tablespoons fresh lemon juice
1 bottle Sauternes
3 tablespoons sugar
4 whole cloves
1 teaspoon pear eau-de-vie, such as
    Poire William (optional)
Vanilla ice cream (optional)
Freshly ground black pepper
Freshly grated lime zest

1. In a medium bowl, toss the pears
with the lemon juice.
2. In a large, shallow, noncorrodible pan, combine the Sauternes, sugar and cloves. Bring to a boil over
moderately high heat. Add the pears.
When the liquid returns to a simmer,

reduce the heat to moderately low and cook until the pears are tender when pierced, 8 to 10 minutes. Remove the pears and set aside. Discard the cloves.

3. Boil the poaching liquid over moderate heat until reduced to ½ cup, 8 to 10 minutes. Remove from the heat and let cool. Stir in the pear eau-de-vie, if using. **(The recipe can be prepared ahead to this point.** Combine the pears and the syrup, cover and refrigerate.)

4. To serve, place 3 pear quarters and a scoop of ice cream on each plate. Sprinkle each serving with 1 tablespoon of the syrup and garnish with a light dusting of pepper and lime zest.

—*W. Peter Prestcott*

PEAR AND FRESH FIG COMPOTE WITH VANILLA ICE CREAM

Chef Marc Meneau of the *Michelin* three-star l'Espérance restaurant, just outside of Vézelay, served this dessert at Le Train Bleu at Bloomingdale's, in New York City.

4 SERVINGS
2 tablespoons unsalted butter
2 large pears, such as Bartlett or Bosc—peeled, cored and sliced ½ inch thick
1 cinnamon stick
1 tablespoon sugar
6 fresh purple figs, halved
1 pint vanilla ice cream

1. In a large skillet, melt the butter over moderately high heat. Add the pear slices and sauté, tossing frequently, until beginning to brown, 5 to 7 minutes. Add ¼ cup of water, the cinnamon stick and the sugar. Reduce

the heat to moderate and simmer gently until the pears are tender when they are pierced with a knife, about 15 minutes.

2. Add the figs and cook until the figs are heated through and the sauce is pink, about 2 minutes.

3. Arrange 3 fig halves on each plate. Fan the pear slices around the figs and spoon the sauce over the fruit. Serve with a scoop of ice cream.

—*Marc Meneau*

GLAZED PINEAPPLE WITH MACADAMIA NUT CRUNCH

8 SERVINGS
1 large ripe pineapple—ends trimmed, skin and eyes removed
1 cup coarsely chopped macadamia nuts
⅓ cup (packed) light brown sugar
Pinch of salt
4 tablespoons unsalted butter, melted

1. Preheat the broiler. Cut the pineapple into 8 slices, each about 1 inch thick. For a decorative presentation, cut notched grooves 1 inch apart on the top of each slice to suggest the grooves in a scallop shell.

2. In a small bowl, combine the nuts, brown sugar and salt. Add the butter and stir until well blended.

3. Place the pineapple slices on a baking sheet lined with foil. Sprinkle a few tablespoons of the nut mixture over each pineapple slice or use to fill each notch.

4. Broil the pineapple slices about 6 inches from the heat until the brown sugar-nut filling starts to caramelize, about 1½ minutes.

—*Marcia Kiesel*

STRAWBERRIES ROMANOFF

6 SERVINGS
2 quarts strawberries, halved or quartered if large
¼ cup plus 1 tablespoon confectioners' sugar
¼ cup plus 1 tablespoon Grand Marnier
½ pint heavy cream, chilled
1 quart Orange Ice Cream (p. 209)
1 navel orange—peel and white pith removed, sectioned

1. In a large bowl, combine the strawberries with ¼ cup of the confectioners' sugar and ¼ cup of the Grand Marnier; toss well. Cover and refrigerate for 1 hour.

2. In a chilled bowl, beat the cream until soft peaks form. Beat in the remaining 1 tablespoon sugar and Grand Marnier; refrigerate for up to 2 hours.

3. To serve, scoop the ice cream into 6 chilled dessert dishes. Spoon the strawberries around the ice cream. Drizzle some of the strawberry juices over the top and garnish with the whipped cream and orange sections.

—*l'Auberge de l'Ill, Illhaeusern, France*

STOCKS & SAUCES

STOCKS & SAUCES

BROWN STOCK

Deep amber, flavorful brown stock forms the basis for many sauces.

MAKES 4 TO 5 QUARTS
6 pounds beef shin with bones
6 pounds veal bones
6 carrots, cut into 2-inch lengths
3 onions—unpeeled, halved and each half stuck with 1 whole clove
3 leeks (white part only), split lengthwise, plus 1 leek (including green top), quartered
2 celery ribs with leaves, cut into 2-inch lengths
1 small white turnip
2 cups coarsely chopped tomatoes, canned or fresh
Bouquet garni: 6 sprigs of parsley, 1 teaspoon thyme, 1 large bay leaf, 7 peppercorns and 2 unpeeled garlic cloves tied in a double thickness of cheesecloth

1. Preheat the oven to 450°. Place the meat and bones in a large roasting pan in 1 or 2 layers, or in 2 roasting pans if necessary. Bake, uncovered, for 30 minutes. Add the carrots and onions and bake, turning occasionally, until the bones are deep brown but not charred, 30 to 60 minutes longer.

2. Transfer the bones and vegetables to a large stockpot. Pour off and discard any fat from the roasting pan. Add 2 to 3 cups of cold water to the pan and deglaze over medium heat, scraping up any browned particles that cling to the bottom. Pour the liquid into the stockpot, add enough additional cold water to cover the bones—about 4 quarts—and bring the water slowly to a simmer over low heat; to insure a clear stock, this slow heating should take about 1 hour. Skim off all the scum that rises to the surface.

3. Add the leeks, celery, turnip, tomatoes, bouquet garni and enough additional water to cover. Simmer, partially covered, over low heat for 5 to 8 hours, skimming the surface occasionally. Add additional water to cover as necessary.

4. Carefully ladle the stock into a large bowl through a colander lined with several thicknesses of dampened cheesecloth. Do not press on the bones and vegetables, or the resulting stock will be cloudy. Refrigerate, uncovered, overnight; then remove any fat from the surface. The stock may be refrigerated for 3 to 4 days, then reboiled, or frozen for several months.

—F&W

CHICKEN STOCK

MAKES ABOUT 4 QUARTS
5 pounds chicken necks, backs and bones
1 calf's foot, split (optional)
2 medium onions, quartered
2 carrots, coarsely chopped
2 celery ribs, coarsely chopped
3 garlic cloves, crushed
3 leeks, green tops only, coarsely chopped
Bouquet garni: 10 parsley stems, ½ teaspoon dried thyme, 10 peppercorns and 1 bay leaf tied in a double thickness of cheesecloth

1. In a large stockpot, combine all the ingredients. Add 4½ quarts of water. Bring to a boil over moderate heat, skimming off the foamy scum as it rises to the surface. Lower the heat to maintain a slow simmer. Cook, skimming occasionally, for 4 hours.

2. Strain the stock through a fine-mesh sieve lined with a double layer of dampened cheesecloth. Let cool to room temperature, then cover and refrigerate. Remove the congealed fat from the top before using.

—F&W

QUICK HOMEMADE BEEF STOCK

MAKES 2 CUPS
1½ to 2 pounds beef short ribs
2 medium onions, coarsely chopped
2 medium carrots, coarsely chopped
2 large celery ribs, coarsely chopped
Bouquet garni: 3 large sprigs of flat Italian parsley, 1 teaspoon thyme, 2 black peppercorns and 1 large bay leaf, tied in a double thickness of cheesecloth

1. Preheat the oven to 500°. Place the short ribs in a heavy roasting pan and cook in the oven, turning occasionally, until lightly browned, about 10 minutes. Add the onions, carrots and celery and cook until the vegetables are tender and lightly browned, about 10 minutes.

2. Transfer the bones and vegetables to a large heavy saucepan and cover with 4 cups of water. Bring to a boil over high heat. Reduce the heat to moderately low, add the bouquet garni and simmer, uncovered, until the stock is reduced to 2 cups, about 1 hour.

3. Strain the stock into a small saucepan and skim off any fat.

—Diana Sturgis

Peach Vanilla Sorbet (p. 213).

Left, a slice of Old-Fashioned Pumpkin Pie (p. 167) and a bowl of Pumpkin Maple Ice Cream (p. 210). Above, Grand Marnier Soufflé (p. 198).

RICH CHICKEN STOCK

Although this deliciously rich stock calls for two whole chickens in addition to chicken parts, the whole birds are removed as soon as they are cooked, so you can eat them as is or use the meat for other dishes, salads or sandwiches. You may substitute additional chicken parts for the whole chickens. Use this stock as a base for soups or sauces.

MAKES ABOUT 3 QUARTS
4 pounds chicken backs, necks and/or wings
2 whole chickens (about 3 pounds each), including neck and gizzards
3 large carrots, sliced
2 large onions, sliced
4 medium leeks—split lengthwise, rinsed and sliced crosswise (or, substitute 1 extra onion)
2 celery ribs with leaves, sliced
Bouquet garni: 8 sprigs of parsley, 1 teaspoon thyme, 1 bay leaf, ½ teaspoon peppercorns and 3 whole cloves tied in a double thickness of cheesecloth

1. Place the chicken parts in a large, heavy stockpot; place the whole chickens on top. Add 6 quarts of cold water and place over low heat. Heat to simmering without stirring; for a clear stock, this should take about 1 hour. While the water is heating, skim off any scum that rises to the surface.

2. Add the carrots, onions, leeks, celery and bouquet garni. Simmer, partially covered, without stirring, for about 45 minutes. Remove both chickens. Continue simmering the stock,

without stirring, for about 4 hours, skimming occasionally. (The meat can be removed from the two chickens as soon as they are cool enough to handle and the bones returned to the pot.)

3. Ladle the stock carefully through a colander lined with several layers of dampened cheesecloth. Strain a second time, if desired, for an even clearer stock. Let cool to room temperature; then cover and refrigerate. Remove the congealed fat from the top. If using the hot stock immediately, remove the fat by first skimming and then blotting the surface with paper towels, or use a degreasing utensil designed for that purpose.

—F&W

WHITE VEAL STOCK

Use this clear, delicate stock to create sauces for veal, chicken or fish dishes.

MAKES 2 TO 3 QUARTS
4½ pounds veal bones
3 pounds veal stew meat, such as shank, breast, neck
2 leeks (white part only), cut into 2-inch lengths
2 medium onions, quartered
2 celery ribs with leaves, cut into 2-inch lengths
2 carrots, cut into 2-inch lengths
Bouquet garni: 6 sprigs of parsley, ½ teaspoon thyme, 1 bay leaf, 2 unpeeled garlic cloves, 3 whole cloves and 4 peppercorns tied in a double thickness of cheesecloth

1. Place the veal bones and meat in a large stockpot. Add enough cold water to cover, about 3 quarts. Cover the pot and bring to a boil over high heat. Lower the heat to moderate and boil gently for 5 minutes. Drain, discarding the water, and rinse the bones

under cold running water. Rinse out the pot. Return the bones and meat to the stockpot and add enough cold water to cover. Bring to a simmer over low heat and skim off any scum that rises to the surface. Add 1 cup cold water and when the liquid has returned to a simmer, skim again. Repeat the cold water-skimming process until the liquid is clear.

2. Add the leeks, onions, celery, carrots and bouquet garni. Simmer, partially covered, for 4 to 5 hours, adding water to cover as necessary.

3. When the stock is ready, carefully ladle it through a colander lined with several thicknesses of dampened cheesecloth into a large bowl. Allow to cool. Cover and refrigerate. After the stock has jelled, remove any fat that has accumulated on the surface.

—F&W

DUCK STOCK

MAKES ABOUT 2 QUARTS
3 duck carcasses
Duck wings
Duck hearts and gizzards
2 medium onions, thickly sliced
2 carrots, thickly sliced
½ cup chopped celery tops
2 medium leeks (green part only), thickly sliced
Bouquet garni: ½ cup fresh parsley stems, 1 teaspoon thyme and 1 bay leaf tied in cheesecloth

1. In a large stockpot, combine the carcasses, wings, hearts, gizzards, onions, carrots, celery tops, leeks and bouquet garni. Add 5 quarts of water and bring to a boil over moderately high heat. Reduce the heat and sim-

Burnt Orange Bavarian (p. 204).

mer gently, skimming from time to time, for 3½ hours, or until reduced to about 2 quarts.

2. Strain through a cheesecloth-lined strainer, pressing hard on the solids to extract all the liquid.

—*Deirdre Davis & Linda Marino*

TURKEY STOCK

Refrigerate the stock, uncovered, overnight. The next day, remove any fat that has congealed on the surface. The stock can be refrigerated for up to 3 days and then reboiled, or it can be frozen for several months.

MAKES ABOUT 9 CUPS
1 turkey carcass
1 teaspoon black peppercorns
1 bay leaf
1 medium onion, quartered
1 carrot, quartered
2 celery ribs, quartered
1 chicken bouillon cube
½ pound turkey or chicken wings (optional)

1. If you are making this with a turkey that was stuffed, scrape as much stuffing as possible from the cavity of the carcass. Cut the carcass as necessary to fit the stockpot. Add 12 cups of cold water and the peppercorns, bay leaf, onion, carrot, celery, bouillon cube and turkey wings, if using. (The additional wings will make the stock more gelatinous and flavorful.)

2. Bring to a boil over high heat. Reduce the heat to moderately low and simmer gently for 3 hours, skimming frequently.

3. Strain the stock through several layers of cheesecloth, pressing hard on the solids to extract as much liquid as possible. Use the stock immediately or refrigerate overnight. Remove any fat from the surface the next day.

—*Molly O'Neill*

QUICK TURKEY STOCK

This is a quick and easy way to make turkey stock with the giblets. Use it as a basting liquid for a roast turkey, or as a deglazing liquid to make a pan gravy.

MAKES 3½ CUPS
3½ cups chicken broth or water
Turkey giblets (neck, heart and gizzard)
1 medium onion, peeled and quartered
1 medium carrot, peeled and quartered
1 celery rib with leaves, coarsely chopped
1 imported bay leaf
Salt and freshly ground pepper

In a large saucepan, combine the broth, turkey giblets, onion, carrot, celery and bay leaf. Bring to a boil over high heat. Reduce the heat to moderately low, cover and simmer for 45 minutes; strain. If there is more than 3½ cups, boil to reduce. If there is less, make up the difference with water. Season with salt and pepper to taste.

—*Arthur Gold & Robert Fizdale*

FISH STOCK

When cleaning whole fish, save the heads and frames for stock; or, inquire at your local fish market. Use this stock for a variety of sauces.

MAKES ABOUT 2 QUARTS
4 pounds fish bones and trimmings (heads, tails, skin)
3 tablespoons vegetable oil
1 medium onion, cut into eighths

1 large celery rib, cut into 1-inch lengths
1 large carrot, cut into 1-inch lengths
Bouquet garni: 3 sprigs of parsley, ½ teaspoon thyme, 1 bay leaf and 8 to 10 peppercorns tied in a double thickness of cheesecloth

1. Rinse the fish bones and trimmings under cold running water to remove any blood; drain.

2. Heat the oil in a large, heavy stockpot. Add the fish bones and trimmings and sauté over moderate heat for 5 minutes, breaking them up occasionally with a wooden spoon. Cook, partially covered, for 5 minutes longer.

3. Add the onion, celery, carrot and bouquet garni. Pour in 3 quarts of cold water. Bring the mixture to a boil over high heat, skimming off any foam from the surface. Reduce the heat to low and simmer, uncovered, for 30 minutes. Strain through a fine sieve lined with several layers of dampened cheesecloth.

—*F&W*

VEGETABLE STOCK

MAKES ABOUT 1½ QUARTS
3 celery ribs, cut into 2-inch lengths
2 large carrots, cut into 2-inch lengths
2 small onions, unpeeled and quartered
1 large boiling potato, cut into 1-inch slices
½ pound mushrooms, roughly chopped
4 small leeks (white part only), split lengthwise
2 small white turnips, peeled and quartered
6 garlic cloves, unpeeled

1½ teaspoons salt
1½ teaspoons Hungarian sweet
   paprika
Bouquet garni: 10 sprigs of parsley,
   1½ teaspoons marjoram, 2 bay
   leaves and 8 peppercorns tied in a
   double thickness of cheesecloth

1. Place all the vegetables in a stockpot. Add the garlic, salt, paprika, bouquet garni and 3 quarts of water and bring to a boil over moderate heat.

2. Reduce the heat to low and simmer the stock, partially covered, until reduced by half, about 1½ hours.

3. Strain through a double thickness of dampened cheesecloth, pressing lightly on the vegetables with the back of a spoon.

—F&W

TOMATO GRAVY

In the South this recipe is traditionally prepared with fresh tomatoes, but if these are unavailable, you can substitute the canned variety. This gravy is delicious with pork chops but can also be served with fried chicken or steak.

MAKES ABOUT 2 CUPS
2 tablespoons fat plus drippings from
   the pan in which the meat was
   cooked
¼ cup minced onion
2 tablespoons all-purpose flour
2 cups peeled, seeded and chopped
   tomatoes with their juice
Up to ¾ cup chicken stock or water
   (optional)
½ teaspoon thyme
1 teaspoon sugar
¼ teaspoon salt
¼ teaspoon freshly ground pepper

1. Being careful to leave the browned bits in the skillet in which

the meat was cooked, pour off all but 2 tablespoons of fat. Heat the fat. Add the onion and sauté over moderate heat until softened and lightly browned, about 2 minutes.

2. Stir in the flour and cook, stirring constantly, until it is well browned, about 3 minutes. Add the tomatoes and stir well to combine. If there is not enough liquid, add the chicken stock or water. Season with thyme, sugar, salt and pepper.

3. Reduce the heat to low and simmer the gravy, stirring occasionally, 20 to 30 minutes. Serve very hot.

—Bill Neal

COUNTRY GRAVY

This traditional southern gravy will go perfectly with your favorite fried chicken. Be sure to reserve the fat and meat drippings in your skillet for use in this recipe.

MAKES ABOUT 2 CUPS
2 tablespoons fat plus drippings from
   the pan in which the chicken was
   fried
½ cup loosely packed julienne strips
   of country ham or prosciutto
2 tablespoons all-purpose flour
2 cups milk

1. Being careful to leave the browned drippings in the pan, pour off all but 2 tablespoons of the cooking fat from the skillet. Add the ham and cook, stirring often, over moderate heat, about 2 minutes. Add the flour and cook, stirring constantly with a whisk, until it is well browned, about 3 minutes.

2. Gradually add the milk to the skillet. Cook, stirring constantly, over low heat; bring the mixture to a gentle boil and simmer until the gravy thickens, 2 to 3 minutes.

—Bill Neal

OLD-FASHIONED PAN GRAVY

This traditional pan gravy can be prepared with any type of meat that will give you sufficient drippings, such as our Standing Rib Roast (page 99).

MAKES ABOUT 2 CUPS
3 tablespoons meat drippings or
   melted beef fat, reserved from a
   roast
3 tablespoons all-purpose flour
3 tablespoons port or Madeira
   (optional)
2 cups Quick Homemade Beef Stock
   (p. 220) or canned broth, warmed
Salt and freshly ground pepper

1. When you have finished cooking your roast, transfer it to a plate and degrease the roasting pan, leaving about 3 tablespoons of meat drippings. Heat the drippings and sprinkle the flour into the pan; blend thoroughly with a wooden spoon or spatula. Cook over moderately low heat, stirring and scraping up any brown bits from the bottom and sides of the pan, until the flour is lightly browned, about 3 minutes. (The color of your roux may appear darker, depending on the color of the meat drippings in the roasting pan.)

2. Whisk in the port or 3 tablespoons of the beef stock and deglaze the pan by boiling over high heat and scraping up any brown bits with a wooden spoon, about 1 minute.

3. Gradually add the warmed beef stock, ½ cup at a time, and continue to cook, whisking constantly. Bring to a boil, reduce the heat and simmer, stirring occasionally, until thickened, about 3 minutes.

4. Strain the gravy into a small

STOCKS & SAUCES

bowl or sauceboat. Add any meat juices that have collected on the platter when you sliced the roast. Season with salt and pepper to taste and serve.

—Diana Sturgis

CREME FRAICHE

MAKES ABOUT 2¼ CUPS
2 cups heavy cream
⅓ cup active-culture buttermilk

1. In a small saucepan, gently heat the cream and buttermilk to just under 100° (higher will kill the culture).
2. Pour into a clean glass jar, cover and place in a saucepan filled with warm (100°) water; or put in a thermos bottle. Allow to stand for 8 to 36 hours, or until thickened, replenishing the warm water from time to time. The longer you culture the cream, the tangier it will become.
3. Refrigerate until chilled. Crème fraîche will keep in the refrigerator for a week to 10 days.

—F&W

BASIC MAYONNAISE

Mayonnaise works best if all the ingredients are at room temperature before you begin. The emulsion (the suspension of the particles of oil within the yolk) will not form if the oil or the yolks are too cold. On a chilly day, warm the bowl and whisk in hot water, then dry well before starting.

MAKES ABOUT 1½ CUPS
3 egg yolks, at room temperature
1 teaspoon Dijon-style mustard
½ teaspoon salt

Pinch of white pepper
1 tablespoon fresh lemon juice
½ cup olive oil mixed with ½ cup light vegetable oil (see Note)
1 tablespoon white wine vinegar
1 tablespoon boiling water

1. In a medium bowl, whisk the egg yolks until they lighten in color and begin to thicken. Beat in the mustard, salt, pepper and lemon juice and continue whisking until the mixture thickens enough to leave a trail when the whisk is drawn across the bottom of the bowl.
2. Very gradually, begin whisking in the oil by droplets. The emulsion will not form if the oil is added too quickly at this stage.
3. Once the emulsion forms and the mayonnaise begins to thicken, you can add the oil more rapidly, but never faster than in a thin stream.
4. After all the oil has been incorporated, whisk in the vinegar and the boiling water. (The vinegar will lighten and flavor the sauce, the boiling water will help stabilize it.) Taste the mayonnaise and adjust the seasonings according to your taste and the planned use. Cover and refrigerate for up to 5 days.
NOTE: We find this combination of oils produces the perfect balance of flavor and lightness for an all-purpose mayonnaise. You can adjust the proportions according to your taste and particular use.

—F&W

LEMON MAYONNAISE

MAKES ABOUT 1½ CUPS
4 egg yolks
1 teaspoon Dijon-style mustard
¾ teaspoon salt
¼ teaspoon freshly ground white pepper
3 tablespoons fresh lemon juice
2 teaspoons freshly grated lemon zest
½ cup extra-virgin olive oil
½ cup safflower oil
1 tablespoon boiling water
2 tablespoons minced parsley

1. In a medium bowl, whisk the egg yolks until thick. Beat in the mustard, salt, white pepper, 1½ tablespoons of the lemon juice and the lemon zest.
2. Very gradually, begin whisking in the oils by droplets. Once an emulsion forms, add the remaining oil in a thin stream, whisking all the while. When all the oil has been incorporated, whisk in the remaining 1½ tablespoons lemon juice, the boiling water and the parsley.

—W. Peter Prestcott

BEURRE BLANC SAUCE

MAKES ABOUT 1½ CUPS
2 to 3 shallots, finely chopped
½ cup distilled white vinegar
2 sticks (8 ounces) lightly salted butter, at room temperature
2 to 3 tablespoons chopped fresh herbs (optional)

In a small heavy saucepan, cook the shallots slowly in the vinegar until only 1 tablespoon of liquid remains. Off the heat, or over very low heat, whisk in the butter 2 tablespoons at a time. Stir in the fresh herbs if used. (This sauce can be kept warm for about 30 minutes in a larger pan of warm water.)

—*Richard Grausman*

AIOLI-MUSTARD MARINADE

Use this as a marinade for grilled meats, especially lamb. Coat the meat with the marinade and let stand, covered, at room temperature for several hours.

If you're pressed for time, you can make this marinade with store-bought mayonnaise. To 1 cup, add the crushed garlic, a little lemon juice, the mustard, thyme and ginger.

MAKES ABOUT 1 CUP

4 to 5 garlic cloves, to taste, crushed
1 egg yolk
Salt
¾ cup olive oil
Fresh lemon juice
1 tablespoon Dijon-style mustard
2 teaspoons thyme
1 tablespoon finely chopped fresh ginger
2 teaspoons dry white wine

Put the garlic in a small mixing bowl. Blend in the egg yolk and a pinch of salt. Gradually whisk in the oil, drop by drop at first until the mixture begins to thicken. Whisk in the remainder in a steady stream. As the sauce thickens, thin out with a little lemon juice to taste. Stir in the mustard, thyme and ginger. Add the wine to thin out slightly. Season with salt to taste.

—*Richard Grausman*

REMOULADE SAUCE

MAKES ABOUT 1½ CUPS

1 cup mayonnaise, preferably homemade
1 teaspoon Dijon-style mustard
½ teaspoon anchovy paste
1 tablespoon minced capers
1 tablespoon minced cornichons (French gherkin pickles)
1 tablespoon minced parsley
1 tablespoon minced fresh chives
2 teaspoons fresh lemon juice

In a bowl, combine the mayonnaise, mustard, anchovy paste, capers, cornichons, parsley, chives and lemon juice with ½ cup of water. Whisk to blend well. Cover and refrigerate until serving time.

—*John Robert Massie*

TAPENADE SAUCE

Tapenade, an anchovy-spiked black olive paste from the south of France, adds a nice sharp flavor to this dipping sauce.

MAKES ABOUT 1 CUP

1 egg yolk
1 garlic clove, minced
½ teaspoon Dijon-style mustard
2 teaspoons fresh lemon juice
1 tablespoon dry white wine
1 tablespoon black olive paste*
1 tablespoon minced parsley
1 cup safflower or other light vegetable oil
*Available at specialty food stores

In a medium bowl, whisk together the egg yolk, garlic, mustard, lemon juice, wine, black olive paste and parsley until blended. Gradually whisk in the oil, then beat in 1 tablespoon of warm water.

—*Anne Disrude*

PESTO

The intensity of any pesto varies with the type and pungency of the basil and garlic used, but included here are tips that will give you a sweet, mild, bright green pesto.

MAKES ABOUT 1 CUP

4 cups (loosely packed) fresh basil leaves
2 large garlic cloves, halved
½ cup toasted walnut halves or pieces
½ teaspoon salt
¼ teaspoon freshly ground pepper
3 tablespoons freshly grated Parmesan cheese
½ cup plus 2 tablespoons extra-virgin olive oil

1. Wash and completely dry the basil leaves (see Tips, below).

2. In a food processor, add half of the basil, garlic, walnuts, salt, pepper and Parmesan cheese. Process for 10 seconds, or until the basil is finely minced. With the machine on, pour in ¼ cup of the olive oil and process for about 10 seconds, until the oil is absorbed. Stop and scrape down the sides of the bowl. Process for 5 seconds longer. With a rubber spatula, remove the pesto to a container. Repeat this procedure with the remaining basil, garlic, walnuts, salt, pepper, Parmesan cheese and ¼ cup olive oil.

3. To store, cover the pesto with the remaining 2 tablespoons of olive oil and place plastic wrap directly on the surface. The pesto will keep, refrigerated, for up to 1 week.

TIPS: If water is left on the leaves, it will make it difficult to efficiently chop the leaves and will turn the mixture black. If time allows, wash the basil the day before; allowing the leaves to rest overnight cuts down on any bitterness.

To ensure efficient chopping, always process the basil with the other dry ingredients before adding the olive oil. The instant the leaves are minced, pour in the oil. Timing in both these steps is important, since overprocessing can destroy the color.

—*Marcia Kiesel*

SALSA TRICOLORE

This piquant sauce, flecked with brightly colored herbs and bits of roasted red pepper and hard-cooked egg, is a quick and delicious oil bath for grilled fish, chicken or meats. It's especially tasty on cold meats or vegetables or with boiled beef. My recipe is freely adapted from a sauce served by Lidia Bastianich at Felidia in New York City.

MAKES ABOUT 2 CUPS
1 medium red bell pepper
1 small red onion, minced (about ½ cup)
1 small celery rib, trimmed and minced (about ⅓ cup)
2 garlic cloves, minced
½ cup chopped Italian flat-leaf parsley
3 to 4 tablespoons chopped fresh chives
2 tablespoons chopped fresh sage or ½ teaspoon dried
1 to 2 teaspoons chopped fresh tarragon (optional)
1 teaspoon salt
½ teaspoon freshly ground black pepper
3 tablespoons balsamic vinegar
2 tablespoons red wine vinegar
¾ cup fruity extra-virgin olive oil
1 hard-cooked egg, finely chopped

1. Roast the pepper under a broiler or directly over a gas flame, turning with tongs, until the skin is charred all over, about 10 minutes. Wrap in foil (or enclose in a paper bag) and let stand for 10 to 15 minutes. Peel off the skin, then remove the stem, seeds and ribs. Cut the pepper into ¼-inch dice and place in a mixing bowl.

2. Add the onion, celery, garlic, parsley, chives, sage, tarragon, salt, black pepper, balsamic and red wine vinegars and the olive oil. Blend well. Stir in the hard-cooked egg. Taste and adjust the seasonings and vinegar-oil balance to your taste. Cover and let mellow at room temperature briefly before using.

—*Richard Sax*

FRESH TOMATO SALSA

This sauce can be spooned over your favorite meats or served simply as a dip with tortilla chips.

MAKES ABOUT 1½ CUPS
5 whole scallions, coarsely chopped
6 large plum tomatoes—peeled, seeded and chopped
1 tablespoon olive oil
½ teaspoon salt
¼ teaspoon ground cumin
¼ teaspoon oregano
Pinch of cayenne pepper

In a large bowl, combine the scallions and tomatoes. Season with the olive oil, salt, cumin, oregano and cayenne. Mix well. Cover and refrigerate for up to 3 hours before serving.

—*Anne Disrude*

VINAIGRETTE DRESSING WITH GARLIC AND FRESH HERBS

Every good cook has a great salad dressing; I like to spike mine with fresh herbs and garlic. Because this creamy vinaigrette is based on an egg yolk, the total yield is more than you will need to serve 6 or 8. Simply refrigerate the remainder in a tightly covered jar and shake to blend well before using.

MAKES ABOUT ¾ CUP
1 egg yolk
1 garlic clove, crushed through a press
1½ teaspoons Dijon-style mustard
2 tablespoons red wine vinegar
½ cup mild olive oil
1 tablespoon minced fresh basil
1 tablespoon minced parsley
¾ teaspoon coarse (kosher) salt
½ teaspoon freshly ground pepper

In a medium bowl, whisk together the egg yolk, garlic, mustard and vinegar until well blended. Gradually whisk in the oil. Blend in the minced basil, parsley, salt and pepper.

—*Lydie Marshall*

WHITE FRENCH DRESSING

MAKES ABOUT 1 CUP
1 medium onion
1 cup mayonnaise, preferably homemade
1 tablespoon fresh lemon juice
4 teaspoons red wine vinegar
1 small garlic clove, minced
½ teaspoon salt
¼ teaspoon freshly ground white pepper

1. In a food processor, puree the onion. Scrape the puree into a fine-mesh strainer set over a medium bowl. Using the back of a spoon, press the puree through the strainer to extract 2 tablespoons of juice. Discard the puree.

2. Add the mayonnaise, lemon juice, vinegar, garlic, salt and pepper to the onion juice. Whisk the dressing until thoroughly blended.

—*Gaidos, Galveston, Texas*

BALSAMIC VINEGAR MIGNONETTE SAUCE

A variation of a classic mignonette, this sauce is best with raw oysters, but it's also good on raw clams and makes a light, tangy dip for cold boiled shrimp.

MAKES ABOUT ⅔ CUP
2 tablespoons minced shallot
1 tablespoon minced carrot
1 tablespoon minced parsley
½ tablespoon coarsely cracked black pepper
¼ cup dry white wine
¼ cup balsamic vinegar

In a small bowl, combine the shallot, carrot, parsley, pepper, wine and vinegar. Serve immediately, or cover and refrigerate for up to 3 hours.

—*Anne Disrude*

TARRAGON-PERNOD BUTTER

This butter can be kept on hand in the freezer for several months. To turn this into a delicious emulsified sauce for roasted shellfish, cut it into pieces and melt slowly over low heat, whisking constantly. When the butter is completely melted and emulsified, transfer to a bowl and serve.

MAKES ABOUT 10 TABLESPOONS
1½ tablespoons chopped shallot
1½ tablespoons chopped fresh tarragon or 2 teaspoons dried
1½ teaspoons tarragon vinegar
1 teaspoon Pernod
½ teaspoon coarsely cracked pepper
1 stick (4 ounces) unsalted butter, cut into pieces

Combine the shallot, tarragon, vinegar, Pernod and pepper in a food processor. Turn the machine on and off until the ingredients are minced but not pureed. Add the butter and process until blended. Transfer the butter to a sheet of plastic wrap and roll into a log about 1½ inches in diameter. Roll up in plastic and twist the ends securely. Freeze until firm, about 1½ hours.

—*Anne Disrude*

RED PEPPER AND HERB BUTTER

This butter can be refrigerated for a couple of days or kept on hand in the freezer for several months. To convert the butter to an emulsified sauce (delicious on roasted shellfish), cut it into pieces and melt it slowly over low heat, whisking constantly. Do not let boil or the sauce will break.

MAKES ABOUT 10 TABLESPOONS
½ red bell pepper, cut into small pieces
2 scallions, chopped
1 tablespoon chopped garlic
½ teaspoon thyme
1 tablespoon chopped parsley
Pinch of cayenne pepper
1 stick (4 ounces) unsalted butter, cut into pieces

Combine the bell pepper, scallions, garlic, thyme, parsley and cayenne in a food processor. Turn the machine on and off until the ingredients are minced but not pureed. Add the butter pieces and process until blended. Transfer the butter to a sheet of plastic wrap and roll into a log shape about 1½ inches in diameter. Roll up in plastic and twist the ends securely. Freeze the butter until firm, about 1½ hours.

—*Anne Disrude*

ROSA RISTORANTE'S PORCINI SAUCE

At the restaurant, this sauce is served with ricotta and spinach ravioli. You can also serve it over plain pasta, as a first course, with freshly grated Parmesan cheese.

MAKES ABOUT 1¾ CUPS
1 ounce dried porcini mushrooms
2 cups heavy cream
3 tablespoons unsalted butter
¼ teaspoon salt
⅛ teaspoon freshly ground pepper

1. In a medium bowl, cover the mushrooms with 1 cup of warm water and let soak for 30 minutes.

2. Strain the mushroom soaking liquid into a medium saucepan through several layers of dampened cheesecloth; set aside. Rinse the mushrooms well. Trim off any sandy stem ends. Coarsely chop the mushrooms and add to the saucepan.

3. Bring the mushroom liquid to a

boil over high heat and cook until reduced to 3 tablespoons, about 7 minutes. Reduce the heat to moderate, add the cream and cook until reduced to 1½ cups, about 7 minutes longer. Remove from the heat and whisk in the butter, 1 tablespoon at a time. Season with the salt and pepper.

—Mario Ricci, Rosa Ristorante Italiano, Baldwin Park, California

THICK COCONUT MILK

Coconut milk is made by pressing a mixture of shredded coconut and hot water through a strainer. The first pressing yields Thick Coconut Milk. A second pressing will yield Thin Coconut Milk (recipe follows). Combining the liquid from both pressings is similar to mixing cream and skim milk to yield whole milk.

MAKES ABOUT 1½ CUPS THICK COCONUT MILK
1 coconut
2 cups hot water (see Note)

1. Preheat the oven to 350°. Place the coconut in a small baking dish and cook until the outer shell cracks in several places, about 30 minutes.
2. Wrap the hot coconut in 3 layers of kitchen towels. Using a small hammer, pound the wrapped coconut until it breaks open.
3. Unwrap the coconut and discard the liquid inside. Using a strong dull knife, pry the hard, outer shell away from the coconut meat. Using a vegetable peeler, remove the thin brown skin from the coconut.
4. Cut the white coconut meat into 1-inch pieces. Place in a food processor and process until shredded (there will be about 3 cups of coconut.)

5. Pour the hot water over the coconut and process for 1 minute. Transfer to a fine strainer set over a large bowl and press with a rubber spatula or wooden spoon. Reserve the shredded coconut to make Thin Coconut Milk (see below).
NOTE: For an even richer coconut milk, use milk instead of water.

THIN COCONUT MILK: Return the reserved shredded coconut to the food processor. Add 2 cups of hot water and process for 1 minute. Transfer the coconut to a fine strainer set over a large bowl and press the mixture through. Yields about 1½ cups.

—Marcia Kiesel

APRICOT SAUCE

MAKES ABOUT 1 CUP
2 ounces dried apricots (⅓ cup)
1 tablespoon dark rum

1. Place the apricots and 1 cup of water in a small saucepan and bring to a boil over low heat. Cover and set aside to soak for 30 minutes.
2. Bring to a simmer, cover and cook until soft, about 20 minutes.
3. Pour the apricots and the liquid into a blender or food processor and puree until smooth. Mix in the rum. Serve warm or at room temperature.

—Diana Sturgis

CHUNKY PINEAPPLE SAUCE

Taste the pineapple before adding it to the sugar syrup; a sweet pineapple may need less syrup and more lemon juice.

MAKES ABOUT 2½ CUPS
1 ripe medium pineapple
½ cup sugar
1 tablespoon fresh lemon juice

1. Cut off the top and bottom of the pineapple. Stand the pineapple upright and slice off a ¼-inch layer all around to remove the rind and all the eyes. Cut out and discard the tough core. Coarsely chop half the pineapple and set aside. Cut the other half of the pineapple into chunks and puree in a food processor.
2. In a medium noncorrodible saucepan, bring the sugar and ¼ cup of water to a boil over high heat. Boil without stirring until the sugar dissolves, about 1 minute. Remove from the heat.
3. Add the pineapple puree, the reserved chopped pineapple and the lemon juice. Gently warm the pineapple sauce over moderately low heat before serving.

—Margaret Fox, Cafe Beaujolais, Mendocino, California

GOLDEN DRIED FRUIT AND COGNAC SAUCE

MAKES ABOUT 3¼ CUPS
¼ pound dried pineapple, cut into large dice
½ pound dried apricots, quartered

¼ *cup currants*
¼ *cup Cognac or brandy*
¼ *cup sugar*
2 tablespoons fresh lemon juice

1. In a food processor, in batches if necessary, process the pineapple and apricots until finely chopped.

2. Transfer the fruit to a medium noncorrodible saucepan. Add the currants, Cognac, sugar, lemon juice and 2 cups of water. Bring to a boil over moderate heat, stirring once or twice. Reduce the heat and simmer, partially covered, stirring occasionally, for about 25 minutes, or until the fruit has absorbed most of the liquid and is tender.

3. Transfer the sauce to a heatproof storage container. Let cool to room temperature, cover and refrigerate. To serve, rewarm over low heat.

—*Michael McLaughlin*

CUSTARD SAUCE

MAKES ABOUT 3 CUPS
6 egg yolks
⅔ *cup sugar*
2½ *cups milk*
1½ *tablespoons brandy*
1 teaspoon vanilla extract

1. In a large bowl, combine the egg yolks and ⅓ cup of the sugar. Beat until the sugar dissolves and the mixture is light colored, about 3 minutes.

2. In a heavy medium saucepan, combine the remaining ⅓ cup sugar and the milk. Bring to a boil. Gradually whisk the milk into the egg yolk mixture in a thin stream.

3. Return the custard to the saucepan. Cook over moderately low heat, stirring constantly, until the custard is thick enough to coat the back of a wooden spoon, about 10 minutes. It

should register 180° on an instant-reading thermometer; do not let the custard boil or the eggs will curdle.

4. Remove from the heat and strain into a bowl. Stir in the brandy and vanilla. Serve warm, at room temperature or chilled. (**The sauce can be made a day ahead.** Cover well and refrigerate.)

—*Diana Sturgis*

BITTERSWEET DOUBLE CHOCOLATE SAUCE

MAKES ABOUT 1 QUART
1½ *sticks (6 ounces) unsalted butter, cut into pieces*
6 ounces dark or semisweet chocolate, coarsely chopped
¾ *cup plus 2 tablespoons sugar*
¾ *cup (firmly packed) unsweetened cocoa powder, sifted*
1 teaspoon freeze-dried instant coffee
½ *teaspoon cinnamon*
½ *cup light corn syrup*
1¼ *cups heavy cream*
1 teaspoon vanilla extract

1. In a heavy medium saucepan, melt the butter and chocolate together over low heat, stirring occasionally, until smooth.

2. Stir in the sugar. Sift in the cocoa and stir well. Add the instant coffee, cinnamon and corn syrup. Slowly whisk in the heavy cream. Bring just to a boil, reduce the heat immediately and simmer for 5 minutes, stirring once or twice and scraping down the sides of the pan with a rubber spatula.

3. Remove from the heat, stir in the

vanilla and pour immediately into a heatproof storage container. Let cool to room temperature, cover and refrigerate. (**The sauce will keep well, refrigerated, for several weeks.**)

4. To serve, remove the desired amount of sauce from the container and reheat in a double boiler, stirring, until hot.

—*Michael McLaughlin*

HOT CHOCOLATE SAUCE

MAKES ABOUT 1½ CUPS
5 ounces semisweet chocolate, coarsely chopped
1⅓ *cups milk*
1 cup sugar
¼ *cup corn syrup*
2 tablespoons instant espresso powder
2 tablespoons unsalted butter, cut into small pieces
Pinch of salt
1 tablespoon brandy

1. In a heavy medium saucepan, combine the chocolate, milk, sugar, corn syrup, espresso powder, butter and salt. Cook over low heat, stirring frequently, until the chocolate and butter melt.

2. Increase the heat to high and bring the mixture to a boil. Cover and boil for 2 minutes. Remove the cover and continue to boil until the temperature reaches 230°, about 3 minutes. Remove from the heat and place the pan in a bowl of cold water to stop the cooking.

3. Beat the chocolate for 1 minute. Let cool for 3 minutes, then beat in the brandy. Reheat in a double boiler before serving.

—*Arthur Gold & Robert Fizdale*

STOCKS & SAUCES

QUICK AND EASY CHOCOLATE SAUCE

MAKES ABOUT 1 CUP

1 teaspoon instant coffee powder
4 tablespoons unsalted butter, cut up
8 ounces bittersweet chocolate,
  broken into 1-inch bits
1 teaspoon vanilla extract

In a small heavy saucepan, dissolve the coffee in 2 tablespoons of hot water. Add the butter, chocolate and vanilla and cook over very low heat, stirring, until the chocolate melts and the sauce is smooth. (**The sauce can be made ahead.** Refrigerated and tightly covered, it will keep for several weeks. Rewarm over very low heat.)
—Diana Sturgis

BUTTERSCOTCH SAUCE

MAKES ABOUT 2½ CUPS

1 stick (4 ounces) unsalted butter
1 cup (packed) light brown sugar
⅓ cup light corn syrup
1½ cups heavy cream
1 tablespoon vanilla extract
1 teaspoon lemon juice, strained

1. In a heavy medium saucepan, melt the butter and brown sugar over moderate heat. Stir in the corn syrup. Whisk in the cream, increase the heat and bring just to a boil. Reduce the heat and simmer, stirring occasionally, until slightly thickened, 15 to 20 minutes.
2. Remove from the heat, stir in the vanilla and lemon juice and pour immediately into a heatproof storage container. Let cool to room temperature, cover and refrigerate. (**The sauce will keep well, refrigerated, for several weeks.**)
3. To use, let return to room temperature, or reheat gently.
—Michael McLaughlin

HOT CARAMEL SAUCE

MAKES ABOUT 1 CUP

4 tablespoons unsalted butter, cut up
⅓ cup granulated sugar
⅓ cup (packed) light brown sugar
½ cup heavy cream

Combine all the ingredients in a heavy medium saucepan. Stir over moderately low heat until the butter melts and the sugar dissolves. Increase the heat to moderately high and boil, stirring, until the sauce thickens slightly and becomes a shade darker, 2 to 3 minutes. Pour at once into a heatproof bowl and let cool slightly.

—Diana Sturgis

CONDIMENTS & PRESERVES

ROASTED SZECHUAN PEPPER-SALT

In addition to its role in several Chinese appetizers, this makes an excellent all-purpose seasoning.

MAKES ABOUT ⅓ CUP
¼ cup coarse (kosher) salt
2 tablespoons Szechuan peppercorns*
*Available at Oriental markets

1. In a large heavy skillet, preferably cast iron, combine the salt and Szechuan peppercorns. Cook, stirring, over moderate heat for about 4 minutes, until the salt turns off-white and the peppercorns smoke fragrantly. (Do not let burn.)

2. Scrape the mixture into a mortar while hot and pound to a powder with a pestle, or pulverize in a spice grinder. Sieve to remove the peppercorn husks. Store in a glass jar away from light and heat.

—Barbara Tropp

CHILI-ORANGE OIL

MAKES ABOUT 3 CUPS
2 cups corn or peanut oil
¼ cup Oriental sesame oil
Zest of 3 large oranges (no white pith), well scrubbed (see Note) and finely minced
½ cup crushed hot pepper
3 tablespoons Chinese salted black beans*
1 to 2 large garlic cloves, to taste, peeled and lightly smashed
*Available at Oriental markets

1. In a heavy medium saucepan, combine the corn and sesame oils. Heat to 250°, or until hot enough to bubble up slowly around a pepper flake.

2. Add the orange zest, hot pepper, black beans and garlic. Remove from the heat, whisk gently to distribute the seasonings and set aside until cool.

3. Transfer the oil and seasonings to a glass jar and store in a cool, dark place. The chili-orange oil will keep almost indefinitely.

NOTE: Oranges are frequently sprayed or subject to pollutants. To wash the peel, use an untreated abrasive pad, a gentle liquid soap and hot tap water, scrubbing lightly until the smell of the orange oil comes to the surface of the peel.

—Barbara Tropp

INDONESIAN SWEET SOY SAUCE (KECAP MANIS)

In a covered jar in the refrigerator, this sauce keeps almost forever. With a little oil, water, garlic and ginger, it makes a fabulous marinade for lamb chops and steaks.

MAKES ABOUT 1½ CUPS
1 cup sugar
1¼ cups light Chinese soy sauce*
2 garlic cloves, bruised
2 large star anise pods*
*Available at Oriental markets

1. In a heavy medium saucepan, cook the sugar over moderately low heat, stirring occasionally, until it melts and caramelizes to a rich brown.

2. Add the soy sauce, garlic, star anise and ¼ cup of water. Cook, stirring, until the caramel and soy are blended. Simmer until slightly thickened, about 15 minutes. Let cool, then pour into a wide-mouthed jar. (Include the garlic and anise.) Cover and refrigerate for up to 2 years.

—Copeland Marks

YELLOW CURRY PASTE

This paste, which is mostly used for chicken curries in Thailand, gets its yellow tinge from turmeric. The use of this spice indicates that the curry has been influenced by the Indian traders who have come to Thailand during the last two centuries.

MAKES ABOUT ½ CUP
8 dried hot red peppers, seeded and broken into pieces, or 2 teaspoons cayenne pepper
1 tablespoon coriander seeds or 1 tablespoon ground coriander
2 teaspoons cuminseed or 2 teaspoons ground cumin
1 teaspoon whole black peppercorns or 1 teaspoon freshly ground black pepper
6 garlic cloves, minced (about 2 tablespoons)
4 shallots, minced (about ¼ cup)
1 stalk of fresh lemon grass*, minced, or grated zest of 1 lemon (about 2 teaspoons)
1 tablespoon minced fresh coriander stems and roots (do not use leaves)
1½ teaspoons turmeric
1 teaspoon ground galangal (laos, ka)* or ½ teaspoon ground ginger
1 teaspoon salt
2 teaspoons shrimp paste (kapi, trassi)* or Chinese shrimp sauce, or 2 teaspoons anchovy paste
2 tablespoons vegetable oil
*Available at Southeast Asian and some Chinese markets

1. In a spice mill or mortar, grind the hot peppers, coriander, cuminseed and black peppercorns to a powder. (Omit this step if using ground spices.)

2. Transfer the ground spices to a

food processor (or continue with the mortar and pestle). Add the garlic, shallots, lemon grass, fresh coriander, turmeric, galangal, salt, shrimp paste and oil. Process to as fine a paste as possible.

3. Transfer the paste to a jar and cap tightly. Store in the refrigerator for up to 3 months.

—*Jennifer Brennan*

GREEN CURRY PASTE

In Thailand, this is one of the hottest curry pastes because large quantities of fresh hot chile peppers are used— and they are not seeded. If you wish a less incendiary paste, remove the seeds and membranes. Alternatively, you may wish to halve the number of fresh green chile peppers and make up the volume with green bell pepper. The results will be different, but milder and equally pleasing.

MAKES ABOUT 1 CUP
10 fresh green serrano peppers or 5 fresh green jalapeño peppers, minced
6 garlic cloves, minced (about 2 tablespoons)
2 shallots, minced (about 2 tablespoons)
¼ cup minced fresh coriander leaves, stems and roots
1 teaspoon coriander seeds or 1 teaspoon ground coriander
1 teaspoon caraway seed or 1 teaspoon ground caraway
1 teaspoon whole black peppercorns or 1 teaspoon freshly ground black pepper
Grated zest of 2 limes (about 4 teaspoons)
1 stalk of fresh lemon grass*, minced, or grated zest of 1 lemon (about 2 teaspoons)

1 teaspoon ground galangal (laos, ka)* or ½ teaspoon ground ginger
1 teaspoon salt
½ teaspoon freshly grated nutmeg
¼ teaspoon ground cloves
1 teaspoon shrimp paste (kapi, trassi)* or Chinese shrimp sauce, or 1 teaspoon anchovy paste
2 tablespoons vegetable oil
*Available at Southeast Asian and some Chinese markets

1. In a food processor, puree the serrano peppers, garlic, shallots and fresh coriander to a juicy paste, stopping occasionally to scrape down the sides of the bowl.

2. In a spice mill or mortar, grind the coriander seeds, caraway and peppercorns to a powder. (Omit this step if using ground spices.) Add the ground spices to the paste in the food processor.

3. Add the lime zest, lemon grass, galangal, salt, nutmeg, cloves, shrimp paste and vegetable oil. Process to a fine paste.

4. Transfer the paste to a jar and cap tightly. Store in the refrigerator for up to 1 month.

—*Jennifer Brennan*

RED CURRY PASTE

This Thai curry paste gets its name, and its color, from the number of dried red chile peppers that are ground into the paste. The Thai do not remove the seeds, and if you can tolerate the heat or are brave enough to try it, leave them in.

MAKES ABOUT ¾ CUP
12 dried hot red peppers, seeded and broken into pieces, or 1 ample tablespoon cayenne pepper
8 pieces of dried galangal (laos, ka)*, broken into smaller pieces or 1½ teaspoons ground ginger

1 tablespoon coriander seeds or 1 tablespoon ground coriander
1 teaspoon caraway seeds or 1 teaspoon ground caraway
1 teaspoon whole black peppercorns or 1 teaspoon freshly ground black pepper
6 garlic cloves, minced (about 2 tablespoons)
4 shallots, minced (about ¼ cup)
3 tablespoons minced fresh coriander stems and roots (do not use leaves)
1 stalk of fresh lemon grass*, minced, or grated zest of 1 lemon (about 2 teaspoons)
Grated zest of 1 lime (about 2 teaspoons)
1 tablespoon paprika
1 teaspoon salt
1 teaspoon shrimp paste (kapi, trassi)* or Chinese shrimp sauce, or 1 teaspoon anchovy paste
¼ cup vegetable oil
*Available at Southeast Asian and some Chinese markets

1. In a spice mill or mortar, grind the hot peppers, galangal, coriander seeds, caraway seeds and peppercorns to a powder. (Omit this step if you are using all ground spices.)

2. Transfer the ground spices to a food processor (or continue with the mortar). Add the garlic, shallots, fresh coriander, lemon grass, lime zest, paprika, salt, shrimp paste and vegetable oil. Process to as fine a paste as possible. (The paste will be rather coarsely textured unless you are using a mortar and pestle.)

3. Transfer the paste to a jar and cap tightly. Store in the refrigerator for up to 3 months.

—*Jennifer Brennan*

CONDIMENTS & PRESERVES

MUSSAMAN CURRY PASTE

This is the Indian-influenced ringer of the Thai curry pastes. It is used to season only beef curries, never other meats or poultry. The robust array of strong spices would overpower a more delicately flavored meat.

MAKES ABOUT ½ CUP

2 tablespoons plus 1 teaspoon vegetable oil
8 garlic cloves, minced (about 2½ tablespoons)
8 shallots, minced (about ½ cup)
5 dried hot red peppers with their seeds, broken into pieces, or 1 teaspoon cayenne pepper
3 whole cloves or ¼ teaspoon ground cloves
½-inch piece of cinnamon stick, broken into fragments, or ½ teaspoon ground cinnamon
Seeds from 6 cardamom pods or ½ teaspoon ground cardamom
1 stalk of fresh lemon grass*, minced, or grated zest of 1 lemon (about 2 teaspoons)
Grated zest of 1 lime (about 2 teaspoons)
1 teaspoon ground galangal (laos, ka)* or ½ teaspoon ground ginger
½ teaspoon freshly grated nutmeg
½ teaspoon shrimp paste (kapi, trassi)* or Chinese shrimp sauce, or ½ teaspoon anchovy paste
*Available at Southeast Asian and some Chinese markets

1. Set a medium skillet over moderate heat and add 1 teaspoon of the oil. Add the minced garlic and shallots and cook, stirring constantly, until they are light brown. Scrape them into a food processor.

2. In a spice mill or mortar, grind the hot peppers, cloves, cinnamon and cardamom seeds to a powder. (Omit this step if using ground spices.)

3. Add the ground spices to the processor. Add the lemon grass, lime zest, galangal, nutmeg, shrimp paste and the remaining 2 tablespoons oil. Process to a fine paste.

4. Transfer the paste to a jar and cap tightly. Store in the refrigerator for up to 3 months.

—*Jennifer Brennan*

SEVEN-DAY PRESERVED LEMON

Preserved lemons are a Moroccan specialty, with a unique flavor that cannot be duplicated with fresh lemon juice or rind. I include here a new seven-day method to replace the traditional month-long preparation.

2 ripe lemons
⅓ cup coarse (kosher) salt
½ cup fresh lemon juice
Olive oil

Scrub the lemons and dry well. Cut each into 8 wedges. Toss with the salt and place in a ½-pint glass jar with a plastic-coated lid. Pour in the lemon juice. Close tightly and let ripen in a warm place for 7 days, shaking the jar each day to distribute the salt and juice. To store, add olive oil to cover and refrigerate for up to 6 months.

—*Paula Wolfert*

MUSTARDS GRILL PICKLED ONIONS

Chef Cindy Pawlcyn suggests serving these onions with smoked meats and fish.

MAKES ABOUT 2 CUPS

1¼ pounds pearl onions
¼ cup olive oil
¾ cup sugar
½ cup red wine vinegar
1 tablespoon ketchup
Pinch of crushed hot pepper

Pinch of freshly ground white pepper

1. Blanch the onions in boiling water for 30 seconds; drain and peel.

2. In a medium skillet, heat the oil. Add the onions and cook over moderate heat, tossing frequently, until golden all over, about 15 minutes.

3. Add the sugar, vinegar, ketchup, hot pepper and white pepper and simmer uncovered for 3 minutes. Let cool and serve at room temperature, or refrigerate, covered, for up to 1 week.

—*Cindy Pawlcyn, Mustards Grill, Napa, California*

SWEET AND SOUR ONIONS

This tangy relish can be made up to a week ahead. Store tightly covered in the refrigerator.

8 SERVINGS

1 pound (1 pint) tiny white pearl onions
1 cup dry white wine
½ cup white wine vinegar
¼ cup tomato paste
3 tablespoons olive oil
2 imported bay leaves
2 tablespoons chopped parsley
½ teaspoon thyme
1 cup currants or raisins
1 teaspoon sugar
½ teaspoon salt
¼ teaspoon freshly ground pepper

1. In a large saucepan of boiling water, blanch the onions for 2 minutes; drain. Rinse under cold running water until cool enough to handle; cut off the root ends and the peel.

2. In a large noncorrodible skillet, combine the wine, vinegar, tomato paste, oil, bay leaves, parsley, thyme, currants, sugar, salt, pepper and ½ cup of water. Bring to a boil, stirring, over moderately high heat.

3. Add the onions. Cover and simmer over moderate heat, stirring occasionally, for 15 minutes. Uncover and continue to cook, stirring frequently, until the onions are tender and the liquid is reduced to a thick sauce, 5 to 10 minutes. (If the onions are tender before the sauce is thick, remove them with a slotted spoon. When the sauce is thick, return the onions to the pan until heated through.) Transfer to a serving dish, spooning the sauce over the onions. Serve warm, at room temperature or chilled.

—*Arthur Gold & Robert Fizdale*

GARLIC AND ONION JAM

This rich, honey-colored jam makes a wonderful sandwich spread (see Lamb and Roasted Eggplant Sandwiches, p. 162) as well as a zesty accompaniment for pâtés and roasted or grilled meats served hot or cold.

MAKES ABOUT 1 CUP
2 large Spanish onions (about 1 pound), coarsely chopped
6 large garlic cloves, coarsely chopped
¼ cup extra-virgin olive oil
1 teaspoon fresh lemon juice
1 teaspoon salt, or to taste
½ teaspoon freshly ground pepper

1. In a heavy medium saucepan, combine the onions, garlic and olive oil. Cover and cook over very low heat, stirring occasionally, until the onions are very soft, golden brown and slightly caramelized, about 1 hour.

2. Transfer the onion mixture to a food processor or blender and puree. Stir in the lemon juice, salt and pepper. Scrape the jam into a small noncorrodible container and let cool completely. (The jam can be covered and

stored in the refrigerator for up to 1 week.)

—*Molly O'Neill*

CAULIFLOWER-CARROT PICKLES IN HONEY-MUSTARD

Blanched in sherry and dressed with sherry vinegar, these elegant pickles are also flavored with mustard, honey and olive oil. They're a good addition to any *tapas* selection and are great with ham or corned beef.

MAKES ABOUT 4 CUPS
1 medium head of cauliflower (about 1½ pounds), separated into 1½-inch florets
4 medium carrots (about ½ pound)
1½ cups dry sherry
⅓ cup plus 1 tablespoon sherry wine vinegar or cider vinegar
3 tablespoons coarse (kosher) salt
1 tablespoon sugar
1 teaspoon tarragon
¼ cup Dijon-style mustard
2 tablespoons honey
⅓ cup olive oil

1. Cut the cauliflorets into halves or quarters (their stems should be about ¼ inch thick). Cut the carrots into 3-by-¼-inch sticks.

2. In a large noncorrodible saucepan, combine the sherry, ⅓ cup of the vinegar, the salt, sugar, tarragon and 2 cups of water. Bring to a boil over high heat. Add the cauliflower and carrots and stir for 1 minute (the water will not return to a simmer).

3. Using a slotted spoon (to leave behind as much of the tarragon as possible), remove the vegetables to a colander to drain; do not rinse. Discard the cooking liquid. Place the vegetables on several layers of paper towels and top with several more; blot well to dry.

4. In a medium bowl, combine the mustard and honey with the remain-

ing 1 tablespoon vinegar. Whisking constantly, add the oil drop by drop and then slowly in a steady stream until all has been added and the dressing is creamy and thick.

5. Add the vegetables, toss well, cover with plastic wrap placed directly on the surface and refrigerate overnight. Toss again before serving.

—*Jim Fobel*

NEW DILL SLICES

I love these crunchy dill slices on hamburgers with mustard, mayonnaise and ketchup. They are also good alone or with almost any sandwich, such as chicken salad.

MAKES ABOUT 2 CUPS
1 pound (4 to 6 medium) pickling cucumbers, such as Kirbys, or regular cucumbers (2 medium)
1 tablespoon plus 1 teaspoon coarse (kosher) salt
3 tablespoons cider vinegar
½ teaspoon dill seed
1 bay leaf
1 garlic clove, thinly sliced
Several small sprigs of fresh dill (optional)

1. If using Kirbys, trim the ends away and cut into ⅛-inch slices. If using regular cucumbers, peel first and then cut into ⅛-inch slices. In a bowl, toss the cucumbers with 1 tablespoon of the salt. Let stand for 1 hour, tossing occasionally. Rinse and drain 3 times with cold water.

2. Meanwhile, in a small noncorrodible saucepan, combine the cider vinegar, dill seed, bay leaf, garlic, remaining 1 teaspoon salt and 1 cup of water. Bring to a boil over moderately high heat. Boil for 1 minute, remove from the heat and let cool to room temperature.

3. With your hands, squeeze out the excess moisture from the cucum-

239

ber slices. Place in a small bowl, add the fresh dill sprigs and the cooled brine. Cover and refrigerate for at least 1 hour, or overnight.

—*Jim Fobel*

KIM CHEE

Although this classic Korean pickle can take up to three weeks to pickle, this version is ready overnight (and happens to taste good after only an hour). It is delicious with grilled beef (such as its traditional partner, Korean *bul goki*) or chicken and perfect with charcoal-broiled hamburgers. Be sure to use the curly-leafed Napa cabbage and *not* the longer, thinner Chinese celery cabbage (which is more fibrous and takes longer to cure).

MAKES ABOUT 5 CUPS
1 medium head of Napa cabbage (about 1¾ pounds)
2 medium pickling cucumbers, such as Kirbys (about ¼ pound each)
¼ cup plus 2 teaspoons coarse (kosher) salt
1 tablespoon grated fresh ginger
1 large garlic clove, crushed through a press
1 tablespoon sugar
1 tablespoon sweet paprika
¼ teaspoon cayenne pepper
1 to 2 tablespoons soy sauce
¼ cup rice vinegar
½ cup sliced scallions (4 to 5 medium)

1. Trim away any wilted or bruised outer leaves from the head of cabbage. Cut the head crosswise into 1½-inch slices. Discard the core end.
2. Trim the ends of the cucumbers, halve them lengthwise and scoop out the seeds. Cut them crosswise into ¼-inch slices.
3. Place the cabbage and cucumbers in a large bowl. Sprinkle on ¼ cup of the salt and toss well. Let rest for 1

hour, tossing occasionally.
4. Fill the bowl with cold water and drain the vegetables into a colander. Repeat this process 3 times to rinse off the salt. Drain well.
5. In a medium bowl, combine the ginger, garlic, sugar, paprika, cayenne, 1 tablespoon of the soy sauce and the remaining 2 teaspoons salt. Stir in the vinegar and 1½ cups of cold water.
6. Add the cabbage, cucumbers and scallions. Toss together, cover with plastic wrap placed directly on the surface and refrigerate overnight. Taste and add 1 more tablespoon soy sauce if desired.

—*Jim Fobel*

PICKLED EGGPLANT AND MUSHROOMS

Good as an antipasto before dinner or lunch, these luscious pickles are also good for picnics and brunch or as a counterpoint to more substantial dishes such as breaded veal cutlets or chicken cacciatore.

MAKES ABOUT 4 CUPS
1½ cups plus 1 tablespoon dry white wine
¼ cup plus 1 tablespoon white wine vinegar
2 large garlic cloves, thinly sliced
1 cinnamon stick
1 bay leaf
1 tablespoon plus ¼ teaspoon oregano
1 tablespoon basil
3 whole cloves
2 tablespoons coarse (kosher) salt
2 tablespoons sugar
1 medium eggplant (about 1 pound), unpeeled and cut into 3-by-½-inch sticks
½ pound small mushrooms or larger mushrooms, halved or quartered
⅓ cup olive oil
Chopped parsley, for garnish

1. In a medium noncorrodible saucepan, combine 1½ cups of the wine, ¼ cup of the vinegar, the garlic, cinnamon, bay leaf, 1 tablespoon of the oregano, the basil, cloves, salt, sugar and 1 cup of water. Bring to a boil over high heat. Reduce the heat to low and simmer for 5 minutes.
2. Add the eggplant and mushrooms to the pickling solution, return to a simmer and cook, stirring occasionally, for 10 minutes.
3. Using a slotted spoon (to leave behind as much of the dried herbs and spices as possible), transfer the eggplant, mushrooms and garlic to a colander; do not rinse. Discard the cooking liquid in the pan and any whole spices in the colander. Place the vegetables in a medium bowl and let cool to room temperature.
4. Add the olive oil, remaining 1 tablespoon wine, 1 tablespoon vinegar and ¼ teaspoon oregano. Stir gently. Cover with plastic wrap placed directly on the surface and refrigerate overnight. To serve, garnish with chopped parsley.

—*Jim Fobel*

FRAGRANT PICKLED BEETS WITH PEARL ONIONS

The sophisticated flavor combination of raspberry vinegar and Zinfandel wine adds fragrance and flavor to these deep red pickles. Try them as a tangy accompaniment to poached salmon, broiled swordfish or grilled pork chops with rosemary.

MAKES ABOUT 3 CUPS
1 cup red Zinfandel wine
3 tablespoons sugar
1 teaspoon whole allspice, cracked
1 teaspoon coarse (kosher) salt
6 ounces tiny, white pearl onions (about 1½ cups), peeled
8 medium beets (about 1 pound), peeled and cut into ¼-inch slices

240

¼ cup raspberry or red wine vinegar

1. In a medium noncorrodible saucepan, combine the wine, sugar, allspice, salt and ¼ cup of water. Bring to a boil over moderately high heat. Add the onions and beets. Partially cover and simmer over low heat until the beets are just tender, about 15 minutes.

2. Transfer the onions, beets and their liquid to a bowl and add the vinegar. Let cool to room temperature. Cover and refrigerate for at least 1 hour, or overnight.

—Jim Fobel

ABBREVIATED BREAD-AND-BUTTER PICKLES

These pickles will satisfy an old-fashioned pickle craving at a moment's notice. Their taste and crunch are traditional; the only thing that's changed is the amount of time that it takes to make them. They are not too sweet and not too sour and are wonderful in tuna or egg salads or alongside baked beans or potato salad.

MAKES ABOUT 4 CUPS
8 medium pickling cucumbers, such as Kirbys (1½ to 2 pounds)
2 medium onions (about ¼ pound each), thinly sliced
6 ice cubes
¼ cup coarse (kosher) salt
1 cup cider vinegar
½ cup sugar
1 tablespoon mustard seed
½ teaspoon celery seed
½ teaspoon turmeric

1. Trim the ends of the cucumbers and cut them into ¼-inch slices (for a truly authentic look, cut the cucumbers with a crinkle-edged cutter).

2. In a large bowl, combine the cucumbers, onions, ice cubes and salt.

Let stand for 1 hour, tossing occasionally. Fill the bowl with cold water and then drain in a colander. Rinse and drain 3 times to rinse off all the salt.

3. In a large noncorrodible saucepan, combine the vinegar, sugar, mustard seed, celery seed and turmeric. Bring to a boil over high heat. Add the vegetables. When the liquid barely begins to simmer again, remove from the heat.

4. Transfer the vegetables and their liquid to a bowl and let cool to room temperature. Cover with plastic wrap placed directly on the surface and refrigerate overnight.

—Jim Fobel

SPICY PINEAPPLE CHUTNEY

In addition to being a lively accompaniment to simple grilled or roasted meats and poultry, this chutney can be used to make an unusual, but delicious, ice cream. To a custard-based vanilla ice cream recipe that will yield 1 quart, add all of the Spicy Pineapple Chutney and ⅓ cup coarsely chopped walnuts. Quick-chill the mixture in a bowl set in ice and water and then freeze in an ice cream maker according to the manufacturers' instructions.

MAKES ABOUT 2½ CUPS
1 large pineapple—peeled, cored and cut into 1- to 2-inch chunks
½ cup golden raisins
⅓ cup white wine vinegar
2 tablespoons fresh lime juice
½ cup sugar
2 tablespoons honey
1½ tablespoons minced fresh ginger
½ teaspoon ground cloves
¼ teaspoon cayenne pepper
3 tablespoons minced fresh mint

1. Place the pineapple in a food processor. Turn the machine on and off quickly until some of the pineapple is pureed and the rest is chopped

into small pieces.

2. In a large noncorrodible saucepan, combine the pineapple, raisins, vinegar, lime juice, sugar, honey, ginger, cloves and cayenne. Bring to a boil, reduce the heat to low and simmer until the mixture is slightly thickened, 10 to 12 minutes. Let cool to room temperature. (**The chutney can be made 2 to 3 days ahead.** Store, covered, in the refrigerator.)

3. Fold the chopped mint into the cooled chutney. Season to taste with additional spices if necessary.

—Marcia Kiesel

MINT JALAPENO JELLY

This fresh jelly is made in small batches and stored in the refrigerator for only a short time. The quantities below make enough to garnish eight lamb chops. The recipe can be easily doubled.

MAKES ABOUT ½ CUP
⅓ cup sugar
¼ teaspoon unflavored gelatin
3 tablespoons shredded fresh mint
1 tablespoon shredded fresh spearmint (if unavailable, increase the mint to 4 tablespoons)
2 large jalapeño peppers, seeded and minced
2 drops of vanilla extract

1. In a small saucepan, combine the sugar and 3 tablespoons of water. Stir over low heat until the sugar completely dissolves.

2. Soften the gelatin in 1 teaspoon of water and add to the saucepan. Increase the heat and bring to a boil.

3. In a small bowl, combine the mint, spearmint and peppers. Pour in the boiling syrup. Let stand until cool, stirring occasionally. Stir in the vanilla. Refrigerate for at least 15 minutes, until chilled, before serving.

—Paula Wolfert

INDEX

chicken with kale and, papillote of, 82
fennel with Parmesan cheese and, braised, 125
mozzarella and tomato salad with, warm, 27
roasted calf's liver with sage cream gravy and, 98

Prunes, compote of apples, apricots and, 215

Pudding. *See also* **Crème brûlée; Custard**
bread
apple, 193
bacon, lettuce and tomato custard, 50
brioche, 193
chocolate, 194
good old-fashioned, 193
brioche and oyster, 156
coconut blancmange with bittersweet chocolate sauce, 204

Pumpkin
cheesecake pie in a gingersnap crust, 166
and ginger soufflé, 198
maple ice cream, 210
mousse (in tulip cups), 200
pie, old-fashioned, 167
seed(s)
and cornbread stuffing, spicy, 157
puree, 17
spicy, corn soup with, 39
walnut ring, 174

Q-R

Quail, tea-and-spice-smoked, 24

Radicchio, in tricolor salad, 134
Ragoût
chicken drumstick, with bell peppers and artichokes, 83
oyster and spinach, 43
Rapini with Italian sausage, 107
Raspberry(-ies)
cardinal sauce, 211
frozen berry yogurt with, 211
in berry puree, grilled squab marinated in, 91
in miniature berry and cherry tartlets, 168
satin (sorbet), 213
snails (cookies), 178
sweet rice with cream and, 192
swirl cheesecake, creamy, 206
Ratatouille with goat cheese, 128
Ravioli, crabmeat, with cream sauce (agnolotti alla Fraccaro), 63
Red kidney bean and mussel salad, 144
Red prawn curry, 77
Red snapper
with fragrant pepper, grilled (tai no sanshoyaki), 55
papillote of, with sage, 56
Relish
pickled onions (Mustards Grill), 238

spicy pineapple chutney, 241
sweet and sour onions, 238
Remoulade sauce, 229
artichoke fritters with, 15
Rice
aromatic, with coconut, dates, fresh coriander and lemon, 153
brown, short-grain, with spicy lentils, 153
chicken with, and olives, 84
and mushroom dressing, double, 157
and mussels with two chiles, tomatoes and garlic, 65
risotto with spring vegetables, 153
salad
bean, corn and, with chili vinaigrette, 139
jambalaya, 143
short-grain, seafood and, with Oriental flavors, 142
shrimp pilau, 154
sweet, with raspberries and cream, 192
and sweet pepper stuffing, 88
roast turkey with pan gravy and, 87
Riesling, frog's legs in, with fresh herbs, 78
Roast beef hash, panhandle, 105
Roquefort cheese, sandwich spread with walnuts, Cognac and, 164
Rosemary, Boston baked beans with maple and, 120
Rum
-lemon glaze, spicy apple chiffon with, 199
-maple bananas, flambéed, 215
Rumanian ciorbă (Ana's), 85

S

Sage
cream gravy, roasted calf's liver with prosciutto and, 98
crumb topping for shellfish, 77
eggplant and tomato with, braised, 125
red snapper with, papillote of, 56
Salad, 132-149
arugula and watercress, with Swiss cheese beignets, 133
bean, corn and rice, with chili vinaigrette, 139
of bitter greens with grapefruit vinaigrette, 132
black bean and bell pepper, 138
cabbage with shrimp (achar udang), 138
chicken
Caesar, 141
and Canadian bacon with toasted pecans, 141
citrus, Sicilian, 132
coleslaw, crisp garlic, 135
of dandelion and fresh goat cheese, 133
fried bean cake and bean sprout (tahu goreng), 137
green, with lemon and fennel, 133

hearts of palm, beet and endive, 136
jambalaya, 143
minted cracked wheat, beefsteak tomatoes with, 138
mozzarella and tomato, with prosciutto, warm, 27
mussel and red bean, 144
of mustard greens and avocado with sweet-hot dressing, 132
The Parrot Restaurant's parrot salad, 138
pear and blue cheese, with Parmesan, 132
Peloponnese, 137
potato
à l'orange with sweet peppers, 139
lightened, 140
scallop
and red pepper, stir-fried, 143
and sweet pepper, with avocado, 149
seafood and short-grain rice with Oriental flavors, 142
with spicy peanut dressing, layered (gado-gado), 140
summer tossed, with mushrooms and fresh and pickled peppers, 134
three-bean macaroni, 139
of tomatoes, fresh and sun-dried, with zucchini and balsamic vinegar, 137
tricolor, 134
turkey and bacon, warm, 142
white bean, Tuscan-style, 149
yellow pickled (achar kuning), 134
zucchini and apple, minted, 136
Salad dressing. *See also* **Mayonnaise; Vinaigrette**
French, white, 230
spicy peanut, layered salad with (gado-gado), 140
Sally's sesame crisps, 179
Salmon
"Auberge de l'Ill," 59
barbecued steaks of, 56
with beurre blanc sauce, grilled fillets of, 56
and chive cakes with coriander butter, 58
and mussel chowder, 44
with oysters and mushrooms, papillote of, 57
with Pernod and mint, en papillote, 57
salmon cabbage sashimi, 23
scallops with scallion cream, 58
skillet-grilled and smoked, 54
smoked, and dill sandwich spread, 164
Salsa
baked beans with, 120
caramelized onion with, 28
fresh tomato, 230
tricolore, 230
Sandwich(es)
grilled smoked turkey and Cheddar, with hot pepper jelly, 163
herbed goat cheese and roasted pepper with olives and watercress, 162

cider apple, 169
flaky pastry for, 170
mushroom-leek, 12
ricotta pesto crescents, 14
Tuscan-style white bean salad, 149

U-V

Upperline's barbecued shrimp, 68
Urab urab (mixed vegetable salad with coconut), 135

Vanilla
 ice cream
  in melon melba, 216
  pear and fresh fig compote with, 217
  vanilla lover's, 208
 papillote of pears with orange and, 216
 peach vanilla sorbet, 213
Veal
 breast of
  stuffed, with mushroom gravy, 94
  stuffed with tuna, rolled, 94
 chops
  herb-pressed, 95
  with sweetbreads in bourbon and morel sauce, 96
 rack of, braised with tarragon, 95
 scallops with braised leeks and glazed carrots, 96
 stock, white, 225
 tonnato with seasoned mayonnaise, cabbage-wrapped, 97
Vegetable(s). *See also specific vegetables*
 chicken, mixed skillet grill with, 82
 fish with lemon and, baked, 54
 fritters, 10-ingredient, 28
 kebabs, seafood and, marinated, 55

pistou, summer, 37
and pork stew, country, 113
ratatouille with goat cheese, 128
risotto with spring, 153
salad
 mixed, with coconut (urab urab), 135
 mixed, with pineapple (asinan), 135
 yellow pickled (achar kuning), 134
and shrimp with tapenade sauce, steamed, 77
soup
 minestra maritata (married soup), 46
 minestrone with artichokes, sausage, pistachios and lemons, 45
stock, 226
Vinaigrette
 chili: bean, corn and rice salad with, 139
 with garlic and fresh herbs, 230
 grapefruit, salad of bitter greens with, 132
 sherry, marinated sirloin with, 100
Vinegar, balsamic
 fresh and sun-dried tomatoes with zucchini and, 137
 mignonette sauce, 231

W-X-Y-Z

Waffle(s)
 banana-pecan, ice cream sundae with pineapple sauce, 196
 chestnut, with chestnut cream, 195
Walnut(s)
 butter crescents, 189
 chocolate cake, 175
 chocolate glaze, 174
 maple crème brûlée, 203

-mocha buttercream, 176
pumpkin ring, 174
sandwich spread with Roquefort, Cognac and, 164
Water chestnuts and shrimp in light cream sauce, 78
Watercress
 and arugula salad, with Swiss cheese beignets, 133
 herbed goat cheese and roasted pepper sandwich with olives and, 162
 in warm turkey and bacon salad, 142
Welsh rarebits, miniature, 14
White bean(s)
 cannellini salad, Tuscan-style, 149
 roasted leg of lamb with mint and, 114
White French dressing, 230
White kidney beans, French-style, 121

Yakitori (glaze-grilled chicken and bell peppers), 80
Yams, baked, with amaretti crumble topping, 129
Yogurt, frozen berry, with cardinal sauce, 211

Zucchini
 and apple salad, minted, 136
 pasta with goat cheese, olives and, spicy, 152
 ribbons with arugula and creamy goat cheese sauce, 27
 roasted pepper soup with, 40
 with tomatoes, fresh and sun-dried, and balsamic vinegar, 137
Zuppa di vongole (clam soup) with garlic toasts, 43
Zuppa di finocchio (fennel soup), 39
Zuppa di funghi (mushroom soup), 40

CONTRIBUTORS

Alyssa Alia is a recipe developer, food stylist and cookbook author.

Jean Anderson is a food and travel writer, cooking teacher (of Portuguese cooking) and cookbook author, whose most recent books are *The Food of Portugal* (Morrow), *Jean Anderson's New Processor Cooking* (Morrow) and, with Elaine Hanna, *The New Doubleday Cookbook* (Doubleday).

Elizabeth Andoh is a cooking teacher (at Culinary Center of New York in Manhattan) and the author of *At Home with Japanese Cooking* (Knopf) and *An American Taste of Japan* (Morrow). She is currently working on a cookbook for Morrow scheduled for publication in spring 1988.

Fio Antognini is chef at Fio's La Fourchette in St. Louis, Missouri.

John Ash is chef/owner of John Ash & Co. in Santa Rosa, California, and is currently working on a cooking video.

Lee Bailey, known to New Yorkers for his stylesetting home furnishings shop in Henri Bendel, writes the Entertaining column for *Food & Wine* and is the author of *Country Weekends, City Food, Good Parties* and the upcoming *Country Desserts* (all from Clarkson Potter).

Nancy Verde Barr is a cooking teacher (at Sakonnet Vineyards in Little Compton, Rhode Island) and food writer, who is currently working on a book on southern Italian cooking for Knopf.

Rose Levy Beranbaum is a cooking teacher (Cordon Rose in Manhattan), cooking equipment designer, consultant and author of *Romantic and Classic Cakes* (Irena Chalmers).

Lisa Brainerd is a freelance recipe developer.

Jennifer Brennan is a food writer and the author of *The Original Thai Cookbook* (Putnam), *The Cuisines of Asia* (St. Martins Press), *One-Dish Meals of Asia* (Times Books) and a forthcoming book tentatively titled *Curries and Bugles—A Cookbook of the British Raj*.

Jason Clevinger is chef at Upperline in New Orleans, Louisiana.

Deirdre Davis & Linda Marino: Deirdre Davis is a food writer and Linda Marino is a food writer and caterer.

Anne Disrude, who prefers to be known simply as a good cook, is a former associate director of *Food & Wine*'s test kitchen.

Ken Dunn created the recipe that appears in this volume while he was chef at American Restaurant in Kansas City, Missouri.

Near Elan is chef at Mama Maria in Boston, Massachusetts.

Jim Fobel is an artist, food and travel writer, food stylist and the author of *Beautiful Food* (Van Nostrand Reinhold) and an upcoming old-fashioned baking book for Ballantine (fall 1987).

Margaret Fox is chef/owner of Cafe Beaujolais in Mendocino, California, and co-author, with John Bear, of a cookbook entitled *Cafe Beaujolais* (Ten Speed Press).

Goffredo Fraccaro is chef at La Riviera in Metairie, Louisiana.

Arthur Gold & Robert Fizdale are duo-pianists, former food columnists for *Vogue*, biographers and the authors of *The Gold and Fizdale Cookbook* (Random House). They are currently working on a biography of Sarah Bernhardt.

Joyce Goldstein is chef at Square One in San Francisco and is working on a cookbook of Mediterranean food for Morrow.

Richard Grausman is a cooking teacher, former U.S. representative of Le Cordon Bleu and food writer currently at work on a cookbook for Workman.

Dorie Greenspan is a freelance food writer.

Susan Grodnick is a food writer, recipe developer and cookbook author whose most recent works are *Seppi Renggli's Four Seasons Spa Cuisine* (Simon & Schuster) and, with Ed Edelman, *The Ideal Cheese Book* (Harper & Row).

Christopher Idone is a food writer, consultant, food stylist and the author of *Glorious Food* (Stewart, Tabori & Chang), *Glorious American Food* (Random House) and the upcoming *Summer Salads* (spring 1987) and *Winter Salads* (fall 1987), both from Random House. Mr. Idone has also recently designed his own line of china and glassware.

Gloria Kaufer Greene is a food writer and the author of *The Jewish Holiday Cookbook* (Times Books).

Marcia Kiesel is the Associate Director of *Food & Wine*'s test kitchen.

Evan Kleiman is chef/owner of Angeli in Los Angeles and co-author, with Viana La Place, of *Cucina Fresca* (Harper & Row).

Karen Lee & Alexandra Branyon: Karen Lee is a caterer, consultant, cooking teacher (Karen Lee's Chinese Cooking Classes in Manhattan) and cookbook author, who has collaborated with playwright and food writer Alaxandra Branyon on *Soup, Salad and Pasta Innovations* (Doubleday) and *Chinese Cooking Secrets* (Doubleday). They are currently working on *Nouvelle Chinoise* scheduled for publication in fall 1987 by MacMillan.

Edda Servi Machlin is a cooking teacher, restaurant consultant and the author of *The Classic Cuisine of the Italian Jews* (Dodd, Mead).

Copeland Marks is a food historian, cooking teacher (at Peter Kump's New York Cooking School) and cookbook author whose most recent book is *The Varied Kitchens of India* (M. Evans). He also has three cookbooks—on the cuisines of Burma, Outer Islands of Indonesia, and Tunisia—in the works.

Lydie Marshall is a cooking teacher (A La Bonne Cocotte in Manhattan) and the author of *Cooking with Lydie Marshall* (Knopf).

John Robert Massie, currently Manager of the Food Center at Ketcham Communications, is a freelance kitchen consultant and former associate director of *Food & Wine*'s test kitchen.

Frank McClelland is chef at Country Inn at Princeton in Princeton, Massachusetts.

Michael McLaughlin is a food writer, cooking teacher,

255